WHAT OTHERS ARE SAYING ABOUT *A TALE OF TWO KINGDOMS:*

Thank you for the manuscript for your new book. You are to be commended for your grasp of the Bible message. You did a lot of study and research. I trust the book will be well received and a blessing to many in coming days.

- Rev. Fred A. Vaughan
retired Fellowship Baptist pastor

I enjoyed reading the various excerpts of your book. The theme of the promised seed is one of the main threads of theology that weaves itself through the entirety of the scriptures. Thank you for tackling the subject and highlighting it. You have done a tremendous amount of work that I think will have an appeal amongst those who are serious students of the Word and those who are involved in theological and pastoral training.

- Rev. Todd Riley
Islington Baptist Church
Toronto, Ontario

A Tale of Two Kingdoms

Heather A. Kendall

Guardian BOOKS

Belleville, Ontario, Canada

A TALE OF TWO KINGDOMS
Copyright © 2006, Heather Kendall

All Rights Reserved. No part of this publication may be reproduced, stored in a retrieval system or transmitted in any form or by any means—electronic, mechanical, photocopy, recording or any other—except for brief quotations in printed reviews, without the prior permission of the author.

All Scripture quotations, unless otherwise specified, are taken from the HOLY BIBLE, NEW INTERNATIONAL VERSION ®. NIV ®. Copyright © 1973, 1978, 1984 by International Bible Society. Used by permission of Zondervan Publishing House. All rights reserved.

Scriptures marked (KJV) are from *The Holy Bible, King James Version.* Copyright © 1977, 1984, Thomas Nelson Inc., Publishers.

Scriptures marked (Phillips) are from *The New Testament in Modern English, Student Ed.* by J.B. Phillips. Copyright © 1972. New York: Macmillan.

Library and Archives Canada Cataloguing in Publication

Kendall, Heather, 1945-
    A tale of two kingdoms / Heather Kendall.

Includes bibliographical references and index.
ISBN 1-55452-003-7
ISBN 1-55452-004-5 (LSI ed.)

    1. Jesus Christ--Kingdom. 2. Devil--Christianity. 3. Salvation--Biblical teaching. I. Title.

BT94.K44 2006   231.7'2   C2005-907835-9

Guardian Books is an imprint of *Essence Publishing,* a Christian Book Publisher dedicated to furthering the work of Christ through the written word. For more information, contact:
20 Hanna Court, Belleville, Ontario, Canada K8P 5J2.
Phone: 1-800-238-6376 • Fax: (613) 962-3055.
E-mail: publishing@essencegroup.com
Internet: www.essencegroup.com

Printed in Canada
by

Guardian BOOKS

*To my family.
Without their help and encouragement,
this book would not have been completed.*

Table of Contents

Foreword 9
Introduction 11

Part 1: Waiting for the Promised Seed

1. The Beginning of the War 17
2. The Development of Satan's Kingdom 29
3. The Founding Fathers of the Faith 41
4. The Establishment of Israel as a Nation 61
5. King David. 85
6. The Northern Kingdom of Israel 111
7. The Southern Kingdom of Judah 141
8. The Fall of Judah 181
9. The Captivity. 199
10. A Second Chance for Israel. 235
11. The Silent Years 257

Part 2: Responding to the Promised Seed

1. The Birth of the Promised Seed 287
2. The Ministry of Jesus 295
3. The Early Church. 333
4. Letters to the Churches 357
5. The Apostolic Fathers. 399

Appendix 415
Timeline of Key People and Events 419
Endnotes. 423
Bibliography 435
Index 439

Maps
Compiled by Debra Kendall

    Figure 1: World of the Founding Fathers 41
    Figure 2: World of Moses 61
    Figure 3: Empire of David and Solomon. 86
    Figure 4: Zion, the City of David 89
    Figure 5: World of Jesus, the Promised Seed 288

Foreword

MANY Christians have benefited much from the teaching of their churches and Sunday schools and have a competent knowledge of many Biblical topics and characters. However, the understanding of the Holy Scriptures could be much enlarged by an introduction to the progressive nature of God's revelation. The organic nature of the Scriptures shows truths that were first presented in seed form, being brought to culmination in the person and work of Christ.

Our author, after years of diligent research, has presented the unfolding history of the Bible as she traced the conflict between the kingdoms of Christ and Satan. In the Apocalypse, all will come to a triumphant conclusion. Maps, diagrams, and background material provide additional resource material to encourage further research. We believe that Heather Kendall's book could prove a blessing to many.

—*Dr. G. A. Adams*
Former Principal,
Toronto Baptist Seminary
and Bible College

Introduction

WHY do God's people disagree on so many different issues? As a young married couple, my husband Barry and I moved from southern Ontario to Sudbury. I am a fourth generation believer whose grandfather and great-grandfather were influential leaders in the Open Plymouth Brethren Church in Toronto. To my surprise, the preacher in Sudbury began to criticize certain teachings of the Brethren. Both my grandfather and Rev. J. R. Boyd believed that Jesus paid the penalty for their sins on the cross. Rev. Boyd was the catalyst that drove me to search the Scriptures for myself. I yearned to know God better and his truths.

Many different people have searched for truth. Scientists conduct experiments so that others can replicate their work and test the validity of the original hypotheses. Philosophers like Descartes and Hume ponder the existence of truth. Historians are detectives, discerning fact from fiction. Religious people cling tenaciously to their particular beliefs and insist that they hold the truth. Obviously, some of those beliefs must be wrong. When two people disagree, one must be in error, perhaps even both. As a result, many deny the reality of objective truth. Instead, truth becomes subjective. In contrast, Jesus told his disciples, "I am the way and the truth and the life. No one comes to the Father except through me" (John 14:6). The God of the Bible declares that he is truth. Therefore, what he says is always true. Yet how do we know that God tells the truth? How do we know that the spiritual realm even exists?

As human beings we are only able to view the physical world around us. We cannot see the spiritual realm. That is why God proves his reliability through physical means. For example, he said, "Let there be lights in the expanse of the sky to separate the day from the night, and let them serve as signs to mark seasons and days and years" (Gen. 1:14). Since time began, people have observed a consistency in how the physical world operates. We are confident that until the end of time the earth will continue to function the same as it does now. Furthermore, in the Scriptures God made many promises that can be validated by history. Therefore we can have confidence that God always keeps his promises and always tells the truth. This includes his description of spiritual realities. The Psalmist writes, "Your promises have been thoroughly tested, and your servant loves them" (Ps. 119:140). His truth is a pearl of great price; it is of immeasurable value; and it is worth the effort to search for it.

The Bible is composed of sixty-six books written over a span of approximately 1500 years. How can a variety of authors writing over such a long time possibly have a unified message? Indeed, does the Bible contain one central truth? Before searching the Scriptures for the answer, each one of us should acknowledge all known assumptions and be willing to discard any bias that proves to be incorrect. If you do this, you will discover that God's purpose for humanity never changes. He wants everyone to know and accept his wonderful gift of salvation. Before creation the Lord knew that all of us would rebel against his authority. In spite of this knowledge, he devised a marvellous plan that would satisfy divine justice and would also demonstrate his love for people. Because of this plan believers would regain the fellowship that they had lost with their Creator. Satan and the fallen angels are continually working to thwart God's plan of salvation. People either accept or reject it.

How did those first Jewish believers respond when they discovered that God's plan included Gentiles? Are you willing to take a trip through time? If you do, you will discover that

God carried out his plan of salvation through Jesus, the promised Seed. This trip is the only way to fully appreciate the unity of the Scriptures. Come! It is time to begin the journey.

Part 1:

Waiting for the Promised Seed

Chapter One

The Beginning of the War

1. The Creator God

WRITING helps me remember what I have learned. While living in Sudbury, I began to write down what I studied about God in his Word. Since I am a visual learner, I needed to write in order to absorb God's truths and make them my own. In contrast, the Lord has no innate need to create anything. Instead creation is an expression of his character.

Long ago God created an innumerable army of angels that can never die. They are spirit beings made to serve and worship God. Knowing that he would be creating people, God also intended angels to be "ministering spirits sent to serve those who will inherit salvation" (Heb. 1:14). Although they are our servants, strangely enough, they are more powerful than we are. They even have the ability to pass from the spirit world into the physical world and take on the shape of our bodies. When the Lord God finished creating the heavens and the earth and everything in them, both visible and invisible, "God saw all that he had made, and it was very good" (Gen. 1:31). This also included Satan.

2. God's Plan for Creation

The Lord created people with the ability to choose whether or not to love and obey him. Knowing that everyone would disobey him and sin, the Triune God devised a plan of salvation that would satisfy divine justice. He was unwilling to lose the love and fellowship of the entire human race. At the appointed time, God the Father sent his Son Jesus to free believers from the bondage of sin and bring them back into fellowship with him. "He saved us, not because of righteous things we had done, but because of his mercy" (Titus 3:5). Jesus is "the Lamb that was slain from the creation of the world" (Rev. 13:8). Because God the Son became the sacrificial lamb to pay for sin, mercy and justice wed at the cross. What a wonderful plan! What else could compare to it? Only by God's grace are rebellious sinners now blameless in his sight. Like Job, we should respond in awe, "I know that you can do all things; no plan of yours can be thwarted" (Job 42:2).

> Because God the Son became the sacrificial lamb to pay for sin, mercy and justice wed at the cross.

For God so loved the world that he gave his one and only Son, that whoever believes in him shall not perish but have eternal life (John 3:16).

The Bible is God's story of his love for people. From Genesis to Revelation we can trace the development of his plan of salvation. Countless times God has proven through fulfilled prophecy that he always tells the truth. For this reason John 3:16 is an excellent theme verse. God loves you and does not want you to perish because of your disobedience to him. His only Son, Jesus, paid the penalty for sinners. If you believe that Jesus took the punishment that you deserve, you will have eternal life. After going on a journey through the Bible, hopefully you will treasure God's gift of salvation even more. It is the pearl of great price.

3. Rebellion in Heaven

Sometimes I wondered whether I took my dog for a walk or if she took me. When she heard the jangling sound of the leash, she jumped up and down with excitement. As soon as I managed to slip the choke collar over her head, she ran out of the house. Like a horse champing at the bit, she begrudgingly consented to sit at the curb before crossing the street. Then she flew off with me in tow. My dog insisted on having her own way. This must be how Satan feels.

> *"You were the model of perfection, full of wisdom and perfect in beauty. You were in Eden, the garden of God...You were anointed as a guardian cherub, for so I ordained you. You were on the holy mount of God; you walked among the fiery stones. You were blameless in your ways from the day you were created till wickedness was found in you...So I drove you in disgrace from the mount of God, and I expelled you, O guardian cherub, from among the fiery stones. Your heart became proud on account of your beauty, and you corrupted your wisdom because of your splendor. So I threw you to the earth"* (Ezek. 28:12-17).

This passage is primarily a lament concerning the fall of the king of Tyre. It is significant, however, that Ezekiel compares the king to a guardian cherub who dwelt on the holy mount of God. That is heaven, where God is worshipped. This angelic being was created to be wise, beautiful, and blameless. Then sometime afterwards, his heart became proud because of his beauty, and this perverted his ability to think wisely (Ezek. 28:17). The proud thoughts in the heart of the king of Tyre reflected the same spirit as this guardian cherub, because both of them thought, "I am a god; I sit on the throne of a god" (Ezek. 28:2). This guardian cherub was also in the Garden of Eden, the place where a serpent enticed Eve to disobey God. According to John, that ancient serpent was called Satan (Rev. 12:9). Thus the beautiful angel who first despised God's authority is Satan.

A similar situation occurs in Isaiah 14 when the Lord compares the king of Babylon to an angelic being who falls from heaven to earth. "How you have fallen from heaven, O morning star, son of the dawn! You have been cast down to the earth" (Isa. 14:12). Satan's sin began in his thought life. He decided, "I will ascend to heaven; I will raise my throne above the stars of God; I will sit enthroned on the mount of assembly, on the utmost heights of the sacred mountain. I will ascend above the tops of the clouds; I will make myself like the Most High" (Isa. 14:13,14). Satan thought that he deserved to sit on the throne of God, because he was so beautiful. The created one became so proud in his heart that he craved the glory, honour, and worship reserved only for the Creator.

> Satan's sin began in his thought-life.

Satan's sin spread like wildfire through the courts of heaven. One-third of the angels followed Satan in disobedience (Rev. 12:4). "And the angels who did not keep their positions of authority but abandoned their own home—these he has kept in darkness, bound with everlasting chains for judgment on the great Day" (Jude 1:6). Likewise, Peter explains, "God did not spare angels when they sinned, but sent them to hell, putting them into gloomy dungeons to be held for judgment" (2 Pet. 2:4). The guardian cherub and his angels became known as Satan and his demons. Judgment is sure. Even now they await the Final Judgment, because God will punish those fallen angels for their disobedience.

4. God's Throne under Attack

Righteousness and justice are the foundation of your throne; love and faithfulness go before you (Ps. 89:14).

Love and faithfulness keep a king safe; through love his throne is made secure (Prov. 20:28).

The first and foremost desire of Satan was to take over the throne of God for himself. To achieve this goal, he had to show that the Lord was not worthy to rule because of being incapable of being just and loving at the same time. Even as an earthly king remains on his throne by maintaining order in the land, likewise God must assert his authority by punishing evil. At the same time a king must be loved and show love in order to be confident that no one is trying to steal his throne. Justice and mercy are equally important foundations for a throne. As F. C. Jennings points out:

> Both justice and mercy are equally important foundations for a throne.

> There must therefore be no lack of either righteousness on the one hand or mercy on the other, for the integrity and maintenance of the Throne of God. Now we may see why Satan ever seeks to drag his victims before the Throne as criminals. If there be an inability to show *mercy*—one speaks with all reverence—God's very throne is of no value to Him. If He is powerless to save those He loves and wills to bless, of what good is His Throne? It lacks power—strength to carry out His will, and He is no longer supreme. But if He pardons convicted criminals—is that righteous? Is not the foundation gone? If He cannot pardon, where is the mercy? If He does, where is the righteousness? It is ever Satan's subtle way to place in a dilemma, and this is a dilemma worthy of being put even before God. Apparently there is no escape, for whichever horn of the dilemma be accepted, the Throne—that Throne he was appointed to guard—is subverted, and since he would himself be as God, *why does not that subversion place it at his own command?*[1]

5. The Temptation of Adam and Eve

God started working through time to carry out his plan of salvation. Satan, puffed up with pride, was thrown from heaven to the beautiful earth created by God. He saw the Lord talking and laughing with Adam and Eve every morning and evening. He could see the sweet communion of those who were in complete agreement emotionally and spiritually with each other. Those two were more than servants of the Lord God. They were his friends. How Satan hated that man and woman! He wanted to destroy the loving friendship that they enjoyed with God. When I was growing up, my family moved around a lot. My dad was a mechanical engineer who called himself an industrial hobo. I never wanted to break up any friendships, but it did take time to make my own friends.

One day when Adam and Eve were walking together near the centre of the garden, they passed close to the forbidden tree, the tree of the knowledge of good and evil. Satan, in the form of a serpent, was nearby and saw Eve gazing at the delicious fruit.

> *He said to the woman, "Did God really say, 'You must not eat from any tree in the garden'?" The woman said to the serpent, "We may eat fruit from the trees in the garden, but God did say, 'You must not eat fruit from the tree that is in the middle of the garden, and you must not touch it, or you will die.'" "You will not surely die," the serpent said to the woman. "For God knows that when you eat of it your eyes will be opened, and you will be like God, knowing good and evil"* (Gen. 3:1-5).

He appealed to Eve's spirit so that she would desire to be like God. Why should she not yearn to usurp the authority of the one who is the Creator of everything? Satan himself coveted the throne of God. "He was instilling the same mind in her that was in himself," Jennings also explains, "whilst loosening her mind from its confidence in the love of God, in His care for her...In the way he leads men he practically says, 'let this mind be in you which was also in me; who, being but a creature, grasped at being as God'"[2]

After some thought Eve took some of the fruit, ate it, turned to Adam, and gave him a piece to eat also. This he did.

The battle lines were drawn, and Adam and Eve were the first human casualties in the war between Satan and the Lord God. No doubt Satan thought that he had succeeded in his plan. The Lord had given Adam and Eve one rule, one test of their obedience, and they had disobeyed. Judgment would be sure. Had not God bound Satan and his demons in everlasting chains of darkness as a result of their disobedience? There was no forgiveness for them. It is true that Satan and his demons could roam about heaven or earth, but they were eternally doomed. If the Lord were to ignore the transgression and show mercy by forgiving Adam and Eve, then Satan would have God right where he wanted him—off the throne.

Satan's plan backfired. The Lord already had worked out his plan for our salvation before he created the world. Consequently we must ask, "Why does God treat angels and people differently?" Although God certainly loves the angels, Satan and his demons are under eternal condemnation. God has to punish them, because his holiness cannot ignore their rebellion. For them justice and mercy are mutually exclusive. Disobedience against the Lord is irreversible and unforgivable. Again we ask, "Why?" The answer appears to hinge on two facts. Angels were created individually to be ministering spirits or servants. In contrast, Adam and Eve were created in God's image and commanded to procreate. Also, God's intent is to treat people like members of his family, not like servants.

> If God punished all of humanity when they sinned, he would never show mercy to any created being.

If God punished all of humanity when they sinned, he would never show mercy to any created being. It is impossible for the Lord to violate his character. He must be merciful. How could God punish everyone he loved? Since Satan knew that disobedience brought punishment, he thought that he had given God an impossible problem to solve. If God did not punish sin in individuals, then he was not righteous. If he never forgave sin, then he did not love. No matter how God reacted, Satan thought, he would win the throne. R. Milligan imagines how the angels probably felt:

> And it is most likely that when man sinned and fell his case was regarded as equally hopeless by all the higher created intelligences of the universe who were cognizant of the fact. They knew that God is just, that he is impartial, and that his government must and will be sustained; and hence it is most likely that all the angels, both good and bad, looked upon man as lost—forever lost—the moment he transgressed in Eden.[3]

6. Paradise Lost

All actions have consequences for good or evil. As a young child I touched a hot element on the stove and was burnt. As soon as Adam and Eve ate the forbidden fruit, they suffered spiritual and physical consequences. After God had created them, he blessed them and said, "Be fruitful and increase in number; fill the earth and subdue it. Rule over the fish of the sea and the birds of the air and over every living creature that moves on the ground" (Gen. 1:28). At that point Adam became king and Eve queen over all living creatures. Even after they were kicked out of the Garden of Eden, they still had authority over their dominion. Meanwhile God had allowed Satan to have control over all of creation that rebelled against him. When Adam and Eve disobeyed God, they rejected his authority and opted out of his kingdom. Since they must be members of either God's kingdom or Satan's, Adam and Eve unwittingly transferred the entire world over to the kingdom of Satan. He became the spiritual king of the earth. John declared that Satan controls the whole world (1 John 5:19). That is why Satan could tell Jesus that all authority over the world had been given to him (Luke 4:6).

> *And I will put enmity between you and the woman, and between your offspring and hers; he will crush your head, and you will strike his heel* (Gen. 3:15).

How often Adam and Eve must have recalled the beautiful garden that was their home no longer. How often they must have pondered the last words of the Lord God just before they were thrown out of the garden. God had not wasted any time addressing their rebellion. He had spoken quietly and firmly to the serpent, and also to Adam and Eve. He told the serpent that the Seed of the woman would crush his head and that he would strike his heel. The promised Seed would be the victor over Satan. God had a plan of salvation. He was not caught off guard, wondering what to do. From that moment on, there are two types of people—those who believe that God will provide for their salvation and those who do not think that they are sinners in need of a Saviour. As a result there will always be friction between God's people and Satan's.

> God had a plan of salvation. He was not caught off guard, wondering what to do.

Adam probably thought, "What does it mean, 'the Seed of the woman'? How will this Seed crush the serpent's head? How will the serpent harm the Seed's heel?" I wonder how forlorn Adam and Eve were when they realized the consequences of their disobedience.

After a while Eve gradually started to get bigger. Then one day she lay down in terrible pain. Soon she held a tiny baby in her arms. Gazing at the child, Eve named her baby Cain. She exclaimed, "With the help of the LORD I have brought forth a man" (Gen. 4:1).

"Is this child a seed? Is this child the Seed that will crush the serpent? What does 'crush the serpent' mean?" they must have wondered. "Does it mean that we can become the friends of God again?"

If they thought that Cain was the promised Seed, many years later their hopes would be cruelly dashed.

7. Cain and Abel

Cain and his brother Abel worked hard to help keep the family alive. Cain became a farmer and Abel a herdsman. One day both of them brought an offering to the Lord. Cain presented some of his crops, while Abel sacrificed the firstborn of his flock. Cain became very angry with God when the Lord was pleased with Abel's offering but not with his. Then God said to Cain, "Why are you angry? Why is your face downcast? If you do what is right, will you not be accepted? But if you do not do what is right, sin is crouching at your door; it desires to have you, but you must master it" (Gen. 4:6,7).

What was the difference between Cain and Abel? As they were growing up, their parents had most certainly told both of them about the Garden of Eden. They knew how Adam and Eve had been deceived by the serpent and had sinned. They heard how God had shed the blood of an animal to cover the naked bodies of their parents and then had kicked them out of the garden. Both boys must have heard about the promise of one who would come to crush the head of the serpent. In the New Testament the Lord acknowledges the faith of Abel and declares him to be righteous (Heb. 11:4). At the very least, Abel must have believed that someday one would be born who would have the power to restore his broken relationship with God. In contrast, Cain lured his brother into the field, attacked him, and killed him. When Adam and Eve had sinned, they hid from the Lord God among the trees of the garden, but not Cain. He thought so little of God that he acted as if nothing out of the ordinary had happened.

The Lord asked, "Where is your brother Abel?"

"I don't know," he replied. "Am I my brother's keeper?" (Gen. 4:9).

The Holy Spirit relates how some people in the early Church had the same heart attitude as Cain. "Yet these men speak abusively against whatever they do not understand; and what things they do understand by instinct, like unreasoning animals—these are the very things that destroy them. Woe to them! They have taken the way of Cain" (Jude 1:10,11).

When God looked into the hearts of Cain and Abel, he saw two different types of people. In Cain he saw one who spoke disrespectfully against the Lord and wanted to act independently of him. In Abel he saw one who had remorse for sin and longed to be restored to fellowship with his Creator. Abel trusted God, and Cain did not. The first human death on earth was the martyrdom of a believer. Since that day so long ago, Abel's blood has been crying out to God from the ground. It will continue to cry out for vengeance until the Final Judgment Day when all will be judged.

> Almost from the beginning there have been two groups of people, believers and non-believers, those obedient to the Lord and those who are not.

Almost from the beginning there have been two groups of people, believers and non-believers, those obedient to the Lord and those who are not. Abel belonged to God's kingdom and Cain to Satan's. God declared Abel to be righteous when he sacrificed a lamb. Abel is assured eternal life with the Lord at the Final Judgment. In contrast, Cain, who was self-seeking and rejected the truth, will receive the wrath and anger of God Almighty. Thousands of years have passed since the first family lived on this earth, but we have the same choices to make as they had. Do you believe that God tells the truth? Will you lovingly obey him? Before God created the world, he worked out a plan of salvation. If you accept his plan, you belong to God's kingdom. If you do not, then you belong to Satan's. The battle lines are drawn. Whose side are you on?

Points to Ponder

1. God created Satan to be good.
2. No one can thwart God's plans.
3. To insist on having your own way means to rebel against God.

4. God planned that the promised Seed would be the victor over Satan.
5. Abel was the first martyr in God's kingdom.

Chapter Two

The Development of Satan's Kingdom

1. The Apostasy of Enoch's Generation

ENOCH was born 622 years after the creation of Adam, and he lived 365 years (Gen. 5). Since time began, Satan has continually tried to thwart God's plan of salvation.

Today there are millions of believers living in many countries. Yet don't we often feel isolated and alone in the workplace? I have. Enoch, however, was in a much more difficult situation than we are. Perhaps he and a few others were the only believers on the entire earth. They were lights shining in the darkness, like you and me.

"See, the Lord is coming with thousands upon thousands of his holy ones to judge everyone, and to convict all the ungodly of all the ungodly acts they have done in the ungodly way, and of all the harsh words ungodly sinners have spoken against him" (Jude 1:14,15).

Enoch walked with God and felt compelled to speak out against the wickedness around him.

Everywhere that Enoch looked, he saw individuals who grumbled and found fault with others. Those people were selfish and boasted about themselves. They flattered others, only if it suited their purpose. Enoch walked with God and felt compelled to speak out against the wickedness around him. He warned his generation that judgment was coming. There was no way that a righteous God could or would allow sin to continue unpunished. The repetition of the word *ungodly* emphasizes the fact that there are two kinds of people, the godly and the ungodly. Likewise, Jude contended with grumblers and faultfinders, godless men who claimed to be believers. Those troublemakers in the early Church needed to hear the same message as Enoch's listeners, since God's desire was for them to repent of their sin. One day the Lord will come back and punish evil. God shows his love for people by warning us of impending disaster, because he wants us to turn from our wicked ways.

2. The Violence of Noah's Generation

For since the creation of the world God's invisible qualities—his eternal power and divine nature—have been clearly seen, being understood from what has been made (Rom. 1:20).

> As every year passed, Satan's kingdom expanded.

No one can say, "It is impossible to know if God exists." Creation reveals the power and divinity of the invisible God. Although the people in Noah's day knew that God existed, they ignored him and refused to thank him for the good things that he gave them. If the ungodly were thankless and spoke harshly against the Lord in Enoch's day, over 900 years later they were even more wicked. For one thing, there were more of them. As every year passed, Satan's kingdom expanded.

Then the Lord said, "My Spirit will not contend with man forever, for he is mortal; his days will be a hundred and twenty years" (Gen. 6:3). God kindly gave them 120 years to turn from their sin before judgment would fall on them. As Matthew

Henry points out, "Justice said, *Cut them down;* but mercy interceded, *Lord, let them alone this year also;* and so far mercy prevailed, that a reprieve was obtained...reprieves are not pardons; though God bear a great while, he will not bear always."[1]

"The LORD was grieved that he had made man on the earth, and his heart was filled with pain" (Gen. 6:6). In the midst of his sorrow the Lord saw Noah, a righteous man, who walked with God. The Lord told Noah that he was going to destroy all the people on the earth because of their violence (Gen. 6:13). To do so would have pleased Satan. Justice would have taken precedence over mercy, and Satan would have won the throne of God. Then God told Noah to build an ark on dry land. It was actually a big barge, large enough to hold eight people and two of every kind of animal (seven of certain kinds that were deemed clean). After many years, the ark was finally completed. During that time Noah had ample opportunity to preach to the people. He warned them that God intended to destroy the earth with a flood—whatever a flood was. Instead of heeding the warning, they jeered at Noah. Life went on as usual. The people certainly did not believe that their world would, or could, be destroyed by water.

3. JUDGMENT ON SIN AND NEW BEGINNINGS

During the flood, God continued to preserve the line of the promised Seed

The reprieve was over. The people watched as all the animals filed into the ark. When Noah and his family entered the ark, anyone else could have joined them, but no one did. "Then the LORD shut him in" (Gen. 7:16). At that point there was a clear distinction between believers and non-believers. For seven days Noah was locked in the barge, and

In that moment the judgment of God was meted out on that unbelieving generation while the ark provided safety for those within.

nothing happened. Imagine how everyone outside was laughing sarcastically!

Then it happened. It started to rain. In that moment the judgment of God was meted out on that unbelieving generation while the ark provided safety for those within. "For forty days the flood kept coming on the earth, and as the waters increased they lifted the ark high above the earth...Every living thing that moved on the earth perished—birds, livestock, wild animals, all the creatures that swarm over the earth, and all mankind" (Gen. 7:17,21).

What a happy day it was for Noah, his wife, his three sons, their wives, and all of the animals when the ground was finally dry and they could leave the ark! In thankfulness Noah built an altar and sacrificed a burnt offering of some clean animals and birds to God. As soon as the Lord smelled the pleasing aroma, he said in his heart, "Never again will I curse the ground because of man, even though every inclination of his heart is evil from childhood. And never again will I destroy all living creatures, as I have done. As long as the earth endures, seedtime and harvest, cold and heat, summer and winter, day and night will never cease" (Gen. 8:21,22). As a sign of this promise God put a rainbow in the clouds. Then God told Noah and his sons, "Be fruitful and increase in number and fill the earth" (Gen. 9:1).

> From Noah would come the promised Seed that would crush the serpent's head, but they had three serious problems—the world, the flesh, and the Devil.

At the age of 601 Noah had a unique opportunity. He and his family could build a new world for themselves. It was a second chance for humanity. From Noah would come the promised Seed that would crush the serpent's head, but they had three serious problems—the world, the flesh, and the Devil. Each of those eight people alive had the power to influence another for good or evil. Believers are to be the salt of the earth (Matt. 5:13), influencing each other for good. Because of the sin of Adam and Eve, every single one of them had a natural bent to sin. Although Noah walked with God and was righteous in the sight of the Lord, he still struggled with his sin nature. Similarly, Paul lamented centuries later, "I know that nothing good lives in me, that is, in my sinful nature. For I have the desire to do what is good, but I cannot carry it out" (Rom. 7:18). Finally, Satan and his demons were as willing as they are today to instill sinful rebellious thoughts into the hearts and minds of Noah and his family. Paul warns believers, "And do not give the devil a foothold" (Eph. 4:27). Between man's innate sinful nature and the influence of others, including people and the wicked angels, the new world established by Noah was doomed to failure. Although the situation appeared to favour Satan and his kingdom, the Lord had a plan for our salvation. The promised Seed would come at the proper time and in the proper place.

4. Trouble in the New World

There was much work for everyone to do in order to survive. As time passed, children were born to Shem, Ham, and Japheth. Being a farmer, Noah decided to plant a vineyard. When the grapes were ripe, he made some wine. One night he became drunk and lay naked in his tent. As Ham passed by his father's tent, he looked in and saw his father lying there, naked and drunk. Immediately he told his two brothers, Shem and Japheth, who picked up a garment and held it up between them. Walking backwards, they entered the tent and covered Noah. Shem and Japheth made sure not to look on their father's nakedness. When Noah woke up and found out what had happened, he said, "Cursed be Canaan!" and also, "Blessed be the Lord, the God of Shem!" (Gen. 9:25,26).

Some may wonder why Noah cursed Canaan. After all, Noah was the one who had sinned by getting drunk. Also, Ham was the one who had actually seen his father lying there naked and drunk. Why did Noah not curse his own son Ham? "The Lord does not look at the things man looks at. Man looks at the outward appearance, but the LORD looks at the heart" (1 Sam. 16:7). In the New Testament God reveals what he saw in Noah's heart: "By faith Noah, when warned about things not yet seen, in holy fear built an ark to save his family. By his faith he condemned the world and became heir of the righteousness that comes by faith" (Heb. 11:7). "Now faith is being sure of what we hope for and certain of what we do not see" (Heb. 11:1). Noah believed in God's existence and that the Lord "rewards those who earnestly seek him" (Heb. 11:6).

> None of us will be completely free of sin until we get to heaven.

Therefore God declared Noah to be righteous and a member of his kingdom, because he had the right heart attitude. Noah would not lose his salvation, although he had sinned. None of us will be completely free of sin until we get to heaven.

On the other hand, notice how Ham acted. Instead of quietly getting a garment and covering his father, he told his brothers so that they could go and have a peek also. He wanted others to see his father in a sinful, weakened state. Do you inwardly chuckle when a good person sins? Beware of the sin of Ham. When the Lord looked into the heart of Canaan, the son of Ham, he saw one who probably approved of his father's behaviour, whereas Ham's other three sons did not. Thus the Lord cursed Canaan for following in his father's footsteps. Canaan became a servant of servants, and the word *Canaan* is synonymous with sin.

Many years later, when the Lord God was ready to lead the children of Israel into the Promised Land, the land flowing with milk and honey, he told them that they would need to cast out seven nations mightier than they were, one of which was Canaan. Lest Israel should become puffed up with pride, the Lord told them, "After the LORD your God has driven them out before you, do not say to yourself, 'The LORD has brought me here to take possession of this land because of my righteousness.' No, it is on account of the wickedness of these

5. The Early Development of Idolatry

When we moved from Sudbury to North Bay, Barry and I sold a small bungalow and bought a large two-storey house. Although we did it to provide more space for our three growing children, we really wanted it for ourselves. Of course, owning the house was not enough. We had to fix it up. This is the kind of attitude that could easily lead to idolatry, if unchecked. I am sure that God is pleased when we take care of the good gifts that he has given us. Nevertheless, a problem arises if those things become more important than he is. Ideas, people, or things can gradually consume more of our thoughts until God no longer matters. This is how idolatry develops.

Ancestral veneration was one of the first steps in a trend away from worship of the one true God. It began with the idea that dead ancestors have the ability to affect your life for good or evil. Worship of the sun, moon, and other heavenly bodies also occurred early in the history of the world. Because there is no written record, however, it is impossible to know which came first. Milligan explains the development of idolatry in this way:

> Sanchoniathon, the oldest Phoenician historian, says that *Chryson* (supposed to be Noah) was the first deified mortal; and that the several members of his family were, after their death, raised to the rank of gods in connection with the heavenly bodies. The Hindoos have a tradition that the *Richis*, who were preserved in the Ark, became after their death the souls of the seven stars of the Great Bear; and that the souls of their wives were, in like manner, transferred to the Pleiades. The ancient Egyptians believed that *Helius*, their first king, had been translated to the Sun. And hence it was that in a short

time the opinion became quite prevalent that all the stars and planets were living beings and proper objects of worship. Other objects of worship were easily added to these newly created divinities, and very soon all animated nature was deified.[2]

6. The Tower of Babel

The world's population gradually increased, and people spread out over the earth. At that time everyone spoke the same language. Some individuals discovered a large plain between the Tigris and Euphrates rivers, which they called the plain of Shinar, meaning "two rivers."[3] Nimrod, the son of Cush and the grandson of Ham, rose to prominence as a mighty warrior whose kingdom was centred in Babylonia. First, Nimrod established four cities in the southern part of the plain, one of which was Babylon. Then branching north to Assyria, he built four more cities, one of which was Nineveh (Gen. 10:8-12). This expansion took place around 2300 B.C.[4] It did not take long for the Assyrians to become a threat to their neighbours, for they quickly "displayed a genius for war."[5]

Nimrod was likely the instigator behind the tower of Babel. One day some men said, "Come, let us build ourselves a city, with a tower that reaches to the heavens, so that we may make a name for ourselves and not be scattered over the face of the whole earth" (Gen. 11:4). They were more interested in becoming famous and self-sufficient in one locality than in obeying God's command to Noah to fill the earth (Gen. 9:1). They did not need or want God. Does this sound familiar? Just as Satan encouraged Eve that she could be like God, he instilled the same desire in these men.

> Just as Satan encouraged Eve that she could be like God, he instilled the same desire in these men.

Situated on a flood plain between two rivers with no rocks, those men made their own bricks. Using tar as mortar, they waterproofed the foundations of the city and the tower. While the men were busy working, the Lord watched and said, "If as one people speaking the same language they have begun to do this, then nothing they plan to do will be impossible for them. Come, let us go down and confuse their language so that they will not understand each other" (Gen. 11:6,7).

When the men could no longer communicate with one another, their plans were foiled. "So the LORD scattered them from there over all the earth, and they stopped building the city" (Gen. 11:8). E. J. Young comments, "The result was that from that time on you had individual nations and individual kingdoms, individual religions, and these more or less counteracted one another."[6] Because of this situation, nobody questioned the union of religion and the state. It became an accepted reality. Many years later this fact would protect the nation of Israel. God could teach them his truth without any danger that it would become corrupted by false religions.

7. The False Need for Pagan Sacrifices

As soon as Adam and Eve disobeyed and sinned, they covered their nakedness with fig leaves and hid from God. After the Lord had explained the consequences of their actions, he killed an animal to make garments for them.[7] Adam and Eve witnessed the meaning of physical death. Because of their sin, blood was shed. The innocent died for the guilty.

Abel was the first person in Scripture who presented a blood sacrifice to God. The Lord accepted his sacrifice, since he knew that Abel had the right heart attitude. On the other hand, when Cain's spiritual descendants embraced the use of blood sacrifices in their worship, they ignored the fact that they were sinners in need of a Saviour; instead they behaved as if God had some innate need to receive such sacrifices. The next step was for them to think, "I have given you what you need. Now you have to give me what I want." In contrast, Aristides, a defender of the faith to Hadrian in A.D. 125-126, emphatically declares that God has no need for sacrifices:

But even the writers and philosophers among them have wrongly alleged that the gods are such as are made in honour of God Almighty. And they err in seeking to liken (them) to God whom man has not at any time seen nor can see unto what He is like. Herein, too (they err) in asserting of deity that any such thing as deficiency can be present to it; as when they say that He receives sacrifice and requires burnt-offering and libation and immolations of men, and temples. But God is not in need, and none of these things is necessary to Him; and it is clear that men err in these things they imagine.[8]

God does teach that those who sacrifice to idols are actually sacrificing to demons. Moses laments, "They made him jealous with their foreign gods and angered him with their detestable idols. They sacrificed to demons, which are not God—gods they had not known, gods that recently appeared, gods your fathers did not fear" (Deut. 32:16,17). God does not teach, however, that demons need sacrifices to survive. Origen, a theologian of the third century A.D., mistakenly writes that demons "must have the nourishment of exhalations and, consequently, are always on the lookout for the savour of burnt sacrifices, blood, and incense."[9] Demons existed long before people began to sacrifice to them, and they exist today without sacrifices.

8. THE LORD'S JUDGMENT ON IDOLATRY

All who make idols are nothing, and the things they treasure are worthless. Those who would speak up for them are blind; they are ignorant to their own shame. Who shapes a god and casts an idol, which can profit him nothing? He and his kind will be put to shame; craftsmen are nothing but men...The blacksmith takes a tool and works with it in the coals; he shapes an idol with hammers, he forges it with the might of his arm...The car-

penter measures with a line and makes an outline with a marker; he roughs it out with chisels and marks it with compasses. He shapes it in the form of man, of man in all his glory, that it may dwell in a shrine. He cut down cedars, or perhaps took a cypress or oak. He let it grow among the trees of the forest, or planted a pine, and the rain made it grow. It is man's fuel for burning; some of it he takes and warms himself, he kindles a fire and bakes bread. But he also fashions a god and worships it; he makes an idol and bows down to it. Half of the wood he burns in the fire; over it he prepares his meal, he roasts his meat and eats his fill. He also warms himself and says, "Ah! I am warm; I see the fire." From the rest he makes a god, his idol; he bows down to it and worships. He prays to it and says, "Save me; you are my god" (Isa. 44:9-17).

From the beginning, Satan has gladly welcomed new followers into his kingdom. They have refused to worship God as Creator or to lovingly obey him. Before Jesus' day, Satan's kingdom expanded rapidly while God's kingdom appeared almost nonexistent. Nevertheless, God was quietly carrying out his plan.

Points to Ponder

1. Self-sufficiency is the opposite of dependence on God.
2. Giving in to temptation leads to sin. Committing that sin makes it easier for a person to yield to another temptation. One who continually gives in to temptation becomes progressively blind to spiritual realities.
3. God does not need blood sacrifices to survive.
4. To sacrifice to an idol means to sacrifice to a demon.
5. In the Old Testament there are more followers in Satan's kingdom than in God's.

Chapter Three

The Founding Fathers of the Faith

1. Abram's Call

*Abram: 1951 B.C. to 1776 B.C. (Gen. 25:7). 1876 B.C.
(For an explanation of dates, see the appendix)*

Figure 1: World of the Founding Fathers

LOOKING back, our move to Sudbury was not a great distance compared to how far others have relocated. For example, our son Stephen and his wife Megan were more like the pioneers than we were. After loading all of their belongings onto a rented truck, they set out for California from Maine. Likewise, Abram left Ur of Babylonia and settled in Haran, a town in Paddan Aram. His elderly father Terah had intended to lead his family all the way to Canaan (Gen. 11:31), but he died in Haran, which was about halfway there. Abram himself had heard the call of the Lord to leave Ur and go to a foreign land (Acts 7:3). Then, at the age of seventy-five, after the death of his father, Abram once again obeyed God, left Haran, and travelled to Canaan, the country west of the Jordan River. His wife Sarai, his nephew Lot, and his servants accompanied him.

God promised Abram, "I will make you into a great nation and I will bless you; I will make your name great, and you will be a blessing. I will bless those who bless you, and whoever curses you I will curse; and all peoples on earth will be blessed through you" (Gen. 12:2,3). Imagine how Abram felt, for God had never promised such blessings to anyone else! He probably expected that the promised Seed would be his son.

When Abram saw in creation the handiwork of the Almighty Creator, he obeyed the Lord and left his home, first in Ur, then in Haran. Both the people of Ur and Haran worshipped the moon.[1] By leaving Haran, Abram turned his back not only on a locality, but also on the worship of the moon. As he travelled from Ur to Canaan, he accomplished something unique for his day. His God accompanied him. Satan had duped the nations into believing that gods were local in nature. Therefore anyone living in a certain town or nation was expected to worship the local gods. To leave that place meant ceasing to be under the jurisdiction of those particular gods. In contrast, Abram obeyed God and went on a long journey even though he had no idea where he was going. By faith he followed the Lord and became a friend of God (2 Chron. 20:7).

> Satan had duped the nations into believing that gods were local in nature.

After arriving in Canaan, the Lord promised Abram, "To your offspring I will give this land" (Gen. 12:7). Abram responded by building an altar to worship God.

2. MELCHIZEDEK

In Canaan the Lord blessed Abram and Lot by increasing their livestock. After they decided to split up, Lot chose to pitch his tents near Sodom. When war broke out, Lot was captured. Someone managed to escape and report to Abram. Immediately Abram and the 318 trained men who were born in his household chased the enemy. After dividing his men to attack, Abram defeated the enemy at night. Then he rescued Lot and the others who had been captured. He also recovered their possessions (Gen. 14).

On his way back home after the battle, Abram met Melchizedek, who was the king of Salem and the priest of God Most High. *Melchizedek* means "king of righteousness," and *Salem* means "peace" (Heb. 7:2). Salem is the oldest recorded name for the city of Jerusalem. After offering Abram bread and wine, Melchizedek blessed him by saying, "Blessed be Abram by God Most High, Creator of heaven and earth. And blessed be God Most High, who delivered your enemies into your hand" (Gen. 14:19,20). According to the Law of Moses, it is wrong for an Israelite king to perform the function of a priest. Many years later, when King Uzziah tried to burn incense to the Lord in the temple, God punished him with incurable leprosy (2 Chron. 26:16-21). Only the promised Seed has the right to combine both offices together. Yet in Abram's day kings often performed both functions simultaneously. Thus it was not unusual for Melchizedek to be the priest-king.

With a thankful heart Abram gave him one-tenth of the spoils. By paying Melchizedek homage, Abram acknowledged his authority. Hebrews 5 and 7 both teach that Jesus was the one who would come and be a priest patterned after the order of Melchizedek. The priesthood of Melchizedek actually foreshadows that of Jesus. "Without father or mother, without genealogy, without beginning of days or end of life, like the Son of God he remains a priest forever" (Heb. 7:3). Since the beginning and the end of Melchizedek's life are not recorded, he is like the Son of God. Similarly, the priesthood of both has no official start or finish. Jesus became a priest like Melchizedek, "not on the basis of a regulation as to his ancestry but on the basis of the power of an indestructible life" (Heb. 7:16). David explains, "The LORD has sworn and will not change his mind: 'You are a priest forever, in the order of Melchizedek'" (Ps. 110:4). Jesus is King and Priest at the same time. He wants to be your Priest-King.

> Jesus is King and Priest at the same time.

3. GOD'S COVENANT WITH ABRAM

On our way to Sudbury, Barry and I decided that it was time to start a family. Sixteen months later Debra was born. We thought that two and one-half years was an ideal space of time between children. Instead, Stephen came three and one-half years later and Philip three and one-half years after that. Praying for the three children increased our faith and dependence on God. Each wait seemed endless. Abram and Sarai, however, were very puzzled. Many years before, back in Ur, the Lord had promised Abram that he would be the father of a great nation. God had even said that all of the people on the earth would be blessed through him. During the centuries some individuals had been waiting for the promised Seed who would be a blessing to all people. Abram probably thought, "Is it possible that I could be the father of the promised Saviour?" Yet as time passed and Sarai remained childless, he told God that his heir would be his servant Eliezer of Damascus.

God replied, "A son coming from your own body will be your heir" (Gen. 15:4). Then God took him outside and asked him to count the stars, if he could. The Lord promised him, "So shall your offspring be" (Gen. 15:5).

As soon as Abram believed, the Lord counted it to him as righteousness. In God's eyes he was declared free from the guilt of sin. He became a child of God and belonged to the kingdom of God. Although he was not called a Christian,

Abram was assured of salvation because of Jesus' death and resurrection. Eusebius, the first Church historian, elaborates, "If any one should assert that all those who have enjoyed the testimony of righteousness, from Abraham himself back to the first man, were Christians in fact if not in name, he would not go beyond the truth."[2] He expands on this thought:

> They did not care about circumcision of the body, neither do we. They did not care about observing Sabbaths nor do we. They did not avoid certain kinds of food, neither did they regard the other distinctions which Moses first delivered to their posterity to be observed as symbols; nor do Christians of the present day do such things. But they also clearly knew the very Christ of God; for it has already been shown that he appeared unto Abraham, that he imparted revelations to Isaac, that he talked with Jacob, that he held converse with Moses and with the prophets that came after...
> So that it is clearly necessary to consider that religion, which has lately been preached to all nations through the teaching of Christ, the first and most ancient of all religions, and the one discovered by those divinely favoured men in the age of Abraham. If it is said that Abraham, a long time afterward, was given the command of circumcision, we reply that nevertheless before this it was so declared that he had received the testimony of righteousness through faith; as the divine word says, "Abraham believed God, and it was counted unto him for righteousness" (Gen. 15:6) [Rom. 4:3, KJV].[3]

Then God told Abram to bring him a heifer, a goat, a ram, a dove, and a pigeon. Abram cut the animals in half, but not the birds. He laid the halves opposite each other. After dark, when Abram was asleep, "a smoking firepot with a blazing torch appeared and passed between the pieces" (Gen. 15:17).

Thus God made a covenant with Abram that was ratified by the blood of those animals. He promised that Abram's descendants would inherit the land of Canaan.

Sometime later, Abram and Sarai were still childless and Sarai knew that she and Abram were not getting any younger. Therefore she persuaded him to follow the custom of the day and take Hagar, her maidservant, as his wife. Abram agreed to the plan, and Hagar conceived (Gen. 16:4). At the age of eighty-six Abram became the father of Ishmael (Gen. 16:16). Taking matters into his own hands and trying to help God give him an heir caused much heartbreak for their family throughout the years. As a result, Abram had to wait thirteen more years before the Lord renewed his promise to him.

4. The Everlasting Covenant, 1852 B.C.

"As for me, this is my covenant with you: You will be the father of many nations. No longer will you be called Abram; your name will be Abraham, for I have made you a father of many nations. I will make you very fruitful; I will make nations of you, and kings will come from you. I will establish my covenant as an everlasting covenant between me and you and your descendants after you for the generations to come, to be your God and the God of your descendants after you. The whole land of Canaan, where you are now an alien, I will give as an everlasting possession to you and your descendants after you; and I will be their God…As for Sarai your wife, you are no longer to call her Sarai; her name will be Sarah. I will bless her and will surely give you a son by her. I will bless her so that she will be the mother of nations; kings of peoples will come from her" (Gen. 17:4-8,15,16).

When Abram was ninety-nine years old, the Lord made an everlasting covenant with him. The Lord told Abram that as a sign of this covenant he must be circumcised and that every eight-day-old male in his house must also be circumcised.

"Any uncircumcised male, who has not been circumcised in the flesh, will be cut off from his people; he has broken my covenant" (Gen. 17:14). Now called Abraham, he showed his faith in God by immediately circumcising himself and every male in his household. Entwined in the everlasting covenant are two sets of promises, one spiritual and the other physical. Concerning the spiritual promises of God, Paul writes:

> *Brothers, let me take an example from everyday life. Just as no one can set aside or add to a human covenant that has been duly established, so it is in this case. The promises were spoken to Abraham and to his seed. The Scripture does not say "and to seeds," meaning many people, but "and to your seed," meaning one person, who is Christ* (Gal. 3:15,16).[4]

The covenant between Abraham and Christ can never be broken or changed. It does not matter what people think about the Lord or how they behave. The promised Seed will come. God will complete his plan. Paul also explains:

> *Therefore, the promise comes by faith, so that it may be by grace and may be guaranteed to all Abraham's offspring—not only to those who are of the law but also to those who are of the faith of Abraham. He is the father of us all. As it is written: "I have made you a father of many nations." He is our father in the sight of God, in whom he believed* (Rom. 4:16,17).

God promised to bestow the blessings of this everlasting covenant on those who have faith in him. By accepting his gift of salvation, they will become Abraham's children in the spiritual sense; race does not matter. Such people will prove the reality of their faith by obeying God's commands with a willing and loving heart attitude.

The New Testament gives us a glimpse into the thought life of Abraham. Although he lived in a tent like a stranger in a foreign land, "he was looking forward to the city with foundations, whose architect and builder is God" (Heb. 11:10). Abraham, his son Isaac, and his grandson Jacob loved God and cared more about spiritual realities than earthly dreams. "Instead, they were longing for a better country—a heavenly one. Therefore God is not ashamed to be called their God, for he has prepared a city for them" (Heb. 11:16). As Philip Mauro explains:

> This gives us clearly to know, *first* that "the promises" exerted a mighty influence over those to whom they were first given…and *second* that the nature of the promises was such as to turn their thoughts *entirely away from the earth*…For those promises had the effect of making even "the land of promise" itself to be to them as a foreign country. For while the land of Canaan was indeed promised to Abraham's natural seed, that promise never was "the hope of Israel." The hope of the gospel which God preached to Abraham was of such a nature that it caused him, and those who were "the heirs with him of the same promise," to declare themselves "strangers and pilgrims *on the earth*."[5]

Concerning the physical promises, earlier God had told Abraham that the boundaries of the Promised Land would be from the River of Egypt to the great river, the Euphrates (Gen. 15:18). Just before his death Joshua told the nation of Israel, "You know with all your heart and soul that not one of all the good promises the LORD your God gave you has failed. Every promise has been fulfilled; not one has failed" (Josh. 23:14). Through the battles of David, Israel actually conquered all the Promised Land. The Israelites possessed everything from the

Shihor River in Egypt to Lebo Hamath in the north (1 Chron. 13:5). David even gained control along the Euphrates River (2 Sam. 8:3-11).

History records how often the nation of Israel vacillated between obedience and disobedience of God. Just before his people entered the Promised Land, God explained the necessity of obedience in order to continue receiving physical blessings (Deut. 27-30). Some people with tunnel vision only considered God's promise of land. They ignored the consequences of disobedience. Thus they easily imagined that the Lord promised to be the tribal god of Israel forever. This attitude can be seen in 2 Esdras, first written in approximately A.D. 70[6] and completed in its final form by A.D. 120.[7]

> All this have I spoken before thee, O Lord, because thou madest the world for our sakes. As for the other people, which also come of Adam, thou hast said that they are nothing, but be like unto spittle: and hast likened the abundance of them unto a drop that falleth from a vessel. And now, O Lord, behold these heathen, which have ever been reputed as nothing, have begun to be lords over us, and to devour us. But we thy people (whom thou hast called thy firstborn, thy only begotten, and thy fervent lover) are given into their hands. If the world now be made for our sakes, why do we not possess an inheritance with the world? how long shall this endure? (2 Esd. 6:55—59, KJV).

This type of thinking is the essence of Zionism, a belief in the intrinsic right of the Jews to reestablish themselves as a nation in Palestine whether they are obedient to the Lord or not. Modern Israelites consider God's promise of land to Abraham as their

The present nation of Israel is a witness of God's mighty power and love, not a fulfillment of this covenant.

birthright. Actually, it is a privilege. For 1900 years God punished his people for rejecting Jesus as their Messiah and their Saviour. Then he mercifully allowed them to go back to the Promised Land, although they still did not acknowledge his Son. The present nation of Israel is a witness of God's mighty power and love, not a fulfillment of this covenant.

5. THE BIRTH OF ISAAC, 1851 B.C.

Nothing can compare to the joy of holding a precious little baby, a gift from God. No wonder Abraham and Sarah were beaming with happiness! They had waited so long. Laughing to himself, Abraham thought, "Will a son be born to a man a hundred years old? Will Sarah bear a child at the age of ninety?" (Gen. 17:17).

Abraham wished that the Lord would bless Ishmael. God responded by saying, "Yes, but your wife Sarah will bear you a son, and you will call him Isaac. I will establish my covenant with him as an everlasting covenant for his descendants after him" (Gen. 17:19).

Soon afterwards Abraham was sitting at the entrance to his tent in the heat of the day. Looking up he saw three men, one of whom was the Lord. Abraham hurriedly prepared a meal for them and stood near them under a tree while they ate. Afterwards the Lord confirmed to Abraham that Sarah would have a son about the same time the following year. Hiding at the entrance to the tent, Sarah heard the conversation. She knew that she was too old to conceive a baby. Laughing to herself, Sarah thought, "After I am worn out and my master is old, will I now have this pleasure?" (Gen. 18:12).

> Hiding at the entrance to the tent, Sarah heard the conversation. She knew that she was too old to conceive a baby.

For many years Abraham and Sarah had waited for the son of promise to be born. Both of them "faced the fact that his

The Founding Fathers of the Faith 51

body was as good as dead—since he was about a hundred years old—and that Sarah's womb was also dead" (Rom. 4:19). Knowing those truths only strengthened their faith in the power of God "to do what he had promised" (Rom. 4:21). At last the day arrived when Isaac was born. When he was eight days old, Abraham circumcised him and Sarah joyfully praised the Lord. "God has brought me laughter, and everyone who hears about this will laugh with me" (Gen. 21:6).

6. The Testing of Abraham and Isaac

Parents who have buried a child have experienced pain similar to Abraham's when God asked him to sacrifice his son. When Isaac had grown up (he was probably a teenager), the Lord came to Abraham and said, "Take your son, your only son, Isaac, whom you love, and go to the region of Moriah. Sacrifice him there as a burnt offering on one of the mountains I will tell you about" (Gen. 22:2).

How ecstatic Satan must have been! If Abraham killed the son of promise, then God would no longer be able to send the promised Seed. Satan would indeed win the throne.

Abraham did not waste any time. He cut wood and saddled his donkey. Taking with him two of his servants and his son Isaac, he began his journey to Mount Moriah. For two days the four of them travelled. On the third day Abraham could finally see the mountain in the distance. He told his servants, "Stay here with the donkey while I and the boy go over there. We will worship and then we will come back to you" (Gen. 22:5).

Imagine how Abraham must have felt! He had waited so long for the birth of this son, who truly was the son of promise. He and Sarah had lovingly watched and guided Isaac as he grew up. Through Isaac's seed would come the one to be his Saviour. Why would the Lord order him to sacrifice Isaac? Yet he knew that he must obey. Abraham remembered the blessings of following God to an unknown land. He grieved over the tensions caused by the birth of Ishmael. "Abraham reasoned that God could raise the dead, and figuratively speaking, he did receive Isaac back from death" (Heb. 11:19). Because the promised Seed would come from Isaac, Abraham knew that his son could not stay dead.

> Because the promised Seed would come from Isaac, Abraham knew that his son could not stay dead.

As they climbed the mountain, Isaac carried the wood for the sacrifice while Abraham held the fire and the knife. Wondering why his father did not bring an animal, Isaac asked, "The fire and wood are here...but where is the lamb for the burnt offering?" (Gen. 22:7).

Abraham replied, "God himself will provide the lamb for the burnt offering, my son" (Gen. 22:8).

Isaac accepted his father's answer, and they continued to climb up the mountain together. After the altar was built, and the wood was arranged on it, Isaac willingly allowed himself to be bound and laid on top of the wood. Just as Abraham was about to kill his son with the knife, he heard a voice calling:

> "Abraham! Abraham!"
> "Here I am," he replied.
> "Do not lay a hand on the boy," he said. "Do not do anything to him. Now I know that you fear God, because you have not withheld from me your son, your only son" (Gen. 22:10-12).

Looking up, Abraham saw a ram caught in a bush. He took Isaac off the altar, placed the ram on it instead, and sacrificed it as a burnt offering. With a thankful heart Abraham named that special place, "The LORD Will Provide" (Gen. 22:14).

Then the angel of the Lord told Abraham that his descendants would be as numerous as the stars in the sky and as the sand on the seashore, because he had been willing to give up Isaac in order to obey God. Looking back from this side of Calvary, we can see a beautiful picture of God the Father sacrificing his only Son Jesus for our sake. From Abraham's point of view, however, he was thankful that he did not have to give

The Founding Fathers of the Faith 53

up the son whom he loved so much and that the line of the promised Seed was preserved.

7. THE BIRTH OF JACOB AND ESAU, 1791 B.C. (GEN. 25:20,26)

No doubt Isaac knew that he was the son of promise and that the Saviour would come through his seed. Unlike his father Abraham, he waited patiently for his son to be born and did not try to take matters into his own hands. For twenty years Isaac and his wife Rebekah waited for a child. When she was finally expecting a baby, she felt so much movement inside her that she asked God what was happening. He answered, "Two nations are in your womb, and two peoples from within you will be separated; one people will be stronger than the other, and the older will serve the younger" (Gen. 25:23).

How excited Rebekah must have been when she told her husband what the Lord had said! Not only was she was having twins, but the line of promise would go through the second child. In due time she gave birth to two boys. Since the first baby was red and hairy, his parents named him Esau. They called the second child Jacob, because he was holding onto Esau's heel. Knowing the Lord's will did not prevent them from playing favourites. Isaac loved Esau, the hunter, and Rebekah loved Jacob, the shepherd. As a result that family suffered a lot of heartache.

8. JACOB'S WRESTLING MATCH WITH GOD

Early in the morning Jacob limped to the ford of the Jabbok, a stream that flows into the Jordan River. The previous night he had sent his family across the ford, but he had remained alone on the north side, where he had wrestled with a man all night. Before daybreak the man touched the socket of his hip and wrenched it out of place.

> *Then the man said, "Let me go, for it is daybreak."*
> *But Jacob replied, "I will not let you go unless you bless me."*

> *The man asked him, "What is your name?"*
>
> *"Jacob," he answered.*
>
> *Then the man said, "Your name will no longer be Jacob, but Israel, because you have struggled with God and with men and have overcome."*
>
> *Jacob said, "Please tell me your name."*
>
> *But he replied, "Why do you ask my name?" Then he blessed him there.*
>
> *So Jacob called the place Peniel, saying, "It is because I saw God face to face, and yet my life was spared"* (Gen. 32:26-30).

As Jacob limped toward the river, perhaps he thought about his past life as well as what had just happened. Named Jacob, meaning "supplanter,"[8] he had lived up to his name. How well he remembered the day Esau had come home starving! As soon as Esau smelled the delicious stew that Jacob was cooking, he asked for some. Instead of feeding his brother, Jacob bargained with him. "First sell me your birthright," he replied.

Esau was so hungry and had so little regard for his birthright as the firstborn male that he cried, "Look, I am about to die. What good is the birthright to me?"
Jacob answered, "Swear to me first" (see Gen. 25:31-33).

In swearing an oath to Jacob, Esau sold his birthright for some bread and lentil stew. He ate, drank, and then left. By his actions Esau displayed contempt for his birthright, a double share of Isaac's legacy (Deut. 21:17).

Many years later, when Isaac was old and going blind, he thought that he was near death. Since Esau was his favourite, he wanted him to receive God's blessing. Isaac must have known that God wanted his special blessing to go to the younger son, Jacob. Isaac, however, asked Esau to hunt some wild game and prepare a meal for him. Then he would bless him. Meanwhile Rebekah was eavesdropping and was determined that Jacob should receive the blessing.

She immediately persuaded Jacob to wear goatskins on his wrists and neck so that he would feel like Esau. Soon Jacob wore Esau's clothes and brought Isaac a tasty meal cooked by his mother. Isaac was sure that the voice was Jacob's, but he thought that the hands were Esau's.

Isaac asked, "Are you really my son Esau?"

"I am," Jacob replied (Gen. 27:24).

After eating the meal, Isaac blessed Jacob. A short time later Esau came in with the game that he had prepared.

> *Isaac trembled violently and said, "Who was it, then, that hunted game and brought it to me? I ate it just before you came and I blessed him—and indeed he will be blessed!"*
>
> *When Esau heard his father's words, he burst out with a loud and bitter cry and said to his father, "Bless me—me too, my father!"*
>
> *But he [Isaac] said, "Your brother came deceitfully and took your blessing."*
>
> *Esau said, "Isn't he rightly named Jacob? He has deceived me these two times: He took my birthright, and now he's taken my blessing!"* (Gen. 27:33-36).

Jacob would have remembered how Esau had angrily wanted to kill him and how he had fled for his life to his relatives in Paddan Aram. Perhaps Jacob thought about that first night on the run. He had had a dream in which he saw a stairway reaching up to heaven, with angels walking up and down it. At the very top was the Lord, who said,

> "I am the LORD, the God of your father Abraham and the God of Isaac. I will give you and your descendants the land on which you are lying. Your descendants will be like the dust of the earth, and you will spread out to the west and to the east, to the north and to the south. All peoples on earth will be blessed through you and your offspring. I am with you and will watch over you wherever you go, and I will bring you back to this land. I will not leave you until I have done what I have promised you" (Gen. 28:13-15).

When he awoke in the morning, Jacob poured oil on the stone that he had used as a pillow and called the place Bethel, meaning "house of God" (Gen. 28:19, NIV). The Lord had said that he was the God of Abraham and Isaac. All of the blessings promised to them would continue through Jacob. That liar and cheat belonged to the line of the promised Seed. God was working out his plan of salvation through Jacob. This should encourage each one of us, for we are all sinners saved by the grace of God.

> That liar and cheat belonged to the line of the promised Seed.

Jacob responded by saying, "If God will be with me and will watch over me on this journey I am taking and will give me food to eat and clothes to wear so that I return safely to my father's house, then the LORD will be my God and this stone that I have set up as a pillar will be God's house, and of all that you give me I will give you a tenth" (Gen. 28:20-22). How presumptuous he was—trying to bargain with God! "If you do what I ask, then I will believe and call you my God."

For the following twenty years, Jacob knew that the Lord had been with him and had blessed him. When he had fled, he had only his shepherd's staff and the clothes on his back. Now he was crossing the river to go back home with two wives, two concubines, eleven sons, servants, and livestock. Nevertheless, he was still terrified of Esau, especially when he heard that Esau was coming to meet him with 400 men. In praying to God for safety, he called the Lord "God of my father Abraham, God of my father Isaac" (Gen. 32:9). Then he sent his servants on ahead with a gift of many animals for Esau. He decided to split his party up into two, so that if Esau attacked one group, the other could escape. Jacob himself was at the rear of everybody else. He stayed alone on the other side of the river because he was still putting himself first.

The Lord had been merciful to Jacob and had blessed him, even though he was a liar and a cheat. At the ford the Lord reminded Jacob of his promise twenty years earlier. In effect

God was saying, "I have kept my end of the bargain, Jacob. It is time for you to submit to me and lovingly acknowledge that I am *your* God, not just the God of your father and your grandfather." Jacob struggled with God and finally begged for God's forgiveness and blessing. As a result he became a changed man. God gave him a new name, Israel, meaning, "He struggles with God" (Gen. 32:28, NIV). Jacob became the father of the race of Israel. How did he show that he was changed? He crossed the river and went to meet Esau face-to-face. He left his family in the rear where they were safer.

9. The Deathbed Blessings of Jacob, 1644 B.C. (Gen. 47:28)

At the age of 147, Jacob was about to die. He had lived the last seventeen years of his life in Egypt with his beloved son Joseph, who had been cruelly sold into slavery by his jealous brothers. Yet the Lord had mightily used Joseph to gain favour with Pharaoh. Joseph had been able to store up seven years worth of food to prepare for the seven years of famine that would follow. In so doing, Joseph not only kept many people from dying of starvation but also protected the line of the promised Seed from extinction.

Before his death, Jacob blessed each of his sons and his two grandsons Ephraim and Manasseh, Joseph's sons. Jacob testified that the Lord had been his shepherd all his life and the Angel who had delivered him from all harm (Gen. 48:15,16). His son Judah received God's special blessing:

> *Judah, your brothers will praise you; your hand will be on the neck of your enemies; your father's sons will bow down to you...The scepter will not depart from Judah, nor the ruler's staff from between his feet, until he comes to whom it belongs and the obedience of the nations is his* (Gen. 49:8-10).

God promised three things to Judah. The family of kings to rule Israel would descend from him; this line would remain unbroken until the arrival of the one to whom the throne belongs; and this future king would have authority over all nations. History records that David of Judah's tribe was placed on the throne of Israel. Until the captivity, David's descendants remained the only kings of Jerusalem. Then, because of the nation's sin, the Babylonians took the people of Judah captive. At their release, Zerubbabel, a descendant of David, became the governor of Judea under the authority of the Medo-Persian Empire. Briefly, when Judea was autonomous under the Maccabees (142 B.C.-63 B.C.), the people preferred to disregard this prophecy and exalt the tribe of Levi.[9] Yet God continued to ensure that the line of David existed until the birth of Jesus. Matthew records the fulfillment of this promise: "A record of the genealogy of Jesus Christ the son of David, the son of Abraham" (Matt. 1:1). The men listed in Matthew 1:12-16 belonged to the royal line authorized by God. Even Joseph, Mary's husband, would have been king. Although not biologically related, Jesus was the official son of Joseph and next in line to rule. Because the nation was disobedient to God, all of those men were unable to sit on David's throne. Only Jesus, as the promised Seed, has the right to the throne. After Jesus' death and resurrection, "God exalted him to the highest place" (Phil. 2:9). Then Jesus had authority to instruct his followers, "Therefore go and make disciples of all nations" (Matt. 28:19). This was a revolutionary idea. The Lord expects people from every race to obey Jesus lovingly, because he is King over all nations, not just Israel.

When God revealed himself to Abraham and his family, he completed an important step in his plan of salvation. Their descendants would become the future nation of Israel. The promised Seed would be born into a nation that knew who God is. In addition to preparing for the future birth of Jesus, God also worked in the hearts of the founding fathers themselves. Abraham, Isaac, and Jacob discovered first-hand that God always keeps his promises in the physical world. As a result, they counted on him to tell the truth about the spiritual realm. They lovingly obeyed the Lord and trusted him to keep his promise to provide for their salvation.

Points to Ponder

1. Abram grew up in a society ignorant of the one true God.
2. By cheerfully tithing, we bring honour to God and acknowledge his providence in supplying all of our needs. This is what Abram did.
3. When God declared Abram righteous, Abram was free from sin's guilt just like us.
4. Whoever trusts and obeys God is a spiritual child of Abraham.
5. God proves his reliability by keeping his promise to Jacob. Over 600 years after Jacob's death, David, who was a descendant of Judah, became king. Then 1000 years after David, Jesus, who was a descendant of David, was born.

Chapter Four

The Establishment of Israel as a Nation

1. The Birth of Moses, 1526 B.C.,

118 years after the death of Jacob

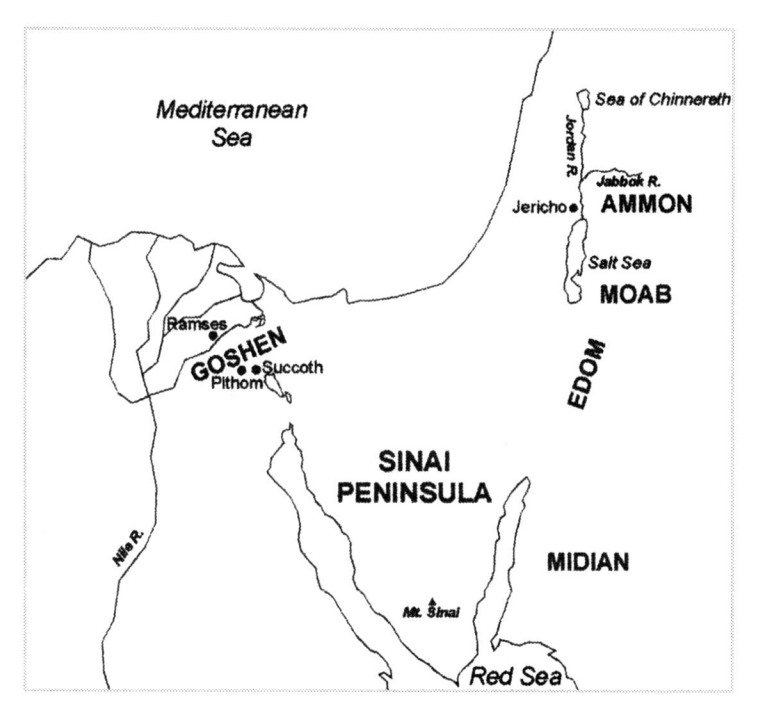

Figure 2: World of Moses

AFTER twenty-seven years working at home, I was no longer qualified to be a computer programmer—the position that I had before moving to Sudbury. Retail was the easiest and quickest way to reenter the workforce. I soon learned that the best guarantee of more hours was to be on call all the time. In other words, my life was not my own. The Israelites certainly felt that way. The present Pharaoh did not remember that Joseph had saved the Egyptians from starvation. When he saw how numerous the Israelites were, he was afraid of them. He did not want them to grow more powerful so that they would fight against Egypt and leave the country. Therefore he made them slaves and forced them to build two cities, Pithom and Rameses. Yet slavery did not stop their phenomenal population explosion. Then the Egyptians feared the Israelites even more and forced them to work harder.

Pharaoh decided, "I will order the Hebrew midwives to kill all the boy babies at birth." Because the midwives feared God, they refused to do it. When the people continued to increase in numbers, Pharaoh desperately ordered all of the Egyptians to throw every newborn Israelite boy into the Nile (see Exod. 1:8-22).

No doubt Satan was thrilled. "Make sure you kill every boy in the tribe of Judah," he thought. Then the boy who was the direct ancestor of the promised Seed would die.

At this time one of the slaves, Amram, from the tribe of Levi, had two children, Aaron and Miriam, and a wife, Jochebed, who was pregnant. By faith Jochebed and Amram hid their baby for three months after he was born (Exod. 2:1-2). They could see that Moses was special, and they did not fear the king's edict (Heb. 11:23). Knowing that she could not conceal her child from the Egyptians forever, Jochebed made a papyrus basket coated with tar and pitch. After placing Moses in it, she put the basket among the reeds at the edge of the Nile River. Miriam watched her brother from a distance to see what would happen (Exod. 2:3-4).

A while later Pharaoh's daughter went down to the Nile to bathe. When she found the child, she felt sorry for him and said, "This is one of the Hebrew babies" (Exod. 2:6).

Approaching the princess, Miriam bravely asked, "Shall I go and get one of the Hebrew women to nurse the baby for you?" (Exod. 2:7).

The princess replied, "Yes, go" (Exod. 2:8).

Surprisingly, the princess paid Jochebed to nurse her own baby. As soon as the child was weaned, Jochebed took him to Pharaoh's daughter, and he became her son. The princess named him Moses, saying, "I drew him out of the water" (Exod. 2:10).

By trying to thwart God's plan to form the nation of Israel, Pharaoh gained a Hebrew grandson. Of course, he did not know it. How else could a Hebrew slave grow up in Pharaoh's court and receive the best education in the land, if it were not for the providence of God?

> By trying to thwart God's plan to form the nation of Israel, Pharaoh gained a Hebrew grandson.

By faith Moses, when he had grown up, refused to be known as the son of Pharaoh's daughter. He chose to be mistreated along with the people of God rather than to enjoy the pleasures of sin for a short time. He regarded disgrace for the sake of Christ as of greater value than the treasures of Egypt, because he was looking ahead to his reward. By faith he left Egypt, not fearing the king's anger; he persevered because he saw him who is invisible (Heb. 11:24-27).

Moses spent the next forty years in the wilderness with Reuel, a priest of Midian (Exod. 2:15-21). Reuel was a descendant of Keturah, Abraham's third wife (Gen. 25:1-4). Through Reuel, Moses learned more about the one true God. For forty years he was educated in the ways of Egypt. Then for forty more years he grew in the knowledge of God. The Lord was gradually carrying out his plan of salvation. At the proper time God would call Moses to be the deliverer of his people.

2. THE PASSOVER, 1446 B.C.

The Lord was finally ready to rescue the Israelites from Egypt. He had prepared Moses from birth for the task of leading the people out of Egypt. God even enabled Moses and his brother Aaron to perform miraculous signs, but Pharaoh still refused to let the Israelites leave. How often they pleaded with Pharaoh! "This is what the LORD, the God of the Hebrews, says: 'Let my people go, so that they may worship me'" (Exod. 9:1). Each time that Pharaoh denied their request, God sent another plague—water turned to blood, frogs, gnats, flies, death of livestock, boils, hail, locusts, and darkness. Then the day came when the Lord told Moses that he would bring one last plague on Egypt, because Pharaoh still would not let the people go (Exod. 11:1).

Moses told the Israelites exactly what to do. First they asked the Egyptians for gifts of gold, silver, and clothing, which they willingly gave. God declared that this month would be the first month of the Israelite year. On the tenth day each man was to take a lamb or a goat for his family. Neighbours were to band together if there were not enough in one family to eat a whole lamb at one meal. The animal chosen had to be a year-old male without defect. At twilight on the fourteenth day of the month, the chosen animals had to be killed. Some of the blood had to be put on the sides and tops of the door frames of the houses where the lambs would be eaten. They were to roast the lamb whole over the fire and eat it with unleavened bread and bitter herbs. They had to eat it with their cloaks tucked into their belts, their sandals on their feet, and their staves in their hands. "Eat it in haste; it is the LORD's Passover" (Exod. 12:11). Any meat not eaten had to be burned. None could be left until the morning (Exod. 12:10).

When the children were growing up, I felt like one of those Israelites. Every Christmas we travelled from northern Ontario to Toronto and Detroit. The day before we left I would be busy packing and also preparing a special dinner. That evening we would celebrate Jesus' birth with our children. Then the next morning we left to visit our families.

On the appointed day everyone was careful to follow God's instructions exactly. At midnight, all of the firstborn in Egypt who were not protected by blood over the door frame died.

Pharaoh immediately ordered Moses and Aaron, "Up! Leave my people, you and the Israelites! Go, worship the LORD as you have requested. Take your flocks and herds, as you have said, and go. And also bless me" (Exod. 12:31,32).

The Egyptians were eager to get rid of the Israelites and urged them to go. "'For otherwise,' they said, 'we will all die!'" (Exod. 12:33). Quickly the Israelites gathered all of their belongings and the gifts that they had received from the Egyptians.

God told Moses, "Consecrate to me every firstborn male. The first offspring of every womb among the Israelites belongs to me, whether man or animal" (Exod. 13:2).

Then Moses instructed the people:

> *In days to come, when your son asks you, "What does this mean?" say to him, "With a mighty hand the LORD brought us out of Egypt, out of the land of slavery. When Pharaoh stubbornly refused to let us go, the LORD killed every firstborn in Egypt, both man and animal. This is why I sacrifice to the LORD the first male offspring of every womb and redeem each of my firstborn sons"* (Exod. 13:14,15).

For the Israelites, the Passover was a vivid lesson on the meaning of the word *redemption*, because they lived through the experience. Just as the Israelites taught their children the significance of the Passover, likewise the Lord expects believers to share their faith with their offspring. The firstborn boys realized that the blood of the lamb without blemish protected them from death. The whole congregation knew that they were rescued from Egypt by the blood of the sacrificial lamb. That blood secured their freedom from slavery. At this point they have no thought that blood must be shed to pay the penalty for their sins. At the Passover God bought the Israelites as his special people. Like the Israelites, believers have been bought with a price—the precious blood of Jesus. Paul calls Christ our Passover Lamb who has been sacrificed (1 Cor. 5:7). Peter writes, "For you know that it was not with perishable things such as silver or gold that you were redeemed from the empty way of life handed down to you from your forefathers, but with the precious blood of Christ, a lamb without blemish or defect" (1 Pet. 1:18,19). Jesus is the superior Passover Lamb. He did not die to free believers from political bondage but from the spiritual bondage of sin.

> Jesus is the superior Passover Lamb. He did not die to free believers from political bondage but from the spiritual bondage of sin.

The Passover was an important step in God's plan. He was about to establish a nation that would be taught important truths about the spiritual realm. They would learn first-hand who God is and what he expects of them. In the past only a few people had waited for the promised Seed to restore their broken relationship with God. Now more people would long for the Saviour to be born. In that day, religion and the state were closely intertwined. By taking advantage of that mindset, God could nurture and lovingly draw many Israelites into his kingdom. When the promised Seed did come, he would find a people prepared to receive him as their Saviour.

3. THE CROSSING OF THE RED SEA, 1446 B.C.

Shortly after the Israelites left, Pharaoh and his officials thought, "What have we done? We have let the Israelites go and have lost their services!" (Exod. 14:5). Immediately Pharaoh gathered all of his horses and chariots, horsemen, and troops to chase after them.

Meanwhile the Lord had been leading his people by a pillar of cloud in the daytime and by a pillar of fire at night (Exod. 13:21-22), first in one direction and then in another. He did it deliberately so that Pharaoh would think that they were wandering around in confusion, not sure where to go. When Pharaoh and his army caught up to them, the Israelites were trapped beside the Red Sea. The cloud moved from the front to the back of the Israelites. For the Egyptians it was dark, while for the Israelites it was light the entire night (Exod. 14:19-20).

God told Moses to raise his hand out over the sea, "and all that night the Lord drove the sea back with a strong east wind and turned it into dry land. The waters were divided, and the Israelites went through the sea on dry ground, with a wall of water on their right and on their left" (Exod. 14:21,22). After the Israelites and the mixed multitude that accompanied them were safely across, God allowed the Egyptian horsemen and chariots to follow them into the sea. The wheels of their chariots started falling off, so the Egyptians had difficulty driving. They cried, "Let's get away from the Israelites! The Lord is fighting for them against Egypt" (Exod. 14:25).

> The miracle of the parting of the waters was salvation to the Israelites and judgment to the Egyptians.

The miracle of the parting of the waters was salvation to the Israelites and judgment to the Egyptians. At daybreak the Lord told Moses to stretch his hand out over the sea, and the waters flowed over the entire Egyptian army that was in the sea. Every single person died (Exod. 14:26-28). "That day the Lord saved Israel from the hands of the Egyptians, and Israel saw the Egyptians lying dead on the shore. And when the Israelites saw the great power the Lord displayed against the Egyptians, the people feared the Lord and put their trust in him and in Moses his servant" (Exod. 14:30,31).

What a victory celebration! Freedom at last! Moses sang a song giving all the praise and glory to God, and later on Miriam led the women in a song. The crossing of the Red Sea was the climax of the Lord's judgments against the false gods of Egypt. Moses sang, "Who among the gods is like you, O Lord? Who is like you—majestic in holiness, awesome in glory, working wonders?" (Exod. 15:11).

To Moses, God is his Saviour. "The Lord is my strength and my song; he has become my salvation" (Exod. 15:2).

To Moses, God is the victorious Warrior. "The LORD is a warrior; the LORD is his name...The enemy boasted, 'I will pursue, I will overtake them. I will divide the spoils; I will gorge myself on them. I will draw my sword and my hand will destroy them.' But you blew with your breath, and the sea covered them. They sank like lead in the mighty waters" (Exod. 15:3,9,10).

To Moses, God is the King of the whole earth. "Your right hand, O LORD, was majestic in power. Your right hand, O LORD, shattered the enemy. In the greatness of your majesty you threw down those who opposed you...Who is like you—majestic in holiness...The LORD will reign for ever and ever" (Exod. 15:6,7,11,18).

To Moses, God is all powerful. He has authority over nature. "By the blast of your nostrils the waters piled up" (Exod. 15:8). He rules over every nation. "You stretched out your right hand and the earth swallowed them...the people of Canaan will melt away; terror and dread will fall upon them" (Exod. 15:12,15,16).

To those who obey him, God is loving and merciful. When the destroyer passed through Egypt, only those firstborn sheltered by the blood were saved. Theoretically, this included Egyptians but they did not obey (Exod. 12:23,29). "In your unfailing love you will lead the people you have redeemed" (Exod. 15:13).

Finally, to Moses, God is the Promise keeper. "You will bring them in and plant them on the mountain of your inheritance—the place, O LORD, you made for your dwelling, the sanctuary, O Lord, your hands established" (Exod. 15:17). God told the truth; he was keeping his promise to Abraham.

4. THE COVENANT AT SINAI, 1446 B.C.

The formation of the nation of Israel is the next step in God's plan of salvation

Now if you obey me fully and keep my covenant, then out of all nations you will be my treasured possession.

The Establishment of Israel as a Nation 69

Although the whole earth is mine, you will be for me a kingdom of priests and a holy nation (Exod. 19:5,6).

In the third month after the Israelites had left Egypt, they arrived at Mount Sinai. Moses went up the mountain to talk to God, who promised that the Israelites would be his treasured possession, a kingdom of priests, and a holy nation. There was, however, one condition. They must obey him fully and keep his covenant. As soon as Moses relayed the message, the people answered without any hesitation, "We will do everything the Lord has said" (Exod. 19:8).

Afterwards God told Moses that he would come on him in a dense cloud. As soon as the people would hear God speak to Moses, they would know that they could always trust Moses' word. For two days the Israelites washed their clothes and consecrated themselves. Then on the third day the Lord came down on the mountain in a thick cloud of smoke. The people saw lightning. They heard thunder and the sound of a very loud trumpet. The whole camp trembled, especially when the mountain shook and the sound of the trumpet grew louder and louder. Moses led them to the foot of the mountain and told them not to go up it, because it was holy. Then God spoke the Ten Commandments.

The Israelites were so afraid that they did not want God to speak to them directly again. Instead they begged Moses, "Speak to us yourself and we will listen. But do not have God speak to us or we will die" (Exod. 20:19).

They stayed far away as Moses once again drew near to God in the thick darkness surrounding the mountain. The Lord spoke to Moses, "Tell the Israelites this: 'You have seen for yourselves that I have spoken to you from heaven: Do not make any gods to be alongside me; do not make for yourselves gods of silver or gods of gold'" (Exod. 20:22,23).

Afterwards God explained in detail the commandments that the Israelites must obey. Those Laws would be the foundation for the new nation of Israel. As soon as Moses came back down the mountain, Moses told the Israelites everything that God had said. They gladly answered, "Everything the LORD has said we will do" (Exod. 24:3).

Moses wrote God's commandments in the Book of the Covenant. The next day he built an altar and a monument of twelve stone pillars—one for each tribe. After he read the Book of the Covenant to everyone, they answered, "We will do everything the LORD has said; we will obey" (Exod. 24:7).

Years later Jesus would shed his blood and become the sacrifice of the new covenant. The Bible is divided into two parts, the Old Testament and the New Testament, meaning the old covenant and the new covenant. The old covenant also required the shedding of blood:

> *This is why even the first covenant was not put into effect without blood. When Moses had proclaimed every commandment of the law to all the people, he took the blood of calves, together with water, scarlet wool and branches of hyssop, and sprinkled the scroll and all the people. He said, "This is the blood of the covenant, which God has commanded you to keep"* (Heb. 9:18-20).

In the covenant at Sinai God promised Israel that they were his special people. He separated them from the rest of the world and its false gods in order to have fellowship with them. This was an important step in the plan of God to obtain our salvation from sin and from the kingdom of Satan. No matter how the Israelites behaved, God would send the promised Seed into this nation. If they disobeyed, they would lose the blessings promised in this covenant, but the long-awaited Saviour, the promised Seed, would still have a family and a nation to whom he would belong. Instead of a few individuals here and there waiting for the promised Seed, many in Israel would be expecting the Saviour's arrival. When his public ministry

> No matter how the Israelites behaved, God would send the promised Seed into this nation.

The Establishment of Israel as a Nation 71

began, those believers could rejoice with God. Concerning Israel's heritage, Paul writes, "Theirs is the adoption as sons; theirs the divine glory, the covenants, the receiving of the law, the temple worship and the promises. Theirs are the patriarchs, and from them is traced the human ancestry of Christ, who is God over all, forever praised! Amen" (Rom. 9:4,5).

After he had spoken the Ten Commandments to all of the people, God told Moses to remind them to not make any gods out of silver or gold. Soon after the covenant had been ratified by the sacrifice of calves, God told Moses to go back up the mountain. There he received two tablets of stone with the Ten Commandments inscribed upon them. For forty days and forty nights God instructed Moses on how to build the tabernacle, what to put in it, what the priests were to wear, and how to consecrate them to his service.

Meanwhile, back at the camp, when the people realized that Moses still had not come back, they begged Aaron to make a god for them. Consequently Aaron asked all of the people to take off their earrings and bring them to him. After melting the gold, he formed it into the shape of a calf. Then the people shouted, "These are your gods, O Israel, who brought you up out of Egypt" (Exod. 32:4).

Less than forty days after the Israelites had willingly and gladly promised to obey all of God's commandments, they did exactly what he had told them never to do. As if that was not bad enough, the mighty power that God had displayed against the Egyptians was attributed to a golden calf.

5. THE PURPOSE OF THE LAW

Those who live according to the sinful nature have their minds set on what that nature desires...The mind of sinful man is death...the sinful mind is hostile to God. It does not submit to God's law, nor can it do so. Those controlled by the sinful nature cannot please God...For if you live according to the sinful nature, you will die (Rom. 8:5-13).

When Adam and Eve broke the one and only command that they had received, death entered the world. They suffered not only physical death but also spiritual death. All of us are under the same condemnation. Because we have inherited the sin nature from them, we are prone to sin. Everyone is born naturally hostile to God and a member of Satan's kingdom.

> *Therefore, just as sin entered the world through one man, and death through sin, and in this way death came to all men, because all sinned—for before the law was given, sin was in the world* (Rom. 5:12,13).

The Lord judges each of us guilty for two reasons. We bear the original guilt of Adam, because we have inherited his sin nature. We are also responsible for the sins that we commit. Since death is the punishment for sin and everyone dies, this proves that sin has been in the world since Eve first ate the forbidden fruit. Yet, before God gave his Law to Israel, how would a person realize that he or she had a sin nature? How would anyone know what sin was? At that time God's only witness was his creation. Sadly, most turned their backs upon God the Creator and worshipped his creation instead. For this reason the heathen were judged as sinners. The Law did not condemn them, because they were ignorant of it.

> *Through the law we become conscious of sin* (Rom. 3:20).

At one point in my retail career, one company took over the operation of some stores from another. The new company had new rules of operation for us to follow. Obviously the purpose of the new way of doing business was to increase sales. It also revealed the heart attitude of the employees. Some became overly aggressive, territorial, and greedy. Others lied. One girl stepped her foot over an imaginary line and looked at me to see how I would react.

Since the Law helps us understand the reality of sin, Paul writes, "What shall we say, then? Is the law sin? Certainly not!

Indeed I would not have known what sin was except through the law. For I would not have known what coveting really was if the law had not said, 'Do not covet'" (Rom. 7:7).

With the establishment of Israel as a nation under the kingship of God, the Lord revealed more of himself to people. Every nation needs laws; otherwise there would be anarchy. In giving the Law to Israel, God also contrasted his holiness with the sinfulness of people. This goal was more important to him than merely sustaining physical peace and stability in the land. From the beginning of time God planned to send his Son, the promised Seed, the one who would be our Saviour and would restore us to fellowship with him. Yet unless we understand what sin is and how we are guilty of sin, why should we want, or understand that we need, a Saviour? The function of the Law is to define sin and to make people aware that they are sinners.

> Yet unless we understand what sin is and how we are guilty of sin, why should we want, or understand that we need, a Saviour?

6. THE DAY OF ATONEMENT

God did not make the children of Israel conscious of their sin and then leave them without hope. After all, if anyone broke the Law, then that person should be punished. Because God loved them and wanted to avert their punishment, he instructed Moses on how to set up an elaborate sacrificial system. The Lord said that if anyone sinned unintentionally and broke any of God's Law, he was guilty. After becoming aware of committing the sin, the person had to present God with a young bull as a sin offering. After the bull was killed, the priest had to put some of the blood on his finger and put it on the horns of the altar. Then he had to pour out the rest of the blood at the base of the altar and burn the fat on the altar. The rest of the bull had to be burned outside the camp. "In this way the priest will make atonement for him for the sin he had committed, and he will be forgiven" (Lev. 4:35). By continually shedding the blood of animals whenever they sinned, the Israelites were constantly reminded that sin causes death. They also learned how God allowed animals to take the punishment that they deserved.

In addition to the regular sacrifices, God told Moses that the tenth day of the seventh month would be the Day of Atonement. This would be the most important day of the year, because it would be the only time when the high priest would enter the Most Holy Place. Everyone gathered together for the sacred meeting while the high priest offered the required sacrifices to the Lord. No one worked on that day. Aaron could not enter the Most Holy Place whenever he pleased, because God was present in the cloud over the atonement cover. On this particular day, however, Aaron was allowed to enter the Most Holy Place in order to perform his high priestly duties.

First Aaron washed and put on the sacred garments of the high priest. Before he could deal with the sins of the people, he had to acknowledge his own sins. He offered a bull for a sin offering "to make atonement for himself and his household" (Lev. 16:6). Then he carried some incense and a censer full of burning coals from the altar into the Most Holy Place. He placed the censer on the floor and poured the incense onto the burning coals. Smoke filled the room immediately so that he was unable to see the atonement cover; otherwise he would die. Then he left to get the bull's blood. He returned to sprinkle some of it on the front of the atonement cover. He also sprinkled some blood with his finger onto the ground, before the cover, seven times.

After leaving the Most Holy Place, Aaron presented the Lord with two goats at the entrance to the tabernacle. Everyone watched as he cast lots to determine which goat would belong to the Lord and which one would be the scapegoat or the goat of removal (Lev. 16:8, NIV). The goat chosen for the Lord was immediately sacrificed as a sin offering. Aaron took some of its blood into the Most Holy Place and sprinkled it in the same manner as he had the bull's blood. No one was allowed into the tabernacle until Aaron came out.

As soon as Aaron finished sprinkling the blood of the bull and the goat, first on the tabernacle and then on the altar, he returned to the live goat. Laying both his hands on its head, he confessed over it "all their sins—and put them on the goat's head" (Lev. 16:21). A man chosen for the job led the goat away into the desert. "The goat will carry on itself all their sins to a solitary place; and the man shall release it in the desert" (Lev. 16:22). Aaron finished the ceremony by retrieving the censer from the Most Holy Place.

The yearly Day of Atonement was significant in the life of the Israelites. The events of that day encouraged them to focus on the fact that their sins were forgiven for one year because of the death of another. "Then, before the LORD, you will be clean from all your sins" (Lev. 16:30). One goat took the punishment that they deserved. Another goat carried their guilt far away. One goat represented the justice of God. Sin must be punished. The other goat showed the mercy of the Lord. The sin of the believer is forgiven. This is the clearest picture so far to illustrate God's plan for our salvation. After the death and resurrection of the promised Seed, God never demanded another payment. Jesus paid the penalty once for all time. Justice and mercy wed at the cross.

> One goat took the punishment that they deserved. Another goat carried their guilt far away.

7. THE TEMPORARY NATURE OF THE OLD COVENANT

The law is only a shadow of the good things that are coming—not the realities themselves. For this reason it can never, by the same sacrifices repeated endlessly year after year, make perfect those who draw near to worship. If it could, would they not have stopped being offered? For the worshipers would have been cleansed once for all, and would no longer have felt guilty for their sins (Heb. 10:1,2).

Sin separates us from God and prevents us from having fellowship with him. The shedding of the blood of bulls and goats was just a temporary measure. The Israelites still felt guilty for their sins. Some, however, were truly sorry for rebelling against God and thanked him for providing a temporary solution. Those people loved the Lord because of his mercy and compassion toward them. They also waited expectantly for the permanent reconciliation that the promised Seed would provide. By establishing the Law and the sacrificial system, God's intent was to show his love in a special way to the Israelites so that they would love him in return. He promised to love a thousand generations of those who love him and keep his commandments (Exod. 20:6). God desires our love more than our sacrifices.

> God desires our love more than our sacrifices.

Many years later, Jesus was in the temple and a teacher of the Law asked him:

> *"Of all the commandments, which is the most important?"*
>
> *"The most important one," answered Jesus, "is this: 'Hear, O Israel, the Lord our God, the Lord is one. Love the Lord your God with all your heart and with all your soul and with all your mind and with all your strength.' The second is this: 'Love your neighbor as yourself.' There is no commandment greater than these."*
>
> *"Well said, teacher," the man replied. "You are right in saying that God is one and there is no other but him. To love him with all your heart, with all your understanding and with all your strength, and to love your neighbor as yourself is more important than all burnt offerings and sacrifices"* (Mark 12:28-33).

God was not surprised when Aaron and the Israelites sinned so quickly after agreeing to obey the Ten Commandments. They had to battle the world, the flesh, and the Devil, just as Noah did. The Israelites honestly thought that they could keep the Law in their own strength. Yet God still made a covenant with them, because he wanted them to have the right heart attitude toward him. God wanted to teach them who he was and how he intended to provide for their salvation. They had to learn through trial and error that they could not possibly keep the Law perfectly and that they needed someone to rescue them from the bondage of sin. "For all have sinned and fall short of the glory of God" (Rom. 3:23). It is impossible for anyone to be restored to fellowship with God by one's own efforts. When some people believed that God would provide a substitute to take their punishment, the Lord looked on them as righteous. Others did not accept this plan of salvation. Give thanks to God that the old covenant was temporary. He did provide a permanent solution, through the death and resurrection of his Son.

8. THE BRONZE SNAKE, 1407 B.C.

For thirty-nine years the Israelites had been wandering around the wilderness wherever God led them. They had followed the pillar of cloud during the day and the pillar of fire at night. He had continually proved his faithfulness and love for them by taking care of their physical needs. Miraculously, their clothes and shoes had never worn out and their stomachs were never empty. Yet the Israelites still complained against God and Moses, just as they had when they first left Egypt. They asked, "Why have you brought us up out of Egypt to die in the desert? There is no bread! There is no water! And we detest this miserable food!" (Num. 21:5).

Because of their whining, unthankful attitude, God sent poisonous snakes among the people to bite them. Many Israelites died. Then they begged Moses, "We sinned when we spoke against the LORD and against you. Pray that the LORD will take the snakes away from us" (Num. 21:7).

How many of us have had the same attitude? How often have I forgotten to thank God for the good gifts that he has given me? After Moses prayed, the Lord answered, "Make a snake and put it up on a pole; anyone who is bitten can look at it and live" (Num. 21:8).

Immediately Moses made a snake out of bronze and put it up on a pole. Anyone who was bitten and looked up at the bronze snake lived. Those who refused to look at it died. In order to live, they had to trust that the Lord was able to heal them. Then they had to obey his instructions and look at the bronze snake. There was nothing that they could do themselves to get better. The Lord saved them in his own power, without their effort. What an object lesson this was for those people, and for us. This is how God would carry out his plan of salvation. Theoretically, if one keeps the Ten Commandments perfectly, then that person will earn his or her own salvation—but no one can. Jesus compared himself to the bronze snake. He told Nicodemus, "Just as Moses lifted up the snake in the desert, so the Son of Man must be lifted up, that everyone who believes in him may have eternal life" (John 3:14,15). There is nothing that we can do to earn our own salvation. Look on the crucified Christ and see in him the one who paid the penalty for your sins. Only then can you know that you have eternal life.

9. THE DECEPTION OF BALAAM, 1407 B.C.

After they captured the land of the Amorites, the Israelites camped on the east side of the Jordan River, across from Jericho. The Moabites were terrified of Israel and appealed to the elders of Midian for help. They cried, "This horde is going to lick up everything around us, as an ox licks up the grass of the field" (Num. 22:4).

In keeping with the custom of the day, Balak, the king of Moab, wanted a soothsayer to curse the Israelites. He sent messengers to Balaam, who lived near the Euphrates River, to say:

> *A people has come out of Egypt; they cover the face of the land and have settled next to me. Now come and put a curse on these people, because they are too powerful for me. Perhaps then I will be able to defeat them and drive them out of the country. For I know that those you bless are blessed, and those you curse are cursed* (Num. 22:5,6).

When Balaam asked God about the situation, the Lord told him not to go with them and not to curse the Israelites, because they were blessed. Since Balaam had refused to go with the Moabite princes, Balak decided to send other princes, even more important than those in the first group. They told Balaam that Balak would reward him handsomely and do whatever he said if he would come back with them and curse the Israelites. Balaam replied, "Even if Balak gives me his palace filled with silver and gold, I could not do anything great or small to go beyond the command of the LORD my God" (Num. 22:18). Although Balaam sounded very devout, he was determined to receive the reward from Balak.

When Balaam finally arrived, Balak lamented:

> *"Did I not send you an urgent summons? Why didn't you come to me? Am I really not able to reward you?"*
> *"Well, I have come to you now,"* Balaam replied. *"But can I say just anything? I must speak only what God puts in my mouth"* (Num. 22:37,38).

Balak took Balaam to three different locations. At each place Balaam asked Balak to build seven altars. On each of the altars, the two of them sacrificed a bull and a ram. The first time Balaam declared, "How can I curse those whom God has not cursed? How can I denounce those whom the LORD has not denounced?" (Num. 23:8). The second time he explained,

"I have received a command to bless; he has blessed, and I cannot change it" (Num. 23:20). The third time he said of Israel, "May those who bless you be blessed and those who curse you be cursed!" (Num. 24:9).

Balak was extremely angry with Balaam by this time. He clapped his hands together and cried, "I summoned you to curse my enemies, but you have blessed them these three times. Now leave at once and go home! I said I would reward you handsomely, but the LORD has kept you from being rewarded" (Num. 24:10,11).

Balaam answered, "Even if Balak gave me his palace filled with silver and gold, I could not do anything of my own accord, good or bad, to go beyond the command of the LORD" (Num. 24:13).

Balaam appeared like a loving, loyal man of God because he kept repeating the Lord's message to Balak. Many years later Jude denounced some godless men in the Church who were hypocrites, because they acted as if they belonged when they did not. "Woe to them!...they have rushed for profit into Balaam's error" (Jude 1:11). Evidently Balaam had his eyes on the money that Balak was offering. He had to figure out how to get it and bless Israel at the same time. John explains to the church at Pergamum how Balaam managed to do this. There were like-minded people in that church "who hold to the teaching of Balaam, who taught Balak to entice the Israelites to sin by eating food sacrificed to idols and by committing sexual immorality" (Rev. 2:14). Publicly Balaam preached the truth of God, but privately he advised, "If you want the Israelites to sin and get into trouble with God, tell your people to befriend them. Involve them in the worship of your gods and in sexually immoral acts. The Lord will punish them, and then you may get your own way." How devious and hypocritical!

> Balaam appeared like a loving, loyal man of God because he kept repeating the Lord's message to Balak.

The Establishment of Israel as a Nation 81

Balak took Balaam's advice. Soon afterwards Moabite women befriended Israelite men. They enticed them to commit sexually immoral acts and to worship Baal (Num. 25:1-3). No doubt Satan was joyful at the infiltration of this false worship into Israel, for he would be able to limit the effectiveness of God's kingdom.

10. THE OLD COVENANT EXPLAINED, 1406 B.C.

See, I set before you today life and prosperity, death and destruction. For I command you today to love the LORD *your God, to walk in his ways, and to keep his commands, decrees and laws; then you will live and increase, and the* LORD *your God will bless you in the land you are entering to possess. But if your heart turns away and you are not obedient, and if you are drawn away to bow down to other gods and worship them, I declare to you this day that you will certainly be destroyed. You will not live long in the land you are crossing the Jordan to enter and possess...Now choose life, so that you and your children may live and that you may love the* LORD *your God, listen to his voice, and hold fast to him. For the* LORD *is your life, and he will give you many years in the land he swore to give to your fathers, Abraham, Isaac and Jacob* (Deut. 30:15-20).

The Israelites were finally preparing to cross the Jordan River and enter the Promised Land. They would become a nation with a land of their own, the land that Abraham, Isaac, and Jacob had lived in as strangers so long ago. God was working out his plan. In order to be happy and prosperous there, they needed to understand the importance of obeying God. Thus this covenant explained in greater detail the one ratified at Sinai. Forty years earlier God had promised the Israelites that they were his special people, but they had to obey him and not worship any other god. Obedience was the prerequisite for blessing. Now God was explaining very clearly how their actions had consequences either for good or evil. Moses advised them, "If you fully obey the LORD your God and carefully follow all his commands I give you today, the LORD your God will set you high above all the nations on earth. All these blessings will come upon you and accompany you if you obey the LORD your God" (Deut. 28:1,2). Moses then described many physical blessings, such as fertile wombs and victory over their enemies. Next he told them, "The LORD will establish you as his holy people, as he promised you on oath, if you keep the commands of the LORD your God and walk in his ways" (Deut. 28:9).

"However," he warned, "if you do not obey the LORD your God and do not carefully follow all his commands and decrees I am giving you today, all these curses will come upon you and overtake you" (Deut. 28:15). Disobedience would bring poor crops, infertile wombs, disease, drought, and defeat by their enemies. Moses explained, "All these curses will come upon you. They will pursue you and overtake you until you are destroyed, because you did not obey the LORD your God and observe the commands and decrees he gave you" (Deut. 28:45). He continued, "You who were as numerous as the stars in the sky will be left but few in number, because you did not obey the LORD your God. Just as it pleased the LORD to make you prosper and increase in number, so it will please him to ruin and destroy you" (Deut. 28:62,63).

> Some of them likely thought that the blessing of the Lord was guaranteed; it was unconditional.

Some of them likely thought that the blessing of the Lord was guaranteed; it was unconditional. One could stubbornly do whatever he or she wanted and still receive God's blessing. Moses, however, objected, "The LORD will never be willing to forgive him; his wrath and zeal will burn against that man" (Deut. 29:20). Yet there was one important ray of hope for those who disobeyed: God delights in showing mercy. If they realized that they had sinned and turned back to the Lord in loving allegiance, then he would forgive them and restore them to the Promised Land. Restoration to the Promised Land would be their reward for repenting of their sin. He never promised them possession of the land unconditionally. After being restored to fellowship with God, Israel could count on his promise. "He will bring you to the land that belonged to your fathers, and you will take possession of it" (Deut. 30:5). This is the same agreement that God had with Abraham, only his test of obedience was circumcision.[1]

Moses also comforted them by saying, "The LORD your God will circumcise your hearts and the hearts of your descendants, so that you may love him with all your heart and with all your soul, and live" (Deut. 30:6). Only God is able to circumcise the heart. He alone is able to remove the desire to sin from a person's heart and replace it with a love for him. This is the heart attitude that God desires us to have. Love willingly obeys. To obey without love is only a superficial outward obedience such as Balaam displayed.

In Deuteronomy 28-30, the Lord was adamant that obedience brings blessing and disobedience yields destruction. Implied in these chapters are two important questions that Moses wanted the Israelites to ask themselves. First, "Do I believe that I can determine my own rules that will please God and that no one is going to change my mind?" To such an attitude the Lord replied, "He will never be forgiven" (see Deut. 29:19-21). This heart attitude led to certain destruction for the individual. Secondly, "Do you love the Lord your God with all your heart and with all your soul?" To such a heart attitude the Lord answered, "You will live. I will bless you and curse your enemies" (see Deut. 30:6-10). The Israelites had two choices, obedience or disobedience.

Everyone today is faced with the same choices. Would you rather trust God's Word and lovingly obey him or ignore him and follow your own ideas? Those who belong to God's kingdom love and obey him; they have a teachable spirit that is willing to be corrected. In contrast, everyone in Satan's kingdom fails to recognize God as the one and only God or to lovingly obey him.

Points to Ponder

1. Before Moses was born, God planned that he would free the Israelites from slavery in Egypt.
2. God demonstrated his sovereign power over all the false gods of Egypt when he sent the ten plagues and freed his people.
3. Sometimes we may feel as if we are wandering around in confusion like the Israelites, but God has a plan for us, just as he did for them.
4. Do we try to obey God in our own strength? We will fail every time, just like the Israelites.
5. Do you want to do your own thing and yet expect the Lord's continued blessing? God does not lie. He cannot condone sin.

Chapter Five

King David

1. A Man after God's Own Heart, 1010-970 B.C.

MY son Philip is artistic. He took all of the drama and theatre technical classes that he could in high school. I still don't understand what made him suddenly want to copy his brother and sister and become a scientist. In grade twelve he overloaded himself with mathematics and science courses. Then he majored in psychology in university, but he soon realized that he had made a mistake. Like Philip, the Israelites also decided to copy the behaviour of others.

The Lord had been their king for almost 400 years, ever since he had delivered the Law to the people at Mount Sinai. After the Israelites entered the Promised Land, they often vacillated between obeying and disobeying God. Periodically he appointed judges to subdue their enemies and rule the people. Then, in 1050 B.C., [1] the people cried to Samuel, "You are old, and your sons do not walk in your ways; now appoint a king to lead us, such as all the other nations have" (1 Sam. 8:5).

Samuel was quite upset and prayed to the Lord, who told him, "Listen to all that the people are saying to you; it is not you they have rejected, but they have rejected me as their king. As they have done from the day I brought them up out of Egypt until this day, forsaking me and serving other gods, so they are doing to you" (1 Sam. 8:7,8).

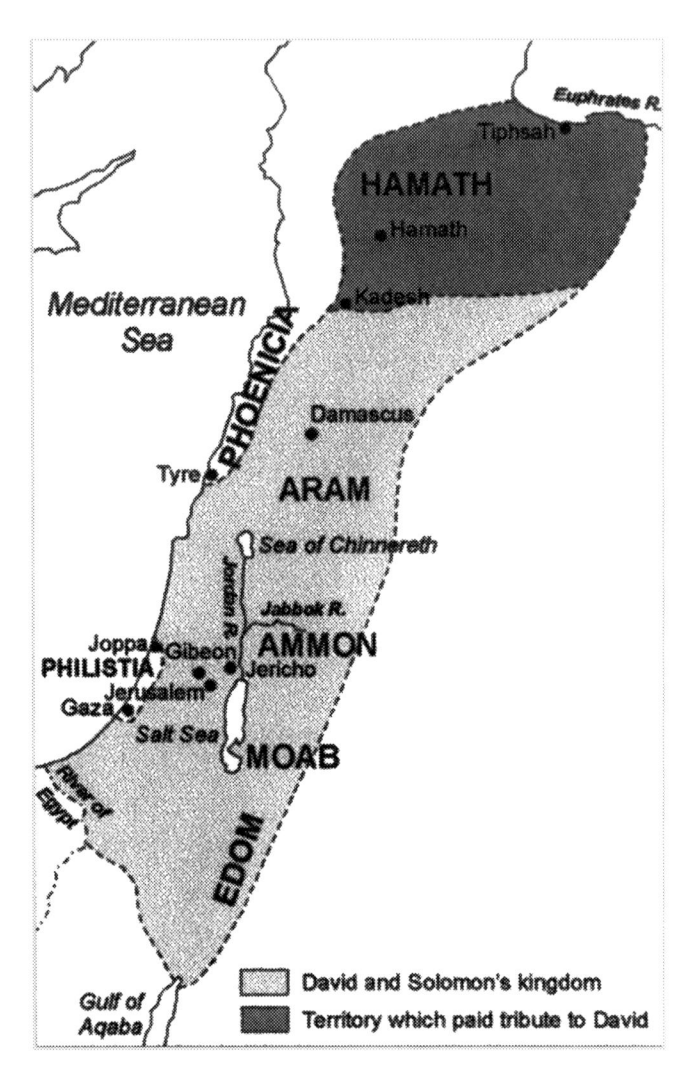

Figure 3: Empire of David and Solomon

As a result, God told Samuel to anoint Saul, the Benjamite, king over Israel. He reigned for forty years. Next the Lord chose David from the tribe of Judah to be king. God began to carry out the next step in his plan of salvation, because David would be the first in a long line of kings descended from Judah. The Israelites would finally see the fulfillment of God's prophecy to Jacob.[2] God always tells the truth and always keeps his promises.

I have found David son of Jesse a man after my own heart; he will do everything I want him to do (Acts 13:22).

Why was David a man after God's own heart? Certainly it was not because he was perfect and had never sinned. One evening when he should have been at war with the rest of his army, he was at home sitting on his rooftop. When he saw a beautiful woman bathing, David sent messengers to go and get her. Bathsheba slept with him and then went back home. Sometime later, she realized that she was pregnant. David immediately ordered her husband to come home from the battlefield, supposedly so that David could receive a report on the progress of the war. In reality David wanted Uriah to sleep with his wife; then he would never suspect that the child was not his.

Uriah, however, refused. He said, "The ark and Israel and Judah are staying in tents, and my master Joab and my lord's men are camped in the open fields. How could I go to my house to eat and drink and lie with my wife? As surely as you live, I will not do such a thing!" (2 Sam. 11:11).

Foiled in his plans, David wrote a letter to his commander Joab and told Uriah to deliver it. He ordered Joab to "put Uriah in the front line where the fighting is fiercest. Then withdraw from him so that he will be struck down and die" (2 Sam. 11:15). Because Uriah refused to be tricked into covering the king's sin, David condemned him to death.

When confronted later by the prophet Nathan, David admitted, "I have sinned against the LORD" (2 Sam. 12:13).

David was a man after God's own heart because he acknowledged his sin and repented of it. He cared what God thought and accepted the consequence of his actions. Although God forgave David, he still had to live with the result of his sin. The child died. With Bathsheba he succumbed to the temptation to abuse his

> Although God forgave David, he still had to live with the result of his sin.

kingly authority. Nevertheless David loved God and wanted to obey him. In fact, he was willing to risk his life for the honour of God.

When David was a boy, the Philistines and the Israelites gathered near Socoh in Judah to fight each other. Only a valley separated the two armies. For forty days Goliath, a giant over nine feet tall (about three metres), entered the valley morning and evening and shouted:

> *"Why do you come out and line up for battle? Am I not a Philistine, and are you not the servants of Saul? Choose a man and have him come down to me. If he is able to fight and kill me, we will become your subjects; but if I overcome him and kill him, you will become our subjects and serve us…This day I defy the ranks of Israel!"* (1 Sam. 17:8-10).

No one responded to the challenge. Everyone, including Saul, was terrified. Meanwhile David had travelled to the battle lines with food for his three eldest brothers. When he heard Goliath yelling defiantly and saw the Israelites running from the giant in fear, David wondered what was going on. He asked, "Who is this uncircumcised Philistine that he should defy the armies of the living God?" (1 Sam. 17:26).

An eavesdropper reported to Saul, who sent for David. When David insisted on fighting Goliath, Saul replied, "You are not able to go out against this Philistine and fight him; you are only a boy, and he has been a fighting man from his youth" (1 Sam. 17:33).

David, however, was not afraid. He retorted, "Your servant has killed both the lion and the bear; this uncircumcised Philistine will be like one of them, because he has defied the armies of the living God" (1 Sam. 17:36). Then Saul allowed David to fight.

Goliath was insulted to see only a boy approaching him with a staff, five smooth stones, and a slingshot. He said to David, "Am I a dog, that you come at me with sticks?" Then he cursed

David by his gods. "Come here…and I'll give your flesh to the birds of the air and the beasts of the field!" (1 Sam. 17:43,44).

David replied:

> *"This day the* LORD *will hand you over to me, and I'll strike you down and cut off your head. Today I will give the carcasses of the Philistine army to the birds of the air and the beasts of the earth, and the whole world will know that there is a God in Israel. All those gathered here will know that it is not by sword or spear that the* LORD *saves; for the battle is the* LORD's, *and he will give all of you into our hands"* (1 Sam. 17:46,47).

Next, while running toward Goliath, David took a stone from his pouch, slung it, and struck him on the forehead. The giant died immediately. David was sure of victory because he fought for God's honour. His heart's desire was for everyone to know the God of Israel. He knew that all other gods are lifeless lies.

2. DAVID CAPTURES JEBUS, 1003 B.C.

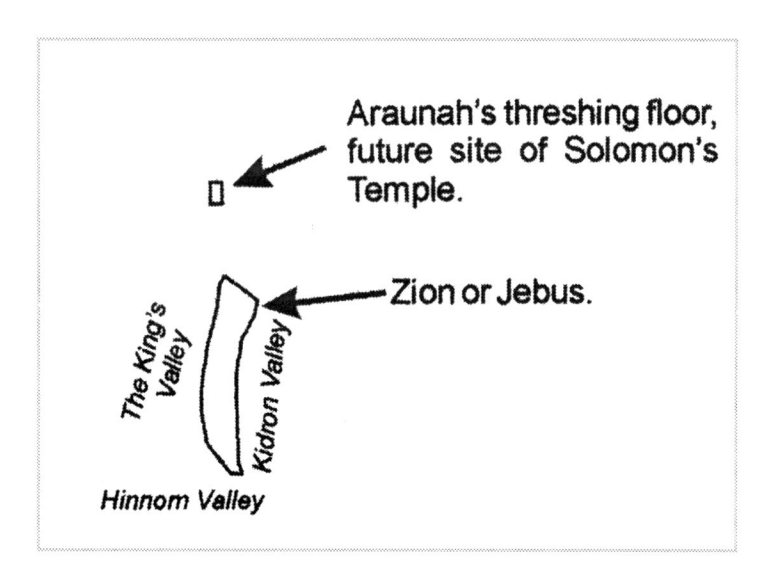

Figure 4: Zion, the City of David

David was king over Judah for seven and one-half years before the other tribes of Israel crowned him king. At that point he decided to move his capital from Hebron to Jerusalem. He probably wanted the city as his capital for security reasons. It was also more centrally located. After Joshua's death, some men of Judah had attacked Jerusalem and had captured it, but the Benjamites were never able to dislodge the Jebusites from Jebus, the southeast hill of Jerusalem. In fact, the Jebusites were extremely self-confident in the security of their mountain stronghold for two reasons. Deep valleys surrounded them on three sides and provided a natural fortress. They also possessed a secret source of water in the event that they were besieged.

Therefore they taunted David, "'You will not get in here; even the blind and the lame can ward you off.' They thought, 'David cannot get in here'" (2 Sam. 5:6).

Meanwhile David informed the Israelites, "Anyone who conquers the Jebusites will have to use the water shaft to reach those 'lame and blind' who are David's enemies" (2 Sam. 5:8). He promised, "Whoever leads the attack on the Jebusites will become commander-in-chief" (1 Chron. 11:6). Joab succeeded, and David kept his word.

> How David knew about the secret water shaft is a mystery.

How David knew about the secret water shaft is a mystery. It began underground at a fountain in the valley and ended up in the centre of the city. That Joab managed to climb up it is quite surprising. Many people wonder if Araunah the Jebusite helped David and Joab, because he was David's friend.[3] Sometime later David bought Araunah's threshing floor as a sacred place to sacrifice to God (2 Sam. 24:21-25). It would later become the site of Solomon's temple. From that time on, Jebus was called the City of David or Zion. This was the next step in the plan of God. The Lord chose Mount Zion as the place where he would reveal more of himself. Thus there are many references to Zion in the psalms and the prophets. David declares, "Great is the LORD, and most worthy of praise, in the city of our God, his holy mountain. It is beautiful in its loftiness, the joy of the whole earth" (Ps. 48:1,2).

3. THE ARK OF GOD

The Lord had given detailed instructions to Moses on how to build the tabernacle and the furniture in it. He told Moses to make a chest out of acacia wood, overlaid inside and out with gold. An atonement cover of pure gold was to fit on top of the box. Two gold cherubim, with wings spread upward, faced each other and looked down. God had said to Moses, "There, above the cover between the two cherubim that are over the ark of the Testimony, I will meet with you and give you all my commands for the Israelites" (Exod. 25:22). Everyone knew that God "sits enthroned between the cherubim" (Ps. 99:1).

Once, when Eli was the high priest and Samuel was his protégé, the Israelites were losing a battle against the Philistines. Because the presence of the Lord was over the ark, they decided to take it to the front lines. They hoped that God's presence would help them defeat the enemy. Instead, the Philistines captured the ark of God and carried it into Dagon's temple, where they put it beside the idol of Dagon. In the morning they found Dagon lying face down on the ground before the ark of the Lord. His head and hands were broken off (1 Sam. 5:4). Everywhere that the ark was taken, people either died or were afflicted with tumours. After seven months, in desperation, the Philistines sent the ark of God back to Israel with gifts. It ended up at Kiriath Jearim, a town in Judah. Needless to say, the Lord proved how powerless the false god Dagon was. No doubt Satan was not pleased.

> Everywhere that the ark was taken, people either died or were afflicted with tumours.

Many years later David called the officers and commanders of Israel together. He said:

> *"If it seems good to you and if it is the will of the LORD our God, let us send word far and wide to the rest of our brothers throughout the territories of Israel, and also to the priests and Levites who are with them in their towns and pasturelands, to come and join us. Let us bring the ark of our God back to us, for we did not inquire of it during the reign of Saul"* (1 Chron. 13:2,3).

Everyone agreed that it was a good idea. Therefore the ark was finally enroute to Zion from Kiriath Jearim. How happy David and all the Israelites were! When the oxen stumbled, Uzzah tried to be helpful by reaching out to steady the ark, but he died as soon as he touched it (1 Chron. 13:9-10).

Angry and afraid of God, David cried out, "How can I ever bring the ark of God to me?" (1 Chron. 13:12). Instead of continuing on to Zion with the ark, he left it with Obed-Edom, a Gittite, for three months.

Then someone reported to David, "The LORD has blessed the household of Obed-Edom and everything he has, because of the ark of God" (2 Sam. 6:12).

Encouraged by that news, David joyfully brought the ark of God from the house of Obed-Edom to Zion. This time he was careful to obey the instructions of the Lord concerning the care of the ark. David said, "No one but the Levites may carry the ark of God, because the LORD chose them to carry the ark of the LORD and to minister before him forever" (1 Chron. 15:2). This is what God had told Moses, and David realized that Uzzah had died because the Lord's instructions were not carried out.

In preparation for its arrival, David had pitched a tent for the ark in Zion (1 Chron. 15:1). David chose some of the Levites to be singers and others to play musical instruments. With great joy, "they brought the ark of God and set it inside the tent that David had pitched for it, and they presented burnt offerings and fellowship offerings before God" (1 Chron. 16:1). David praised God in a psalm. In so doing, he offered the sacrifice of praise, much like we do.

4. THE WORSHIP OF THE LORD IN ZION

The Creator God chose Mount Zion as his dwelling place. Although "the Most High does not live in houses made by men" (Acts 7:48), he promised to meet with his people in the tent erected by David. Accordingly, from that day on some of the Levites ministered "before the ark of the LORD, to make petition, to give thanks, and to praise the LORD, the God of Israel" (1 Chron. 16:4). Here at the tent pitched by David in Zion, the Lord was worshipped in the same way that we worship today. Prayers of petition, thanksgiving, and praise were offered to God. The people sang to the Lord. They worshipped him corporately in spirit and in truth. In David's tent we find the beginning of church-like worship.

> In David's tent we find the beginning of church-like worship.

Jesus said, "True worshipers will worship the Father in spirit and truth, for they are the kind of worshipers the Father seeks. God is spirit, and his worshipers must worship in spirit and in truth" (John 4:23,24).

David had spent much time alone with God throughout the years. He knew how to worship God in spirit and in truth. Once he prayed, "O Lord, open my lips, and my mouth will declare your praise. You do not delight in sacrifice, or I would bring it; you do not take pleasure in burnt offerings. The sacrifices of God are a broken spirit; a broken and contrite heart, O God, you will not despise" (Ps. 51:15-17). God wants us to worship him out of loving obedience. He delights when a person is sorrowful over his or her sin and asks for forgiveness. He does not delight in the sacrifice of animals.

At that time, the tabernacle was at Gibeon. According to God's instructions to Moses, the ark should have been placed in the Most Holy Place. Only the high priest could enter that room, and just once a year, on the Day of Atonement. As a result, the Israelites would visibly sense a great gulf separating them from God. This situation emphasized their sinfulness and God's holiness. In contrast, when the ark was in David's tent at Zion, the Israelites could fellowship directly with God in spirit and in truth. What a picture of the New Testament Church! Since God allowed David to worship him in this way, the word *Zion* carries spiritual overtones. George Smith points out:

> Chiefly it is to be observed that this sojourn of the ark on Mount Zion is the foundation of the many references in the Psalms and the Prophets to *Zion, as the dwelling place of Jehovah,* and is what gives to the terms "Zion" and "Mount Zion" their high spiritual meaning…when God speaks by His prophets concerning things to come in the Kingdom of Christ, He never says "I will build again the Temple of Solomon which I destroyed," but "I will build again the Tabernacle of David which is fallen down."[4]

Although David had fellowship with God in front of the ark at Zion, he did not neglect to follow the Law. God still required that sacrifices continue on the altar in front of the tabernacle at Gibeon. Because the promised Saviour had not yet come, the Israelites still needed to be reminded daily that blood must be shed to atone for sin.

5. The Covenant with David

> *The LORD declares to you that the LORD himself will establish a house for you: When your days are over and you rest with your fathers, I will raise up your offspring to succeed you, who will come from your own body, and I will establish his kingdom. He is the one who will build a house for my Name, and I will establish the throne of*

his kingdom forever. I will be his father, and he will be my son. When he does wrong, I will punish him with the rod of men, with floggings inflicted by men. But my love will never be taken away from him, as I took it away from Saul, whom I removed from before you. Your house and your kingdom will endure forever before me; your throne will be established forever (2 Sam. 7:11-16).

After David was living in Zion and was at peace with his enemies, he thought, "Here I am, living in a palace of cedar, while the ark of God remains in a tent" (2 Sam. 7:2).

At first the prophet Nathan encouraged David to build a permanent house for the Lord, until God spoke to him. Then, instead of advising David to go ahead with it, he directed David's attention toward the eternal kingdom of the promised Seed. The expression *when your days are over and you rest with your fathers* indicates that the promised Seed would establish his kingdom sometime after David's death. God would be his Father, and he would be the Son of the Most High. Miraculously, the promised Seed would also be David's direct descendant. This person "will build a house for my Name." In other words, the promised Seed would build a spiritual temple. Paul explains to the Corinthian believers, "For we are the temple of the living God" (2 Cor. 6:16). Every local church today is God's spiritual temple.

At the same time, Nathan told David that one of his sons would build a house for God. Sometime later God told David that his son Solomon would be the one to build the temple in Jerusalem. Although his son would sin, the kingdom would not be taken away from him or his descendants. The Lord calls these promises a covenant. David testifies, "You said, 'I have made a covenant with my chosen one. I have sworn to David my servant, "I will establish your line forever and make your throne firm through all generations"'" (Ps. 89:3,4).

The Lord *swore an oath to David, a sure oath that he will not revoke: "One of your own descendants I will place on your throne—if your sons keep my covenant and the statutes I teach them, then their sons will sit on your throne for ever and ever." For the* LORD *has chosen Zion, he has desired it for his dwelling: "This is my resting place for ever and ever; here I will sit enthroned, for I have desired it"* (Ps. 132:11-14).

Here God implies that the promises were to be fulfilled on two levels, one spiritual and the other physical. Under no circumstances would God back down on his plan to place the promised Seed on the throne of David. No matter how David's descendants behaved, one would come in the future to build a house for God's name, to sit on David's throne, and to establish an eternal kingdom. In contrast, David's sons had a condition attached to their continued blessing. In order to remain on the throne, they had to obey God and keep the covenant of Sinai.

Moreover, the Lord chose Zion as his resting place. He desired to dwell there forever, because it was the place where the Israelites gathered to worship him in spirit and in truth. God was pleased that David had brought the ark of God to Zion. There he sat enthroned between the cherubim. Since the beginning of time, the heart's desire of the Lord has been to regain his fellowship with sinful people. In Zion God found those who wanted to love, honour, and worship him because of who he is.

God first described himself as Father in the covenant with David. He called both Solomon and the promised Seed his sons. Imagine how David felt! It was possible for fallen humanity to be restored to such close fellowship with God the Father that he would call a created man his son and part of his family. David exclaimed, "Is this your usual way of dealing with man, O Sovereign LORD?" (2 Sam. 7:19).

6. The Last Words of David, 970 B.C.

Just before his death, David reminded his son Solomon to walk with God and obey God's commandments. Then the Lord could keep his promise to David. "If your descendants watch how they live, and if they walk faithfully before me with all their heart and soul, you will never fail to have a man on the throne of Israel" (1 Kings 2:4). The implication is that if David's descendants fail to keep God's Law, then they would lose the throne. David also realized that God had chosen Israel as his special people in order to prepare for the arrival of the promised Seed. His Saviour would be his descendant. Special blessings, both physical and spiritual, were granted to the Israelites because the promised Seed would be a Jew. Yet in his dying words David is more concerned with spiritual realities than physical promises.

> *The Spirit of the LORD spoke through me; his word was on my tongue. The God of Israel spoke, the Rock of Israel said to me: "When one rules over men in righteousness, when he rules in the fear of God, he is like the light of morning at sunrise on a cloudless morning, like the brightness after rain that brings the grass from the earth." Is not my house right with God? Has he not made with me an everlasting covenant, arranged and secured in every part? Will he not bring to fruition my salvation and grant me my every desire? But evil men are all to be cast aside like thorns, which are not gathered with the hand. Whoever touches thorns uses a tool of iron or the shaft of a spear; they are burned up where they lie* (2 Sam. 23:2-7).

There is only one who reigns over us in righteousness because he has never sinned. There is only one who is like the morning light at sunrise because of his purity. His name is Jesus. These last words of David echo Psalm 72, a prayer of David for Solomon. In it David also prophesied about King Jesus:

> *He will judge your people in righteousness…He will endure as long as the sun, as long as the moon, through all generations. He will be…like showers watering the earth…He will rule from sea to sea and from the River to the ends of the earth…All nations will be blessed through him, and they will call him blessed* (Ps. 72:2-17).

This is the one that Abraham waited for, the promised Seed of the Garden of Eden, the Saviour who would take away his sin and restore him to fellowship with God. What a wonderful plan! The Saviour would also be our King.

As David was dying, he first looked to the coming King and then he turned his thoughts toward his own need for salvation. "Is not my house right with God?" (2 Sam. 23:5). In other words, "Am I not ready to die? My sins have been forgiven, and I am reconciled to God." Many years before David had prayed for God to forgive his sins:

> *Show me your ways, O* Lord, *teach me your paths; guide me in your truth and teach me, for you are God my Savior, and my hope is in you all day long. Remember, O* Lord, *your great mercy and love, for they are from of old…For the sake of your name, O* Lord, *forgive my iniquity, though it is great…Look upon my affliction and my distress and take away all my sins* (Ps. 25:4-18).

David had complete confidence that God would provide for his salvation. He asks, "Will he not bring to fruition my salvation?" (2 Sam. 23:5).

> David had complete confidence that God would provide for his salvation.

David knew that God's everlasting covenant with him was arranged and secured in every part (2 Sam. 23:5). These are *the sure mercies of David.* God invites everyone to appropriate these promises. "Incline your ear, and come unto me: hear, and your soul shall live; and I will make an everlasting covenant with you, *even* the sure mercies of David" (Isa. 55:3, KJV). Just as the fulfillment of the everlasting covenant with Abraham would be Christ (Gal. 3:16), the King promised in the everlasting covenant with David would also be Christ. The Holy Spirit confirms the fact that the resurrection of Jesus from the dead is the fulfillment of the sure mercies of David. "The fact that God raised him [Jesus] from the dead, never to decay, is stated in these words: 'I will give you the holy and sure blessings promised to David.' So it is stated elsewhere: 'You will not let your Holy One see decay'" (Acts 13:34,35). Because of the death and resurrection of Jesus, "the forgiveness of sins is proclaimed to you" (Acts 13:38). Everyone who believes is declared righteous in God's sight.

Isaiah explains how to claim those promises. "Seek the LORD while he may be found; call on him while he is near. Let the wicked forsake his way and the evil man his thoughts. Let him turn to the LORD, and he will have mercy on him, and to our God, for he will freely pardon" (Isa. 55:6,7). David testified that he had claimed the everlasting covenant for himself. "Praise the LORD, O my soul; all my inmost being, praise his holy name. Praise the LORD, O my soul, and forget not all his benefits—who forgives all your sins and heals all your diseases, who redeems your life from the pit and crowns you with love and compassion" (Ps. 103:1-4).

David finished his dying words by remembering the fate of evil individuals, those who do not accept the salvation offered by the coming King. He said that they would be cast aside and that they would be burned up where they lie (2 Sam. 23:6,7). Once again God emphasized two types of people, believers and non-believers, those who accept the salvation offered by God and those who do not.

7. THE PLAN OF GOD AS REVEALED IN THE PSALMS

The psalms are Israel's songs written to express the emotions and understanding of the authors about God. Likewise, this book is my attempt to put into writing what I understand about God. Unlike them, this book is not authorized by God to be part of the Scriptures. Hopefully my words are true and I have not contradicted clear teaching in the Bible. David wrote many of these psalms that reveal important truths about Jesus and God's plan of salvation. He knew that the nation of Israel was an important part of God's plan. When he first heard of God's covenant with him, David reacted by wondering:

> *And who is like your people Israel—the one nation on earth that God went out to redeem as a people for himself, and to make a name for himself, and to perform great and awesome wonders by driving out nations and their gods from before your people, whom you redeemed from Egypt? You have established your people Israel as your very own forever, and you, O LORD, have become their God* (2 Sam. 7:23,24).

The Lord had redeemed the Israelites from the Egyptians. He had given them the Promised Land of Canaan to live in. He had become their very own God. Was the God of the universe to be only the God of Israel? Was he to be only another tribal deity? Did the Creator put Israel on a pedestal, forever above other nations, no matter how they treated him? Is that what this covenant was all about? These are questions that David may have often pondered. In his psalms David revealed his understanding of who Jesus is, how Jesus would accomplish our salvation, and how Israel fits into God's plan.

> Was the God of the universe to be only the God of Israel?

7a. Psalm 2

> *Why do the nations conspire and the peoples plot in vain? The kings of the earth take their stand and the rulers gather together against the LORD and against his Anointed One* (Ps. 2:1,2).

Because the Hebrew language does not have one word denoting a king who has been anointed, the Israelites did not use the word *Messiah* until they learned Aramaic in Babylon.[5] Although David was not familiar with the word *Messiah*, he did write this psalm about the promised Seed who would be not only the Saviour but also the anointed King. God laughs at the futile attempts of people to rebel against him and his Anointed (Ps. 2:4). He insists, "I have installed my King on Zion, my holy hill" (Ps. 2:6).

The Lord's Anointed is not only a King but also his Son (Ps. 2:7). Through the prophet Nathan, David knew that someday one of his descendants would become a King with an eternal kingdom. God would call this person his Son. God the Father says to his Son, "Ask of me, and I will make the nations your inheritance, the ends of the earth your possession. You will rule them with an iron scepter; you will dash them to pieces like pottery" (Ps. 2:8,9). As King on Zion, the Messiah has authority over all nations. That is why David advises rulers, "Serve the LORD with fear and rejoice with trembling…Blessed are all who take refuge in him" (Ps. 2:11,12). Anyone who rejects the Lord will be destroyed.

When David wrote this psalm, he may not have known when or how the Messiah would receive his throne. David only knew that he himself would be dead (2 Sam. 7:12). After Jesus' resurrection, God declared the fulfillment of this prophecy by quoting Psalm 2. One night the Sadducees put Peter and John in jail for preaching the resurrection of Jesus from the dead. On their release they prayed with other believers about the harassment that they were experiencing. Through the Holy Spirit, the apostles and the other believers prayed:

> *You spoke by the Holy Spirit through the mouth of your servant, our father David: "Why do the nations rage and the peoples plot in vain? The kings of the earth take their stand and the rulers gather together against the Lord and against his Anointed One." Indeed Herod and Pontius Pilate met together with the Gentiles and the people of*

Israel in this city to conspire against your holy servant Jesus, whom you anointed…Now, Lord, consider their threats and enable your servants to speak your word with great boldness (Acts 4:25-29).

The Sanhedrin, the Jewish high council, had desperately tried to find Jesus guilty of wrongdoing. Eventually the Son of God appeared before a mob filled with hatred and yelling, "Crucify him! Crucify him!" (Matt. 27:22-23). It was the week of Passover, and Jerusalem was filled with people from many different countries. They were part of the mob, along with the citizens of Judea and Galilee. The Jewish hierarchy likely thought that in killing Jesus they could be rid of him. In actual fact they were merely carrying out the eternal plan of God, because the death of his Son was the only way to satisfy divine justice. Jesus is the only person who has never sinned. "God made him who had no sin to be sin for us" (2 Cor. 5:21).

Peter and John testified, "They did what your power and will had decided beforehand should happen" (Acts 4:28). Before the earth was created, God the Father, Son, and Holy Spirit agreed that God the Son would come into the world to save sinners (1 Tim. 1:15). Jesus warned his disciples that he must go to Jerusalem and that he must be killed, but on the third day he would be raised to life (Matt. 16:21). God was not surprised at the enmity against his Son. When he hung there on the cross, Jesus suffered not only physical torture but also the spiritual anguish of being totally separated from God the Father. Yet in the midst of all his grief, God was able to laugh (Ps. 2:4). Humanity had exacted the worst that they could on the Messiah. They had killed him, but Jesus did not stay dead. Instead, the King was installed on Zion (Ps. 2:6). One Sabbath Paul preached in the synagogue at Pisidian Antioch, "We tell you the good news: What God promised our fathers he has fulfilled for us, their children, by raising up Jesus. As it is written in the second Psalm: 'You are my Son; today I have become your Father'" (Acts 13:32,33). Good news! Jesus came back to life; he is not dead. The resurrection of Jesus is proof that he is the Son of God and that he is the fulfillment of Psalm 2. Who would ever think that a king could begin reigning by dying on a cross? Yet if God is telling the truth, Jesus is ruling today over all of the nations of the world. At his Second Coming the reality of his present reign will be visible to all.

> Who would ever think that a king could begin reigning by dying on a cross?

John states, "Out of his mouth comes a sharp sword with which to strike down the nations. 'He will rule them with an iron scepter'" (Rev. 19:15). The writer to the Hebrews declares, "For the word of God is living and active. Sharper than any double-edged sword, it penetrates even to dividing soul and spirit, joints and marrow; it judges the thoughts and attitudes of the heart" (Heb. 4:12). The source of Jesus' power is the unchangeable true Word of God. It is sharper than a two-edged sword. By the Word he rules with authority over all things. This includes the angels, good and bad, and every person, past, present, and future. He is our Messiah, chosen by God before the foundation of the world.

Although his power is real, we cannot always see it. Instead it is human nature to focus on the effects of Satan's kingdom—the sin, the pain, and the suffering around us. Satan would love for believers to turn their eyes away from God Almighty and the truths proclaimed in the Bible. He would prefer your worship, but he is happy if you believe any lie and not the truth. He does not want you to love God. We need faith to trust in the mighty power of Jesus. We must believe God when he says that King Jesus has inherited all of the nations of the earth and that he possesses the earth (Ps. 2:8).

7b. Psalm 16

I have set the LORD always before me. Because he is at my right hand, I will not be shaken. Therefore my heart is glad and my tongue rejoices; my body also will rest secure, because you will not abandon me to the grave, nor will you let your Holy One see decay. You have made known to me the path of life; you will fill me with joy in your presence, with eternal pleasures at your right hand (Ps. 16:8-11).

On the day of Pentecost Peter preached to God-fearing Jews from every nation on earth. He reminded them of the many miracles that God had performed through Jesus. Next he said, "This man was handed over to you by God's set purpose and foreknowledge; and you, with the help of wicked men, put him to death by nailing him to the cross. But God raised him from the dead, freeing him from the agony of death, because it was impossible for death to keep its hold on him" (Acts 2:23,24). Peter then quoted Psalm 16:8-11 to explain that David was prophesying about Jesus when he wrote the psalm. Peter reminded the Jews that David had died and was buried, and that he was still dead. This was a very important fact. David could not have been talking about himself in Psalm 16, because his body had obviously decayed long ago. It was also important in relation to God's covenant with David, because the Messiah could not sit on David's throne unless David himself was dead (2 Sam. 7:12). Through Peter, God revealed David's thoughts. "But he [David] was a prophet and knew that God had promised him on oath that he would place one of his descendants on his throne. Seeing what was ahead, he [David] spoke of the resurrection of the Christ, that he was not abandoned to the grave, nor did his body see decay" (Acts 2:30,31).

> Did God tell the truth? Did Jesus receive David's throne at his resurrection? If he did not, then God is a liar.

David actually knew that the Messiah would receive his throne by rising from the dead! Peter told his audience that they were witnesses of the resurrection. He encouraged them to believe the truth of David's words. At his resurrection Jesus was "exalted to the right hand of God" (Acts 2:33).

Did God tell the truth? Did Jesus receive David's throne at his resurrection? If he did not, then God is a liar.

7c. Psalm 110

> *The LORD says to my Lord: "Sit at my right hand until I make your enemies a footstool for your feet"* (Ps. 110:1).

The writer to the Hebrews quoted this verse (Heb. 1:13). In past times God had spoken through the prophets. Now he speaks through his Son (see Heb. 1:1-2). "After he [Jesus] had provided purification for sins, he sat down at the right hand of the Majesty in heaven" (Heb. 1:3). Concerning the throne of Jesus, the Lord promises, "Your throne, O God, will last for ever and ever, and righteousness will be the scepter of your kingdom" (Heb. 1:8). As F. F. Bruce points out, "The throne of David is now absorbed in the heavenly throne of glory and grace."[6] Henry writes of Jesus:

> III. He was to be advanced to the highest honour, and entrusted with an absolute sovereign power, both in heaven and in earth; *Sit thou at my right hand*. Sitting is a resting posture; after his services and sufferings, he entered into rest from all his labours. It is a ruling posture; he sits to give law, to give judgment: it is a remaining posture; he sits like a king for ever: sitting at the right hand of God denotes both his dignity and his dominion, the honour put upon him, and the trust reposed in him, by the Father…
> IV. All his enemies were in due time to be made his footstool…Even Christ himself has enemies that fight against his kingdom and subjects, his honour and interest, in the world: there are those that will not have him to reign over them, and thereby they join themselves to Satan, who will not have him to reign at all…He shall reign till it is done; and all

their might and malice shall not give the least disturbance to his government. His sitting at God's right hand is a pledge to him of his setting his feet, at last, on the necks of all his enemies.[7]

David's confession that the Messiah was also his Lord is obviously very important, because Jesus brought the issue up with the Pharisees. Three of the gospels record this conversation (Matt. 22:41-45; Mark 12:35-37; Luke 20:41-44).

> *While the Pharisees were gathered together, Jesus asked them, "What do you think about the Christ? Whose son is he?"*
> *"The son of David," they replied.*
> *He said to them, "How is it then that David, speaking by the Spirit, calls him 'Lord'? For he says, 'The Lord said to my Lord: "Sit at my right hand until I put your enemies under your feet."' If then David calls him 'Lord,' how can he be his son?" No one could say a word in reply, and from that day on no one dared to ask him any more questions* (Matt. 22:41-45).

When Jesus asked the Pharisees, the teachers of the Law, whose son the Christ was, they thought that this was an easy question. In their own catechisms they answered, "The son of David." They had no problem in thinking of the Messiah[8] as a human being, but Jesus knew that this was only a half-truth. Yes, Jesus is fully human, because he is a descendant of David through his mother Mary. Jesus, however, probed further, "Why does David through the Holy Spirit call the Christ 'Lord?'" Matthew used the same Greek word *kurios* for God the Father as for God the Son.[9] Jesus wanted the Pharisees to realize that the Messiah is also fully God. He is the Son of God. Not one of the Pharisees replied to his question. They either did not know or they did not believe that the Messiah was God, but the rest of the crowd listened with delight (Mark 12:37).

On the day of Pentecost Peter quoted Psalm 110:1 and then declared its fulfillment. "God has made this Jesus, whom you crucified, both Lord and Christ" (Acts 2:36). This is a marvellous truth. Christ is not only the son of David, but also the Son of God. David was probably mystified how this could be, because it seemed to be a contradiction. By faith David believed that God would accomplish what seemed naturally impossible.

> Christ is not only the son of David, but also the Son of God.

7d. Psalm 22

It is exciting to plan a trip. Of course, my family thinks that I cram too much into each day. No matter what the weather is like, we try our best to complete the to-do list. This backfired on me one summer. We continued with our plans although I was completely soaked by rain. It was worth it! I found bear grass in Waterton Lakes National Park. Standing in the pouring rain, Barry and Debra deliberately pointed rather nonchalantly at the white flower while I happily took a picture.

At some point in time everyone has probably pondered about some particular event in the future and has tried to imagine what will happen. Because Jesus is God, he did not have to wonder what would take place when he came to earth. He knew (John 18:4). Yet like us he did meditate on the future, and he had thousands of years to do it. This psalm reveals the heart of the Saviour as he looked ahead to what he would endure in order to obtain our salvation.

> *My God, my God, why have you forsaken me? Why are you so far from saving me, so far from the words of my groaning?* (Ps. 22:1).

The emotional suffering of being separated from his Father was much harder for Jesus to bear than the physical pain. That

> The emotional suffering of being separated from his Father was much harder for Jesus to bear than the physical pain.

is why he cried out, "My God, my God, why have you forsaken me?" (Matt. 27:46). The Saviour acknowledged that God is on his throne and the deliverer of those that put their trust in him. He declared, "Yet you are enthroned as the Holy One; you are the praise of Israel. In you our fathers put their trust; they trusted and you delivered them. They cried to you and were saved; in you they trusted and were not disappointed" (Ps. 22:3-5). The Saviour experienced the scorn of men and the hatred of the people. "All who see me mock me" (Ps. 22:7).

They jeered, "He trusts in the LORD; let the LORD rescue him" (Ps. 22:8). The chief priests and the Pharisees were very pleased with themselves. As they watched Jesus die, they mocked, "He saved others…but he can't save himself! He's the King of Israel! Let him come down now from the cross, and we will believe in him. He trusts in God. Let God rescue him now if he wants him, for he said, 'I am the Son of God'" (Matt. 27:42,43).

The Saviour prophesied, "Dogs have surrounded me; a band of evil men has encircled me, they have pierced my hands and my feet. I can count all my bones; people stare and gloat over me. They divide my garments among them and cast lots for my clothing" (Ps. 22:16-18). The Roman soldiers led Jesus to Golgotha, meaning "the Place of the Skull" (Matt. 27:33). There they nailed his hands and feet to a cross (John 20:25). After lifting him up to crucify him, they cast lots for his clothing (Matt. 27:35). Crucifixion was the Roman death penalty. David would have been unfamiliar with such a death, because the Israelites stoned offenders. At times they did hang a dead body up as a spectacle afterwards. The Holy Spirit showed him the pain and suffering that his Saviour would have to bear in order to pay the punishment for his sins.

The Saviour cried triumphantly, "You who fear the LORD, praise him! All you descendants of Jacob, honor him! Revere him, all you descendants of Israel! For he has not despised or disdained the suffering of the afflicted one; he has not hidden his face from him but has listened to his cry for help" (Ps. 22:23,24). David knew that all praise and honour belonged to the Lord. As soon as God the Father would accept the sacrifice of his Son, the penalty for sin would be paid. God would listen to his Son's cry for help. Because of Jesus' death and resurrection, "all the ends of the earth will remember and turn to the LORD, and all the families of the nations will bow down before him, for dominion belongs to the LORD and he rules over the nations" (Ps. 22:27,28). God has a special place in his heart for the Israelites, because they would proclaim his plan of salvation to a needy world. The rest of us would never have heard of God's love without the faithfulness of those first Jewish believers. Jesus is King over the entire earth, but especially over his own.

The Saviour announced, "Posterity will serve him; future generations will be told about the Lord. They will proclaim his righteousness to a people yet unborn—for he has done it" (Ps. 22:30,31). The gospel has gone forth continuously and with great power ever since Calvary. Many have believed that the blood of Jesus covers their sins. By faith David could be as sure of his salvation as we are today, because he knew that God would not let him down. *He has done it.* The Saviour would accomplish God's plan to restore fellowship between him and those who would trust him. John records, "Later, knowing that all was now completed, and so that the Scripture would be fulfilled, Jesus said, 'I am thirsty'" (John 19:28). After receiving a drink of wine vinegar on a sponge, Jesus said, "It is finished" (John 19:30). Then he deliberately gave up his spirit and died.

In David we see a man after God's own heart. As a result, the Lord blessed him with insight into how Jesus would obtain his salvation; he felt the suffering of his Saviour. Because God the Father would accept the sacrifice of his Son, David knew that his sins were forgiven and that he had immediate fellowship with God. He also understood that people from all over the world would accept God's salvation. David, however, had no idea exactly how everyone would hear about Jesus, for he lived in a society in which religion and the state were unified.

Points to Ponder

1. Sin sometimes has long-lasting physical consequences, even if one repents and is forgiven.
2. God is pleased when a believer places his or her highest priority on defending and upholding God's honour.
3. David believed that the promised Seed would be fully God and fully man.
4. David was assured of his salvation as much as believers are today.
5. David believed that the Messiah would begin his reign by dying 1000 years before it happened.

Chapter Six

The Northern Kingdom of Israel

1. The Division of Israel, 930 B.C.[1]

MANY times I have asked various members of my family to give me ideas for presents. Others have often asked me the same question. All of us realize that there are limits to any request. If one of the children teasingly asked for a car, I would respond with, "How about a dinky car?" In contrast, God's resources are infinite. When the Lord asked Solomon what he wanted, he was very pleased with Solomon's response. Instead of focusing on physical desires, Solomon asked for wisdom to rule and to distinguish right from wrong. God gladly granted his wish and also promised him riches and honour. For forty years Solomon ruled over all the kings from the Euphrates River to the Egyptian border. Kings sought his advice and admired how wealthy he was. During his rule, Israel reached its peak politically. It has never had such influence again.

There was, however, one serious problem. Solomon loved many foreign women. He married 700 women and took 300 others as concubines. Under their influence Solomon worshipped Ashtoreth, the goddess of the Sidonians, Molech, the god of the Ammonites, and Chemosh, the god of the Moabites. Twice God warned Solomon to stop worshipping other gods, but Solomon would not listen. God finally told Solomon that he would lose his kingdom. Yet, for the sake of David and Jerusalem, it would happen to Solomon's son and not to Solomon himself. His son would end up ruling only one tribe of Israel (1 Kings 11:11-13). God punished Solomon but kept his promise to Judah and to David.[2] God always tells the truth.

Then one day Jeroboam, an Ephraimite, was leaving Jerusalem when Ahijah, the prophet of Shiloh, met him. When they were alone, Ahijah ripped his new cloak into twelve pieces and said:

> *"Take ten pieces for yourself, for this is what the* LORD, *the God of Israel, says: 'See, I am going to tear the kingdom out of Solomon's hand and give you ten tribes. But for the sake of my servant David and the city of Jerusalem, which I have chosen out of all the tribes of Israel, he will have one tribe...However, as for you, I will take you, and you will rule over all that your heart desires; you will be king over Israel. If you do whatever I command you and walk in my ways and do what is right in my eyes by keeping my statutes and commands, as David my servant did, I will be with you. I will build you a dynasty as enduring as the one I built for David and will give Israel to you'"* (1 Kings 11:31-38).

After Solomon's death, his son Rehoboam became king of Israel. The line of Judah appeared secure on the throne of Israel, and David was definitely dead. I wonder how many Israelites were waiting for the promised Seed. Instead, politics and earthly concerns seemed to be occupying the minds of the people. Shortly after Rehoboam became king, Jeroboam and all of Israel approached Rehoboam and complained about the hard labour that Solomon had demanded of them. They promised Rehoboam that they would serve him if he made their load lighter. Wanting time to think, Rehoboam said, "Go away for three days and then come back to me" (1 Kings 12:5).

As soon as the people went away, Rehoboam asked his father's advisors what to do. They answered, "If today you will be a servant to these people and serve them and give them a favorable answer, they will always be your servants" (1 Kings 12:7).

Rehoboam did not like their advice. When he asked some of his friends, they answered, "Tell these people who have said to you, 'Your father put a heavy yoke on us, but make our yoke lighter'—tell them, 'My little finger is thicker than my father's waist. My father laid on you a heavy yoke; I will make it even heavier. My father scourged you with whips; I will scourge you with scorpions'" (1 Kings 12:10,11).

Soon the people returned to hear the king's answer. Rehoboam spoke harshly. "My father made your yoke heavy; I will make it even heavier. My father scourged you with whips; I will scourge you with scorpions" (1 Kings 12:14).

After hearing those cruel words, they retorted, "What share do we have in David, what part in Jesse's son? To your tents, O Israel! Look after your own house, O David!" (1 Kings 12:16).

Since Solomon had refused to stop sinning, God allowed Rehoboam to listen to the bad advice of his friends. Therefore Israel became split into the northern kingdom of Israel, consisting of ten tribes, and the southern kingdom of Judah, including those from the tribes of Benjamin, Simeon, and Levi who lived there. As Israel's first king, Jeroboam was very wise politically but not spiritually. He thought, "If these people go up to offer sacrifices at the temple of the LORD in Jerusalem, they will again give their allegiance to their lord, Rehoboam king of Judah. They will kill me and return to King Rehoboam" (1 Kings 12:27).

> Since Solomon had refused to stop sinning, God allowed Rehoboam to listen to the bad advice of his friends.

Jeroboam was unwilling to sever the close relationship between religion and the state. He convinced the Israelites that it was too much trouble to travel all the way to Jerusalem to worship the Lord. That is why he made two golden calves. He placed one close to the southernmost border of Israel, at Bethel, and one in the far north, at Dan. Then Jeroboam proclaimed, "Here are your gods, O Israel, who brought you up out of Egypt" (1 Kings 12:28).

God had ordained the tribe of Levi to be the workers in the temple and the line of Aaron, a Levite, to be the priests. Instead Jeroboam chose whomever he wanted to become priests in the shrines that he built. Although God promised to bless Jeroboam if he obeyed, Jeroboam chose to lead the Israelites astray into worshipping idols. He obviously did not believe God's promise to build him an enduring dynasty. Satan must have been glad that the nation of Israel was weakened and that the promised Seed would only come to Judah.

2. Elijah on Mount Carmel, 865 B.C.

Reign of Ahab: 874-853 B.C.[3]

In the succeeding years not one king of Israel loved the Lord, but the wickedest one of all was Ahab. Not only did he continue to commit the sins of Jeroboam, but he also married Jezebel, daughter of the king of Sidon, who taught him to worship Baal. In Samaria, the capital of Israel, Ahab built a temple for the worship of Baal and an Asherah pole. Because of Ahab's sin, Elijah informed him, "As the Lord, the God of Israel, lives, whom I serve, there will be neither dew nor rain in the next few years except at my word" (1 Kings 17:1). For three and one-half years it did not rain in Israel (Jas. 5:17). The famine was so severe that Ahab searched everywhere for Elijah, but he could not be found.

One day God finally told Elijah to go to Ahab, who angrily said, "Is that you, you troubler of Israel?" (1 Kings 18:17).

Elijah replied:

> *"I have not made trouble for Israel...But you and your father's family have. You have abandoned the Lord's commands and have followed the Baals. Now summon the people from all over Israel to meet me on Mount Carmel. And bring the four hundred and fifty prophets of Baal and the four hundred prophets of Asherah, who eat at Jezebel's table"* (1 Kings 18:18,19).

After everyone was gathered on the mountain, Elijah spoke to the people:

> *"How long will you waver between two opinions? If the LORD is God, follow him; but if Baal is God, follow him." But the people said nothing. Then Elijah said to them, "I am the only one of the LORD's prophets left, but Baal has four hundred and fifty prophets. Get two bulls for us. Let them choose one for themselves, and let them cut it into pieces and put it on the wood but not set fire to it. I will prepare the other bull and put it on the wood but not set fire to it. Then you call on the name of your god, and I will call on the name of the LORD. The god who answers by fire—he is God." Then all the people said, "What you say is good"* (1 Kings 18:21-24).

The prophets of Baal chose one of the bulls and prepared it. From morning until noon they danced around the altar and shouted, "O Baal, answer us!" (1 Kings 18:26). Nothing happened.

By noon, Elijah teased them, "Shout louder!...Surely he is a god! Perhaps he is in deep thought, or busy, or traveling. Maybe he is sleeping and must be awakened" (1 Kings 18:27). The priests shouted louder and cut themselves with swords and spears. By the evening still nothing had happened. No one answered or paid attention to the priests of Baal. Then Elijah took twelve stones, one for each of the twelve tribes of Israel, and built an altar in the name of the Lord. After he dug a large trench around it, he arranged the wood on top of the altar. He cut up the bull and laid it on top of the wood. He ordered the people to fill four large jars with water and to pour them on the offering and on the wood. "Do it again," he said, and they did it again. "Do it a third time," he ordered, and they did it the third time (1 Kings 18:34). There was so much water that it filled the trench. Next Elijah prayed, "O LORD, God of Abraham, Isaac and Israel, let it be known today that you are God in Israel and that I am your servant and have done all these things at your command. Answer me, O LORD, answer me, so these people will know that you, O LORD, are God, and that you are turning their hearts back again" (1 Kings 18:36,37).

Immediately the fire of the Lord "burned up the sacrifice, the wood, the stones and the soil, and also licked up the water in the trench" (1 Kings 18:38). The people fell to the ground and cried, "The LORD—he is God! The LORD—he is God!" (1 Kings 18:39). At once Elijah ordered the Israelites to seize all the prophets of Baal and kill them. Shortly afterwards the sky grew black, and the rain finally fell again on Israel.

In founding the nation of Israel, Moses had often warned the Israelites never to make an idol and worship it, for God is a consuming fire (Deut. 4:23,24). Through Elijah, the consuming fire of God's judgment was meted out on those false prophets. Elijah himself was filled with the fire of zeal for God's honour. "Everyone will be salted with fire" (Mark 9:49). Do you want the fire of God's judgment upon you or the fire of the Holy Spirit within you? When God looks into each person's heart, he either sees one who loves him and is obedient to him or one who is not.

3. THE THREAT OF ASSYRIA, 841 B.C.[4]

Joram, the son of Ahab, was king of Israel.

One day Elisha sent a student from his prophet's school to find Jehu at Ramoth Gilead. After the two of them were alone in a house, the prophet poured oil on Jehu's head and said:

> *"This is what the LORD, the God of Israel, says: 'I anoint you king over the LORD's people Israel. You are to destroy the house of Ahab your master, and I will avenge the blood of my servants the prophets and the blood of all the*

Lord's *servants shed by Jezebel. The whole house of Ahab will perish. I will cut off from Ahab every last male in Israel—slave or free...As for Jezebel, dogs will devour her on the plot of ground at Jezreel, and no one will bury her'"* (2 Kings 9:6-10).

Then the prophet quickly ran out of the house. God ordained Jehu to wipe out the house of Ahab because he had introduced Baal worship to Israel. The other army officers wondered what had happened. Soon Jehu admitted, "Here is what he told me: 'This is what the Lord says: I anoint you king over Israel'" (2 Kings 9:12).

Then the officers blew the trumpet and shouted, "Jehu is king!" (2 Kings 9:13).

Meanwhile, recovering from battle wounds received while fighting the Arameans, King Joram was resting at Jezreel with his nephew, Ahaziah, king of Judah. Jehu quickly climbed into his chariot and rode to Jezreel. The lookout of the city reported to Joram, "The driving is like that of Jehu son of Nimshi—he drives like a madman" (2 Kings 9:20). Immediately Joram and Ahaziah hitched up their chariots and rode out to meet him.

> *When Joram saw Jehu he asked, "Have you come in peace, Jehu?"*
> *"How can there be peace," Jehu replied, "as long as all the idolatry and witchcraft of your mother Jezebel abound?"*
> *Joram turned about and fled, calling out to Ahaziah, "Treachery, Ahaziah!"* (2 Kings 9:22,23).

With his bow and arrow Jehu shot and killed Joram. One of the soldiers with Jehu wounded Ahaziah, who later died of the wound. When Jehu reached Jezreel, he asked some eunuchs to throw Jezebel from the wall of the city.[5]

Naturally, because he had killed a Sidonian princess and the king of Judah, Jehu would find no allies in those two countries. Sidon, a city in Phoenicia, on the Mediterranean

> Since enemies surrounded Jehu, he chose to find an ally in Assyria.

Sea, was located northwest of Israel while Judah was situated to the southeast. To the southwest lay Philistia, a perennial enemy of Israel. Aram, positioned to the northeast, was more intent on war than on peace. At that time God allowed Aram to conquer all of Gilead (2 Kings 10:32,33). Since enemies surrounded Jehu, he chose to find an ally in Assyria. Therefore he willingly paid Shalmaneser III tribute.[6] This was the first inroad Assyria had into Israel. How sad that Jehu did not ask God for protection from his enemies.

4. The Prophets: Proclaiming the Word of God

For almost 400 years some prophets left a written record of God's message to the kingdoms of Israel and Judah. We will continue our journey through time by considering these books, which were authorized by God to deal primarily with the issues of their day. Many years later Paul reminded Timothy that the Scriptures are "able to make you wise for salvation through faith in Christ Jesus" (2 Tim. 3:15). This includes the Old Testament. While reading, we must determine the purpose of each book. Does God explain more about his plan of salvation? We must continually keep the words of the prophets in their proper historical context.

5. Jonah: The First Missionary

Date written: about 785-760 B.C.[7]
Reign of Jeroboam II: 793-753 B.C.[7]

One day God told Jonah, the prophet from Gath Hepher in Israel, "Go to the great city of Nineveh and preach against it, because its wickedness has come up before me" (Jonah 1:2).

Instead of obeying, Jonah ran in the opposite direction.

In Joppa he boarded a ship headed for Tarshish. Jonah was probably not eager to go to the capital of the nation that had sunk its fangs into them (thanks to Jehu). Besides, why would the Assyrians listen to the God of Israel? They had their own gods. After Jonah climbed on board the ship, he went below deck and promptly fell asleep.

> *The captain went to him and said, "How can you sleep? Get up and call on your god! Maybe he will take notice of us, and we will not perish."*
>
> *Then the sailors said to each other, "Come, let us cast lots to find out who is responsible for this calamity." They cast lots and the lot fell on Jonah. So they asked him, "Tell us, who is responsible for making all this trouble for us? What do you do? Where do you come from? What is your country? From what people are you?"*
>
> *He answered, "I am a Hebrew and I worship the* LORD, *the God of heaven, who made the sea and the land"*
> (Jonah 1:6-9).

The sailors were terrified when they found out that Jonah was running from the Lord. Although they did not want to do it, eventually they threw Jonah overboard. Immediately the sea grew calm. Yet God did not allow Jonah to die because of his disobedience. He wanted him to go to Nineveh. As a result, Jonah was safe in the belly of a large fish for three days and three nights. As soon as Jonah finally yielded to the will of God, the fish vomited him onto dry land. Once again God told Jonah to go to Nineveh. This time Jonah obeyed. After entering the city, he cried out, "Forty more days and Nineveh will be overturned" (Jonah 3:4).

For three days he walked through the city and preached to the people. The Ninevites believed God and fasted in sorrow over their sin. News of this situation soon reached the king of Assyria, who also covered himself with sackcloth and fasted. The entire city shook with sorrow over God's message. Then the king[8] decreed:

> *Do not let any man or beast, herd or flock, taste anything; do not let them eat or drink. But let man and beast be covered with sackcloth. Let everyone call urgently on God. Let them give up their evil ways and their violence. Who knows? God may yet relent and with compassion turn from his fierce anger so that we will not perish* (Jonah 3:7-9).

After Jonah finished preaching, he left Nineveh and sat down outside the city to see what would happen. When the forty days had passed and the city was still standing, Jonah was very angry. He prayed, "O LORD, is this not what I said when I was still at home? That is why I was so quick to flee to Tarshish. I knew that you are a gracious and compassionate God, slow to anger and abounding in love, a God who relents from sending calamity. Now, O LORD, take away my life, for it is better for me to die than to live" (Jonah 4:2,3).

> *If at anytime I announce that a nation or kingdom is to be uprooted, torn down and destroyed, and if that nation I warned repents of its evil, then I will relent and not inflict on it the disaster I had planned. And if at another time I announce that a nation or kingdom is to be built up and planted, and if it does evil in my sight and does not obey me, then I will reconsider the good I had intended to do for it* (Jer. 18:7-10).

Although Jonah's message was one of judgment, he realized that mercy would override justice if the people repented of their sin. God's promise of judgment was actually conditional. God's dealings with Nineveh are a good example of how he treats nations. Normally people are happy when good overcomes evil. The opposite is harder to accept. Yet the Lord makes it clear that if a nation continues in evil, then he will change the good that he intends for that nation to evil. Jonah obviously thought that God had no business showing compassion on the Assyrians. It would be a conflict of interest for the Lord to have mercy on Israel's enemies, because in that day religion and the state were closely intertwined. Instead, God showed that he cares for all countries, not just Israel. This was an important revelation into God's character and plan of salvation. He knows every individual, and his plan includes people from all races.

The Lord said, "But Nineveh has more than a hundred and twenty thousand people who cannot tell their right hand from their left, and many cattle as well. Should I not be concerned about that great city?" (Jonah 4:11).

Satan was probably angry about God's actions. For a time his stronghold was under the Lord's control. Instead of killing those Assyrians while they belonged to Satan's kingdom, God forgave them and accepted them as his own people. God's plan of salvation included them. How comforting to know that no one is too wicked to become a child of God! Although the Assyrians were ruthless warriors, forever trying to expand their borders, God still loved them. Because of Jonah's witness, the Israelites had sixty more years to repent of their sin. During those years the Assyrians likely kept busy trying to keep their borders intact.[8] Meanwhile Jeroboam II was able to restore Israel's boundaries to those of Solomon's day. God blessed Israel materially during the years of grace while he waited for them to throw away their idols.

6. Amos: Rejecting Ritualistic Religion

Date of ministry: about 760-750 B.C.[9]

Amos finished prophesying 28 years before the fall of Israel and 212 years before the edict of Cyrus. Amos was a shepherd from Tekoa in Judah when the Lord called him to go to Bethel in Israel. He went to the prosperous land of Jeroboam II, where the people brought sacrifices to God every morning and regularly held religious feasts. Outwardly they appeared to worship the Lord, but in their hearts they did not care what he thought. They still bowed down to the idols that Jeroboam, the first king of Israel, had erected over 170 years before.[10] This is a danger that has often troubled me—probably because I accepted the Lord as my Saviour at the age of nine. It is too easy to assume that children brought up in the Church are believers. Sadly, they may only be going through the motion of worship, like the Israelites did.

> *Woe to you who long for the day of the LORD! Why do you long for the day of the LORD? That day will be darkness, not light. It will be as though a man fled from a lion only to meet a bear, as though he entered his house and rested his hand on the wall only to have a snake bite him. Will not the day of the LORD be darkness, not light—pitch-dark, without a ray of brightness?* (Amos 5:18-20).

The Israelites waited expectantly for the day of the Lord, because then God would destroy all their enemies. Likely they knew how Joel, an earlier prophet for the people of Judah, had described it as a day of celebration and victory for God's people.[11] If the Israelites thought that they would be excluded from the judgment of God, they were sorely mistaken. God said, "You only have I chosen of all the families of the earth; therefore I will punish you for all your sins" (Amos 3:2). Peter echoes a similar thought, "For it is time for judgment to begin with the family of God; and if it begins with us, what will the outcome be for those who do not obey the gospel of God?" (1 Pet. 4:17). The Lord expects love and obedience from those to whom he has revealed himself.

God reminded them of their sins—bragging about their offerings for the Lord, forcing the poor to give them grain, oppressing the righteous, taking bribes, and depriving the poor of justice in the courts. For the sin of idolatry Israel would be sent into exile. The Lord warned them, "You have lifted up the shrine of your king, the pedestal of your idols, the star of your god—which you made for yourselves. Therefore I will send you into exile beyond Damascus" (Amos 5:26,27). Amos lamented, "Fallen is Virgin Israel, never to rise again, deserted in her own land, with no one to lift her up" (Amos 5:2).

God promised to raise up a nation that would oppress the entire land of Israel (Amos 6:14). Amos pleaded with the Israelites to repent of their sins. As with Nineveh, the Lord would love to show mercy to his chosen people. Yet the only way that Israel could change God's judgment was to listen and obey the advice of Amos. "Seek good, not evil, that you may live. Then the LORD God Almighty will be with you, just as you say he is. Hate evil, love good; maintain justice in the courts. Perhaps the LORD God Almighty will have mercy on the remnant of Joseph" (Amos 5:14,15).

The people stubbornly ignored what Amos said. The prophet Amaziah said, "Get out, you seer! Go back to the land of Judah. Earn your bread there and do your prophesying there. Don't prophesy anymore at Bethel, because this is the king's sanctuary and the temple of the kingdom" (Amos 7:12,13). How different from Nineveh's reaction!

> *"Surely the eyes of the Sovereign LORD are on the sinful kingdom. I will destroy it from the face of the earth—yet I will not totally destroy the house of Jacob...For I will give the command, and I will shake the house of Israel among all the nations as grain is shaken in a sieve, and not a pebble will reach the ground"* (Amos 9:8,9).

When the Lord destroyed other nations such as the Philistines, the Ammonites, and the Moabites, they disappeared from the face of the earth. Because of God's covenant with Abraham, Israel would not be like those other nations. Instead he would scatter a remnant of them among all the nations.[12] He would gladly give them an opportunity to repent of their sin.

> *"In that day I will restore David's fallen tent. I will repair its broken places, restore its ruins, and build it as it used*

to be, so that they may possess the remnant of Edom and all the nations that bear my name" (Amos 9:11,12).

While Amos was preaching, the line of David was reigning on the throne of Judah. The people of Judah were worshipping in Solomon's temple according to God's Law. In contrast, those in Israel continued to worship God in front of false idols. That is why Amos lamented over David's fallen tent. He knew that the Israelites worshipped God but their worship was mere ritual and outward show. Their hearts were far from God. They did not love him or want to obey him. They only looked as if they did.

Over 200 years had passed since the death of David. In David's tent the worshippers had loved and adored the Lord. They had worshipped him in spirit and in truth with joyful hearts, because God was their God and they belonged to him.[13] God wanted the Israelites to repent of their sin and worship him the same way David had. Even if they refused to repent, God would continue to confirm the covenant mercies promised to David. Although Israel would be scattered throughout the Assyrian Empire, God's covenant with David still remained intact. No matter how the Israelites acted, the promised Seed would be born to the line of Judah at the appointed time. No one can thwart God's plan of salvation.

This prophecy also involved the Gentiles—anyone who did not observe the beliefs and practices of the Jews. Many years later the apostles held a council at Jerusalem to discuss the Gentiles who had accepted God's salvation in Jesus. James spoke:

"Brothers, listen to me. Simon has described to us how God at first showed his concern by taking from the Gentiles a people for himself. The words of the prophets

are in agreement with this, as it is written: 'After this I will return and rebuild David's fallen tent. Its ruins I will rebuild, and I will restore it, that the remnant of men may seek the Lord, and all the Gentiles who bear my name, says the Lord who does these things'...It is my judgment, therefore, that we should not make it difficult for the Gentiles who are turning to God" (Acts 15:13-19).

The apostles agreed that the gospel of Jesus transcended political boundaries. In many different countries God was busy saving people from their sins and restoring them to fellowship with him. Those people worshipped God in spirit and in truth, just as David had.

"I will bring back my exiled people Israel; they will rebuild the ruined cities and live in them. They will plant vineyards and drink their wine; they will make gardens and eat their fruit. I will plant Israel in their own land, never again to be uprooted from the land I have given them" (Amos 9:14,15).

God promised to bring back his exiled people to the Promised Land, where they would rebuild the cities and live in them. Over 200 years later Cyrus published his edict allowing the Israelites to return to their own land. Most of those who returned truly loved God. This situation was in keeping with the covenant at Sinai. Before they crossed the Jordan River, Moses told the Israelites that they would go into exile if they disobeyed God and they would return to their land if they repented. How trustworthy God is! He keeps his promises. Although God was willing to plant the Israelites securely in their land forever, obedience to him is the prerequisite for its continued possession. God must apply the law for nations to Israel, just as he did to Nineveh in Jonah's day (Jer. 18:7-10). If the Israelites did not maintain the right heart attitude toward the Lord after he had restored them to the land, then the good that God had intended for them would turn to evil.

7. Hosea: The Love of God

Date of ministry: 753-715 B.C.[14]

Hosea prophesied for 31 years before the fall of Israel and for 7 years afterward. He finished prophesying 177 years before the edict of Cyrus.

God had chosen the Israelites to be his special people, but their hearts had strayed from him to worshipping idols. The words of Amos only hardened their hearts to continue in their sin; they did not repent. Amaziah even kicked Amos out of the land. Around the same time the Lord expressed his love for Israel through Hosea, a prophet of God who lived in Israel. For many years he preached to the people by his words and by his actions. "Hear the word of the Lord, you Israelites, because the Lord has a charge to bring against you who live in the land: 'There is no faithfulness, no love, no acknowledgment of God in the land. There is only cursing, lying and murder, stealing and adultery; they break all bounds, and bloodshed follows bloodshed'" (Hos. 4:1,2). Hosea made sure that the Israelites knew exactly why God would abandon them. True love kindly but firmly warns people about the consequences of continuing in sin; true love wants to change the rebellious heart to one of loving obedience.

Once someone at work was talking about becoming a mother. She decided to never teach her children any religious beliefs. Instead she preferred to let them choose for themselves. She was oblivious to the fact that she was influencing them for evil. If we really love our children and the Lord, we will want them to learn the Scriptures. Then we will pray that the Holy Spirit will open their spiritual eyes to understand. Through Hosea, God lamented:

> "Israel cries out to me, 'O our God, we acknowledge you!' But Israel has rejected what is good; an enemy will pursue him…With their silver and gold they make idols for themselves to their own destruction. Throw out your calf-idol, O Samaria! My anger burns against them. How long will they be incapable of purity? They are from Israel!

This calf—a craftsman has made it; it is not God. It will be broken in pieces, that calf of Samaria" (Hos. 8:2-6).

With their lips they cried to God, but in their hearts they continued to worship idols. Because of their sin the Israelites would be expelled from the Promised Land; they would return to Egypt and eat unclean food in Assyria (Hos. 9:3). Hosea warned them:

The people who live in Samaria fear for the calf-idol of Beth Aven. Its people will mourn over it, and so will its idolatrous priests, those who had rejoiced over its splendor, because it is taken from them into exile. It will be carried to Assyria as tribute for the great king. Ephraim will be disgraced; Israel will be ashamed of its wooden idols. Samaria and its king will float away like a twig on the surface of the waters (Hos. 10:5-7).

How Hosea longed for his audience to repent of their sins! "Return, O Israel, to the LORD your God. Your sins have been your downfall! Take words with you and return to the LORD. Say to him: 'Forgive all our sins and receive us graciously, that we may offer the fruit of our lips'" (Hos. 14:1,2).

God also told Hosea to marry a prostitute. His wife, Gomer, was guilty of unfaithfulness to her husband just as Israel was unfaithful to God. Eventually Hosea and Gomer had three children. Through their names Hosea preached to the Israelites, because in that day people paid attention to the meaning of names. When Gomer had a second child, God said, "Call her Lo- Ruhamah, for I will no longer show love to the house of Israel, that I should at all forgive them. Yet I will show love to the house of Judah; and I will save them—not by bow, sword or battle, or by horses and horsemen, but by the LORD their God" (Hos. 1:6,7). Then when she had a third child, God said, "Call him Lo-Ammi, for you are not my people, and I am not your God" (Hos. 1:9). Lo-Ruhamah means, "not loved" and Lo-Ammi means, "not my people." God would no longer love them or call them his people. From their perspective God would abandon them. Sin has consequences.

Yet this situation was not permanent. One day Judah and Israel would be reunited as one country under one leader.

> *"Yet the Israelites will be like the sand on the seashore, which cannot be measured or counted. In the place where it was said to them, 'You are not my people,' they will be called 'sons of the living God.' The people of Judah and the people of Israel will be reunited, and they will appoint one leader and will come up out of the land"* (Hos. 1:10,11).

> *"I will plant her for myself in the land; I will show my love to the one I called 'Not my loved one.' I will say to those called 'Not my people,' 'You are my people'; and they will say, 'You are my God'"* (Hos. 2:23).

In the physical realm, this happened after Cyrus decreed that anyone in the Medo-Persian Empire could return to the Promised Land. God's people from Israel and Judah were reunited politically and religiously under Zerubbabel. Many years later Jesus would unite Jewish believers in the spiritual realm. He would offer them forgiveness of sins by his blood.

Like Amos, Hosea also prophesied about the Gentiles—the rest of the world not chosen by God and apparently not loved. Many years later Paul would preach:

> *What if he did this to make the riches of his glory known to the objects of his mercy, whom he prepared in advance for glory—even us, whom he also called, not only from the Jews but also from the Gentiles? As he says in Hosea: "I will call them 'my people' who are not my people; and I will call her 'my loved one' who is not my loved one"* (Rom. 9:23-25).

Gentiles, as well as the Jews, could become the loved ones of God. This means that race is not important for salvation.

Anyone, anywhere, may become a believer and a member of God's kingdom. Through Hosea, God pointed to the gospel age. What a wonderful plan!

After the death of Jeroboam II in 753 B.C., the nation was continually plagued with political instability and with the ever-present threat of Assyria. Perhaps some wondered if the Lord had rejected them permanently. Although judgment was coming because the Israelites refused to repent, the Lord used Hosea's life to demonstrate how much he loved them. God told Hosea to continue loving his wife. Another man loved Gomer, and she was committing adultery with him. Yet God told Hosea, "Love her as the LORD loves the Israelites, though they turn to other gods and love the sacred raisin cakes" (Hos. 3:1). Hosea showed how worthless Gomer was by only paying fifteen shekels of silver and ten bushels of barley to get her back (Hos. 3:2). Gomer was forced to be faithful to her husband for a certain period of time. By doing without other men, she became an object lesson for Hosea to explain:

> *For the Israelites will live many days without king or prince, without sacrifice or sacred stones, without ephod or idol. Afterward the Israelites will return and seek the* LORD *their God and David their king. They will come trembling to the* LORD *and to his blessings in the last days* (Hos. 3:4,5).

Hosea's audience had rejected God, but he would never forsake them. He was working out his plan of salvation. Although they had forsaken God, his temple, and the Messiah, the Lord reminded them of his covenant with David. For a long time they would lose everything that they cherished—their king, their sacrifices, their precious stones, and their idols. Then sometime in the future they would seek God.

Loving him with their whole hearts and begging for his mercy, they would come trembling to God and to the Messiah, the promised Seed who would reign on David's throne. To the Israelites, God, the temple, and the political Messiah of David's line were inseparable parts of a glorious future. In the mindset of that day, religion and the state must be unified. One could not function without the other. Therefore when the Lord returned them to the Promised Land about 200 years later, they expected that the promised Ruler would come with them. They did not realize that they would have to wait over 500 more years before the Messiah would enter his temple. Even then, he did not come as a political ruler but as a spiritual leader.

8. MICAH

Date of ministry: 742-687 B.C.[15]

Micah prophesied for 20 years before the fall of Israel and for 35 years afterward. He finished prophesying 101 years before the fall of Jerusalem and 149 years before the edict of Cyrus. He is primarily a prophet of Judah and the contemporary of Isaiah. He is, however, one of only three prophets who wrote directly to Israel.

8a. The necessity of repenting

Micah warned Israel that Samaria, its capital, would be destroyed and that all of her idols would be broken to pieces (Micah 1:6,7). Micah of Moresheth was so upset at Israel's sin that he cried, "Because of this I will weep and wail; I will go about barefoot and naked. I will howl like a jackal and moan like an owl. For her wound is incurable" (Micah 1:8,9).

Through Micah, God warned them, "I am planning disaster against this people, from which you cannot save yourselves. You will no longer walk proudly, for it will be a time of calamity" (Micah 2:3).

Some false prophets replied, "Do not prophesy about these things; disgrace will not overtake us" (Micah 2:6).

Micah did not listen. Instead he continued to warn Israel and Judah of impending disaster. "Then they will cry out to the LORD, but he will not answer them" (Micah 3:4).

> The Israelites were sure that God would never destroy them since they were his special people.

The Israelites were sure that God would never destroy them since they were his special people. He dwelt among them. It did not matter how they behaved. Yet eventually the Lord would punish the Israelites for their sin. The Assyrians would scatter them throughout the Assyrian Empire. Because of God's covenant with Abraham and with David, the Israelites could say, "Do not gloat over me, my enemy! Though I have fallen, I will rise. Though I sit in darkness, the LORD will be my light. Because I have sinned against him, I will bear the LORD's wrath, until he pleads my case and establishes my right" (Micah 7:8,9). The Israelites would return to the Promised Land, because they would acknowledge their sin. The basis of their restoration would be the mercy of God.

8b. The Forgiveness of God

Who is a God like you, who pardons sin and forgives the transgression of the remnant of his inheritance? You do not stay angry forever but delight to show mercy. You will again have compassion on us; you will tread our sins underfoot and hurl all our iniquities into the depths of the sea (Micah 7:18,19).

When the Israelites would return to the Promised Land, many of them would shout for joy over God's wonderful salvation.

Although they would appreciate their physical restoration to the land, they would be more thankful that the Lord had forgiven their sins. They would enjoy fellowship with their Creator. Today we can sing the same song of forgiveness. That is why Henry writes, "God's people are pardoned people, and to this they owe their all. When God *pardons* sin, he *passes it by*, does not punish it as justly he might, nor deal with the sinner according to the desert of it."[16] God is merciful, because he does not temporarily forgive our sin. His forgiveness lasts forever. "He casts them *into the sea*, not near the shore-side, where they may appear again next low water, but into the *depth of the sea*, never to rise again. *All their sins* shall be cast there without exception, for when God forgives *sin*, he forgives all." [16]

> God is merciful, because he does not temporarily forgive our sin. His forgiveness lasts forever.

8c. The Messiah's Birthplace

"But you, Bethlehem Ephrathah, though you are small among the clans of Judah, out of you will come for me one who will be ruler over Israel, whose origins are from of old, from ancient times" (Micah 5:2).

How amazing that God names the birthplace of Jesus around 700 years before his birth! Many years before, Moses had explained to the Israelites how to distinguish truth from error. "You may say to yourselves, 'How can we know when a message has not been spoken by the LORD?' If what a prophet proclaims in the name of the LORD does not take place or come true, that is a message the LORD has not spoken. That prophet has spoken presumptuously. Do not be afraid of him" (Deut. 18:21,22). In contrast, God always tells the truth and always keeps his promises. When Jesus was born in Bethlehem, God proved that Micah was his true prophet. Therefore we can rely on Micah's words concerning the spiritual realm. The little baby born in Bethlehem is eternal. His *origins are from of old, from ancient times*. Jesus has no beginning and no end, because he is God. As a result, Jesus is the one who unites the Scriptures. He is the one who spoke face to face with believers in the Old Testament. T. T. Shields is overjoyed that Jesus is God's visible witness in this world:

> When Jesus was born in Bethlehem, God proved that Micah was his true prophet.

> How delightful it is to turn the pages of the Bible and see Him stepping down the centuries, making Himself known here a little, and there a little, communicating Himself to Adam, to Enoch, to Noah, to Abraham, to Isaac, Jacob, Joseph, Moses, Joshua, and David, and all the prophets! Have you ever noticed, in reading the Bible, how, as you turn from one book to another, there is no break in its continuity? It is the same Voice, the voice of Him Who is contemporary with all ages; and Who speaks as an eyewitness of all the events recorded! "His goings forth have been from of old, from everlasting." The margin has it, "From the days of eternity."[17]

8d. The Messiah's Kingdom

In the last days the mountain of the LORD*'s temple will be established as chief among the mountains; it will be raised above the hills, and peoples will stream to it. Many nations will come and say, "Come, let us go up to the mountain of the* LORD*, to the house of the God of Jacob. He will teach us his ways, so that we may walk in his paths." The law will go out from Zion, the word of the* LORD *from Jerusalem* (Micah 4:1,2).

When Micah wrote, most people only considered worshipping their local deity. Yet someday people from many different nations would travel to Jerusalem to worship the Lord. While true worship of the one and only God was located in Jerusalem, others worshipped their false gods at their own mountain shrines (Ezek. 18:5,6). In Jesus' day, because many devout Jews from all over the world expected the arrival of the Messiah, they actually moved to Jerusalem to await his coming. "Now there were staying in Jerusalem God-fearing Jews from every nation under heaven" (Acts 2:5). What a wonderful fulfillment of Micah's prophecy. People flooded into Jerusalem to worship the Lord.[18]

The Jews have always had a mindset that unites religion with the state. For this reason they have assumed that their own political supremacy over the world will coincide with the universal worship of the one true God. Today they still hope that the Messiah will bring them political peace and will enlarge their sphere of influence over all nations. Because this has not happened yet, they are still waiting for their Utopia on earth. Thus it is understandable how a Jewish Biblical scholar, Dr. Kac, interprets the phrase *in the last days*. "The phrase 'latter days' always refers in the Old Testament to the time of Israel's final and complete national restoration and spiritual redemption."[19] Such a statement encourages the hope of Israel for future world dominance, both politically and spiritually. Yet is Dr. Kac correct? Is what he claims always true? Consider Jeremiah's words to the people of Judah living in Jerusalem before its fall in 586 B.C. False prophets continually insisted that no harm would come to the people (Jer. 23:17). Instead Jeremiah warned them, "The anger of the LORD shall not return, until he have executed, and till he have performed the thoughts of his heart: in the latter days ye shall consider it perfectly" (Jer. 23:20, KJV). In other words, "In days to come, when Nebuchadnezzar has conquered Jerusalem and dragged its citizens off to Babylon, you will understand the truth of my words."

"The law will go out from Zion, the word of the LORD from Jerusalem." Luke records, "And repentance and forgiveness of sins will be preached in his name to all nations, beginning at Jerusalem" (Luke 24:47). After Jesus' death and resurrection the disciples preached the good news of sins forgiven to those who repented. This gospel spread throughout the Roman Empire, mainly because many believing Jews witnessed to others when they went back home.

> *He will judge between many peoples and will settle disputes for strong nations far and wide. They will beat their swords into plowshares and their spears into pruning hooks. Nation will not take up sword against nation, nor will they train for war anymore* (Micah 4:3).

What a beautiful picture of peace! It portrayed what life would be like during the time of Jesus. It was the era of the Pax Romana. The Bethel Series paints a vivid picture of the world in Jesus' day:

> Not before or since in the annals of recorded human history has the world enjoyed such an extended period of peace. To be sure, there was a jockeying for power within Rome's own house and maybe small skirmishes and uprisings to be put down in different parts of the sprawling empire. But during the peace of Rome, no people lived with paralyzing fear that an enemy was about to vanquish them. Caesar's subjects, wherever they were, could scan the horizons and see no signs of an enemy anywhere. For Rome ruled with a strong hand, and there was no nation big enough or powerful enough to threaten that rule. Peace and quiet reigned! How easy then for the world to hear the good news of God's love in Christ.[20]

> *All the nations may walk in the name of their gods; we will walk in the name of the LORD our God for ever and ever* (Micah 4:5).

According to Roman law each nation was allowed to worship its own god. At first Christianity was considered a sect of the Jewish religion by the Romans and the Jews. Thus they had the freedom to worship and to evangelize other Jews. In J. Ironside Still's words:

> Roman law permitted the people of a subject state to continue the religion they had at the time they were conquered, but did not permit them to adopt any other except the Roman. The religion of the Jews was thus protected by Roman law, and their religion was defined by their Scriptures, which were, so to speak, the *Charter of their religious rights.* Roman law could not therefore refuse its protection to any form of the Jewish religion that was "according to the Scriptures."[21]

> *"I will make the lame a remnant, those driven away a strong nation. The LORD will rule over them in Mount Zion from that day and forever"* (Micah 4:7).

Micah 4:1-7 is a description of the world in Jesus' day and of his impact on it. During Jesus' lifetime, thousands flocked to him, and he ruled over them in the spiritual realm. Jesus proved his spiritual power by the miracles that he performed in the physical world. For example, when four friends lowered a paralytic through the roof of a house, Jesus saw their faith and determination to have him heal their friend. Jesus responded by saying, "Son, your sins are forgiven" (Mark 2:5). Jesus knew that the Pharisees present revolted at his presuming to forgive sins.

> *He said to them, "Why are you thinking these things? Which is easier: to say to the paralytic, 'Your sins are forgiven,' or to say, 'Get up, take your mat and walk'? But that you may know that the Son of Man has authority on earth*

to forgive sins..." He said to the paralytic, "I tell you, get up, take your mat and go home." He got up, took his mat and walked out in full view of them all (Mark 2:8-12).

9. THE FALL OF ISRAEL

722 B.C. The fall of Samaria, the capital of Israel, is 136 years before the fall of Jerusalem[22]
Reign of Tiglath-Pileser III of Assyria: 745-727 B.C.[22]

The time for mercy was over. Because the Israelites refused to repent of their sins, God allowed the Assyrians to conquer them. During his reign Tiglath-Pileser III had successfully conquered many nations from Egypt to Babylonia and as far north as Armenia.[23] Such a large area was very difficult to control. As long as each country paid its tribute on time, it retained its local autonomy. If anyone refused to pay, then Assyria would have to wage another war against the offending nation. In order to solve this problem, Tiglath-Pileser III developed the policy of deporting conquered people to foreign lands and repopulating the vacant country with strangers. By mixing up the races the Assyrians hoped to squash racial loyalty. According to Will Durant, "Revolts came nevertheless, and Assyria had to keep herself always ready for war."[24]

> By mixing up the races the Assyrians hoped to squash racial loyalty.

From 730 to 728 B.C. Tiglath-Pileser III conquered Gilead and Galilee in Israel and deported the people to Assyria.[25] In the seventh year of Hoshea, the last king of Israel, Shalmaneser V, the son of Tiglath-Pileser III, laid siege to Samaria,[22] but he was unable to conquer it before his death. Two years later, in 722 B.C., "Sargon II, an officer in the army, made himself king by a Napoleonic *coup d'état*." [23] He then conquered Samaria and carried 28,290 people from the city into captivity. [22] Imitating Tiglath-Pileser III, Sargon II scattered the Israelites throughout the Assyrian Empire and imported foreigners into Samaria. "All this took place because the Israelites had sinned against the LORD their God...They rejected his decrees and the covenant he had made with their fathers and the warnings he had given them. They followed worthless idols and themselves became worthless" (2 Kings 17:7,15). How ecstatic Satan must have been!

10. NAHUM: JUDGMENT ON ASSYRIA

Date written: sometime between 663-612 B.C.[26]

Nahum prophesied to Judah at least fifty-nine years after the fall of Israel. The Assyrian Empire reached its peak during the reign of Ashurbanipal (668-626 B.C.). Soon after his death, the Babylonians began to assert themselves.[27]

> *The LORD has given a command concerning you, Nineveh: "You will have no descendants to bear your name. I will destroy the carved images and cast idols that are in the temple of your gods. I will prepare your grave, for you are vile"* (Nahum 1:14).

> *Nothing can heal your wound; your injury is fatal. Everyone who hears the news about you claps his hands at your fall, for who has not felt your endless cruelty?* (Nahum 3:19).

God warned Assyria once again of impending judgment. Unlike the people in Jonah's day, they refused to repent. Therefore this time God would destroy Assyria completely. In 612 B.C., the Babylonians, Medes, and Scythians united to fight against the Assyrians. Durant writes, "At one blow Assyria disappeared from history...Not a stone remained visible of all the temples with which Assyria's pious warriors had sought to beautify their greatest capital. Even Ashur, the everlasting god, was dead."[28] In contrast, although the Israelites were scattered throughout the Assyrian Empire, they had a sure hope of returning to the Promised Land. Nahum prophesied, "The LORD will restore the splendor of Jacob like the splendor of Israel, though destroyers have laid them waste and have ruined their vines" (Nahum 2:2). God always tells the truth and always keeps his promises. He will complete his plan of salvation.

> In contrast, although the Israelites were scattered throughout the Assyrian Empire, they had a sure hope of returning to the Promised Land.

Points to Ponder

1. God works out his sovereign will through the good and bad choices that we make.
2. God used Jonah although he was extremely reluctant and vocally opposed to the task.
3. Amos taught that true worship begins with the proper heart attitude toward God. Race does not matter.
4. Through Hosea, God demonstrates how much he loves sinners.
5. According to Micah, God yearns for people to repent of their sin so that he can forgive them.

Chapter Seven

The Southern Kingdom of Judah

1. The Valley of Jehoshaphat

Reign of Jehoshaphat: 872-848 B.C.[1]

BARRY'S dad, Syd, had been home sick for a few days. He was shocked when his nephew Don showed up at the door and told him not to bother going back to work. Syd had trusted his older brother Jack, Don's father, to provide identical legal benefits to the brothers who owned shares in the family printing company. Jack did not. At the age of sixty-nine, Syd thought that he could work as long as he wanted. Then when he stopped, he would receive a pension for life. Instead Jack had arranged for his own pension and had ignored the needs of his brothers. After spending his entire working life at the printing company, Syd could not go back to retrieve personal pictures. Of course, he had no farewell party. More importantly, he owned a substantial part of the company and yet received no regular income from it. Because Jack and Don were self-serving, the family was torn apart—hurt and angry forever. Likewise Rehoboam, David's grandson, had angered the northern tribes of Israel by his cruel words. As a result, in 930 B.C., the kingdom was split into two.[2]

    Some kings in the southern kingdom of Judah loved God, but others did not. Jehoshaphat made a serious error in judgment when he became an ally of Ahab, the wickedest king of the north. In spite of this Jehoshaphat was one of the good kings who loved God. One day some men warned Jehoshaphat that a vast army was approaching from Edom. Jehoshaphat was quite alarmed and wanted God's guidance, but first he asked all of the people to fast. Because they feared the enemy, everyone, including the women and children, gathered together at the temple. Then Jehoshaphat prayed:

> "O LORD, *God of our fathers, are you not the God who is in heaven? You rule over all the kingdoms of the nations. Power and might are in your hand, and no one can withstand you. O our God, did you not drive out the inhabitants of this land before your people Israel and give it forever to the descendants of Abraham your friend? They have lived in it and have built in it a sanctuary for your Name, saying, 'If calamity comes upon us, whether the sword of judgment, or plague or famine, we will stand in your presence before this temple that bears your Name and will cry out to you in our distress, and you will hear us and save us.' But now here are men from Ammon, Moab and Mount Seir, whose territory you would not allow Israel to invade when they came from Egypt; so they turned away from them and did not destroy them. See how they are repaying us by coming to drive us out of the possession you gave us as an inheritance. O our God, will you not judge them? For we have no power to face this vast army that is attacking us. We do not know what to do, but our eyes are upon you"* (2 Chron. 20:6-12).

God responded through the prophet Jahaziel, who was in the crowd:

> *"Do not be afraid or discouraged because of this vast army. For the battle is not yours, but God's. Tomorrow march down against them. They will be climbing up by the Pass of Ziz, and you will find them at the end of the gorge in the Desert of Jeruel. You will not have to fight this battle. Take up your positions; stand firm and see*

the deliverance the LORD *will give you, O Judah and Jerusalem. Do not be afraid; do not be discouraged. Go out to face them tomorrow, and the* LORD *will be with you"* (2 Chron. 20:15-17).

In faith Jehoshaphat chose some men to march in front of the army and sing praises to God. They sang, "Give thanks to the LORD, for his love endures forever" (2 Chron. 20:21).

God was with them as he had promised. While the army of Judah approached the battlefield, the Ammonites and the Moabites began fighting the Edomites. Once all of the Edomites were dead, they began to fight each other. When the soldiers from Judah arrived at the battlefield, they saw a vast army of dead bodies. They spent the next three days collecting the plunder (2 Chron. 20:25). Because the battle belonged to God, Judah did not need to fight. What a testing ground for faith! What a valley of praise! Four days later Jehoshaphat and all his army gathered in the valley to praise the Lord. Then they joyfully returned to Jerusalem. Meanwhile the other nations nearby were afraid of God, because he had fought against Judah's enemies (2 Chron. 20:29).

> Jehoshaphat won the battle without anyone lifting a sword against the enemy.

The Lord delights in proving through the physical world how he works in the spiritual realm. Jehoshaphat won the battle without anyone lifting a sword against the enemy. If God can take care of such physical difficulties, how much more is he able and willing to provide for every spiritual need? Many years before, Joshua had exhorted the Israelites to choose the Lord over the false gods of their enemies (Josh. 24:15). Everyone has the same choice to make. Do you want reassurance that God is fighting for you and not against you? Trust God, because he always tells the truth and always keeps his promises. If you are his child, the battle belongs to God, not you.

2. Athaliah

Reign of Athaliah: 841-835 B.C.[3]

It is surprising that good King Jehoshaphat allowed his son Jehoram to marry Athaliah, the daughter of Ahab, the wicked king of Israel. In those days Judah and Israel became close allies. After Jehoram's death, his son Ahaziah continued to be friends with his Uncle Joram, king of Israel. Then one day, while Ahaziah was visiting Joram, an unexpected adversary killed both of them.[4] On hearing of her son's death, Athaliah coveted the throne of Judah for herself. She immediately murdered the whole royal family, the descendants of David. At least she thought that she had succeeded in her evil plan.

> On hearing of her son's death, Athaliah coveted the throne of Judah for herself.

The Lord, however, would keep his covenant with David. He would send the Messiah through David's line. In the providence of God, Athaliah's daughter, Jehosheba, was married to a priest whose name was Jehoiada. As soon as Jehosheba realized that her nephew Joash was in danger, she grabbed him and his nurse and hid them in the temple for six years. When Joash was seven years old, his uncle Jehoiada crowned him the rightful king of Judah. How surprised Athaliah was when she heard the cheering of the people and saw her grandchild standing at the entrance to the temple!

"Treason! Treason!" she shouted (2 Chron. 23:13).

As she tried to escape out of the city, the troops killed her. Then everyone made a covenant with Jehoiada and Joash to be God's people. To prove their sincerity, they tore down the temple of Baal and killed Mattan, Baal's priest. Through Athaliah, Satan tried to thwart God's plan to send the promised Seed. He almost wiped out the line of David completely. Once again God demonstrated his power over Satan and his false gods.

3. Joel: Two Sides to God's Judgment

Date of ministry: about 835-796 B.C.[5] He finished prophesying 74 years before the fall of Israel, 210 years before the fall of Jerusalem, and 258 years before the edict of Cyrus.

> *Before them the earth shakes, the sky trembles, the sun and moon are darkened, and the stars no longer shine (Joel 2:10).*

When a judge announces his verdict, the accused will be either freed or punished. Similarly, when God judges the heart, he either blesses or curses the person. There are always two sides to judgment. The Lord often uses the figurative language of this verse to signify his judgment on particular nations. For example, when Isaiah prophesies about the fall of Babylon, he writes, "The stars of heaven and their constellations will not show their light. The rising sun will be darkened and the moon will not give its light" (Isa. 13:10). Many years later Jesus quoted Isaiah to warn his disciples about the destruction of Jerusalem in A.D. 70 (Matt. 24:29). In Joel, God illustrates how his judgments lead to punishment for some and blessing for others.

> *What the locust swarm has left the great locusts have eaten; what the great locusts have left the young locusts have eaten; what the young locusts have left other locusts have eaten (Joel 1:4).*

> *Before them fire devours, behind them a flame blazes. Before them the land is like the garden of Eden, behind them, a desert waste—nothing escapes them. They have the appearance of horses; they gallop along like cavalry. With a noise like that of chariots they leap over the mountaintops, like a crackling fire consuming stubble, like a mighty army drawn up for battle. At the sight of them, nations are in anguish; every face turns pale. They*

charge like warriors; they scale walls like soldiers. They all march in line, not swerving from their course. They do not jostle each other; each marches straight ahead. They plunge through defenses without breaking ranks. They rush upon the city; they run along the wall. They climb into the houses; like thieves they enter through the windows (Joel 2:3-9).

In Joel's day Judah suffered the worst invasion of locusts in the memory of the people. Joel asked incredulously, "Has anything like this ever happened in your days or in the days of your forefathers?" (Joel 1:2).

"Why should it happen now?" some may have asked. "How could God allow locusts to destroy our land and our livelihood?"

Ever since Adam and Eve sinned, natural disasters have been a common occurrence. Believers suffer as well as nonbelievers. Sometimes God allows these troubles as a penalty for sin, but not always. For example, it is wrong to assume that every person who is sick is being punished for some sin. Once, when I had breast cancer, a stranger implied that my disease was the result of sin.

On the other hand, before the Israelites entered the Promised Land, Moses taught them to always obey God. If they did not obey, then the Lord would allow certain judgments to fall on them—one of which was locusts (Deut. 28:38). Therefore Joel pleaded with them, "Rend your heart and not your garments. Return to the LORD your God, for he is gracious and compassionate, slow to anger and abounding in love, and he relents from sending calamity" (Joel 2:13). Joel knew that God was punishing Judah by sending locusts to devour the vegetation. How God longs for his people to repent of their sin!

Joel begged them to humble themselves and pray, "Spare your people, O LORD. Do not make your inheritance an object of scorn, a byword among the nations. Why should they say among the peoples, 'Where is their God?'" (Joel 2:17). Sometimes people gloat over the sin or troubles of others because it makes them feel superior. Remember the sin of Ham.[6]

The Southern Kingdom of Judah

Then the Lord promised, "I will repay you for the years the locusts have eaten...You will have plenty to eat, until you are full, and you will praise the name of the LORD your God, who has worked wonders for you; never again will my people be shamed" (Joel 2:25,26). In the Old Testament, whenever God warned his people of impending judgment, he always reassured them of a future deliverance.

> In the Old Testament, whenever God warned his people of impending judgment, he always reassured them of a future deliverance.

"And afterward, I will pour out my Spirit on all people. Your sons and daughters will prophesy, your old men will dream dreams, your young men will see visions. Even on my servants, both men and women, I will pour out my Spirit in those days. I will show wonders in the heavens and on the earth, blood and fire and billows of smoke. The sun will be turned to darkness and the moon to blood before the coming of the great and dreadful day of the LORD. And everyone who calls on the name of the LORD will be saved; for on Mount Zion and in Jerusalem there will be deliverance, as the LORD has said, among the survivors whom the LORD calls" (Joel 2:28-32).

Sounding like a violent wind and looking like tongues of fire, the Holy Spirit came down and filled believers with his power on the day of Pentecost (Acts 2:2,3). After a crowd had gathered because of the noise, all of the believers immediately spoke in many different languages.

Amazed and perplexed, they asked one another, "What does this mean?"
Some, however, made fun of them and said, "They have had too much wine."
Then Peter stood up with the Eleven, raised his voice

> *and addressed the crowd: "Fellow Jews and all of you who live in Jerusalem, let me explain this to you; listen carefully to what I say. These men are not drunk, as you suppose. It's only nine in the morning!"* (Acts 2:12-15).

Peter informed the crowd that Jesus whom they had crucified was both Lord and Christ. Realizing that they had killed the long-awaited Messiah, they were broken-hearted. They asked Peter and the other apostles:

> *"Brothers, what shall we do?"*
> *Peter replied, "Repent and be baptized, every one of you, in the name of Jesus Christ for the forgiveness of your sins. And you will receive the gift of the Holy Spirit. The promise is for you and your children and for all who are far off—for all whom the Lord our God will call"* (Acts 2:37-39).

About 3000 people responded to Peter's sermon and were baptized (Acts 2:41). This was the fulfillment of Joel 2:28-32. As Joel had prophesied, many people were filled with the Holy Spirit, both young and old, men and women. A great number joyfully witnessed to their friends and neighbours of Jesus' death and resurrection. When Joel prophesied about the day of Pentecost, he used the imagery of the sun darkening and the moon turning to blood. There are always two sides to God's judgment. In the physical realm, when the Lord destroyed the earth by a flood, he saved Noah and his family. Whenever one nation is destroyed, another prospers. In the spiritual realm, God judges our heart attitude toward him. The day of Pentecost was full of joy for the new believers. In contrast, that day was horrible spiritually for those who rejected the salvation offered by Jesus. At the end of time those who have rejected him will suffer eternal punishment while those who lovingly obey him will receive eternal life (Matt. 25:46).

Many times throughout history the Holy Spirit has come

down in power and swept through various countries with the fires of revival. Then thousands have accepted Christ as their Saviour and have given God the glory. What a happy day! "There is rejoicing in the presence of the angels of God over one sinner who repents" (Luke 15:10). In contrast, God is very sad whenever people reject the plea of his prophets to repent of their sins.

> *"In those days and at that time, when I restore the fortunes of Judah and Jerusalem, I will gather all nations and bring them down to the Valley of Jehoshaphat. There I will enter into judgment against them concerning my inheritance, my people Israel, for they scattered my people among the nations and divided up my land"* (Joel 3:1,2).

The Valley of Jehoshaphat was a day of rejoicing for God's people but a day of great sorrow for the enemy. The army of Judah did not even have to lift a sword in battle.[7] Through Joel, God promised his people a similar day after the captivity. All the nations that had mistreated them would disappear from the face of the earth. Then his people would praise the Lord for his goodness to them. In a similar fashion another day is coming—the end of time. God will challenge the wicked (those people who refused to love and trust him) to be ready for battle.

> *Proclaim this among the nations: Prepare for war! Rouse the warriors! Let all the fighting men draw near and attack. Beat your plowshares into swords and your pruning hooks into spears. Let the weakling say, "I am strong!" Come quickly, all you nations from every side, and assemble there* (Joel 3:9-11).

All the forces of Satan's kingdom, both human and demonic, continually delude themselves into thinking that they can conquer God. In these verses God challenges them to prepare for war. Henry points out, "Thus does a God of almighty power *bid defiance* to all the opposition of the powers of darkness...let them *assemble and come*, and *gather themselves together;* but he that sits in heaven shall laugh at them, and, while he thus calls them, he has them in derision."[8]

> *"Let the nations be roused; let them advance into the Valley of Jehoshaphat, for there I will sit to judge all the nations on every side. Swing the sickle, for the harvest is ripe. Come, trample the grapes, for the winepress is full and the vats overflow—so great is their wickedness!"* (Joel 3:12,13).

Quite often Jesus spoke to the people in parables, which he would explain afterwards to his disciples. On one occasion he compared the kingdom of heaven to a man who sowed good seed in his field. While everyone slept, an enemy sowed weeds among the wheat. As soon as the servants discovered the weeds, they asked the owner:

> *"Sir, didn't you sow good seed in your field? Where then did the weeds come from?"*
> *"An enemy did this,"* he replied.
> The servants asked him, *"Do you want us to go and pull them up?"*
> *"No,"* he answered, *"because while you are pulling the weeds, you may root up the wheat with them. Let both grow together until the harvest. At that time I will tell the harvesters: First collect the weeds and tie them in bundles to be burned; then gather the wheat and bring it into my barn"* (Matt. 13:27-30).

Privately Jesus told his disciples, "The harvest is the end of the age, and the harvesters are angels" (Matt. 13:39). At the end of time the angels "will weed out of his kingdom everything that causes sin and all who do evil" (Matt. 13:41). The angels will swing sickles and gather everyone to God's judgment seat. They will throw the weeds "into the fiery furnace, where there will be weeping and gnashing of teeth. Then the righteous will shine like the sun in the kingdom of their Father" (Matt. 13:42,43).

> *Multitudes, multitudes in the valley of decision! For the day of the LORD is near in the valley of decision. The sun and moon will be darkened, and the stars no longer shine. The LORD will roar from Zion and thunder from Jerusalem; the earth and the sky will tremble. But the LORD will be a refuge for his people, a stronghold for the people of Israel* (Joel 3:14-16).

There are two types of people, those who believe that God tells the truth and those who do not. For believers the valley of decision will be like the Valley of Jehoshaphat, a valley of praise, a wonderful place. Not so for non-believers; instead the valley of decision will be a place of horror. Will you allow the Lord to be your refuge? If you do, then the Lord will fight the battle for you. Only praise him the way that Jehoshaphat did.

> *"Then you will know that I, the LORD your God, dwell in Zion, my holy hill. Jerusalem will be holy; never again will foreigners invade her"* (Joel 3:17).

Isaiah echoes a similar thought, "Awake, awake, O Zion, clothe yourself with strength. Put on your garments of splendor, O Jerusalem, the holy city. The uncircumcised and defiled will not enter you again" (Isa. 52:1). In the New Jerusalem, the heavenly Jerusalem, there will be no sin and nothing to fear, ever. God will complete his plan. Paradise will be restored. Only then will Satan never be able to sever the relationship between the Lord and his people.

4. Isaiah

Date of ministry: 740-681 B.C.[9]
Reign of Uzziah (Azariah): 792-740 B.C.[3]

Isaiah began prophesying 18 years before the fall of Israel, 154 years before the fall of Jerusalem, and 202 years before the edict of Cyrus. While the Lord was blessing the northern kingdom of Israel during the reign of Jeroboam II (2 Kings 14:25), he also was providing material prosperity to Uzziah and the southern kingdom of Judah.

> *As long as he sought the* LORD, *God gave him success. He went to war against the Philistines and broke down the walls of Gath, Jabneh and Ashdod. He then rebuilt towns near Ashdod and elsewhere among the Philistines. God helped him against the Philistines and against the Arabs who lived in Gur Baal and against the Meunites. The Ammonites brought tribute to Uzziah, and his fame spread as far as the border of Egypt, because he had become very powerful* (2 Chron. 26:5-8).

4a. Isaiah's Call

> *"'Be ever hearing, but never understanding; be ever seeing, but never perceiving.' Make the heart of this people calloused; make their ears dull and close their eyes. Otherwise they might see with their eyes, hear with their ears, understand with their hearts, and turn and be healed"* (Isa. 6:9,10).

In the year that King Uzziah died, Isaiah saw the Lord seated on his throne. Two seraphs called to each other, "Holy, holy, holy is the LORD Almighty; the whole earth is full of his glory" (Isa. 6:3).

Isaiah cried, "Woe is me!...I am ruined! For I am a man of unclean lips, and I live among a people of unclean lips, and my eyes have seen the King, the LORD Almighty" (Isa. 6:5).

The Southern Kingdom of Judah 153

Then one of the seraphs touched Isaiah's lips with a live coal from the altar and said, "See, this has touched your lips; your guilt is taken away and your sin atoned for" (Isa. 6:7).

Next Isaiah heard the Lord's voice asking, "Whom shall I send? And who will go for us?" Isaiah answered, "Here am I. Send me!" (Isa. 6:8).

Isaiah saw the holy God in a vision and acknowledged that he and his people were sinners in need of the Saviour. In referring to the blinding of eyes and deadening of hearts, John explains, "Isaiah said this because he saw Jesus' glory and spoke about him" (John 12:41). As soon as Isaiah believed that his sins were atoned for, the Lord took away his guilt. Then Isaiah willingly became God's messenger. He was troubled by the message, however. "Be ever hearing, but never understanding; be ever seeing, but never perceiving."

"For how long, O Lord?" asked Isaiah (Isa. 6:11).

God told him that he must preach that message until the land was devastated and the people were carted off into captivity, but there was hope. "And though a tenth remains in the land, it will again be laid waste. But as the terebinth and oak leave stumps when they are cut down, so the holy seed will be the stump in the land" (Isa. 6:13). God's people would not be utterly destroyed. He would always leave a remnant, some of whom would be waiting for the Saviour. The line of the promised Seed would be preserved, and God would carry out his plan of salvation.

> Some would believe in God's gift of salvation, but others would not.

What a difficult truth Isaiah was called to preach! Both Jesus and Paul were faced with same situation (John 12:37; Acts 28:24). Some would believe in God's gift of salvation, but others would not. This is a principle expressed throughout Scripture. When people are presented with the holiness and glory of the Lord, some are like Isaiah. Through the mercy of God, they are horrified by their sin and beg for forgiveness. In contrast, God hardens the hearts of others "through the delusive glamour of sin" (Heb. 3:13, Phillips) so that they reject his gift of salvation.

4b. The Salvation of the Lord, Isaiah 1-5

From birth Isaiah was a reminder of God's promised salvation, because his name means "the salvation of Jehovah."[10] Then God blessed Isaiah as an adult with greater insight into his wonderful plan of salvation. That is why Isaiah entreats God's people, "Turn to me and be saved, all you ends of the earth; for I am God, and there is no other" (Isa. 45:22).

Like the other prophets, Isaiah first reminded the people of their sins so that they would see their need for a Saviour. Through Isaiah, God lamented, "I reared children and brought them up, but they have rebelled against me. The ox knows his master, the donkey his owner's manger, but Israel does not know, my people do not understand" (Isa. 1:2,3). Even the ox and the donkey are smarter than the people of Judah. Those animals at least acknowledge their masters. God sadly chided, "The multitude of your sacrifices—what are they to me?...I have no pleasure in the blood of bulls and lambs and goats...Stop bringing meaningless offerings! Your incense is detestable to me. New Moons, Sabbaths and convocations—I cannot bear your evil assemblies" (Isa. 1:11-13). Externally the people of Judah appeared to be worshipping the Lord, but inwardly they were rebelling. They had the same heart attitude as the Israelites in the north.

Consequently Isaiah preached, "Stop doing wrong, learn to do right! Seek justice, encourage the oppressed. Defend the cause of the fatherless, plead the case of the widow" (Isa. 1:16,17). In other words, show that you love God by loving other people. Isaiah also warned them, "Woe to those who call evil good and good evil, who put darkness for light and light for darkness, who put bitter for sweet and sweet for bitter" (Isa. 5:20). It is a sin for people to disregard God's Law and make up their own rules contrary to him. Because of their sins the Lord would judge them. "Therefore my people will go into exile for lack of understanding; their men of rank will die of hunger and their masses will be parched with thirst" (Isa. 5:13).

> *"Though your sins are like scarlet, they shall be as white as snow; though they are red as crimson, they shall be like wool. If you are willing and obedient, you will eat the best from the land; but if you resist and rebel, you will be devoured by the sword"* (Isa. 1:18-20).

Because the Lord loved them so much, he tried to reason with them. He offered them a spiritual salvation. If they were willing and obedient, he would wash away their sins and make them as white as snow. If they accepted God's terms for salvation in the spiritual realm, then he did promise to bless them in the physical world. As Henry writes:

> He does not say, "If you be *perfectly* obedient," but, "If you be *willingly* so;" for if there be a willing mind, it is accepted...The greatest sinners, if they truly repent, shall have their sins forgiven them, and so have their consciences pacified and purified. Though our sins have been as scarlet and crimson, a deep dye, a double dye, first in the wool of original corruption, and afterwards in the many threads of actual transgression, though we have been often dipped, by our many backslidings, into sin, and though we have lain long soaking in it, as the cloth does in the scarlet dye, yet pardoning mercy will thoroughly discharge the stain.[11]

God is just as willing today to cleanse you of your sin, as he was so long ago for them. The people of Judah had two choices. They could either accept the salvation offered and live, or resist and die a spiritual death. We have the same choices today.

4c. Immanuel, Isaiah 7-12, 732 B.C.[12]

Reign of Ahaz: 740-724 B.C.[13]

When the allied forces of Aram and Israel marched against Jerusalem, "the hearts of Ahaz and his people were shaken, as the trees of the forest are shaken by the wind" (Isa. 7:2). Isaiah found Ahaz and told him:

> *"Be careful, keep calm and don't be afraid. Do not lose heart because of these two smoldering stubs of firewood—because of the fierce anger of Rezin and Aram and the son of Remaliah. Aram, Ephraim and Remaliah's son have plotted your ruin, saying, 'Let us invade Judah; let us tear it apart and divide it among ourselves, and make the son of Tabeel king over it.' Yet this is what the Sovereign LORD says: 'It will not take place, it will not happen'"* (Isa. 7:4-7).

When God, through Isaiah, offered to give Ahaz a sign to encourage him, Ahaz replied, "I will not ask; I will not put the LORD to the test" (Isa. 7:12). Undaunted, Isaiah offered him a sign anyway:

> *"The virgin will be with child and will give birth to a son, and will call him Immanuel. He will eat curds and honey when he knows enough to reject the wrong and choose the right. But before the boy knows enough to reject the wrong and choose the right, the land of the two kings you dread will be laid waste"* (Isa. 7:14-16).

Many years later, Joseph of Nazareth pondered what to do about Mary, his fiancée. When he discovered that she was pregnant, he knew that he had the right to have her stoned to death for being unfaithful to him, but he preferred "to divorce her quietly" (Matt. 1:19). One night while appearing to Joseph in a dream, an angel of the Lord said, "Joseph son of David, do not be afraid to take Mary home as your wife, because what is conceived in her is from the Holy Spirit. She will give birth to a son, and you are to give him the name Jesus, because he will save his people from their sins" (Matt. 1:20,21).

According to Matthew, Mary's pregnancy was the fulfillment of this prophecy: "The virgin will be with child and will give birth to a son, and they will call him Immanuel—which means, 'God with us'" (Matt. 1:23). After waking up, Joseph immediately took Mary as his wife.

Regrettably, Ahaz did not care about the Lord's promises. Instead of trusting God, he sent messengers to Tiglath-Pileser III to say, "I am your servant and vassal. Come up and save me out of the hand of the king of Aram and of the king of Israel, who are attacking me" (2 Kings 16:7). He even sent gold and silver from the temple as a gift for the king of Assyria. Then "Tiglath-Pileser king of Assyria came to him, but he gave him trouble instead of help" (2 Chron. 28:20). Remembering how Aram had defeated them earlier in battle (2 Chron. 28:5), Ahaz also decided, "Since the gods of the kings of Aram have helped them, I will sacrifice to them so they will help me" (2 Chron. 28:23). He was willing to do anything except trust the Lord. This included closing the temple and setting up altars for false gods in Jerusalem (2 Chron. 28:24).

Because of Ahaz, Tiglath-Pileser III attacked Damascus and destroyed it (2 Kings 16:9). He continued by capturing all of Israel east of the Jordan River from 730 to 728 B.C.[12] Ahaz succeeded in bringing the threat of Assyria closer to Judah. Although Ahaz rejected the Lord, Isaiah's prophecy came true. Within four years Aram was captured and Israel was in the process of being devastated. Those two countries did not succeed in conquering Judah.

> Ahaz succeeded in bringing the threat of Assyria closer to Judah.

God was still with Judah even though his people followed other gods.

> *For to us a child is born, to us a son is given, and the government will be on his shoulders. And he will be called Wonderful Counselor, Mighty God, Everlasting Father, Prince of Peace. Of the increase of his government and peace there will be no end. He will reign on David's throne and over his kingdom, establishing and upholding it with justice and righteousness from that time on and forever. The zeal of the* Lord *Almighty will accomplish this* (Isa. 9:6,7).

E. J. Young explains the significance of the words *child* and *son* in this way:

> The word "child" is masculine, and it means that a boy child has been born. Why then does the prophet use the word "son"? Is this not mere redundancy? No, I think not. I think the prophet wants to tell us that not only is there a real Child born who is an heir to David's throne, but in addition there is an unique Son given to us, and he reflects upon the 7th chapter, "Behold a virgin is with child and will bring forth a son and call his name Immanuel," and notice that it is said this Son is given to us. John reflects upon this when he says, "God so loved the world that he gave us his only begotten Son"—it is that Son that is referred to here. The writer to the Hebrews says, "God has spoken in a son"; it is the Son of God, in other words. There is given to us for our salvation a human being, a Child who sits upon the throne of David, a Child is born for us, but a Son is given to us. In the coming of this Child there is a Son.[14]

The promised Seed is coming. The one who is fully God and fully man will rule *from that time on and forever*. When he comes, he will reign in the spiritual realm. "The people walking in darkness have seen a great light" (Isa. 9:2). How the people will rejoice at his presence! He will shatter "the yoke that burdens them, the bar across their shoulders, the rod of their oppressor" (Isa. 9:4). Jesus entreats, "Come to me, all you who are weary and burdened, and I will give you rest. Take my yoke upon you and learn from me, for I am gentle and humble in heart, and you will find rest for your souls. For my yoke is easy and my burden is light" (Matt. 11:28-30). Sadly, because of the mindset that religion and the state are intertwined, the people expected the Messiah to be a great political leader. They are still waiting.

At that time the meaning of every child's name was very important. Therefore for God to name his son Wonderful Counsellor, the Mighty God, the Everlasting Father, and the Prince of Peace was quite significant. "Now as I read that 6th verse it seems to me to tell very clearly that these are the names of the child," continues Young, "and as soon as you say that, you realize that the child is not only extraordinary but the child is a divine Child."[15] Isaiah must have pondered those names. Only God could accomplish such an impossible task. How could the son of David be the Son of God? Isaiah trusted God when he said, "The zeal of the LORD Almighty will accomplish this" (Isa. 9:7).

> *A shoot will come up from the stump of Jesse; from his roots a Branch will bear fruit* (Isa. 11:1).

Although the land would be devastated and the people of Judah would be carted off to Babylon, God would not forget his promise to David. Just as some trees have the ability to grow again after they have been axed down, the Messiah would still spring from the seed of Jesse—no matter how hopeless the situation seemed. A tiny vulnerable shoot would grow up to become the Branch. In the same way Jesus, as the Branch, would become a baby. He would be born to poor parents and placed in a manger, the feeding trough for animals.

Then, as an adult, crowds would chase after him. He would heal their diseases, perform many miracles, and preach the good news of salvation. At his death and resurrection Jesus would bear much fruit—the salvation of believers, past, present, and future. John quotes Jesus, "I am the Root and the Offspring of David, and the bright Morning Star" (Rev. 22:16). The Branch is fully God—the root of David's source of life. He is also fully man—a descendant of David.

In Isaiah 11:2-5, God describes the Messiah's character. He will rule with righteousness and faithfulness. "Righteousness will be his belt and faithfulness the sash round his waist" (Isa. 11:5). His only weapon is his mouth. "He will strike the earth with the rod of his mouth" (Isa. 11:4). He will not judge by outward appearance but by the inner thoughts and motives of his subjects. "He will not judge by what he sees with his eyes, or decide by what he hears with his ears; but with righteousness he will judge the needy" (Isa. 11:3,4).

> *The wolf will live with the lamb, the leopard will lie down with the goat, the calf and the lion and the yearling together; and a little child will lead them...They will neither harm nor destroy on all my holy mountain, for the earth will be full of the knowledge of the* LORD *as the waters cover the sea* (Isa. 11:6-9).

After God had created the heaven and the earth, he saw that everything that he had made was good. This included all the animals. Then, after Adam and Eve sinned, the animals were changed also. When the Messiah comes, he will restore fellowship between people and God. The Lord, however, has not forgotten animals. He looks forward to the future when paradise will be restored. In it there will be no sin ever. Once again he will create animals, and they will never have to live in a sin-filled world. God says, "Behold, I will create new heavens and a new earth (Isa. 65:17).

Through Isaiah, the Lord describes the new earth, "The wolf and the lamb will feed together, and the lion will eat straw like the ox, but dust will be the serpent's food. They will neither harm nor destroy on all my holy mountain" (Isa. 65:25). Paul explains, "We know that the whole creation has been groaning as in the pains of childbirth right up to the present time" (Rom. 8:22). When paradise is restored on the new earth, even animals will be changed from their present state. Only the new earth will truly be *full of the knowledge of the* LORD *as the waters cover the sea,* because sin will never exist there.

> *In that day the Root of Jesse will stand as a banner for the peoples; the nations will rally to him, and his place of rest will be glorious* (Isa. 11:10).

The Messiah will be like a magnet drawing many different people from all over the world. Jesus promises, "But I, when I am lifted up from the earth, will draw all men to myself" (John 12:32). When they come to him, they will find peace for their souls.

> The Messiah will be like a magnet drawing many different people from all over the world.

His place of rest will be glorious. What could be more glorious than having your sins forgiven and having your fellowship restored with the Creator? Paul uses this verse to encourage the Jews to accept Gentiles as fellow believers:

> *Accept one another, then, just as Christ accepted you, in order to bring praise to God. For I tell you that Christ has become a servant of the Jews on behalf of God's truth, to confirm the promises made to the patriarchs so that the Gentiles may glorify God for his mercy, as it is written...And again, Isaiah says, "The Root of Jesse will*

spring up, one who will arise to rule over the nations; the Gentiles will hope in him" (Rom. 15:7-12).

John Urquhart ponders this truth:

> This, then, was the hope of the Old Testament...It was not a blessing which was to come men knew not whence, nor how. They looked for the Messiah. The hope of Israel and of all peoples lay in Him. He alone would touch the world's heart and roll away the world's burden. And the work which He began, He should continue. His influence was pictured as going on broadening and deepening through all after time: "His name shall be continued as long as the sun; and men shall be blessed in Him: all nations shall call him blessed" (Ps. lxxii. 17).[16]

> *In that day the Lord will reach out his hand a second time to reclaim the remnant that is left of his people* (Isa. 11:11).

Long ago there was a highway for Israel when they came up from Egypt (Isa. 11:16). Likewise, there would be one for the remnant who would return from many countries to Judah after the Babylonian exile. Then many years later in Jesus' day, God would gather the Israelites a second time from the four corners of the earth (Isa. 11:12). Indeed, many Israelites did assemble in Jerusalem at that time, because they awaited the arrival of the Messiah. Caesar unwittingly prepared their way, since his roads made travelling easier than in the past. The Bethel Series elaborates on this point:

> Caesar Augustus was a worried man. As he surveyed the vast expanses of the world he ruled, he feared rebellion from within. Hence, he commanded that 10,000 laborers be secured to build a network of military roads from one end of his domain to the other.

Then let the uprising come, and Caesar's legions would march quickly to the trouble spots and strike down the insurgents who challenged Roman rule.

How strange that these very roads, built to speed Caesar's soldiers on the way to battle, should be the pathways used by the messengers of God on a mission of peace.

When the last two acts of God's divine drama had been played—one on Calvary's hill and the other in an empty tomb—it was **Christ's** legions who marched on Caesar's roads bringing the electrifying news of their crucified and risen Lord to the far-flung ends of the Roman world. It was the fullness of time.[17]

Eventually many of those new believers returned home and testified joyfully, "Surely God is my salvation; I will trust and not be afraid. The LORD, the LORD, is my strength and my song; he has become my salvation. With joy you will draw water from the wells of salvation" (Isa. 12:2,3).

4d. A Panoramic View of History, Isaiah 13-35

The earth is defiled by its people; they have disobeyed the laws, violated the statutes and broken the everlasting covenant. Therefore a curse consumes the earth; its people must bear their guilt (Isa. 24:5,6).

Come near, you nations, and listen; pay attention, you peoples! Let the earth hear, and all that is in it, the world, and all that comes out of it! The LORD is angry with all nations; his wrath is upon all their armies. He will totally destroy them (Isa. 34:1,2).

As Creator, God has authority over every country in the world. Each nation consists of the total number of citizens within its borders. In these chapters God warned many different countries of their impending doom. When God punished a country for its sin, every individual within its borders suffered the consequences. "It will be the same for priest as for people, for master as for servant, for mistress as for maid, for seller as for buyer, for borrower as for lender, for debtor as for creditor" (Isa. 24:2). The Lord is ultimately appealing to each one of us. Every person has the same choice to make as Isaiah's audience had—either acknowledge the Creator and worship him alone or refuse to love and obey him.

Although God is long-suffering and merciful, in the end justice must prevail. For those who continue to flaunt his advances, the day of the Lord is coming. Jerusalem would face its own judgment day. "The Lord, the LORD Almighty, has a day of tumult and trampling and terror in the Valley of Vision" (Isa. 22:5). In Isaiah's day the Assyrians were the world power to fear, not the Babylonians. Yet God knew that the Babylonians would be the country to punish Judah for its sins. Afterwards, because of pride in its own strength, Babylon would be destroyed by the Medes (Isa. 13:17-19). That event is described as the day of the Lord, "a cruel day, with wrath and fierce anger—to make the land desolate and destroy the sinners within it" (Isa. 13:9). After the demise of Babylon, God promised to restore Israel to the Promised Land. "The LORD will have compassion on Jacob; once again he will choose Israel and will settle them in their own land" (Isa. 14:1). Likewise, the very last generation to live on this earth will face its own judgment day. "See, the LORD is going to lay waste the earth and devastate it; he will ruin its face and scatter its inhabitants...The earth will be completely laid waste and totally plundered" (Isa. 24:1,3).

> *In that day the LORD will punish the powers in the heavens above and the kings on the earth below. They will be herded together like prisoners bound in a dungeon; they will be shut up in prison and be punished after many days* (Isa. 24:21,22).[18]

Is physical death the final punishment of the wicked? Where is Tiglath-Pileser III now? Where is Hitler or the king of

Babylon now? Like believers who have died, they are presently in the intermediate state between death and the final consummation of this earth. Unlike believers, who are in heaven, they are in a temporary prison for those who have rejected God. Isaiah told his audience that a welcoming party would meet the king of Babylon after his death:

> *The grave below is all astir to meet you at your coming; it rouses the spirits of the departed to greet you—all those who were leaders in the world; it makes them rise from their thrones—all those who were kings over the nations. They will all respond, they will say to you, "You also have become weak, as we are; you have become like us"* (Isa. 14:9,10).

All non-believers from Cain to the present time who have died are powerless. Their souls await the final sentence of their Creator. What is worse than physical death and impotence of the soul? God created people in his image to have fellowship with him, "but your iniquities have separated you from your God" (Isa. 59:2). The Final Judgment is eternal separation from God. Jesus told his disciples what he will say to non-believers on judgment day. "'Depart from me, you who are cursed, into the eternal fire prepared for the devil and his angels.'…Then they will go away to eternal punishment, but the righteous to eternal life" (Matt. 25:41,46).

> **What is worse than physical death and impotence of the soul?**

> *Strengthen the feeble hands, steady the knees that give way; say to those with fearful hearts, "Be strong, do not fear; your God will come, he will come with vengeance; with divine retribution he will come to save you." Then will the eyes of the blind be opened and the ears of the deaf unstopped. Then will the lame leap like a deer, and the mute tongue shout for joy* (Isa. 35:3-6).

When John the Baptist was languishing in prison, he needed reassurance that Jesus was the Messiah. Therefore he sent two of his disciples to Jesus with the question, "Are you the one who was to come, or should we expect someone else?" (Luke 7:18).

Jesus lovingly replied, "Go back and report to John what you have seen and heard: The blind receive sight, the lame walk, those who have leprosy are cured, the deaf hear, the dead are raised, and the good news is preached to the poor. Blessed is the man who does not fall away on account of me" (Luke 7:22,23). In other words, "John, be strong, and keep the faith. I have not forgotten you. In fact Isaiah's prophecy has come true. The miracles are proof that I am indeed the Messiah."

For non-believers the judgment of God results in physical death, impotence of the soul, and eternal separation from the Creator. It is true that believers suffer physical hardship and death in this present world. John did. Yet the Holy Spirit provides the strength and grace to persevere joyfully. At the Final Judgment believers will cry tears of joy and leap with gladness.

> *On this mountain he will destroy the shroud that enfolds all peoples, the sheet that covers all nations; he will swallow up death forever. The Sovereign* LORD *will wipe away the tears from all faces; he will remove the disgrace of his people from all the earth* (Isa. 25:7,8).

> *But your dead will live; their bodies will rise. You who dwell in the dust, wake up and shout for joy* (Isa. 26:19).

God promises, "I will ransom them from the power of the grave; I will redeem them from death. Where, O death, are your plagues? Where, O grave, is your destruction?" (Hos. 13:14). When the purposes of the Lord are completed for this present world, marvellous blessings await the believer. They will rise physically to receive new immortal bodies. No longer will death hold sway over them. Do you want to be included with the redeemed? Then believe that the promised Seed has paid the penalty for your sins.

4e. The Threat of Sennacherib, Isaiah 36, 37, 701 B.C.[19]

Reign of Hezekiah, king of Judah: 725-697 B.C.[20]
Reign of Sennacherib, king of Assyria: 705-681 B.C.[19]

Filled with pride, the kings of Assyria thought that they were unbeatable. After one city fell, they attacked another, then another, until entire countries were under their authority. That is why Sennacherib thought:

> *"By the strength of my hand I have done this, and by my wisdom, because I have understanding. I removed the boundaries of nations, I plundered their treasures; like a mighty one I subdued their kings. As one reaches into a nest, so my hand reached for the wealth of the nations; as men gather abandoned eggs, so I gathered all the countries; not one flapped a wing, or opened its mouth to chirp"* (Isa. 10:13,14).

Sennacherib attributed his success in war to his gods. Obviously they must be more powerful than the gods of other countries. After attacking all the fortified cities of Judah and capturing them, he was ready to conquer Jerusalem. Speaking to the besieged people on the walls of Jerusalem, his field commander shouted:

> *"Do not let Hezekiah persuade you to trust in the* LORD *when he says, 'The* LORD *will surely deliver us; this city will not be given into the hand of the king of Assyria.'...Has the god of any nation ever delivered his land from the hand of the king of Assyria? Where are the gods of Hamath and Arpad? Where are the gods of Sepharvaim? Have they rescued Samaria from my hand? Who of all the gods of these countries has been able to save his land*

> Sennacherib attributed his success in war to his gods. Obviously they must be more powerful than the gods of other countries.

from me? How then can the L<small>ORD</small> *deliver Jerusalem from my hand?"* (Isa. 36:15-20).

After tearing his clothes and putting on sackcloth, King Hezekiah went to the temple. He also sent messengers to tell Isaiah:

> *"This day is a day of distress and rebuke and disgrace, as when children come to the point of birth and there is no strength to deliver them. It may be that the* L<small>ORD</small> *your God will hear the words of the field commander, whom his master, the king of Assyria, has sent to ridicule the living God, and that he will rebuke him for the words the* L<small>ORD</small> *your God has heard. Therefore pray for the remnant that still survives"* (Isa. 37:3,4).

The Lord replied through Isaiah, "Do not be afraid of what you have heard—those words with which the underlings of the king of Assyria have blasphemed me. Listen! I am going to put a spirit in him so that when he hears a certain report, he will return to his own country, and there I will have him cut down with the sword" (Isa. 37:6,7).

When Sennacherib heard a rumour that the king of Egypt was coming to fight against him, he wrote a letter to Hezekiah. In it he said, "Do not let the god you depend on deceive you when he says, 'Jerusalem will not be handed over to the king of Assyria.' Surely you have heard what the kings of Assyria have done to all the countries, destroying them completely. And will you be delivered?" (Isa. 37:10,11).

After receiving the letter, Hezekiah took it to the temple and prayed:

> *"O* L<small>ORD</small> *Almighty, God of Israel, enthroned between the cherubim, you alone are God over all the kingdoms of the earth. You have made heaven and earth. Give ear, O* L<small>ORD</small>, *and hear; open your eyes, O* L<small>ORD</small>, *and see; listen to all the words Sennacherib has sent to insult the living*

> *God. It is true, O LORD, that the Assyrian kings have laid waste all these peoples and their lands. They have thrown their gods into the fire and destroyed them, for they were not gods but only wood and stone, fashioned by human hands. Now, O LORD our God, deliver us from his hand, so that all kingdoms on earth may know that you alone, O LORD, are God"* (Isa. 37:16-20).

Again Isaiah sent Hezekiah a message. "'He will not enter this city or shoot an arrow here. He will not come before it with shield or build a siege ramp against it. By the way that he came he will return; he will not enter this city,' declares the LORD. 'I will defend this city and save it, for my sake and for the sake of David my servant!'" (Isa. 37:33-35).

Both God's honour and his promise to David to send the Messiah were at stake. If Satan had his way, Judah would be completely destroyed and God would not be able to send the promised Seed. That night the angel of the Lord killed 185,000 men in the Assyrian camp. Those who woke up in the morning found all the dead bodies. Sennacherib packed up the camp and returned to Nineveh (Isa. 37:36,37). Truly the Lord did fight for his people! In fulfillment of Isaiah's prophecy, Sennacherib was murdered twenty years later with a sword by his two sons while he worshipped in the temple of Nisroch.

4f. The Redeemer, Isaiah 40-53

> *"I say: My purpose will stand, and I will do all that I please"* (Isa. 46:10).

How comforting Isaiah's words should have been to his listeners, who were squirming under the oppression of Assyria. How much more would the captives in Babylon over 100 years later cling with hope to God's promises. In these chapters God emphasized the fact that he is the one and only God. Frequently he reminded them that he is the Redeemer.[21] Just as often he told them that the nation of Israel is his servant.[22] When the situation appeared hopeless at the fall of Jerusalem, the first reaction of the captives would be, "The LORD has forsaken me, the Lord has forgotten me" (Isa. 49:14). Yet, because of Isaiah's words, many in Judah would be comforted and would wait for God to redeem them.

Intertwined in these chapters are two sets of promises, one spiritual and the other physical. By being trustworthy in redeeming them from physical bondage, the Lord intended them to look forward with anticipation to the coming of the Servant, the tender plant (Isa. 53:2, KJV), who would rescue them from the spiritual bondage of sin. Long ago God had demonstrated his power to redeem the Israelites by rescuing them from Egypt. Once again he promised to redeem them from physical bondage—this time from Babylon. Isaiah preached, "Leave Babylon, flee from the Babylonians! Announce this with shouts of joy and proclaim it. Send it out to the ends of the earth; say, 'The Lord has redeemed his servant Jacob'" (Isa. 48:20).

> *He [Cyrus] is my shepherd and will accomplish all that I please; he will say of Jerusalem, "Let it be rebuilt," and of the temple, "Let its foundations be laid"* (Isa. 44:28).

> *I will raise up Cyrus in my righteousness: I will make all his ways straight. He will rebuild my city and set my exiles free, but not for a price or reward* (Isa. 45:13).

God would accomplish their physical redemption by allowing the Medes and Persians to conquer Babylon. Then Cyrus, king of Persia, would voluntarily, and with no strings attached, encourage the people of Israel and Judah to go back to the Promised Land. The edict of Cyrus that allowed God's people to return to their homeland was an important step in the plan of God. The Israelites could only worship properly, according to the Law of God, if they were free to publicly sacrifice animals at the temple. Jesus needed to be born into a nation that visibly worshipped the one and only God according to his commandments. As the exiles returned home, they would sing for joy at being allowed to worship God again in Zion. "The ransomed of the LORD will return. They will enter Zion with singing; everlasting joy will crown their heads. Gladness and joy will overtake them, and sorrow and sighing will flee away" (Isa. 51:11). What an object lesson! Because the Lord would instill in a heathen king the desire to be kind toward Israel, the people would be free to sing this song of freedom.

> Yet Israel had more to look forward to than physical freedom, as precious as that was.

Yet Israel had more to look forward to than physical freedom, as precious as that was. Those sensitive to God's Word would eagerly await the fulfillment of his spiritual promises. They would wait for their Saviour to come and free them from the spiritual bondage of sin. For example, many years later Zechariah, being filled with the Holy Spirit, prophesies about his son, John the Baptist. "And you, my child, will be called a prophet of the Most High; for you will go on before the Lord to prepare the way for him, to give his people the knowledge of salvation through the forgiveness of their sins" (Luke 1:76,77). Seeing God work in the physical realm was meant to strengthen their hope for him to accomplish what he promised in the spiritual realm.

> *Comfort, comfort my people, says your God. Speak tenderly to Jerusalem, and proclaim to her that her hard service has been completed, that her sin has been paid for, that she has received from the LORD's hand double for all her sins* (Isa. 40:1,2).

How would God accomplish their spiritual redemption? At this point God introduced the Servant. He called the promised

Seed, the everlasting King, a Servant. This is what the Servant is like. "He will not shout or cry out, or raise his voice in the streets. A bruised reed he will not break, and a smoldering wick he will not snuff out. In faithfulness he will bring forth justice; he will not falter or be discouraged till he establishes justice on earth" (Isa. 42:2-4). After Jesus healed the sick, he made a point of "warning them not to tell who he was" in order to fulfill the prophecy of the Servant (Matt. 12:16). This is how the Servant would pay the penalty required to secure the salvation of believers:

> *But he was pierced for our transgressions, he was crushed for our iniquities; the punishment that brought us peace was upon him, and by his wounds we are healed. We all, like sheep, have gone astray, each of us has turned to his own way; and the* LORD *has laid on him the iniquity of us all. He was oppressed and afflicted, yet he did not open his mouth; he was led like a lamb to the slaughter, and as a sheep before her shearers is silent, so he did not open his mouth. By oppression and judgment, he was taken away. And who can speak of his descendants? For he was cut off from the land of the living; for the transgression of my people he was stricken. He was assigned a grave with the wicked, and with the rich in his death, though he had done no violence, nor was any deceit in his mouth. Yet it was the* LORD's *will to crush him and cause him to suffer, and though the* LORD *makes his life a guilt offering, he will see his offspring and prolong his days, and the will of the* LORD *will prosper in his hand. After the suffering of his soul, he will see the light of life and be satisfied; by his knowledge my righteous servant will justify many, and he will bear their iniquities* (Isa. 53:5-11).

This is one of the most precious chapters in the Old Testament, because God explains exactly how he will pay the penalty for sin. Since his holiness demands justice, sin must be punished. The Servant "was cut off from the land of the living." In other words, he died. "He was pierced for our transgressions." He paid the punishment that we deserve. In his death he offered himself as a guilt offering for our sins. He not only substituted himself for us; he did it willingly. "He was oppressed and afflicted, yet he did not open his mouth." By means of the Lord Jesus, God satisfies divine justice and yet shows mercy to those he loves. *He bore the sin of many.* Truly our God reigns. Do you believe him? God always tells the truth and always keeps his promises.

> *"It is too small a thing for you to be my servant to restore the tribes of Jacob and bring back those of Israel I have kept. I will also make you a light for the Gentiles, that you may bring my salvation to the ends of the earth"* (Isa. 49:6).

It is a huge mistake for the Israelites to focus their thoughts only on their physical restoration to the Promised Land. "It is too small a thing." The Servant would be the Redeemer, not just for Israel, but also for the whole world. Likewise the nation of Israel, as the servant, would carry the good news of salvation from sin to every country.

4g. Fellowship Restored with the Creator, Isaiah 54-66

> *"Come, all you who are thirsty, come to the waters; and you who have no money, come, buy and eat! Come, buy wine and milk without money and without cost. Why spend money on what is not bread, and your labor on what does not satisfy? Listen, listen to me, and eat what is good, and your soul will delight in the richest of fare"* (Isa. 55:1,2).

Do you want your soul to delight in the richest of fare and live in intimate communion with your Maker? Do you thirst to be reconciled to God? Everyone past, present, and future has rebelled against the Lord. Yet in these verses God invites all. It does not cost anything to accept this gracious offer. On the contrary, this salvation is free. It is impossible for anyone to receive it by paying money or by working for it. Perhaps you are asking, "How can this be? Nobody gets something for nothing in this world." The amazing fact is that while salvation costs us nothing, it cost God everything. He is the one who paid the price. The only thing that we must do is accept his gift by asking him to give us the willingness to repent of our sins—in other words, to be sorry for and determined to turn away from our sins. Believers admit that they have been rebellious God-haters. With thankful, loving hearts they accept God's gift of salvation.

> The amazing fact is that while salvation costs us nothing, it cost God everything.

I remember the evening when the Lord opened my eyes and drew me with the cords of love to accept Jesus as my Saviour. I was only nine years old. It was during a sermon on the broad way to hell and the narrow path that leads to heaven (Matt. 7:13-14). Even as a child I was a thinker. Accepting Jesus to avoid hell seemed rather selfish. I guess that I was not sure of my salvation, because I did not tell anyone for two years.

Isaiah continually pointed out the sins of his own generation to them. He asked, "Whom are you mocking? At whom do you sneer and stick out your tongue? Are you not a brood of rebels, the offspring of liars? You burn with lust among the oaks and under every spreading tree; you sacrifice your children in the ravines and under the overhanging crags" (Isa. 57:4,5). He also implored, "Seek the Lord while he may be found; call on him while he is near. Let the wicked forsake his way and the evil man his thoughts. Let him turn to the Lord, and he will have mercy on him, and to our God, for he will freely pardon" (Isa. 55:6,7).

Those who accepted God's free gift of salvation awaited the coming of the promised Seed, the Servant, the one who would be their Saviour. They looked forward to the cross, whereas we look back. All of us, however, are saved by the same terms and by the same everlasting covenant that can never be revoked because it is dependent on the precious blood of Jesus, the Son of God. Many years later the captives in Babylon could have the reassurance that God had not forsaken them permanently. He would be their Redeemer not only in a spiritual sense but also in the physical realm. How glad they must have been to hear God's promise! "Foreigners will rebuild your walls, and their kings will serve you. Though in anger I struck you, in favor I will show you compassion" (Isa. 60:10).

> *The Spirit of the Sovereign* LORD *is on me, because the* LORD *has anointed me to preach good news to the poor. He has sent me to bind up the brokenhearted, to proclaim freedom for the captives and release from darkness for the prisoners, to proclaim the year of the* LORD's *favor and the day of vengeance of our God, to comfort all who mourn, and provide for those who grieve in Zion—to bestow on them a crown of beauty instead of ashes, the oil of gladness instead of mourning, and a garment of praise instead of a spirit of despair. They will be called oaks of righteousness, a planting of the* LORD *for the display of his splendor* (Isa. 61:1-3).

One Sabbath Jesus went into the synagogue at Nazareth. After being handed the scroll of Isaiah, he read, "The Spirit of the Lord is on me, because he has anointed me to preach good news to the poor. He has sent me to proclaim freedom for the prisoners and recovery of sight for the blind, to release the oppressed, to proclaim the year of the Lord's favor" (Luke 4:18,19). After sitting down, he said, "Today this scripture is fulfilled in your hearing" (Luke 4:21).

As he continued to speak to them, the people were amazed and praised him. Finally the day had arrived when the spiritual redemption promised in the Old Testament was no longer just a promise but an accomplished fact. The Holy Spirit anointed Jesus to be the bearer of good news. He would free us from the punishment and guilt of sin. What a comfort to those who mourned over their separation from God! Such news evokes praise from the believer. Consider, for example, Mary of Nazareth. "My soul glorifies the Lord and my spirit rejoices in God my Savior" (Luke 1:46,47).

What do you think of when you ponder the phrase *the day of vengeance of our God*? Do you think of a battlefield strewn with dead bodies, mangled and bloody? Most people do. Whenever each great world power has collapsed, it has been a day of judgment involving a terrible carnage. It is true that God has punished people in the past by means of war. He will continue to do so in the future until the end of time. It is wise, however, to remember that the battle is not only raging in the physical world but in the spiritual realm as well. Scripture does not record the rest of Jesus' sermon that day in Nazareth, but one thing is certain: his topic dealt with the spiritual realm rather than the physical. Does the gospel have anything to do with vengeance? Was there a day of vengeance in the spiritual realm during the time of Jesus? Yes! Jesus declared, "Now is the time for judgment on this world; now the prince of this world will be driven out. But I, when I am lifted up from the earth, will draw all men to myself" (John 12:31,32). The vengeance of God Almighty was concentrated against Jesus as he hung bleeding and dying on the cross. For believers, Jesus is like a lightning rod, absorbing the wrath of God. Paul writes, "Since we have now been justified by his blood, how much more shall we be saved from God's wrath through him!" (Rom. 5:9). What a wonderful day of vengeance that was. Once, and for all eternity, God dealt with my sin. Jesus paid the penalty that I deserve. Sorrow will turn to joy in the heart of every believer who accepts God's plan for salvation from sin.

> *Who is this coming from Edom, from Bozrah, with his garments stained crimson? Who is this, robed in splendor, striding forward in the greatness of his strength?*
> *"It is I, speaking in righteousness, mighty to save."*
> *Why are your garments red, like those of one treading the winepress?*
> *"I have trodden the winepress alone; from the nations no one was with me. I trampled them in my anger and trod them down in my wrath; their blood splattered my garments, and I stained all my clothing. For the day of vengeance was in my heart, and the year of my redemption has come. I looked, but there was no one to help, I was appalled that no one gave support; so my own arm worked salvation for me, and my own wrath sustained me. I trampled the nations in my anger; in my wrath I made them drunk and poured their blood on the ground"* (Isa. 63:1-6).

In these verses Isaiah has a conversation with God. Its primary purpose is to comfort Isaiah's audience. They knew of Bozrah, a city in Edom. Just as there had been enmity between the brothers Jacob and Esau, there continued to be animosity between the two countries. Therefore the people of Judah would be encouraged, because one day God would punish Edom for its sins. In that day of battle the victor would be the Lord.

God also painted a picture of the battle that Jesus won at Calvary. "I looked, but there was no one to help." On the day of vengeance, Christ battled Satan completely alone. The disciples had deserted him; even God the Father had. Standing alone and covered with blood, Jesus is "mighty to save." How precious is God's salvation! When Jesus shed his blood on the cross, he accomplished our spiritual redemption. He paid the price necessary to rescue believers from Satan's kingdom.[23] Paul writes, "In him we have redemption through his blood, the forgiveness of sins, in accordance with the riches of God's grace that he lavished on us with all wisdom and understanding" (Eph. 1:7,8). Henry points out, "Our Lord Jesus wrought out our redemption, in a holy zeal for the honour of his Father, the happiness of mankind, and a holy indignation at the daring attempts Satan had made upon both; this zeal and indignation upheld him throughout his whole undertaking."[24] Truly Jesus Christ was the mighty Conqueror on that day.

Yet another day of vengeance and redemption is coming. For believers it will be joyous, whereas for non-believers it will be a time of horror and sorrow. God's judgment has two sides, blessing and cursing. On the cross Jesus accomplished the spiritual redemption of believers. At the end of time he will change their bodies into glorified ones like his. Paul explains, "And we eagerly await a Savior from there [heaven], the Lord Jesus Christ, who, by the power that enables him to bring everything under his control, will transform our lowly bodies so that they will be like his glorious body" (Phil. 3:20,21). God calls this event "the redemption of our bodies" (Rom. 8:23). In contrast, for non-believers that day will be extremely painful. "I have trodden the winepress alone...I trampled them in my anger and trod them down in my wrath...I trampled the nations in my anger; in my wrath I made them drunk and poured their blood on the ground" (Isa. 63:3-6). At the end of time the Word of God, who is Jesus, will tread "the winepress of the fury of the wrath of God Almighty" (Rev. 19:15). With his mouth as a sword he will "strike down the nations" (Rev. 19:15). There shall be no escape. Everyone will die—"all people, free and slave, small and great" (Rev. 19:18).

God exhorts everyone to accept his gift of salvation. The Lord will keep his promise to send the promised Seed. The Saviour will be successful on his day of battle at Calvary. Satan will be forever defeated, because God always tells the truth. There are two types of people, believers and non-believers, those who love the Lord and those who do not. When the Final Judgment Day comes, will you be prepared to meet your Maker? I hope so.

4h. The Eternal Reward of the Redeemed

Your gates will always stand open, they will never be shut, day or night (Isa. 60:11).

No longer will violence be heard in your land, nor ruin or destruction within your borders, but you will call your walls Salvation and your gates Praise. The sun will no more be your light by day, nor will the brightness of the moon shine on you, for the LORD *will be your everlasting light, and your God will be your glory. Your sun will never set again, and your moon will wane no more; the* LORD *will be your everlasting light, and your days of sorrow will end. Then will all your people be righteous and they will possess the land forever* (Isa. 60:18-21).

These verses describe the new heaven and new earth. John echoes Isaiah:

I did not see a temple in the city, because the Lord God Almighty and the Lamb are its temple. The city does not need the sun or the moon to shine on it, for the glory of God gives it light, and the Lamb is its lamp. The nations will walk by its light, and the kings of the earth will bring their splendor into it. On no day will its gates ever be shut, for there will be no night there. The glory and honor of the nations will be brought into it. Nothing impure will ever enter it, nor will anyone who does what is shameful or deceitful, but only those whose names are written in the Lamb's book of life (Rev. 21:22-27).

In the new heaven and new earth there will never be any crying (Isa. 65:17,19). John echoes, "He will wipe every tear from their eyes. There will be no more death or mourning or crying or pain, for the old order of things has passed away" (Rev. 21:4). Isaiah testified, "Since ancient times no one has heard, no ear has perceived, no eye has seen any God besides you, who acts on behalf of those who wait for him" (Isa. 64:4). Paul exclaims, "No eye has seen, no ear has heard, no mind has conceived what God has prepared for those who love him—but God has revealed it to us by his Spirit" (1 Cor. 2:9,10). Isaiah tasted of "the deep things of God" (1 Cor. 2:10) and caught a glimpse of the eternal blessings of believers. Because God has kept all of his promises so far, believers can count on seeing him one day in the new heaven and new earth.

> Because God has kept all of his promises so far, believers can count on seeing him one day in the new heaven and new earth.

Points to Ponder

1. God never allows our choices to thwart his sovereign will. Consider Athaliah and Sennacherib.
2. Everyone who has ever lived must make a decision for or against trusting the Lord.
3. The hearts of those who reject God's salvation are hardened more and more by sin.
4. This present earth will never be free of sin.
5. God is more concerned with the spiritual redemption of humanity than with anyone's physical prosperity.

Chapter Eight

The Fall of Judah

1. Zephaniah: Mighty to Save

Date of ministry: 640-621 B.C.[1] He finished prophesying 35 years before the fall of Jerusalem and 83 years before the edict of Cyrus.

LIFE was good for Barry and me. We were living in North Bay and enjoying it. We liked our house. We were involved in our church and busy in the Lord's work. Then Barry came home from work with the bad news that his job was to be eliminated in about a year. Our imagination ran wild that year. We kept hoping that the news wasn't true, but it was. Fourteen months later Barry received his termination letter.

The people of Judah were forewarned many more years than we were. Like us, however, time was running out. The axe would indeed fall.

> *The great day of the LORD is near—near and coming quickly. Listen! The cry on the day of the LORD will be bitter, the shouting of the warrior there. That day will be a day of wrath, a day of distress and anguish, a day of trouble and ruin, a day of darkness and gloom, a day of clouds and blackness, a day of trumpet and battle cry against the fortified cities and against the corner towers. I will bring distress on the people and they will walk like blind men, because they have sinned against the LORD…In the fire of his jealousy the whole world will be*

consumed, for he will make a sudden end of all who live in the earth (Zeph. 1:14-18).

The day of the Lord was very near when Judah and all the surrounding countries would be judged for their sins. That is why God pleaded with his people to stop sinning. "Seek the LORD, all you humble of the land, you who do what he commands. Seek righteousness, seek humility; perhaps you will be sheltered on the day of the LORD's anger" (Zeph. 2:3).

Zephaniah compared Judah's fate with those of the surrounding countries. "Surely Moab will become like Sodom, the Ammonites like Gomorrah—a place of weeds and salt pits, a wasteland forever" (Zeph. 2:9). Assyria would become "a lair for wild beasts" (Zeph. 2:15). All of the other countries would be destroyed. "No one will be left—no one at all" (Zeph. 3:6). In contrast, God would save a remnant of Judah who were meek and humble and who trusted him. Zephaniah prophesied, "The remnant of Israel will do no wrong; they will speak no lies, nor will deceit be found in their mouths. They will eat and lie down and no one will make them afraid" (Zeph. 3:13). Judah would become an object lesson for the whole world. Unlike other nations that would disappear, it would survive. God surely is "mighty to save" (Zeph. 3:17). As a result, everyone living would praise and honour Judah. All nations would acknowledge God's mighty power in restoring the people of Judah to the Promised Land. What the Lord did so long ago for his people should encourage us today, because God never changes. He upholds his honour by always keeping his promises. He is still *mighty to save*. He only asks us to believe his Word and have faith in his Son Jesus.

When Zephaniah warned Judah of imminent trouble, he also hinted at the end of time. "He will make a sudden end of all who live in the earth." According to Henry, the day of the Lord for that generation was "a specimen of the day of judgment, a kind of doom's-day, as the last destruction of Jerusalem by the Romans is represented to be in our Saviour's prediction concerning it."[2] On that day God will judge everyone. While believers will find the Lord mighty to save, non-believers will be forced to admit their rejection of God and his gift of salvation.

2. Jeremiah

Date of ministry: 627-586 B.C.[3] He prophesied for 41 years before the fall of Jerusalem and for a short time afterwards. He finished prophesying 48 years before the edict of Cyrus. Reign of Josiah: 640-609 B.C.[4]

2a. The Old Covenant Broken

Jeremiah lived during the tumultuous last years of the kingdom of Judah. Since the Lord called him to preach when he was young, he said, "Ah, Sovereign Lord…I do not know how to speak; I am only a child" (Jer. 1:6).

The Lord replied, "Do not say, 'I am only a child.' You must go to everyone I send you to and say whatever I command you. Do not be afraid of them, for I am with you and will rescue you" (Jer. 1:7).

Through Jeremiah, God reminded the people of the old covenant:

> *"Cursed is the man who does not obey the terms of this covenant—the terms I commanded your forefathers when I brought them out of Egypt, out of the iron-smelting furnace…Obey me and do everything I command you, and you will be my people, and I will be your God. Then I will fulfill the oath I swore to your forefathers, to give them a land flowing with milk and honey"* (Jer. 11:3-5).

Ever since Moses' day, most of God's people had refused to listen to the Lord. Instead each generation had "followed the stubbornness of their evil hearts" (Jer. 11:8). That is why God would soon allow the Babylonians to conquer Judah. Then in shock the people would ask Jeremiah, "Why has the LORD our God done all this to us?" (Jer. 5:19).

God instructed Jeremiah to reply, "As you have forsaken me and served foreign gods in your own land, so now you will serve foreigners in a land not your own" (Jer. 5:19).

God is merciful and patient, but eventually unrepentant sin must be punished. He told Jeremiah not to pray for the people any more, because he would not listen. The land would become a wasteland while the people would be captives in Babylon for seventy years. Eventually Jeremiah would be imprisoned for his preaching. He would even endure the hardship of rationed food in a besieged Jerusalem.

> *"Cries of fear are heard—terror, not peace. Ask and see: Can a man bear children? Then why do I see every strong man with his hands on his stomach like a woman in labor, every face turned deathly pale? How awful that day will be! None will be like it. It will be a time of trouble for Jacob, but he will be saved out of it"* (Jer. 30:5-7).

One day the Babylonians would enter Jerusalem and capture it. Judgment would befall the people of Judah. At that time every man would act like a woman in labour; their pain would overwhelm them. When it was too late, the people of Judah would know that Jeremiah had told them the truth. The false prophets had only preached a message of peace because it was the popular expectation. Nevertheless, like a woman in labour, their sorrow would be temporary. God promised to rescue them. The fall of Jerusalem and the captivity were certainly times of trouble for Jacob. Likewise, the destruction of Jerusalem in A.D. 70 was a time of unparalleled trouble for the Jewish people. In order to comfort them, Jeremiah reminded them that the Messiah would indeed come (Jer. 23:5,6; 30:8,9; 33:15,16).

> *"In that day," declares the LORD Almighty, "I will break the yoke off their necks and will tear off their bonds; no longer will foreigners enslave them. Instead, they will serve the LORD their God and David their king, whom I will raise up for them"* (Jer. 30:8,9).

Although the Lord would punish them for their sin, they had a sure hope of restoration to the land. "No longer will foreigners enslave them." At this point most of the people were blind to spiritual realities and only concerned with the physical world. As a result they merely looked forward to a day of political salvation. For a brief time under the Maccabees the nation did achieve independence again.[5] Jesus, however, came to save them from spiritual death. He would restore those who trusted in him to fellowship with their Creator. This spiritual restoration was much more important to God than their physical return to the Promised Land. "They will serve the LORD their God and David their king." This is a reference to the Messiah. No matter how wicked the people of Judah had become, the Lord would always keep his promise to send the everlasting King, whose kingdom would never end. He would keep his covenant with David. Jeremiah's audience assumed that the promised Seed would be their political leader. After the captivity, the exiles must have been very disappointed when their governor Zerubbabel was not the Messiah.

2b. The New Covenant Promised

> *"The time is coming," declares the LORD, "when I will make a new covenant with the house of Israel and with the house of Judah. It will not be like the covenant I made with their forefathers when I took them by the hand to lead them out of Egypt, because they broke my*

> covenant, though I was a husband to them," declares the
> LORD. "This is the covenant that I will make with the
> house of Israel after that time," declares the LORD. "I will
> put my law in their minds and write it on their hearts. I
> will be their God, and they will be my people. No longer
> will a man teach his neighbor, or a man his brother, say-
> ing, 'Know the LORD,' because they will all know me,
> from the least of them to the greatest," declares the LORD.
> "For I will forgive their wickedness and will remember
> their sins no more" (Jer. 31:31-34).

It is impossible for anyone to obey God perfectly. Some of God's people tried to keep the Law in their own strength while others ignored the Lord and chased after false gods. That is why God continually pointed out their sin and their need for the Saviour. Only the promised Seed could truly restore them to fellowship with God. To those who lovingly tried to obey the Lord, this was good news. The Saviour would replace the old covenant with a new one ratified by his blood. No longer would the Law be only an external set of rules. The knowledge of the Lord would be internal—written in the hearts and minds of believers. Many years later, when Jesus walked through the land of Israel, his first concern was to preach to the lost sheep of Israel (Matt. 10:6). His mission was "to seek and to save what was lost" (Luke 19:10). He wanted to reach those Jews who were patiently waiting for their Saviour to be born, for they would be overjoyed at his arrival. Israel was the nation especially prepared by God to receive the promised Seed. If anyone would be waiting for the Saviour's arrival to satisfy divine justice, it would be a Jew.

The people of Judah had the following proverb: "The fathers have eaten sour grapes, and the children's teeth are set on edge" (Jer. 31:29). Such thinking upset Jeremiah. At Mount Sinai when God spoke the Ten Commandments to the children of Israel, he said, "For I, the LORD your God, am a jealous God, punishing the children for the sin of the fathers to the third and fourth generation of those who hate me" (Exod.

20:5). It is easy to understand how wicked parents quite naturally teach their children their own set of values. By acting on those values, the children become guilty of sin in their own right. As a result, three or four generations may commit the same sins. Everyone is responsible for his or her own sins and will be punished for such. God explained, "Instead, everyone will die for his own sin; whoever eats sour grapes—his own teeth will be set on edge" (Jer. 31:30). This is the essence of the new covenant. It is a covenant for individuals within Israel, not for everybody. According to George B. Fletcher:

> This is the essence of the new covenant. It is a covenant for individuals within Israel, not for everybody.

> Jeremiah's prophecy of the New Covenant (Jer. 31:31-34) was fulfilled and established in Christ, as is testified to by the words of the institution of the Lord's Supper in Luke 22:20 and I Cor. 11:25. Moreover, there is no other Old Testament prophecy to the exposition of which four chapters of the New are devoted; and the fulfillment of which we celebrate every time we sit down to the Lord's Table (II Cor. 3 and Heb. 8 to 10).[6]

This is what the LORD *says, he who appoints the sun to shine by day, who decrees the moon and stars to shine by night, who stirs up the sea so that its waves roar— the* LORD *Almighty is his name: "Only if these decrees vanish from my sight," declares the* LORD, *"will the descendants of Israel ever cease to be a nation before me." This is what the* LORD *says: "Only if the heavens above can be measured and the foundations of the earth below be searched out will I reject all the descendants of Israel because of all they have done"* (Jer. 31:35-37).

Nothing would deter God from initiating the new covenant. The Lord promised never to reject all the descendants of Israel. It is as sure as the fact that the sun, moon, and stars exist.

> The Lord promised never to reject all the descendants of Israel. It is as sure as the fact that the sun, moon, and stars exist.

Between A.D. 70 and 1948, there was no country on earth called Israel. Yet did God's promise fail, that the descendants of Israel would never cease to be a nation? Before condemning him as a liar, we must consider the spiritual realm. Paul points out, "For not all who are descended from Israel are Israel. Nor because they are his descendants are they all Abraham's children" (Rom. 9:6,7). Many years before, God reminded Elijah of the believing remnant in his day (1 Kings 19:18). There will always be a remnant of believers who will be a nation in the eyes of the Lord. This is the true Israel of the new covenant. In the physical realm it takes time to populate a country so that it is large enough to become a nation. Isaiah remarks, "Can a country be born in a day or a nation be brought forth in a moment?" (Isa. 66:8). In the spiritual realm, it happened on the day of Pentecost when about 3000 people trusted God to forgive their sins (Acts 2:41). Others accepted God's wonderful gift of salvation in the days to follow (Acts 2:47). What a population explosion!

> *Circumcise yourselves to the* LORD, *circumcise your hearts, you men of Judah and people of Jerusalem, or my wrath will break out and burn like fire because of the evil you have done—burn with no one to quench it* (Jer. 4:4).

In the physical realm every male had to be circumcised by having a piece of flesh cut off. Likewise, in the spiritual realm everyone must be circumcised in the heart by removing hatred toward God and replacing it with love for him. That is why Jeremiah pleaded, "O Jerusalem, wash the evil from your heart and be saved. How long will you harbor wicked thoughts?" (Jer. 4:14). Many years later Paul explains, "A man is not a Jew if he is only one outwardly, nor is circumcision merely outward and physical. No, a man is a Jew if he is one inwardly; and circumcision is circumcision of the heart, by the Spirit, not by the written code. Such a man's praise is not from men, but from God" (Rom. 2:28,29). In order to be a member of the spiritual nation of Israel, the Holy Spirit must circumcise the believer's heart. How comforting to know that we are not responsible for circumcising ourselves! The Holy Spirit will do it.

Jeremiah told his audience that God is the fountain of living water (Jer. 2:13; 17:13). This means that God is the only source of spiritual life. He desired to give Jeremiah's audience the living water as much as he wants to give it to each of us today. At the well of Sychar Jesus told the woman of Samaria, "If you knew the gift of God and who it is that asks you for a drink, you would have asked him and he would have given you living water" (John 4:10). Everyone who has been circumcised in the heart belongs to the spiritual nation of Israel and possesses the living water.

2c. Condemnation on Babylon

Reign of Nebuchadnezzar: 604-561 B.C.[7]

> *This is what the LORD says: "See, I will stir up the spirit of a destroyer against Babylon and the people of Leb Kamai. I will send foreigners to Babylon to winnow her and to devastate her land; they will oppose her on every side in the day of her disaster"* (Jer. 51:1,2).

In Jeremiah's day the Babylonians replaced the Assyrians as the world power to fear. Soon even Jerusalem would succumb to their superior strength. Yet the kingdom of Babylon was only temporary. In God's time the Medes and Persians would conquer it.

> *"I am against you, O destroying mountain, you who destroy the whole earth," declares the* LORD. *"I will stretch out my hand against you, roll you off the cliffs, and make you a burned-out mountain. No rock will be taken from you for a cornerstone, nor any stone for a foundation, for you will be desolate forever," declares the* LORD (Jer. 51:25,26).

Until Nebuchadnezzar built the temple of Bel Merodach on top of it, the tower of Babel had been the highest point in the plain of Shinar. Through Jeremiah, God promised to burn Nebuchadnezzar's tower, the sacred mountain where the Babylonians worshipped their gods. According to Urquhart, some scholars speculate that Nebuchadnezzar's tower was struck by lightning, because it actually looks like a burned-out mountain.[8] In the eyes of the Lord it was a destroying mountain for two reasons. First, when the Babylonians chose to worship Bel and the other minor deities, they forever rejected fellowship with the one true God. The people were lost spiritually. Secondly, in the physical realm they conquered many nations, including Judah, and even credited their military success to those false gods. "You will be desolate forever." To this day no one else has ever worshipped there, and nobody ever will.

> *Babylon, the jewel of kingdoms, the glory of the Babylonians' pride, will be overthrown by God like Sodom and Gomorrah. She will never be inhabited or lived in through all generations; no Arab will pitch his tent there, no shepherd will rest his flocks there* (Isa. 13:19,20).

Although some years later the Medes and Persians did conquer Babylon, the city itself still existed for many centuries. It gradually deteriorated, however, to the point where it became uninhabitable. The ancient city of Babylon now lies in ruins. According to Werner Keller, "The little Arab settlement of 'Babil' preserves in its name the memory of the proud city: but it lies some miles north of the ruins."[9] God always tells the truth and always keeps his promises.

3. Habakkuk: Living by Faith

Date of ministry: 612-589 B.C.[10] He finished prophesying 3 years before the fall of Jerusalem and 51 years before the edict of Cyrus.

In May 1998 I wrote the first draft of this section in my book. The previous July Barry and I had moved back to southern Ontario from North Bay. That September I was diagnosed with breast cancer. We had no children at home, because we had left Philip in North Bay for grade twelve. Since Barry had a two-hour commute to work, he was gone twelve hours every day. This meant that I was alone in a strange place most of the time. In October I had an operation. From November until May, I underwent chemotherapy. Then during the month of January I travelled on the subway from my mother-in-law's to a Toronto hospital for radiation. Having chemotherapy and radiation at the same time made me extremely tired. By May I was at the lowest point in my life physically and emotionally, but Habakkuk was my inspiration. His testimony is also mine.

Habakkuk was upset about a problem that bothers many people. He cried out to God, "Why do you tolerate wrong?...The wicked hem in the righteous, so that justice is perverted" (Hab. 1:3,4). "It is not fair," he thought.

The Lord answered, "Look at the nations and watch—and be utterly amazed. For I am going to do something in your days that you would not believe, even if you were told. I am raising up the Babylonians, that ruthless and impetuous people, who sweep across the whole earth to seize dwelling places not their own" (Hab. 1:5,6). Judgment would come to those who had perverted God's Law.

After thinking about the Lord's answer, Habakkuk had another problem. The righteous would suffer along with the wicked when the Babylonians conquered Judah. He asked God, "Why are you silent while the wicked swallow up those more righteous than themselves? You have made men like fish in the sea, like sea creatures that have no ruler" (Hab. 1:13,14).

> *Write down the revelation and make it plain on tablets so that a herald may run with it. For the revelation awaits an appointed time; it speaks of the end and will not prove false. Though it [he] linger, wait for it [him]; it [he] will certainly come and will not delay* (Hab. 2:2,3).

> God knows that his loved ones sometimes hurt through no fault of their own.

God knows that his loved ones sometimes hurt through no fault of their own. Therefore he asks them to have patience. He has not abandoned the righteous. They must wait for the end. God has a plan, which "will certainly come and will not delay." Through Habakkuk, God promised, "You came out to deliver your people, to save your anointed one. You crushed the leader of the land of wickedness, you stripped him from head to foot" (Hab. 3:13). This is the end that God wanted them to focus their thoughts on. Although Babylon would come and destroy their land, a remnant would return, and Babylon would fall. The Lord would prove how much he loved his people by taking care of them in captivity and by restoring them to the Promised Land.

Nevertheless, God was more concerned with their spiritual needs than with their physical ones. Spiritual reconciliation with the Creator is more important than temporal blessing. Some people eagerly waited for the promised Seed, the Saviour. Knowing that he would come at the appointed time was a tremendous comfort.

The believers of the early Church joyfully accepted persecution, because they expected the soon return of Christ. As time passed, they were perplexed, but God reminded them to be patient. Jesus will return. The end will come. "He who is coming will come and will not delay. But my righteous one will live by faith. And if he shrinks back, I will not be pleased with him" (Heb. 10:37,38). Those who trust the Lord to save them from their sins live by faith. They know that their compassionate, loving God has their best interests at heart.

The believers in Habakkuk's day looked forward to the restoration of Israel and to the First Coming of the Saviour. Those in our day look forward to the Second Coming of Jesus. Do not be discouraged! Although the Church has been waiting for almost 2000 years, Jesus will come back. God always tells the truth and always keeps his promises.

> *"The righteous will live by his faith"* (Hab. 2:4).

David lamented, "Do not bring your servant into judgment, for no one living is righteous before you" (Ps. 143:2). He depended on God's righteousness to save him. Those who accept God's verdict of guilty know that they are sinners and are not capable of making themselves righteous or pure. That is why Paul writes, "For in the gospel a righteousness from God is revealed, a righteousness that is by faith from first to last, just as it is written: 'The righteous will live by faith'" (Rom. 1:17). When the Lord looks at a believer, he sees the righteousness of Christ. Paul explains further, "Clearly no one is justified before God by the law, because, 'The righteous will live by faith'" (Gal. 3:11). Habakkuk did not depend on his ability to keep the Law perfectly. He knew that he could not. Therefore he lived by faith and waited for God's salvation. This was credited to him as righteousness.

> *"For the earth will be filled with the knowledge of the glory of the* LORD, *as the waters cover the sea"* (Hab. 2:14).

When the two Israelite spies met Rahab in Jericho, she told them, "I know that the LORD has given this land to you and that a great fear of you has fallen on us, so that all who live in this country are melting in fear because of you" (Josh. 2:9).

Although forty years had passed since God had delivered the Israelites from Egypt, the Canaanites were still overwhelmed with fear of the Lord. The whole world had heard how God had rescued his people and had destroyed their enemies. Similarly, when God would destroy the Babylonians and restore Israel to the Promised Land, the whole world would acknowledge the mighty power of God. Likewise, after Jesus' death and resurrection, news of God's mighty power spread throughout the world. Finally, only in the new heaven and earth will there be no sin. Then and only then will the whole earth truly be filled with the knowledge of the Lord.

> *"But the* LORD *is in his holy temple; let all the earth be silent before him"* (Hab. 2:20).

Habakkuk is relevant to every generation, because he turns eyes away from worthless idols to focus on the Lord of Glory, who is the one in control. Do not worry; keep the faith. Only rest, assured that the Lord knows the end from the beginning. There will be an end! Solomon reminds us, "There is a time for everything, and a season for every activity under heaven" (Eccl. 3:1). Nothing in the physical realm lasts forever—not the good times or the bad—not even life itself.

Yet I will rejoice in the LORD*, I will be joyful in God my Savior* (Hab. 3:18).

> The Lord does not want us just to grit our teeth while we bear the pain and sorrow.

Habakkuk ends his book by praising God. The Lord does not want us just to grit our teeth while we bear the pain and sorrow. He certainly does not want us to become bitter against him. He wants us by faith to patiently wait for the end and to experience the joy of his salvation, day by day.

4. The Threat of Babylon

Reign of Jehoiakim, king of Judah: 609-598 B.C.[11]
Reign of Nebuchadnezzar, king of Babylon: 604-561 B.C.[7]

After King Josiah was killed in a battle with Neco, king of Egypt, his son Jehoahaz became king. Three months later, probably to flaunt his power, Neco forced Jehoahaz into slavery and took him to Egypt. Then he appointed the brother of Jehoahaz, Eliakim, to be king. Neco even changed Eliakim's name to Jehoiakim and demanded that he pay tribute.

Sent by his father, Nabopolassar, in 605 B.C., Nebuchadnezzar defeated Neco, drove him out of Asia, and annexed Syria (Aram) to the Babylonian Empire.[7] After Egypt's defeat, Nebuchadnezzar was free to attack Jerusalem. He besieged the city and succeeded in capturing Jehoiakim. Then Nebuchadnezzar raided the temple of God and carried off some of its treasures to put in his god's temple in Babylonia (Dan. 1:2). Daniel and some others from the nobility were also deported. It appears as if Nebuchadnezzar intended to take Jehoiakim to Babylon and then changed his mind (2 Chron. 36:6). Instead Jehoiakim became his vassal and remained the king of Jerusalem. I wonder if Nebuchadnezzar later regretted that decision. Only the restraining mercy of God kept Nebuchadnezzar from burning Jerusalem to the ground at that time. No doubt Satan was saying, "Kill them! Burn that temple! Destroy that city!"

> Only the restraining mercy of God kept Nebuchadnezzar from burning Jerusalem to the ground at that time.

In 602 B.C. Jehoiakim rebelled against the king of Babylon,[7] but he did not succeed. Although Jehoiakim remained king for another five years, he eventually died in shame. Jeremiah prophesied that Jehoiakim would "have the burial of a donkey—dragged away and thrown outside the gates of Jerusalem" (Jer. 22:19).

In 598 B.C. the son of Jehoiakim, Jehoiachin, became king for three months.[11] When Nebuchadnezzar laid siege to Jerusalem, Jehoiachin and many other nobles decided to surrender. "He carried into exile all Jerusalem: all the officers and fighting men, and all the craftsmen and artisans—a total of ten thousand. Only the poorest people of the land were left" (2 Kings 24:14). Nebuchadnezzar also took all the treasure from the temple, including the gold articles that Solomon had made. In those days Ezekiel went into exile. Then Nebuchadnezzar appointed Mattaniah, son of Josiah and uncle of Jehoiachin, to be king and changed his name to Zedekiah. He reigned for eleven years, until 586 B.C.[11] For twenty-three difficult years the people of Jerusalem continued to ignore the Lord. They endured taxes to pay tribute money; they suffered famine when they were besieged; some of their citizens became captives of Babylon. "Surely these things happened to Judah according to the LORD's command" (2 Kings 24:3).

5. The Fall of Jerusalem

586 B.C.[11]

Although Nebuchadnezzar had already captured many of the people, those remaining with Zedekiah would not believe that the king of Babylon would eventually win. Jeremiah warned them, "Do not deceive yourselves, thinking, 'The Babylonians will surely leave us.' They will not! Even if you were to defeat the entire Babylonian army that is attacking you and only wounded men were left in their tents, they would come out and burn this city down" (Jer. 37:9,10). God even advised that wicked generation how to escape the coming disaster. "Whoever stays in this city will die by the sword, famine or plague, but who-

> God even advised that wicked generation how to escape the coming disaster.

ever goes over to the Babylonians will live. He will escape with his life; he will live" (Jer. 38:2).

The officials of Jerusalem wanted to kill Jeremiah for speaking treason. After putting him in the bottom of an empty well, Jeremiah sank into the mud. As soon as someone told Zedekiah what had happened, he ordered some men to pull Jeremiah out of the well. He kept him in prison, however (Jer. 38:6-13).

In 588 B.C. Nebuchadnezzar laid siege to Jerusalem.[7] For two years the people were imprisoned in the city. By then the famine was so severe that the people had nothing to eat. The Babylonians finally managed to make a hole in the city wall and entered Jerusalem. Zedekiah and his army were terrified. That night they escaped and fled toward the Jordan valley, but the Babylonians soon captured them in the plains of Jericho. Meanwhile Nebuzaradan, commander of the imperial guard, broke down all the walls of Jerusalem; he stole everything valuable from the temple of the Lord; then he burnt the entire city, including the temple. Those who had listened to Jeremiah had already surrendered to the Babylonians. Nebuzaradan captured the rest who had survived the famine, the sword, and the fire. Next he led the chief priest Seraiah, the officials, and any others left in Jerusalem to Nebuchadnezzar at Riblah in Hamath. There the king of Babylon had Seraiah, all the officials, and sixty others executed (2 Kings 25:18-21). Zedekiah was forced to watch while his sons and all the nobles of Judah were killed. "Then he put out Zedekiah's eyes and bound him with bronze shackles to take him to Babylon" (Jer. 39:7).

Some of the poorest people remained in the land and worked in the vineyards and fields. Gedaliah, who was appointed by Nebuchadnezzar to be the governor, encouraged them, "Do not be afraid of the Babylonian officials...Settle down in the land and serve the king of Babylon, and it will go well with you" (2 Kings 25:24).

Then, since Gedaliah was not a descendant of David, Ishmael conspired with ten men and murdered him seven months later. Afterwards, fearing for their lives, the people fled to Egypt and took Jeremiah with them. The land of Judah, which was once so prosperous, lay vacant for seventy years (2 Chron. 36:21). Only 4600 people ended up living in Babylon (Jer. 52:30). Satan must have been ecstatic. Surely the line of the promised Seed was eradicated! Yet God had a plan. He would once again free his people, just as he had in Egypt.

Points to Ponder

1. God gives plenty of warning before he punishes unrepentant people for their sin.
2. Even believers sometimes commit the sin of self-righteousness and act as if God has no business punishing them.
3. Although believers often fall short of God's expectations, he never forsakes his own.
4. God gives supernatural strength to those who trust him in difficult times.
5. The God of Scripture is the only source of spiritual life.

Chapter Nine

The Captivity

1. Obadiah: Judgment on Edom

586 B.C.[1] He prophesied just after the fall of Jerusalem and 48 years before the edict of Cyrus.

MY dad was so sad that I wanted to marry a non-believer. He wrote me a letter, which I promptly threw in the garbage. My uncle, who had married Barry and me, was shocked to see the word *atheist* on the marriage license. He said that he would have stood in front of the church and refused to marry us if he had known. Soon afterwards I claimed God's promise to move a mountain if I would have faith like a mustard seed (Matt. 17:20). I prayed that God would move the mountain of Barry's unbelief. Miraculously, he saved Barry eighteen months after our wedding. My dad was overjoyed. We were also reconciled to my uncle, who felt that God had overruled in allowing the marriage to take place. Instead of accepting God's forgiveness for marrying a non-believer, I was plagued with false guilt for many years. I became a spiritual captive of my own making, because there was nothing that I could do to correct the past. One Sunday morning a sermon on how Jesus set the captives free finally opened my eyes to the truth. I am a sinner saved by grace. I can do nothing to atone for the past. Jesus did it all.

Like me, the exiles wept. How could the Babylonians possibly expect them to sing songs of joy? Yet they continually demanded, "Sing us one of the songs of Zion!" (Ps. 137:3).

The exiles longed for Jerusalem. They cried, "If I forget you, O Jerusalem, may my right hand forget its skill. May my tongue cling to the roof of my mouth if I do not remember you, if I do not consider Jerusalem my highest joy" (Ps. 137:5,6).

With sorrow the people of Judah remembered how the Edomites had reacted to their tragedy. Instead of being sympathetic for the plight of a relative, they had cried against Jerusalem. "Tear it down...tear it down to its foundations!" (Ps. 137:7).

Long ago Jacob had cheated his brother Esau out of his inheritance and his blessing.[2] "It's payback time!" they thought. Thus the Edomites rejoiced over the misfortune of the people of Judah (Obad. 1:12). Waiting for an opportunity to take advantage of the situation, they stood by and watched (Obad. 1:11). Some Edomites managed to steal from the people (Obad. 1:13). Others killed those who were trying to escape (Obad. 1:14). A few even tried to ingratiate themselves with the Babylonians by capturing the runaways and handing them over to the enemy (Obad. 1:14). It was too painful to remember how the Edomites had treated them. At this point the Edomites were proud and self-satisfied. Like the Jebusites of old, they trusted in their mountain fortresses to keep them safe. They thought, "Who can bring me down to the ground?" (Obad. 1:3).

The Lord answered, "See, I will make you small among the nations; you will be utterly despised. The pride of your heart has deceived you, you who live in the clefts of the rocks and make your home on the heights" (Obad. 1:2,3). God would punish the Edomites. "As you have done, it will be done to you; your deeds will return upon your own head" (Obad. 1:15).

To encourage the sorrowful exiles, God reminded them that their situation was not permanent. Unlike the Edomites who would eventually disappear from the earth, the Israelites would be restored to the Promised Land and would prosper materially and spiritually. Through Obadiah, the Lord declared, "But on Mount Zion will be deliverance; it will be holy, and the house of Jacob will possess its inheritance. The house of Jacob will be a fire and the house of Joseph a flame; the house of Esau will be stubble, and they will set it on fire and consume it. There will be no survivors from the house of Esau" (Obad. 1:17,18). When the Israelites would return to their land, they would also possess Edom. Under the Maccabees the Jews finally did conquer the Edomites.[3] Victory was sure for the Israelites in the physical realm, because God always tells the truth and always keeps his promises.

The Israelites would also experience victory in the spiritual realm. Obadiah preached, "Deliverers will go up on Mount Zion to govern the mountains of Esau. And the kingdom will be the LORD's" (Obad. 1:21). After the Jews captured the Edomites, they forced Judaism on them.[3]

This is not the kind of worship that God desires. Long ago David had worshipped the Lord in spirit and in truth.[4] When the Messiah would come to establish his kingdom, the worship of the one true God would overshadow all false worship. The good news of salvation in Christ would spread throughout the world. Then people from many different countries would accept God's gift of salvation from sin. Their heart attitude would be one of loving obedience to the Lord.

2. Life in Babylon

This is what the LORD Almighty, the God of Israel, says to all those I carried into exile from Jerusalem to Babylon: "Build houses and settle down; plant gardens and eat what they produce. Marry and have sons and daughters; find wives for your sons and give your daughters in marriage, so that they too may have sons and daughters. Increase in number there; do not decrease. Also, seek the peace and prosperity of the city to which I have carried you into exile. Pray to the LORD for it, because if it prospers, you too will prosper" (Jer. 29:4-7).

In 597 B.C. Nebuchadnezzar had carried Jehoiachin and many other nobles, including Ezekiel, into exile.[5] Soon afterwards Jeremiah wrote a letter to the captives. In it he told them that the Lord expected them to live contented, quiet, and peaceable lives in Babylon. They were to obey the laws of the land and not to dwell on the fact that they were displaced from their homeland (Jer. 29:5-9). Jeremiah reminded them not to expect a speedy return to the Promised Land, because their exile would last for seventy years (Jer. 29:10). Thankfully, this captivity was quite different from the cruel slavery that their ancestors had endured in Egypt over 800 years before. That is why Keller comments, "Nowhere is there any mention of their having to make bricks by the Euphrates. Yet Babylon ran what was probably the greatest brick-making industry in the world at that time. For never was there so much building going on in Mesopotamia as under Nebuchadnezzar."[6]

When God told the exiles to carry on with the everyday activities of life, they knew that they must earn a living. Since Babylon was famous as a centre of commerce, the exiles soon began to work as merchants. How often the prophets had denounced the sins of shopkeepers! Long ago Hosea had lamented, "The merchant uses dishonest scales; he loves to defraud" (Hos. 12:7). Yet God allowed them to enter a profession fraught with the temptation to sin. This was an important step in God's plan to protect his people from assimilation into Babylonian society. As Keller points out:

> The switch over to this hitherto forbidden profession was extremely clever—a fact that is seldom properly understood. For it proved to be in the last resort, when added to a tenacious attachment to their old faith, the best guarantee of the continuance of Israel as a people. As farmers and settlers scattered throughout a foreign land they would have intermarried and interbred with people of other races and in a few generations would have been absorbed and would have disappeared. This new

profession demanded that their houses should be in more or less large societies, within which they could build themselves into a community and devote themselves to their religious practices. It gave them cohesion and continuity.[7]

In addition to the need for a new livelihood, the exiles had another problem. They were far from home and unable to worship any longer at the temple. At first they probably gathered by the banks of the river, just as Lydia did in Paul's day (Acts 16:13,14). Eventually they built synagogues where they could pray and read God's Word together. In the words of D. A. Rausch, the origin of the synagogues has been "traditionally traced to the period of the Babylonian exile when the Jewish people were deprived of the temple and assembled together for worship in a strange land...When the exiles returned and rebuilt the temple, it is believed that the synagogue continued as an institution of Palestinian Judaism."[8] In those synagogues the Jews worshipped God in spirit and in truth, exactly like the early believers in the New Testament Church and like us today. The first Christians recognized the connection between the two institutions. According to Loraine Boettner:

> In regard to the meaning of the Greek word *ekklesia*, translated "church," it is well to keep in mind that in the Septuagint, which was a Greek translation of the Old Testament and which was in common use in Palestine in Jesus' day, the word *ekklesia* is used about 70 times to render the Hebrew word *quahal*, assembly or congregation. This translation was made in Alexandria, Egypt, about 150 B. C., by a group of 70 scholars, whence it received its name.

Consequently the Jewish people were familiar with this rendering and naturally would have connected the New Testament Church with the assembly or congregation of Israel as it had existed in Old Testament times.[9]

Like Abraham of old, God travelled with the people of Judah to a foreign country. This is not surprising, but it is amazing that the Babylonians allowed the exiles freedom to worship the one true God. In 605 B.C. Nebuchadnezzar had taken Daniel and a few other young nobles to Babylon. Sometime later Shadrach, Meshach, and Abednego refused to bow down to a ninety-foot high idol made of gold. When God saved them from certain death in the fiery furnace, Nebuchadnezzar ordered, "Therefore I decree that the people of any nation or language who say anything against the God of Shadrach, Meshach and Abednego be cut into pieces and their houses be turned into piles of rubble, for no other god can save in this way" (Dan. 3:29).

Because of the courage of those three men, Nebuchadnezzar remained true to his word. He allowed the captives to worship the one true God. Although Nebuchadnezzar did respect the Lord, obviously this did not prevent him from eventually conquering Jerusalem. Nevertheless God was able to safeguard his people while they worshipped him in a foreign land.

3. Ezekiel

Date of ministry: 593-571 B.C.[10] *He prophesied to the exiles for 7 years before the fall of Jerusalem. His ministry ended 33 years before the edict of Cyrus and 396 years before Antiochus Epiphanes began to reign.*

3a. The Coming Judgment

"This is what the Sovereign Lord *says to the land of Israel: The end! The end has come upon the four corners of the land. The end is now upon you and I will unleash my*

anger against you. I will judge you according to your conduct and repay you for all your detestable practices. I will not look on you with pity or spare you" (Ezek. 7:2-4).

Soon after Ezekiel was captured, Jeremiah wrote a letter to the captives. He urged them to make a life for themselves in Babylon, because they would be there for seventy years. Then for seven years Ezekiel warned the exiles that Jerusalem was about to fall. Some believed the Word of the Lord and were concerned for their loved ones back in Jerusalem. Like Jeremiah, Ezekiel strenuously objected to the idea that children were punished for their father's sins. He exclaims, "What do you people mean by quoting this proverb about the land of Israel: 'The fathers eat sour grapes, and the children's teeth are set on edge'?" (Ezek. 18:2).

Twice God insisted, "The soul who sins is the one who will die" (Ezek. 18:4,20). Each person is responsible for his or her own attitude to God. The Lord explained, "The son will not share the guilt of the father, nor will the father share the guilt of the son. The righteousness of the righteous man will be credited to him, and the wickedness of the wicked will be charged against him" (Ezek. 18:20). Then God pleaded, "Do I take any pleasure in the death of the wicked?...Rather, am I not pleased when they turn from their ways and live?" (Ezek. 18:23).

> *Now the glory of the God of Israel went up from above the cherubim, where it had been, and moved to the threshold of the temple. Then the* Lord *called to the man clothed in linen who had the writing kit at his side and said to him, "Go throughout the city of Jerusalem and put a mark on the foreheads of those who grieve and lament over all the detestable things that are done in it." As I listened, he said to the others, "Follow him through the city and kill, without showing pity or compassion. Slaughter old men, young men and maidens, women and children, but do not touch anyone who has the mark. Begin at my sanctuary"* (Ezek. 9:3-6).

How comforting those words were to believers who had loved ones back in Jerusalem! Anyone who grieved for the sins of the people would be safe. The remnant of believers in Jerusalem endured the same hardships that the others suffered. The Lord, however, knew his own. Believers in Jerusalem carried God's mark on their forehead so that he could protect them from a violent death. Nevertheless, it is unwise to assume that God will always protect his children from the sword. Paul tells the Corinthian Christians that God "set his seal of ownership on us, and put his Spirit in our hearts as a deposit, guaranteeing what is to come" (2 Cor. 1:22). Yet Paul was beheaded because of his faith in Christ. Likewise, John comforts the persecuted Christians of his day by saying, "Do not harm the land or the sea or the trees until we put a seal on the foreheads of the servants of our God" (Rev. 7:3).

> Believers in Jerusalem carried God's mark on their forehead so that he could protect them from a violent death.

Most of the believers had likely heeded Jeremiah's advice and had surrendered while they had the chance (Jer. 38:2). A few may have refused to leave Jeremiah, who was in prison, and God protected them. It is amazing that Nebuchadnezzar remembered Jeremiah in the midst of the conquest. He ordered his commander Nebuzaradan to look after Jeremiah, not to harm him, and to do whatever he asked (Jer. 39:11,12). Because God wanted a remnant to be the nucleus of a reconstituted Israel, he kept some of them from dying. Even a few of the wicked may have escaped death by heeding Jeremiah's advice.

> *Then the word of the LORD came to me: "Son of man, the people living in those ruins in the land of Israel are saying, 'Abraham was only one man, yet he possessed the land. But we are many; surely the land has been given to us as our possession'"* (Ezek. 33:23,24).

Many people refused to believe that God would actually destroy Jerusalem. In response to this Zionism, God replied, "Since you eat meat with the blood still in it and look to your idols and shed blood, should you then possess the land? You rely on your sword, you do detestable things, and each of you defiles his neighbor's wife. Should you then possess the land?" (Ezek. 33:25,26). As Louis A. DeCaro explains:

> Many people refused to believe that God would actually destroy Jerusalem.

> Ezekiel rejected the arrogant claims of the political and secularist Zionists of his time. He demonstrated that their claim to territoriality in the name of Abraham and covenant promises was nullified due to disobedience to covenant conditions...The fundamental question of Israel and Biblical prophecy was best understood by the believing remnant who alone could authentically say, "this is that which was spoken by the prophet" as did Peter on the day of Pentecost. Anointed by the Spirit and renewed in spiritual understanding, Israel's believing remnant experienced covenant blessings and covenant continuity. Their prophetic witness, expressed through the voice of the Apostles, brought to the surface the incompetence of Israel's leaders in understanding prophecy.[11]

3b. A New Spirit within Every Believer

"Rid yourselves of all the offences you have committed, and get a new heart and a new spirit. Why will you die, O house of Israel? For I take no pleasure in the death of anyone, declares the Sovereign LORD. *Repent and live!"* (Ezek. 18:31,32).

"I will give you a new heart and put a new spirit in you; I will remove from you your heart of stone and give you

a heart of flesh. And I will put my Spirit in you and move you to follow my decrees and be careful to keep my laws. You will live in the land I gave your forefathers; you will be my people, and I will be your God" (Ezek. 36:26-28).

What a precious gift of God, a new heart and a new spirit! There was only one way for the people of Judah to receive this gift—by repenting of their sins. Furthermore, anyone in Ezekiel's audience could count on receiving this new heart and new spirit immediately. In Moses' day the Israelites had promised to obey God in their own strength. How often they failed! In contrast, when the exiles would return to the Promised Land, the Holy Spirit would live inside believers and enable them to obey God. They would have a heart of flesh, not of stone. Henry writes:

> Their hearts shall no longer be, as they have been, dead and dry, and hard and heavy, as a stone; no longer incapable of bearing good fruit, so that the good seed is lost upon it, as it was on the *stony ground*...he will make their hearts sensible of spiritual pains and spiritual pleasures; will make them tender, and apt to receive impressions; this is God's work, it is his gift, his gift by promise.[12]

Ezekiel invited the exiles to accept God's gift of the Holy Spirit.

Ezekiel invited the exiles to accept God's gift of the Holy Spirit. Likely some did and others did not. He knew that without the Holy Spirit dwelling within himself, he was utterly incapable of waiting for the promised Seed to be his Saviour. Indeed, he would have no desire or ability to teach others about God. The only way that any of us can understand spiritual realities is through the work of the Holy Spirit. He also works in every believer to make us more like Christ.

"Prophesy to these bones and say to them, 'Dry bones, Hear the word of the LORD! This is what the Sovereign LORD says to these bones: I will make breath enter you, and you will come to life. I will attach tendons to you and make flesh come upon you and cover you with skin; I will put breath in you, and you will come to life. Then you will know that I am the LORD'" (Ezek. 37:4-6).

To further emphasize the miracle that he would perform, God painted a word picture. In defeating Israel and Judah, both Assyria and Babylon suffered from the delusion that their gods were more powerful than the God of Israel. Whenever they conquered a country, they assumed that they had also destroyed the god of the land. Satan must have been ecstatic the day that Jerusalem fell. Like a broken eggshell the people of Judah were scattered—some to Babylon and others to Egypt. Who would ever expect them to be reinstated to their land? Only God has the power to put those bones back together and infuse life into them. No other god has ever revived its scattered citizens and then restored them to their own land.

The exiles were so discouraged that they cried, "Our bones are dried up and our hope is gone; we are cut off" (Ezek. 37:11).

God lovingly replied:

"O my people, I am going to open your graves and bring you up from them; I will bring you back to the land of Israel. Then you, my people, will know that I am the LORD, when I open your graves and bring you up from them. I will put my Spirit in you and you will live, and I will settle you in your own land. Then you will know that I the LORD have spoken, and I have done it" (Ezek. 37:12-14).

Ever since the fall of the northern kingdom, the Israelites had been dispersed among the nations. Yet God promised that once again both the northern and the southern kingdoms would become one country. He said, "There will be one king over all of them and they will never again be two nations or be divided into two kingdoms" (Ezek. 37:22).

After the edict of Cyrus, people from what had been the Assyrian and Babylonian empires did eventually go back to the Promised Land. Their numbers, however, were small, and their return was gradual. They occupied only a small portion of the land originally assigned to the tribe of Judah.

3c. The Shepherd King, Ezekiel 34, 37

> *"My servant David will be king over them, and they will all have one shepherd...David my servant will be their prince forever. I will make a covenant of peace with them; it will be an everlasting covenant. I will establish them and increase their numbers, and I will put my sanctuary among them forever"* (Ezek. 37:24-26).

In these two chapters God reinforced the concept of the Messiah as the Shepherd King. What a strange idea for the people of Judah! In those days kings were authoritarian, and their word was law. No king felt the need to lead his people to accept his ideas. He merely dictated what would happen. In contrast, a shepherd would sacrifice his own well-being for the sake of the sheep. He led his flock to green pastures and cool waters (Psalm 23:2), and he protected them against wild animals that would prey on them. The coming Shepherd King would not only rule with authority over his people, but he would also sacrifice himself for them. He would also be the fulfillment of the everlasting covenant promised by God to David. His reign would never end. Many years later Jesus would explain to some Pharisees that he is the Good Shepherd. He told them, "I am the gate; whoever enters through me will be saved. He will come in and go out, and find pasture…The good shepherd lays down his life for the sheep" (John 10:9-11). Jesus is the fulfillment of Ezekiel's prophesies. He is the son of David, the King who is also the Good Shepherd. There is only one way to heaven. Jesus is the gate to the Father.

> *"For this is what the Sovereign LORD says: I myself will search for my sheep and look after them. As a shepherd looks after his scattered flock when he is with them, so will I look after my sheep. I will rescue them from all the places where they were scattered on a day of clouds and darkness. I will bring them out from the nations and gather them from the countries, and I will bring them into their own land. I will pasture them on the mountains of Israel"* (Ezek. 34:11-13).

Every shepherd counts his flock and will not rest until each sheep is safely in the fold. Likewise God promised to search for his people who were lost in foreign lands and bring them back to the pasturelands of Israel. By proving to be a faithful shepherd in the physical realm, God intended to strengthen their faith so that they would wait for the promised Seed, the Saviour. Knowing that he keeps his promises in this visible world, do you count on God to be your Good Shepherd in the spiritual realm?

3d. Gog and Magog, Ezekiel 38, 39

> *The word of the LORD came to me: "Son of man, set your face against Gog, of the land of Magog, the chief prince of Meshech and Tubal; prophesy against him and say: 'This is what the Sovereign LORD says: I am against you, O Gog, chief prince of Meshech and Tubal'"* (Ezek. 38:1-3).

If Ezekiel had finished his prophecy at chapter 37, the people of Judah would finally have had good reason to expect Utopia on earth. Not only would they be living in the Promised Land, but they would also be united spiritually to the Lord. His Holy Spirit would be living in many of them and enabling them to obey. The Messiah would restore fellowship between them and their God. Not surprisingly, the exiles would suffer from the same problems that plagued Noah—the world, the flesh, and the devil. Many in the first generation would love the Lord, but what about the second? That is why God warned the exiles that life would not be rosy forever once they were back home. An enemy would confront them. Yet who is Gog, and where is Magog? Evidently the words *Gog* and *Magog* represent a future king and kingdom. History attests that Antiochus Epiphanes fulfilled the prophecies of Gog and Magog. Fletcher explains how:

> The history of the inter-Biblical period of the Seleucidae adequately fulfills all Ezekiel 38 and 39 requires, as is evident from the following considerations:
> (1) The armies of Gog would come from the north (39:2): Syria was located north of Palestine.
> (2) Gog would attack a "people gathered out of the nations" (38:8) and "Dwelling safely" (38:14). Palestine was resettled after their return from captivity and the Jews enjoyed a large measure of peace and prosperity.
> (3) The armies would be large (38:15,16). In the wars of the Macabees [sic Maccabees], the Jews were constantly opposed by numerically superior forces. With 10,000 men Judas Maccabeus confronted the

Syrians with 60,000 infantry and 5,000 calvary [sic cavalry], and was victorious.

(4) History records that Antiochus Epiphanes sent a huge force against Judea under three generals, and so sure were they of victory that Grecian merchants were already in the camp in order to buy up the Jewish soldier-captives as slaves (38:13).

(5) The Scythians were famous for their skilful use of the horse, bow and arrow: they answer to the descriptions of the prophecy (38:4,5;39:9,19).

(6) History records they took the "silver and gold" from the house of the Lord (38:13).

(7) "Antiochus had an army made up of the very nations here named, and many others. These people had been at variance with one another, and yet in combination against Israel" (Comprehensive Commentary—see Ezek. 38:4-6).

(8) History declares that again and again, as if by a miracle, Jehovah, in answer to prayer, caused the armies of the Maccabees to triumph over the superior forces of Syria under Antiochus (38:21;39:3).

(9) In the miraculous defeats of Antiochus Epiphanes by Judas Maccabeus, the Syrians were obliged to leave thousands of dead on the field of battle, and their wooden weapons of warfare provided firewood for months (39:9-12).[13]

Although this prophecy is primarily about Antiochus Epiphanes, Revelation 20 records a secondary but even more significant fulfillment. This time the mysterious Gog and Magog are the nations in the four corners of the earth. In other words, they are countries outside the scope of recorded Biblical history. Near the end of time, Satan will deceive those nations "to gather them for battle" (Rev. 20:7,8). Like Syria, those antichristian nations will hate believers and will attempt to destroy the Church worldwide. Pray for patient endurance and faithfulness.[14]

3e. God's Plans for the Future, Ezekiel 40-48

573 B.C. (Ezek. 40:1). Daniel was in his thirty-third year and Ezekiel was in his twenty-fifth year of captivity.

In this section God develops three different ideas. His first concern was for the people to build a temple once they had returned from captivity. Then, while describing this physical temple, God looks forward to his spiritual temple, the Church. The picture of the Holy Spirit like an uncrossable river illustrates how God will build his Church. Finally, this vision leads to a glimpse of the new heaven and new earth.

> *"Now let them put away from me their prostitution and the lifeless idols of their kings, and I will live among them forever. Son of man, describe the temple to the people of Israel, that they may be ashamed of their sins. Let them consider the plan, and if they are ashamed of all they have done, make known to them the design of the temple—its arrangement, its exits and entrances—its whole design and all its regulations and laws. Write these down before them so that they may be faithful to its design and follow all its regulations"* (Ezek. 43:9-11).

One day God took Ezekiel, in a vision, to the land of Israel and set him on a very high mountain. There the Lord encouraged Ezekiel to reveal the plan for a new temple to the people, if they would forsake their idols and repent of their sins. It is not surprising to find God instructing Ezekiel on the division of the Promised Land or on the physical attributes of the temple. He did exactly the same thing for Moses. Likewise, David received instructions on how to build the temple that Solomon eventually built. Now a new generation needed to be taught the proper way to worship. God has

> God has always been very particular about how and where his people should worship him.

always been very particular about how and where his people should worship him. The plans that the Lord had for his people and for the Promised Land must have been very reassuring to those captives.

> *"This is what the Sovereign LORD says: No foreigner uncircumcised in heart and flesh is to enter my sanctuary, not even the foreigners who live among the Israelites"* (Ezek. 44:9).

God also looks ahead to his spiritual temple, the Church. Most Israelites were concerned only with the outward rituals of religion. They thought that they were pleasing to God as long as they were circumcised in the flesh. The Lord, however, attached more importance on a proper heart attitude. Only those who were circumcised in the heart by the Holy Spirit would be welcome in God's spiritual sanctuary, the Church. True fellowship between God and his people involves not only an outward obedience but also an inner love.

> *The man brought me back to the entrance of the temple, and I saw water coming out from under the threshold of the temple towards the east (for the temple faced east). The water was coming down from under the south side of the temple, south of the altar. He then brought me out through the north gate and led me round the outside to the outer gate facing east, and the water was flowing from the south side. As the man went eastward with a measuring line in his hand, he measured off a thousand cubits and then led me through water that was ankle-deep. He measured off another thousand cubits and led me through water that was knee-deep. He measured off another thousand and led me through water that was up to the waist. He measured off another thousand, but now it was a river that I could not cross, because the water had risen and was deep enough to swim in—a river that no one could cross* (Ezek. 47:1-5).

Ezekiel must have thought, "What is going on, Lord? Where is all this water coming from? There was never an underground stream in Solomon's temple."

Obviously, this is not ordinary water. In fact, the New Testament teaches that water is a symbol of the Holy Spirit. John writes:

> *On the last and greatest day of the Feast, Jesus stood and said in a loud voice, "If anyone is thirsty, let him come to me and drink. Whoever believes in me, as the Scripture has said, streams of living water will flow from within him." By this he meant the Spirit, whom those who believed in him were later to receive. Up to that time the Spirit had not been given, since Jesus had not yet been glorified* (John 7:37-39).

Jesus offered to quench the spiritual thirst of anyone who would ask. He also promised that streams of living water would flow from believers. Did he mean that he could not satisfy their needs until he had been glorified? In other words, did his listeners have to wait until after his death, resurrection, and triumphant return to heaven to have their sins forgiven and receive the gift of the Holy Spirit? What does it mean, "up to that time the Spirit had not been given"? How could Ezekiel plead with his audience to repent and receive the indwelling of the Holy Spirit if he had not been given?[15] Preceding the creation of the world, God the Father, Son, and Holy Spirit had agreed what part each would play to accomplish our salvation. Evidently, the Holy Spirit could not begin his special task until Jesus had completed his.

Before Pentecost, the Holy Spirit was like a dripping tap. He dwelt in the prophets and worked through them, but not much happened. How frustrated Moses, Jeremiah, Ezekiel, and all of the other prophets must have been! They pleaded over and over again, "Repent!" Very few people listened to their message. Even the joyful exiles did not have a lasting influence on their children. Because they feared their neighbours, they were also slow to build the temple. Before Pentecost God allowed Satan to have a greater influence in the world than the Holy Spirit had. Afterwards the roles were reversed. The tap burst. At that point the full power of the Holy Spirit was unleashed into the world. After God rescued the Israelites from Egypt and from Babylon, knowledge of God's mighty power spread throughout the earth. In contrast, after Pentecost love of the Lord quickly filled many hearts. The first believers in the early Church eagerly taught the good news of salvation from sin through Jesus. Because they travelled all over the Roman Empire, today there are believers throughout the entire world.

> Before Pentecost God allowed Satan to have a greater influence in the world than the Holy Spirit had.

Ezekiel saw a tiny stream flow from under the temple and gradually grow until it became an uncrossable river. The New Testament confirms that this is exactly what happened. Mauro points out that the old dispensation was centred in the temple. "Therefore, it was fitting that the new dispensation should start at that place, and move out thence into the world which it was to overspread."[16] Moreover he writes:

> Luke records the Lord's commandment to His disciples to tarry in the city of Jerusalem until they should be endued with power from on high, Luke 24:49. The brief record of this verse does not state whether or not the Lord designated any particular place in Jerusalem where they were to await the promised enduement; but the further record given in verses 52, 53 of *what they did in obedience to the Lord's commands*, supplies this information. For we read that "they worshipped Him and returned to Jerusalem with great joy, and were *continually in the Temple* praising and blessing God" (Luke 24:52,53).[17]

On the day of Pentecost, a group of 120 believers (Acts 1:15) had probably participated in the early morning service to celebrate the Feast of Harvest. According to Mauro, "This service being concluded, they would naturally be 'sitting' in their customary place; and then it was that 'suddenly' out of heaven came that sound 'as of a rushing, mighty wind.'"[18]

After Peter's sermon about 3000 more believed, were filled with the Holy Spirit, and joined the Church. At Pentecost the living water of the Holy Spirit began to flow into believers with great power. As time passed, the power of the Holy Spirit would continue to pour into even more people until eventually the entire world would marvel. From then until the present day, the Holy Spirit maintains his mission to flood believers with God's power. Surely he has become like an uncrossable river! Through the Holy Spirit, God continues to build his Church, the spiritual temple.

> At Pentecost the living water of the Holy Spirit began to flow into believers with great power.

Furthermore, this section also looks ahead to the new heaven and new earth. Ezekiel saw fruit trees growing on both banks of the river. "Their fruit will serve for food and their leaves for healing" (Ezek. 47:12). Likewise in the new heaven, "on each side of the river stood the tree of life...And the leaves of the tree are for the healing of the nations" (Rev. 22:2). In addition, aliens are to live among the native-born Israelites and to inherit land (Ezek. 47:21-23). There is no difference between Jew and Gentile in the Church, and both will receive an inheritance in the new earth. Ezekiel ends with a vision of the city of God similar to the one in Revelation 21. Thus this section begins with a description of a physical temple, alludes to the spiritual temple, the Church, and ends with a vision of the new heaven and new earth.

4. Daniel

Date of ministry: 605-536 B.C. [19] *He finished prophesying 2 years after the edict of Cyrus and 361 years before Antiochus Epiphanes began to reign.*

4a. The King of Kings, Daniel 2, 603 B.C.

In 605 B.C. Nebuchadnezzar had besieged Jerusalem and had carried Daniel and some others from the royal family off to Babylon. [20] On their arrival Nebuchadnezzar ordered the chief of his court officials to set apart some of the captives. They must be "young men without any physical defect, handsome, showing aptitude for every kind of learning, well informed, quick to understand, and qualified to serve in the king's palace" (Dan. 1:4). Daniel and his friends Shadrach, Meshach, and Abednego were chosen to become wise counsellors for the king.

Two years later Nebuchadnezzar had trouble sleeping. The next day he ordered the magicians, enchanters, sorcerers, and astrologers to tell him his dream and then explain what it meant. Daniel and his friends were not there. When the king threatened to kill those present if they did not co-operate, they cried, "There is not a man on earth who can do what the king asks! No king, however great and mighty, has ever asked such a thing of any magician or enchanter or astrologer. What the king asks is too difficult. No one can reveal it to the king except the gods, and they do not live among men" (Dan. 2:10,11).

The king furiously ordered the execution of all the wise men, including Daniel and his friends. Upon hearing what had happened, Daniel immediately went to Nebuchadnezzar and asked for time to figure out the dream and its meaning. Shadrach, Meshach, and Abednego prayed with Daniel for mercy from God so that they would not be executed. During the night God revealed the dream and its interpretation to Daniel. The next morning, after thanking God for revealing the dream, Daniel approached the king. He explained to him that only the God of heaven is able to solve such a mystery. Then Daniel said:

"You looked, O king, and there before you stood a large statue—an enormous, dazzling statue, awesome in appearance. The head of the statue was made of pure gold, its chest and arms of silver, its belly and thighs of bronze, its legs of iron, its feet partly of iron and partly of baked clay. While you were watching, a rock was cut out, but not by human hands. It struck the statue on its feet of iron and clay and smashed them. Then the iron, the clay, the bronze, the silver and the gold were broken to pieces at the same time and became like chaff on a threshing floor in the summer. The wind swept them away without leaving a trace. But the rock that struck the statue became a huge mountain and filled the whole earth" (Dan. 2:31-35).

Daniel explained to Nebuchadnezzar that his kingdom was the first of four world empires. During the time of the fourth empire, God would set up a kingdom that would never be destroyed. "It will crush all those kingdoms and bring them to an end, but it will itself endure forever" (Dan. 2:44). It is interesting that God revealed his plans to a heathen emperor. The Lord wanted Nebuchadnezzar to realize that man-made empires only exist by God's permission. Moreover, every worldly kingdom has an end. Only the kingdom of God is eternal.

> Moreover, every worldly kingdom has an end. Only the kingdom of God is eternal.

Nebuchadnezzar thought that he was the king of kings. Daniel, however, told him, "The God of heaven has given you dominion and power and might and glory" (Dan. 2:37).

The Lord would work out his plan of salvation through those four kingdoms, which history has revealed to be Babylon, Medo-Persia, Greece, and Rome. Did the Messiah set up his kingdom during the time of the fourth world empire? Can we count on God to tell the truth? When Jesus walked through Galilee, he proclaimed, "The time has come...The kingdom of

God is near. Repent and believe the good news!" (Mark 1:15).

Did Jesus tell the truth when he announced that the kingdom would soon appear? God promised that he would set up a kingdom during the time of the Roman Empire, and Jesus announced that he was about to set up a kingdom. Because it never happened in the physical realm, we must examine the spiritual realm before dismissing God as an untrustworthy liar. Jesus often taught his disciples what the kingdom of heaven was like. Near the end of his time on earth, Jesus was pleased at Peter's confession that he was the promised Messiah. Immediately Jesus linked the Church with the kingdom of heaven. He promised Peter that nothing would prevent the growth of the Church. As the leader of the Church, Peter would hold the keys to the kingdom of heaven (Matt. 16:18-19).[21]

4b. The Kingdom of Light and the Kingdom of Darkness, Daniel 7

Daniel was deeply troubled by his dreams, probably because he found out that God's people would suffer tribulation after they were back in the Promised Land. God, however, intended to comfort him with the knowledge that the persecution would be short-lived. In his dream Daniel saw the following three great political beasts: a lion with the wings of an eagle, representing Babylon; a bear with three ribs sticking out of its mouth, representing Medo-Persia; and a leopard with four wings and four heads, representing Greece. As frightening and formidable as these three evil beasts were, God worked out his plan of salvation through them. In the city of Babylon the people of Judah were able to retain their national identity. Although forced to live in captivity, they maintained their uniqueness by living as an ethnic group. After Cyrus conquered Babylon, he encouraged the people of Judah and any other Israelite to repopulate the Promised Land. Finally, Alexander the Great left Palestine a legacy of the Greek language. Because of this, the Septuagint (the Jewish Old Testament) and the New Testament were written in Greek. In Jesus' day most people understood Greek. Therefore the gospel was easily spread by word of mouth to many different countries. God will complete his plan of salvation in spite of Satan's best efforts to thwart him.

After the death of Alexander the Great in 323 B.C., the vast Greek Empire was divided up among his generals. Ptolemaeus gained dominion over Egypt and Palestine until 311 B.C. when Antigonus of Phrygia seized control of Palestine. Meanwhile, in 321 B.C., the son of the general Antiochus, Seleucus Nicator, began to rule Babylon. For 22 years Alexander's generals fought among themselves for power over the various regions of the empire. Then, at the battle of Ipsus in 301 B.C., Antigonus died. Afterwards Alexander's empire was divided into four main kingdoms. That is why the leopard has four heads (Dan. 7:6). Seleucus obtained Syria, Cappadocia, Mesopotamia, and Armenia, while Ptolemaeus regained Palestine.[22] For the next 100 years, the Seleucid kings of Syria coveted Palestine, mainly because it contained an important trade route, but they were unsuccessful in wresting the region from the Ptolemaic kings of Egypt. Seleucus and his successors were also very annoyed that Ptolemaeus gained a reward from the battle of Ipsus although he had showed up too late to fight.[23]

> *"After that, in my vision at night I looked, and there before me was a fourth beast—terrifying and frightening and very powerful. It had large iron teeth; it crushed and devoured its victims and trampled underfoot whatever was left. It was different from all the former beasts, and it had ten horns. While I was thinking about the horns, there before me was another horn, a little one, which came up among them; and three of the first horns were uprooted before it. This horn had eyes like the eyes of a man and a mouth that spoke boastfully"* (Dan. 7:7,8).

Nebuchadnezzar's dream in Daniel 2 proclaimed the arrival of God's eternal kingdom. In contrast, Daniel's dream portrayed the arrival of the little horn whose kingdom would be the antithesis of God's. This king would have "a mouth that spoke boastfully." He would speak despicably against God, oppress the saints, and try to change God's Law (Dan. 7:25). History records that the next kingdom to rule Judea after the Ptolemaic Empire was the Seleucid Empire (198 B.C.-142 B.C.). It is worthwhile noting that both of these empires were essentially a continuation of the Greek Empire. At first the reign of the Ptolemies was not any different than the rule of Alexander the Great. Most of the time the Jews enjoyed peace and prosperity. Then in 198 B.C., because of Ptolemaic persecution, the Jews assisted Antiochus III, the Seleucid king, in expelling the Ptolemies from Palestine. Therefore the fourth beast, the Seleucid Empire, gained control over the reconstituted Israel.[24]

Antiochus Epiphanes was the Seleucid king who deliberately tried to wipe out Judaism and force the Jews to worship Greek gods. In the New Testament a similar person is revealed—the man of lawlessness. "He will oppose and will exalt himself over everything that is called God or is worshiped, so that he sets himself up in God's temple, proclaiming himself to be God" (2 Thess. 2:4). Likewise, the political beast of Revelation will utter proud words and blasphemies and make war with the saints (Rev. 13:5-7). While the primary fulfillment of Daniel 7 is the reign of terror caused by Antiochus Epiphanes, the man of sin will possess the same characteristics. The culmination of such evil will be seen at the end of the world in the political beast. Because the kingdom of Satan is always busy actively trying to destroy the kingdom of God, believers must endure severe persecution at times.

The political beast in Revelation 13 contains elements of the first three beasts from Daniel's dream. John writes, "The beast I saw resembled a leopard, but had feet like those of a bear and a mouth like that of a lion" (Rev. 13:2). The most harmful assault that Satan can make against God and his people will represent the combined characteristics of the leopard, bear, and lion attacking simultaneously. The worst that the head of such a government can do is enslave or kill the saints. Satan cannot destroy a believer's citizenship in the kingdom of God or keep one from experiencing the joys of heaven.

> *"As I looked, thrones were set in place, and the Ancient of Days took his seat. His clothing was as white as snow; the hair of his head was white like wool. His throne was flaming with fire, and its wheels were all ablaze. A river of fire was flowing, coming out from before him. Thousands upon thousands attended him; ten thousand times ten thousand stood before him. The court was seated, and the books were opened"* (Dan. 7:9,10).

Daniel was privileged to behold the throne room of heaven. All the boastful words of the little horn, the emissary of Satan, were powerless against the authority of the Ancient of Days. "I kept looking until the beast was slain and its body destroyed and thrown into the blazing fire" (Dan. 7:11). Similarly, at the end of time, "the beast was captured, and with him the false prophet…The two of them were thrown alive into the fiery lake of burning sulfur" (Rev. 19:20). Thus both Antiochus Epiphanes and Antichrist end up in the Lake of Fire. True, the little horn did receive power to persecute the saints "for a time, times and half a time" (Dan. 7:25). Satan, however, is limited not only in his type of kingdom but also in its duration. The little horn will only be a despot for a short time. Charles. D. Alexander ponders:

> The period denoted "time, times and a half" must be regarded not as a period measurable by man, but as hidden in the divine counsel…It was never the intention of Almighty God who has reserved to

Himself the secrets of the times and seasons (Acts 1.7), to allow man to anticipate the time schedule which omnipotent wisdom has decreed, for this would invade the region of faith. It is enough that the great Architect of Time has placed all things within His own power, and the calendar is no substitute for humble adoring faith. The message...is that the trials and tribulations of the people of God down the ages have an end, just as they had a beginning.[25]

"In my vision at night I looked, and there before me was one like a son of man, coming with the clouds of heaven. He approached the Ancient of Days and was led into his presence. He was given authority, glory and sovereign power; all peoples, nations and men of every language worshiped him. His dominion is an everlasting dominion that will not pass away, and his kingdom is one that will never be destroyed" (Dan. 7:13,14).

Through other prophets the Lord had prepared his people for the birth, death, and resurrection of the promised Seed. How appropriate it is for God to give us a vision of the coronation of the King! What a triumphant moment when the Son of Man approached the Ancient of Days to receive the kingdom! At that time the Lord Jesus was given authority over "all peoples, nations and men of every language." His rule would be universal and everlasting. In contrast, every empire of Satan is temporary and is eventually destroyed. Many years later John had a vision of the same ceremony. By what right did the Lamb of God open the scroll and receive all authority in heaven and in earth? The four living creatures and the twenty-four elders sang, "You are worthy to take the scroll and to open its seals, because you were slain, and with your blood you purchased men for God from every tribe and language and people and nation. You have made them to be a kingdom and priests to serve our God, and they will reign on the earth" (Rev. 5:9,10). When Jesus ascended to the Father, he went to receive the glory and honour due him. By his death and resurrection he received the right to rule. What a day of rejoicing that must have been in heaven!

4c. Antiochus Epiphanes

Reign of Antiochus, king of the Seleucid Empire: 175-164 B.C.[26]

"A stern-faced king, a master of intrigue, will arise. He will become very strong, but not by his own power. He will cause astounding devastation and will succeed in whatever he does. He will destroy the mighty men and the holy people. He will cause deceit to prosper, and he will consider himself superior. When they feel secure, he will destroy many and take his stand against the Prince of princes. Yet he will be destroyed, but not by human power" (Dan. 8:23-25).

"His armed forces will rise up to desecrate the temple fortress and will abolish the daily sacrifice. Then they will set up the abomination that causes desolation" (Dan. 11:31).

Through Daniel, God names two future world kingdoms, Medo-Persia and Greece (Dan. 8:20,21). Afterwards the kingdom of Greece will split into four and "a stern-faced king, a master of intrigue, will arise." History reveals that this ruler was Antiochus Epiphanes. Moreover, Daniel 11 is remarkable because it reveals future conflicts and intrigues—particularly those of Syria and Egypt. In it the history of Antiochus Epiphanes is described in detail. He was a vile person who invaded Israel when the people felt safe (Dan. 11:21). He blasphemed the only true God and exalted himself

> He blasphemed the only true God and exalted himself above all gods.

above all gods. Some would give in to his corruption, while others who trusted the Lord would resist him (Dan 11:32). God is truly all-knowing.

The Lord's primary purpose was to warn the generation that would be living at the time of Antiochus Epiphanes. The phrase *the abomination that causes desolation* is repeated in the New Testament, however. "So when you see standing in the holy place 'the abomination that causes desolation,' spoken of through the prophet Daniel—let the reader understand—then let those who are in Judea flee to the mountains" (Matt. 24:15,16). Likewise, "When you see 'the abomination that causes desolation' standing where it does not belong—let the reader understand—then let those who are in Judea flee to the mountains" (Mark 13:14). These verses are a clue that a similar desecration to the temple would occur again in history. When the Roman legion under Titus sacked Jerusalem in A.D. 70,[27] God fulfilled this prophecy.

4d. The Birth Announcement of the Promised Seed

"Seventy 'sevens' are decreed for your people and your holy city to finish transgression, to put an end to sin, to atone for wickedness, to bring in everlasting righteousness, to seal up vision and prophecy and to anoint the most holy. Know and understand this: From the issuing of the decree to restore and rebuild Jerusalem until the Anointed One, the ruler, comes, there will be seven 'sevens,' and sixty-two 'sevens.' It will be rebuilt with streets and a trench, but in times of trouble. After the sixty-two 'sevens,' the Anointed One will be cut off and will have nothing" (Dan. 9:24-26).

After reading the book of Jeremiah, Daniel realized that the seventy years of captivity were drawing to a close. Fasting in sackcloth and ashes, he admitted to the Lord, "All Israel has transgressed your law and turned away, refusing to obey you" (Dan. 9:11). Daniel knew that God was just in punishing

Israel, but he still pleaded with the Lord to forgive the sins of his people:

> *"Give ear, O God, and hear; open your eyes and see the desolation of the city that bears your Name. We do not make requests of you because we are righteous, but because of your great mercy. O Lord, listen! O Lord, forgive! O Lord, hear and act! For your sake, O my God, do not delay, because your city and your people bear your Name"* (Dan. 9:18,19).

While Daniel was praying, the angel Gabriel appeared to him. God loved Daniel and wanted him to understand what would happen in the future. The restoration of Israel was only one step towards the fulfillment of God's plan of salvation. The promised Seed would put an end to sin, make atonement for wickedness, and usher in everlasting righteousness. Expectant parents know the approximate due date for the birth of their child. Similarly, God gave Israel the due date for the birth of his Son. The countdown to the birth would begin with the decree allowing the Israelites to restore and rebuild Jerusalem. The ruler would appear 483 years later.

> Expectant parents know the approximate due date for the birth of their child.

Scholars disagree about which decree God meant. In 538 B.C. Cyrus decreed that anyone who wanted to return to Jerusalem to build the temple of God was allowed to go (Ezra 1:1). Then in 458 B.C. Artaxerxes decreed that Ezra could go to teach the people the Law of God.[28] Finally, in 445 B.C., Artaxerxes decreed that Nehemiah could go to build the walls of the city of Jerusalem. [28] This was accomplished in fifty-two days (Neh. 6:15). Differences of opinion occur, because there are two problems. The Jewish calendar differs from the Roman calendar, and nobody knows the exact date of Jesus' birth. The point is that Jesus was born at the appointed time. If Jesus, or someone else living at that time, was not the Messiah, then God has failed to keep his promise. Because the Lord told Daniel when to expect the promised Seed, Henry rightly concludes that the time for his birth is long past. Knowing the birthdate encouraged believers in Jesus' day to wait expectantly. It may have been the reason for so many people flocking to Jerusalem. Henry also points out that this prophecy condemns non-believers who continue to wait for the Messiah's arrival. "For reckon these seventy weeks from which of the commandments to build Jerusalem we please, it is certain that they are expired above 1500 years ago." [29]

The seventy sevens or 490 years are divided into three sections. During the first 49 years the temple would be rebuilt and Jerusalem would be restored. For the next 434 years God would be silent, because He did not have anything new to say. He expected that Israel would wait and watch for the birth of his Son.

The last seven years of this prophecy concern the Messiah's purpose on earth. Sometime after the 483 years, "the Anointed One will be cut off" (Dan. 9:26). In other words, he would die. This is how the promised Seed would complete his part of God's plan to obtain our salvation. By dying and rising again, the Saviour would finish six important tasks in the spiritual realm.

> By dying and rising again, the Saviour would finish six important tasks in the spiritual realm.

The Messiah would *finish transgression*. *Finish* is the Hebrew word *kala*, meaning "to shut, restrain, finish."[30] *Transgression* is the Hebrew word *pesha*, meaning "transgression, rebellion."[31] Ever since the rebellion of Adam and Eve in the Garden of Eden, Satan has been busy building his own kingdom on earth. Until the time of Christ most people remained rebellious to their Creator. Relatively few actually loved God or desired to fellowship with him. Because of Jesus' death and resurrection, God is able to contain the rebellion. As time passes many more people are turning to the Lord.

Moreover, faith in the only true God is no longer limited to one nation. Paul writes, "All over the world this gospel is bearing fruit and growing, just as it has been doing among you since the day you heard it" (Col. 1:6). People from many different countries are hearing the good news of salvation in Christ and want to have fellowship restored with their Creator. The result is an increase in the proportion of believers to non-believers. The kingdom of God is gaining power while the kingdom of Satan is weakening.

The Messiah would *put an end to sin*. "But now he has appeared once for all at the end of the ages to do away with sin by the sacrifice of himself...so Christ was sacrificed once to take away the sins of many people" (Heb. 9:26-28). In the Old Testament the priests continually sacrificed animals in order to ask God to forgive their sins. Because of Jesus' one sacrifice, God will forever pardon anyone who asks for forgiveness. Through the Messiah, God would solve the problem of sin, which has plagued the world ever since Adam and Eve rebelled.

The Messiah would *atone for wickedness*. John writes, "He [Jesus] is the atoning sacrifice for our sins, and not only for ours but also for the sins of the whole world" (1 John 2:2). Jesus substituted himself for us and took the punishment that we deserve. Whoever believes that Jesus paid the penalty for his or her own sins is reconciled to God. That person is no longer God's enemy. This is how God would solve the problem of sin. Jesus is the Peacemaker, providing a way for everyone in the world to have peace with God, not just the people of Israel.

The Messiah would *bring in everlasting righteousness*. Paul writes, "But now a righteousness from God, apart from the law, has been made known, to which the Law and the Prophets testify. This righteousness from God comes through faith in Jesus Christ to all who believe" (Rom. 3:21,22). When God looks at believers, he only sees the righteousness of his Son. He does not require any more punishment for their sins, because Jesus has already paid the penalty—once and for always. Therefore by faith believers are assured everlasting life. "Whoever believes in the Son has eternal life" (John 3:36).

The Messiah would *seal up vision and prophecy*. Jesus says, "Do not think that I have come to abolish the Law or the Prophets; I have not come to abolish them but to fulfill them" (Matt. 5:17). After his resurrection, Jesus was walking along the road to Emmaus with two sad and distraught believers. Not recognizing him, they could not believe that this stranger was ignorant of the recent crucifixion of their Master. Finally he said, "How foolish you are, and how slow of heart to believe all that the prophets have spoken! Did not the Christ have to suffer these things and then enter his glory?" (Luke 24:25,26). Then Jesus showed them that Moses and the prophets had foretold the Messiah's death. He explained that Jesus had accomplished the requirements of those prophecies. Thus he confirmed that those prophecies were true.

The Messiah would *anoint the most holy*. *Anoint* is the Hebrew word *mashach*, meaning "to smear, anoint."[32] When the tabernacle was first set up, Moses anointed it and everything in it with oil to consecrate it for God's service (Ex. 40:9). Afterwards the glory of the Lord filled the tabernacle, and God dwelt in the most holy place (Ex. 40:35). Likewise, believers are anointed with the Holy Spirit and set apart for God's service. Paul states, "He anointed us, set his seal of ownership on us, and put his Spirit in our hearts as a deposit, guaranteeing what is to come" (2 Cor. 1:21,22). "Therefore, I urge you, brothers, in view of God's mercy, to offer your bodies as living sacrifices, holy and pleasing to God" (Rom. 12:1). Such a person will be "useful to the Master and prepared to do any good work" (2 Tim. 2:21). God would increase his influence in the world by mobilizing a mighty army filled with the Holy Spirit. These believers would do his bidding eagerly. This most holy army is the Church.

> *"The people of the ruler who will come will destroy the city and the sanctuary. The end will come like a flood:*

War will continue until the end, and desolations have been decreed. He will confirm a covenant with many for one 'seven.' In the middle of the 'seven' he will put an end to sacrifice and offering. And on a wing of the temple he will set up an abomination that causes desolation, until the end that is decreed is poured out on him" (Dan. 9:26,27).

In these verses God has intertwined two promises, the destruction of Jerusalem and the sacrificial death of the Messiah. Daniel must have been mystified. Perhaps he thought, "The Anointed One is supposed to bring peace and honour to Israel. How can this be?"

Halfway through the last week, "he will put an end to sacrifice and offering." For three and one-half years Jesus preached the good news of the coming kingdom throughout Judea and Galilee. Afterwards at Calvary he presented himself as the perfect sacrifice to God, "because it is impossible for the blood of bulls and goats to take away sins" (Heb. 10:4). By shedding his blood Jesus paid the penalty for sin and satisfied divine justice. Since Calvary, nobody needs to sacrifice animals. To do so is an insult to the forgiving power of God and to the effectiveness of Jesus' sacrifice.

> Since Calvary, nobody needs to sacrifice animals. To do so is an insult to the forgiving power of God and to the effectiveness of Jesus' sacrifice.

Sadly, some Jewish people would continue to follow the sacrifices of Moses and would reject the perfect sacrifice of Jesus. That is why God would make sure that they were unable to continue with this affront to his plan of salvation. The temple must be destroyed. By rejecting the Messiah during those seven years, the non-believing Jews of that generation sealed their own fate. It is only by the grace of God that they had forty more years after the resurrection to repent before the destruction of Jerusalem. In A. R. Fausset's words:

The closing one week (or seven years) includes the 3 1/2 years of Jesus' own preaching to the Jews and 3 1/2 of the apostles' preaching to the Jews only; then the persecution as to Stephen drove the evangelists from Jerusalem to Samaria...Jerusalem was not actually destroyed till A.D. 70 but virtually and theocratically was "dead" A.D. 33, 3 1/2 years after Christ's death, having failed to use that respite of grace...*in the day* that Adam *sinned* he *died*, though his actual death was long subsequent.[33]

Daniel did not understand everything that he had heard. Nevertheless he must have realized the implications of what God had revealed to him. After the Israelites returned from captivity to the Promised Land, they would have to wait a very long time before the Messiah's birth. They must also expect persecution sometime in the future. Daniel asked the angel, "My lord, what will the outcome of all this be?" (Dan. 12:8).

The angel told him that those who remained faithful until the persecution was over would be blessed, and it would not last longer than 1290 days (Dan. 12:11,12). Some may attempt to count the days and hold God accountable, just as Jonah did at Nineveh. The Lord, however, has the right to choose the exact time to end the tribulation. Therefore he uses the expression, "for a time, times and half a time" (Dan. 7:25; 12:7; Rev. 12:14). The angel closed by saying, "As for you, go your way till the end. You will rest, and then at the end of the days you will rise to receive your allotted inheritance" (Dan. 12:13).

Although confused, Daniel believed that God keeps his promises. The Messiah would be born at the appointed time; his kingdom would be eternal; and there would be no more sin. Daniel himself would come back to life sometime in the future. These promises are the hope of every believer.

Points to Ponder

1. Like the Edomites, no one can hide from God.
2. God expects us, like the people of Judah, to be flexible and contented when our circumstances change throughout our life.
3. God knows each person intimately, including the smallest detail of our lives. This should be comforting for a believer but unnerving for a non-believer.
4. Like Ezekiel, we need the Holy Spirit working in our hearts in order to understand spiritual realities.
5. Through Daniel, God outlines his solution to the problem of sin. The result will be an eternal kingdom free of sin, and everlasting judgment for Satan and his followers.

Chapter Ten

A Second Chance for Israel

1. The Edict of Cyrus

*God is carrying out his plan of salvation when he restores the Israelites to the Promised Land.
Reign of Cyrus, king of Persia: 558-529 B.C.[1]*

AFTER twenty-five years in northern Ontario, Barry sadly left his family and boarded a bus for Toronto and a new job. Meanwhile Philip and I remained in North Bay to sell the house. Quite often we drove down to my mother-in-law's house with a station wagon full of boxes. She very kindly allowed us to fill up one room and then another and another. It was six months before Barry and I relocated to our own house in Innisfil. We felt like the Israelites returning to the Promised Land, although our move was bittersweet.

I wonder how God's people reacted in 538 B.C. when Cyrus succeeded in assimilating the Babylonian Empire into his kingdom.[2] It is amazing that in the first year of his reign over Babylon this heathen king desired to show favour to a small group of people called Israelites. Cyrus announced:

> "The LORD, the God of heaven, has given me all the kingdoms of the earth and he has appointed me to build a temple for him at Jerusalem in Judah. Anyone of his people among you—may his God be with him, and let him go up to Jerusalem in Judah and build the temple of the

Lord, the God of Israel, the God who is in Jerusalem" (Ezra 1:2,3).

Many Israelites gladly prepared for their journey back home. Their neighbours gave them gifts of gold, silver, livestock, and money. Zerubbabel, the political leader descended from David, and the high priest, Joshua, led 42,358 Israelites and 7,337 servants back to the Promised Land (Ezra 2:64,65). As they walked, they laughed and sang songs of joy. They felt as if they were dreaming. They praised God by saying, "The Lord has done great things for us, and we are filled with joy" (Ps. 126:3).

Soon the people enthusiastically settled in their own towns. Some gladly donated freewill offerings to help rebuild the temple. Then seven months later everyone gathered at Jerusalem to celebrate the Feast of Tabernacles. Although afraid of trouble from their neighbours, they offered the morning and evening sacrifices as prescribed in the Law of Moses. The people eagerly began worshipping God, even though the foundation of the temple was not yet laid. Twice God had kept his promise and had rescued Israel from foreign domination—first Egypt, and then Babylon. Twice the nations were compelled to acknowledge the mighty power of the God of Israel. After the exiles had left Babylon, other people exclaimed, "The Lord has done great things for them" (Ps. 126:2).

> Returning the Israelites to the Promised Land was a necessary step in God's plan of salvation.

The return of the exiles to the Promised Land was an excellent witness of God's power. It was also proof that God always tells the truth and always keeps his promises. Returning the Israelites to the Promised Land was a necessary step in God's plan of salvation. If he is able to restore a nation scattered throughout the Medo-Persian Empire, then he can certainly carry out his plan in the spiritual realm. The promised Seed needed a family and a country in which to be born. Therefore God chose Bethlehem of Judea to be Jesus' birthplace. The promised Seed had to grow up in a country where God's Law was acknowledged and where God was worshipped.

Two years later when the builders had finished laying the foundation of the temple, the priests blew trumpets, and the Levites clanged the cymbals. "With praise and thanksgiving they sang to the LORD: 'He is good; his love to Israel endures forever'" (Ezra 3:11).

At first everyone shouted joyfully, until those who remembered Solomon's temple cried out in sorrow. They likely felt as if this building could not possibly replace the original temple because it would not be as big or beautiful. "No one could distinguish the sound of the shouts of joy from the sound of weeping, because the people made so much noise. And the sound was heard far away" (Ezra 3:13). Meanwhile their neighbours tried to discourage the building of the temple by making the people afraid. "They hired counselors to work against them and frustrate their plans" (Ezra 4:5). Thus their enemies effectively stopped the work for many years.

2. HAGGAI: BUILDING THE TEMPLE

Date written: 520 B.C.[3] He prophesied 18 years after the edict of Cyrus. Reign of Darius, king of Persia: 521-485 B.C.[2]

Although the people knew that the Lord wanted them to build the temple, they kept procrastinating. They thought, "The time has not yet come for the LORD's house to be built" (Haggai 1:2).

Through Haggai, God rebuked them:

> *"Give careful thought to your ways. You have planted much, but have harvested little. You eat, but never have enough. You drink, but never have your fill. You put on clothes, but are not warm. You earn wages, only to put them in a purse with holes in it...Give careful thought*

to your ways. Go up into the mountains and bring down timber and build the house, so that I may take pleasure in it and be honored...You expected much, but see, it turned out to be little. What you brought home, I blew away. Why?...Because of my house, which remains a ruin, while each of you is busy with his own house" (Haggai 1:5-9).

Then the governor Zerubbabel, the high priest Joshua, and all of the people listened to Haggai, obeyed God, and began to build the temple.

"This is what the LORD *Almighty says: 'In a little while I will once more shake the heavens and the earth, the sea and the dry land. I will shake all nations, and the desired of all nations will come, and I will fill this house with glory,' says the* LORD *Almighty. 'The silver is mine and the gold is mine,' declares the* LORD *Almighty. 'The glory of this present house will be greater than the glory of the former house,' says the* LORD *Almighty. 'And in this place I will grant peace,' declares the* LORD *Almighty"* (Haggai 2:6-9).

Although Zerubbabel's temple would not be as ornate as Solomon's, it was destined for the greatest honour of all.

The promised Seed, the Saviour, is *the desired of all nations*. Only he can crush the power of Satan and restore fellowship between God and people. Although Zerubbabel's temple would not be as ornate as Solomon's, it was destined for the greatest honour of all. The glorious promised Seed would walk through its doors. In that place many would find peace with God by trusting in Jesus as their Saviour.

3. Zechariah

Chapters 1-8 written: about 520-518 B.C. Chapters 9-14 written: about 480 B.C.[4] He began to prophesy 18 years after the edict of Cyrus. He finished his ministry 305 years before Antiochus Epiphanes began to reign.

3a. Building the Temple

God raised up Zechariah as well as Haggai to encourage the Israelites to finish building the temple. Through Zechariah, God said, "I will return to Jerusalem with mercy, and there my house will be rebuilt" (Zech. 1:16). The Lord promised to be a protecting wall of fire around the city and to dwell there (Zech. 2:5). They need not fear their enemies because they are "the apple of his eye" (Zech. 2:8).

When Satan wanted to harm the high priest Joshua spiritually, he accused Joshua of wrongdoing. God replied, "The LORD rebuke you, Satan! The LORD, who has chosen Jerusalem, rebuke you! Is not this man a burning stick snatched from the fire?" (Zech. 3:2). Then God told Joshua, "See, I have taken away your sin, and I will put rich garments on you" (Zech. 3:4).

Joshua knew that God had forgiven his sins. Although Jesus had not yet paid the penalty for them, Joshua was no longer guilty in the eyes of the Lord. As a result, God figuratively saw Joshua wearing clean clothes, not dirty ones. The Lord also promised, "I will remove the sin of this land in a single day" (Zech. 3:9). This happened the day that Jesus died on the cross.

Both Zerubbabel and Joshua were chosen by God to build the temple. Zerubbabel was the political leader while Joshua was the spiritual leader. They were like two olive trees planted by God to be his special servants (Zech. 4:12-14). He would make sure that they could accomplish the task of building the temple by protecting them from any opposition. Similarly, the two witnesses in Revelation are described as two olive trees (Rev. 11:4). Like Zerubbabel and Joshua, God will anoint them for a special task—to preach the Scriptures to the last generation living in Jerusalem.

How would Zerubbabel and Joshua accomplish the work? The Lord told Zerubbabel, "Not by might nor by power, but by my Spirit" (Zech. 4:6). In case Zerubbabel might be ashamed of the new temple, the Lord encouraged him, "Who despises the day of small things? Men will rejoice when they see the plumb line in the hand of Zerubbabel" (Zech. 4:10).

Zechariah told Joshua that he and his associates were symbols of future events—the coming Branch (Zech. 3:8). Sometime later three exiles from Babylon arrived with silver and gold for the temple. Instead of using those precious metals as the exiles had intended, the Lord instructed Zechariah to fashion a crown out of them and to "set it on the head of the high priest, Joshua son of Jehozadak" (Zech. 6:11). Then the Lord said, "Here is the man whose name is the Branch, and he will branch out from his place and build the temple of the LORD. It is he who will build the temple of the LORD, and he will be clothed with majesty and will sit and rule on his throne. And he will be a priest on his throne. And there will be a harmony between the two" (Zech. 6:12,13).

No other Israelite priest ever wore a crown in Scripture. Even then Joshua only wore it long enough for God to paint a picture of his Son, the Branch, who would be the Priest King. Jesus taught his disciples, "I am the vine; you are the branches. If a man remains in me and I in him, he will bear much fruit; apart from me you can do nothing" (John 15:5). As the Branch, Jesus is the sole source of everlasting life. The Lord commissioned Joshua to build the physical temple. In contrast, Jesus is busy building a spiritual temple whose blocks are believers. Paul writes, "Don't you know that you yourselves are God's temple and that God's Spirit lives in you?" (1 Cor. 3:16).

518 B.C. (Zech. 7:1)

When the people needed more encouragement to go on with the work, God said, "Let your hands be strong so that the temple may be built" (Zech. 8:9). Through Zechariah, God told them not to be afraid and instructed them, "So now I have determined to do good again to Jerusalem and Judah. Do not be afraid... Speak the truth to each other, and render true and sound judgment in your courts; do not plot evil against your neighbor, and do not love to swear falsely. I hate all this" (Zech. 8:15-17). Looking into the future, God could see himself dwelling in the completed temple while old men and women sat in the streets and children played there (Zech. 8:4-5).

516 B.C. (Ezra 6:15)

The Israelites prospered under the preaching of Haggai and Zechariah so that they finished building the temple. They joyfully dedicated the house of God. "And they installed the priests in their divisions and the Levites in their groups for the service of God at Jerusalem" (Ezra 6:18).

3b.Two Spiritual Realities, Zechariah 5-6

Zechariah was blessed because the Lord revealed two important spiritual realities to him. True, the curse of sin does blanket the whole world, but God is more powerful. In order to encourage Zechariah, God showed him a huge flying scroll with words on it. Zechariah wrote, "This is the curse that is going out over the whole land; for according to what it says on one side, every thief will be banished, and according to what it says on the other, everyone who swears falsely will be banished" (Zech. 5:3). In other words, sinners will be punished.

Then Zechariah saw wickedness personified as a woman in a covered basket and carried off to Babylon. False religion would build a house for wickedness there (Zech. 5:6-11). As long as this world exists, Satan will always have his places of worship, just as God has his. The woman, however, was pushed into the basket, carried to Babylon, and put in place. Similarly, Satan has set bounds defined by God. Although the kingdom of Satan does exist, the Lord is in control. Zechariah

> As long as this world exists, Satan will always have his places of worship, just as God has his.

saw four chariots, representing the four spirits of heaven, leave the presence of God and cover the whole earth (Zech. 6:1-5). Notice the similarity to the four horsemen in Revelation 6. The red, black, white, and dappled chariots are powerful, and God will accomplish his purposes no matter what Satan does. The promised Seed will be born.

3c. The Judgment and Salvation of God, Zechariah 9-14

> *"Though I scatter them among the peoples, yet in distant lands they will remember me. They and their children will survive, and they will return. I will bring them back from Egypt and gather them from Assyria"* (Zech. 10:9,10).

God honoured his promise to provide salvation in the physical realm to those who repented of their sin. Thus in Zechariah's day the Israelites were free to return to the Promised Land. Many, however, chose to remain where they were living. To encourage those who were struggling in Judah, God promised that more of them would return. Some returned from Babylon with Ezra in 458 B.C.[5] He taught them the Law of God so that they would lovingly obey the Lord. Others came home with Nehemiah when he left Babylon to build the walls of Jerusalem in 445 B.C.[5] Unlike the mass exodus from Egypt under Moses, this return was gradual and depended on the individual desires of each person. According to Henry, "Some think that this was literally fulfilled when Ptolemaeus Philadelphus king of Egypt sent 120,000 Jews out of his country into their own land, as was the promise of *gathering them* out of Assyria by Alexander the son of Antiochus Epiphanes."[6]

In Zechariah 9-13, God gives Zechariah a glimpse into the last week of Jesus' life. This week is the climax of God's plan of salvation in the spiritual realm. His Son would die and rise again. Through the death and resurrection of Jesus, the promised Seed would pay the penalty for sin and would restore those who believe to fellowship with God.

> *Rejoice greatly, O Daughter of Zion! Shout, Daughter of Jerusalem! See, your king comes to you, righteous and having salvation, gentle and riding on a donkey, on a colt, the foal of a donkey* (Zech. 9:9).

Five days before the Passover, Jesus sent two of his disciples into Bethphage to borrow a colt on which no one had ever ridden. After the disciples threw their cloaks over the back of the colt, Jesus sat on it. As he rode toward Jerusalem, a crowd gathered to shout, "'Hosanna!' 'Blessed is he who comes in the name of the Lord!' 'Blessed is the coming kingdom of our father David!' 'Hosanna in the highest!'" (Mark 11:9,10). Many people threw cloaks or branches on the road for Jesus to ride over. What a way for the King of kings to claim his kingdom! He rode on a lowly donkey instead of a mighty horse or beautiful chariot. When Jesus entered Jerusalem on that day, he fulfilled this prophecy (John 12:14,15).

> *Therefore the people wander like sheep oppressed for lack of a shepherd* (Zech. 10:2).

For three and one-half years crowds often gathered to hear Jesus speak or watch him heal the sick. Matthew records, "When he saw the crowds, he had compassion on them, because they were harassed and helpless, like sheep without a shepherd" (Matt. 9:36).

> *As for you, because of the blood of my covenant with you, I will free your prisoners from the waterless pit* (Zech. 9:11).

At the last supper, after offering his disciples a cup of wine, Jesus said, "This is my blood of the covenant, which is poured out for many for the forgiveness of sins" (Matt. 26:28). [7] What assurance Zechariah had! The King was coming who would pay the penalty for his sins.

> *"Awake, O sword, against my shepherd, against the man who is close to me!" declares the* Lord *Almighty. "Strike the shepherd, and the sheep will be scattered, and I will turn my hand against the little ones"* (Zech. 13:7).

As they were walking to the Garden of Gethsemane after the last supper, Jesus warned his disciples that they would desert him. Just before he was arrested, Jesus told them, "You will all fall away...for it is written: 'I will strike the shepherd, and the sheep will be scattered'" (Mark 14:27).

Peter was shocked. "Even if all fall away, I will not," he insisted (Mark 14:29). The other disciples agreed with Peter. Yet, when a group of priests and teachers of the Law arrived a little while later to arrest Jesus, all of them ran away.

> *I told them, "If you think it best, give me my pay; but if not, keep it." So they paid me thirty pieces of silver. And the* Lord *said to me, "Throw it to the potter"—the handsome price at which they priced me! So I took the thirty pieces of silver and threw them into the house of the* Lord *to the potter* (Zech. 11:12,13).

Judas Iscariot was thoroughly disgusted when Mary of Bethany poured a vial of very expensive perfume on Jesus' feet six days before the Passover (John 12:1-11). Immediately he approached the chief priests and offered to betray Jesus. In return they promised to pay him thirty pieces of silver. "He consented, and watched for an opportunity to hand Jesus over to them when no crowd was present" (Luke 22:6). Consequently, on the night of the Passover, Judas guided a motley crew into the Garden of Gethsemane. "Judas said, 'Greetings, Rabbi!' and kissed him. Jesus replied, 'Friend, do what you came for.'" (Matt. 26:49,50).

Judas later regretted what he had done, but it was too late. When the priests refused to take back the money, he threw the coins down, left the temple, and hanged himself (Matt. 27:3-5). The chief priests could not put the silver into the treasury, because it was blood money. Unwittingly they fulfilled prophecy. "So they decided to use the money to buy the potter's field as a burial place for foreigners" (Matt. 27:7).

"And I will pour out on the house of David and the inhabitants of Jerusalem a spirit of grace and supplication. They will look on me, the one they have pierced, and they will mourn for him as one mourns for an only child, and grieve bitterly for him as one grieves for a firstborn son" (Zech. 12:10).

The Jews did not want the dead bodies of the three criminals left on the crosses during the Sabbath. Pilate agreed, therefore, to have the soldiers break their legs and remove them. Finding Jesus already dead, "instead, one of the soldiers pierced Jesus' side with a spear, bringing a sudden flow of blood and water" (John 19:34). John testifies that the soldiers fulfilled this prophecy. "They will look on the one they have pierced" (John 19:37).

At Pentecost many Jews were very upset after Peter explained that Jesus, who was crucified, is both Lord and Christ. They cried, "Brothers, what shall we do?" (Acts 2:37). On that day about 3000 people mourned for their sins and asked God for forgiveness (Acts 2:41).

At the end of time everyone, whether dead or alive, will see the Second Coming of Jesus. Many people will mourn as soon as they realize that the claims of Jesus are true and that they have rejected God's invitation for salvation. John promises, "Look, he is coming with the clouds, and every eye will see him, even those who pierced him; and all the peoples of the earth will mourn because of him. So shall it be! Amen" (Rev. 1:7).

> *"On that day a fountain will be opened to the house of David and the inhabitants of Jerusalem, to cleanse them from sin and impurity"* (Zech. 13:1).

John declares, "The blood of Jesus, his Son, purifies us from all sin" (1 John 1:7). How can you know that the penalty for your sins has been paid? If God tells the truth, the shed blood of Jesus satisfies divine justice. If you confess that Jesus was punished in your place, then God will cleanse you of your sins. Zechariah paints a word picture of a fountain filled with Jesus' blood and poured over the believer. In a spiritual sense each one of us must be cleansed in the fountain of Jesus' blood.

> *The word of the LORD is against the land of Hadrach and will rest upon Damascus—for the eyes of men and all the tribes of Israel are on the LORD* (Zech. 9:1).

Reign of Antiochus Epiphanes, king of the Seleucid Empire: 175 B.C.-164 B.C. [8]

Intertwined in these chapters is another theme—the judgment of God against non-believers. God focuses on Antiochus Epiphanes as well as those living at the end of the world. When Zechariah preached, Israel had no quarrel with Syria, because they were both under Persian domination. In retrospect, Antiochus Epiphanes would be the next most dangerous threat coming upon Israel from Syria. Hopefully the generation that would suffer from his attacks would be comforted by this prophecy. The Lord promised the destruction of those forces that joined with Antiochus. God would consume Tyre by fire, and the Philistines would be devastated (Zech. 9:4-6).

Then the L‍ord will appear over them; his arrow will flash like lightning. The Sovereign L‍ord will sound the trumpet; he will march in the storms of the south, and the L‍ord Almighty will shield them. They will destroy and overcome with slingstones…The L‍ord their God will save them on that day as the flock of his people (Zech. 9:14-16).

God promised to march with them to battle, to shield them, to destroy the enemy, and to save his people. "They will sparkle in his land like jewels in a crown" (Zech. 9:16). Although both Jerusalem and Judah would be besieged (Zech. 12:2), God would rescue them and would destroy the nations that attacked them. He promised, "On that day I will set out to destroy all the nations that attack Jerusalem" (Zech. 12:9). Through the valiant faith of the Maccabees, God would allow Israel to reconquer the Promised Land. [9]

Then the L‍ord will go out and fight against those nations, as he fights in the day of battle. On that day his feet will stand on the Mount of Olives, east of Jerusalem, and the Mount of Olives will be split in two from east to west, forming a great valley, with half of the mountain moving north and half moving south (Zech. 14:3,4).

In Antiochus' time there was no earthquake. From then until now the Mount of Olives has remained intact. Therefore the battle mentioned in this passage must be in the future. Just as God fought for his people to defeat Antiochus Epiphanes, he will fight again at the end of time. While Ezekiel was in Babylon, God showed him in a vision the glory of the Lord standing on the mountain east of Jerusalem (Ezek. 11:23). Likewise, sometime in the future Jesus will once more stand, in the spiritual realm, on the Mount of Olives and look down on his beloved city. Will he be weeping because of their unbelief as he did so long ago? At his word there will be a great earthquake, and the survivors will flee to safety (Zech. 14:5). This is the same earthquake described in Revelation 11, which will cause many in Jerusalem to be saved. This natural disaster will be judgment for some but salvation for others.

> *It will be a unique day, without daytime or nighttime— a day known to the* LORD. *When evening comes, there will be light* (Zech. 14:7).

The unique day that believers have been waiting for is the Second Coming of Christ. "Two men will be in the field; one will be taken and the other left. Two women will be grinding with a hand mill; one will be taken and the other left" (Matt. 24:40,41). There will be no mistaking that day. At the shout of the archangel Jesus will appear in the sky with all of his angels and everyone will see him (Rev. 1:7). Jesus will come as a judge, gathering the redeemed to himself and leaving the non-believers to suffer the wrath of Almighty God. "For the Son of Man is going to come in his Father's glory with his angels, and then he will reward each person according to what he has done" (Matt. 16:27).

> *Then the survivors from all the nations that have attacked Jerusalem will go up year after year to worship the King, the* LORD *Almighty, and to celebrate the Feast of Tabernacles* (Zech. 14:16).

At the end of time there will be no survivors (Rev. 16:17-21; Rev. 20:9). That is why the survivors mentioned in this verse must be those spared during the time of the Maccabees. More importantly, to reinstitute the sacrificial system near the end of time would be an insult to the blood of Jesus. God destroyed the temple in A.D. 70 to prevent the continuation of animal sacrifices. Why would he ever encourage them again? Therefore this picture of the universal worship of God at Jerusalem must be a promise for Old Testament times. In order for these expectations to be fulfilled, the Israelites had to be obedient to the commands of God. That is why Fletcher points out:

> The prophecies both of good and evil to Israel after the captivity were *conditional* and the good and evil came in proportion to their obedience or disobedience. This prophecy of other people coming to Jerusalem to keep the feast of tabernacles is in line with the other predictions of Jewish headship and greatness, of which their coming would be an acknowledgment. But as the Jews never attained the headship, the other nations were never brought into such relations to them. Jerusalem did not become the Mecca of the nations; for it was not worthy. [10]

And on that day there will no longer be a Canaanite in the house of the LORD Almighty (Zech. 14:21).

The word *Canaanite* is synonymous with sin. [11] Zechariah ended his book with a glimpse into eternity where God's house would be completely free of sin. Non-believers will not be allowed to enter God's dwelling place. Only in the new heaven and new earth will there be an absence of sin. [12]

4. ESTHER: SAVED FROM DESTRUCTION

God carried out his plan of salvation by protecting his people from annihilation. Esther influenced Xerxes from 479 to 474 B.C. [13]
She became queen 59 years after the edict of Cyrus and 37 years after the temple had been built. After her influence ended, Ezra taught the people God's Law 16 years later, and Nehemiah built the walls of Jerusalem 29 years later.
Reign of Ahasuerus (Xerxes I), king of Persia: 485-465 B.C. [2]

No doubt Satan was furious that many Israelites were back in the Promised Land. He must have been upset that they had actually finished building the temple. He was probably glad that some, like Mordecai and Esther, had chosen not to return. Satan certainly did not want to take a chance on the promised Seed being born. Therefore it is not surprising to find Haman, a Persian nobleman, hatching a plot to exterminate the Jews.

One day Xerxes decided to honour Haman by ordering the other royal officials in Susa to kneel down before him. Now Haman was angry when Mordecai refused to do it. Only killing Mordecai did not satisfy him. He wanted to kill all of the Jews throughout the kingdom. Therefore Haman complained to Xerxes that there was a group of people in the Persian Empire who follow their own customs and who do not obey the king's laws. He said, "It is not in the king's best interest to tolerate them. If it pleases the king, let a decree be issued to destroy them, and I will put ten thousand talents of silver into the royal treasury for the men who carry out this business" (Esther 3:8,9).

Xerxes did not ask the identity of those people. He merely handed Haman his signet ring and told him to do whatever he wanted. Haman proceeded to order the annihilation of all Jews on one particular day eleven months later. Messengers travelled throughout the empire and informed everyone of the king's decree. Then Jews everywhere fasted and mourned—except for Esther, Mordecai's cousin. She had no idea what was happening, because as queen she was secluded within the palace. Mordecai had taken care of her after the death of her parents. Before Xerxes had chosen her to be his queen, Mordecai had insisted that she not reveal her true identity. As a result neither Haman nor Xerxes knew that the queen was a Jewess.

Soon Esther's servants told her that Mordecai was dressed in sackcloth and ashes and was sitting at the king's gate. She sent one of her servants to ask Mordecai what was wrong, because she was not allowed to talk to him directly. The servant returned with an urgent request for Esther to enter the king's presence, "to beg for mercy and plead with him for her people" (Esther 4:8). Through the servant, Esther replied:

> *"All the king's officials and the people of the royal provinces know that for any man or woman who approaches the king in the inner court without being summoned the king has but one law: that he be put to death. The only exception to this is for the king to extend the golden scepter to him and spare his life. But thirty days have passed since I was called to go to the king"* (Esther 4:11).

Mordecai made sure that Esther understood the seriousness of the situation. If she failed to stand up for the Jews, they would be saved in another way. She and her family would die, however. He asked, "And who knows but that you have come to royal position for such a time as this?" (Esther 4:14).

Then Esther responded, "Go, gather together all the Jews who are in Susa, and fast for me. Do not eat or drink for three days, night or day. I and my maids will fast as you do. When this is done, I will go to the king, even though it is against the law. And if I perish, I perish" (Esther 4:16).

Three days later Esther approached Xerxes in the throne room. "He was pleased with her and held out to her the gold scepter that was in his hand. So Esther approached and touched the tip of the scepter" (Esther 5:2). Because of Esther's courage, God worked through her to spare his people. Instead of being destroyed on the appointed day, the Jews were allowed to defend themselves, to kill anyone who attacked them, and to collect plunder from their enemies. As for Haman, he was hanged on the gallows that he had prepared for Mordecai. Once again Satan's plans were thwarted and the line of the promised Seed was protected.

> Because of Esther's courage, God worked through her to spare his people.

5. Malachi: the Coming of the Lord

Date written: about 430 B.C. [14] *He prophesied 108 years after the edict of Cyrus, 28 years after Ezra taught the people the Law of God, and 15 years after Nehemiah built the walls.*

The Jews had a second chance to please God, and like Noah they failed. The world, the flesh, and the devil prevented them from realizing their dreams. Instead of blessing the people, God said, "I will send a curse upon you, and I will curse your blessings. Yes, I have already cursed them, because you have not set your heart to honor me" (Mal. 2:2). The Lord explained why he was so upset:

> "A son honors his father, and a servant his master. If I am a father, where is the honor due me? If I am a master, where is the respect due me?...It is you, O priests, who show contempt for my name. But you ask, 'How have we shown contempt for your name?' You place defiled food on my altar. But you ask, 'How have we defiled you?' By saying that the LORD's table is contemptible. When you bring blind animals for sacrifice, is that not wrong? When you sacrifice crippled or diseased animals, is that not wrong? Try offering them to your governor! Would he be pleased with you? Would he accept you?" (Mal. 1:6-8).

In fact, God was so exasperated that he said, "Oh, that one of you would shut the temple doors, so that you would not light useless fires on my altar! I am not pleased with you...and I will accept no offering from your hands" (Mal. 1:10). Through Malachi, God pleaded with them, "I the Lord do not change. So you, O descendants of Jacob, are not destroyed. Ever since the time of your forefathers you have turned away from my decrees and have not kept them. Return to me, and I will return to you" (Mal. 3:6,7).

> "My name will be great among the nations, from the rising to the setting of the sun" (Mal. 1:11).

A Second Chance for Israel

Discouraged by the lack of proper worship from the Jews, God looked forward to the day when the Gentiles would revere his name. Since Jesus' time, people from many different nationalities have praised the name of the Lord.

> *"See, I will send my messenger, who will prepare the way before me. Then suddenly the Lord you are seeking will come to his temple; the messenger of the covenant, whom you desire, will come," says the* LORD *Almighty* (Mal. 3:1).

> Discouraged by the lack of proper worship from the Jews, God looked forward to the day when the Gentiles would revere his name.

God did not promise Israel restoration to the land, because they were already there. Instead he prophesied the arrival of his messenger who would prepare the way for the promised Seed. Over 400 years later crowds flocked to the Jordan River to hear John the Baptist, the son of Zechariah, preach "a baptism of repentance for the forgiveness of sins" (Luke 3:3). Everyone wondered if he was the Messiah. Some priests and Levites even came from Jerusalem to ask him, "Are you the Christ?" He admitted to them that he was not the Christ, or Elijah, or the Prophet. Instead John the Baptist answered, "I am the voice of one calling in the desert, 'Make straight the way for the Lord'" (John 1:23).

Around six months after John the Baptist started preaching, Jesus began his public ministry. Then the promised Seed, the desire of all nations, came to his temple in Jerusalem.

> *But who can endure the day of his coming? Who can stand when he appears? For he will be like a refiner's fire or a launderer's soap* (Mal. 3:2).

After entering the courts of the temple, Jesus was disgusted to find men selling cattle, sheep, and doves while others changed money. With a whip he drove the animals and their owners from the temple. "He scattered the coins of the money changers and overturned their tables. To those who sold doves he said, 'Get these out of here! How dare you turn my Father's house into a market!'" (John 2:15,16).

> *"Surely the day is coming; it will burn like a furnace. All the arrogant and every evildoer will be stubble, and that day that is coming will set them on fire," says the* LORD *Almighty. "Not a root or a branch will be left to them. But for you who revere my name, the sun of righteousness will rise with healing in its wings. And you will go out and leap like calves released from the stall"* (Mal. 4:1,2).

God promised to send the prophet Elijah before the "great and dreadful day of the LORD" (Mal. 4:5). In speaking of John the Baptist to a crowd, Jesus said, "And if you are willing to accept it, he is the Elijah who was to come" (Matt. 11:14).

Malachi also connects Elijah's coming to a day of burning and judgment. Peter warns, "By the same word the present heavens and earth are reserved for fire, being kept for the day of judgment and destruction of ungodly men" (2 Pet. 3:7). At the end of time the world will be destroyed by fire. It is not surprising, therefore, to find that the two witnesses in Revelation 11 possess the powers of Elijah.

Points to Ponder

1. God understands that his people have enemies who want to hinder his work. Therefore he uses people like Haggai and Zechariah to encourage believers not to give up.

2. Through Haggai, God chides his people, because they put their own needs over God's glory. Then they wonder why they are having financial trouble.

3. Through Zechariah, God reveals specific events in the last week of Jesus' life 500 years before it happened. God is indeed all-knowing.

4. Satan used the most powerful person in the Persian Empire to prevent the birth of the promised Seed, but God proved that he is King of kings by using Esther to save the Jews.

5. In Malachi, God is thoroughly disgusted at half-hearted worship. He wants our all or nothing.

Chapter Eleven

The Silent Years

430-6/5 B.C. The Israelites had known the Law of God for over 1000 years. He had periodically given them the written Word through the prophets. Now for over 400 years God would be silent. He expected that his people would wait patiently for the arrival of the promised Seed.

1. False Writings

ONCE, when I lived in North Bay, one of my pastors and I were talking about the end times. He thought that the apostolic fathers should know the truth better than anyone, because they lived near the time of Jesus. He wondered exactly what they wrote on that subject. I told him that I would do some research and let him know. As a result I travelled to Toronto a few times and spent hours in several theological libraries. Immersing myself in those ancient sermons was exciting.

On one occasion I decided to find out about Jewish writings during the 400 years between the Old and New Testaments. I discovered that from 200 B.C. to A.D. 100 a peculiar style of Jewish writing arose. This collection of books became known as the *Pseudepigrapha* or false writings. In the Old Testament God had occasionally authorized some prophets to write about the end times. For example, Malachi promises that one day the world will burn like a furnace (Mal. 4:1). God did not, however, sanction the false writings. Those authors eagerly awaited the arrival of the Messiah and his kingdom, but they erred when they expected that current events would soon fulfill prophecy. Those writings also added to the Old Testament teaching on the Messiah.

There are two important ways to distinguish the divinely inspired Scriptures from those false writings. The latter did not plead with their audience to repent of their sins. They never longed for the promised Seed to take away their sin and restore them to fellowship with their Creator. Instead they had a perplexing problem. The false writers could not understand why the righteous were suffering at the hands of the wicked and were not enjoying the benefits of a peaceful kingdom. In the words of G. E. Ladd, "The righteous can only patiently suffer while waiting a future salvation...Their problem rests in the very fact that there is a righteous remnant which is overwhelmed by undeserved evil."[1] Moreover none of the writers claimed to speak in the name of the Lord. They did not even use their own names; instead they pretended to be a famous person from the past. According to William J. Deane, most Jews failed to question the accuracy of those authors. "A writer who ventured to appropriate a celebrated title would take care to satisfy the expectations raised by his pseudonym, and readers would believe that no one would dare to challenge comparison with a great original who was not qualified to sustain the character assumed."[2] The ideas of these false writers permeated Jewish society and influenced the thinking of most Jews.

2. ENOCH: CHAPTERS 1-36, 106, 107

170 B.C.[3] Written in Palestine, Enoch contains 4 different books whose authors used the pseudonym Enoch.
Reign of Antiochus Epiphanes, king of the Seleucid Empire: 175-164 B.C.[3]

Situated between the Seleucid Empire to the north and Egypt to the south, Judea was caught between two strong powers determined to beat each other into submission.[4] At this time the Seleucids had ruled Palestine for twenty-eight years, and the present king was Antiochus Epiphanes. Yet, on his way home after conquering much of Egypt, he invaded Jerusalem, plundered the temple, and persecuted some of the people.

> And [he] entered proudly into the sanctuary, and took away the golden altar, and the candlestick of light, and all the vessels thereof...He took also the silver and the gold, and the precious vessels: also he took the hidden treasures which he found. And when he had taken all away, he went into his own land, having made a great massacre, and spoken very proudly. Therefore there was great mourning in Israel...all the house of Jacob was covered with confusion (1 Macc. 1:21-28, KJV).

The Jews were in shock. In order to comfort them the false Enoch wrote:

Chapters 1-5: Parable of Enoch on the Future Lot of the Wicked and the Righteous.

Enoch 1

1. The words of the blessing of Enoch, wherewith he blessed the elect [and] righteous, who will be living in the day of tribulation, when all the wicked [and godless] are to be removed.

8. But with the righteous He will make peace, and will protect the elect, and mercy shall be upon them. And they shall all belong to God, and they shall be prospered, and they shall [all] be blessed. [And He will help them all], and light shall appear unto them, [and He will make peace with them].

9. And behold! He cometh with ten thousands of [His] holy ones to execute judgement upon all, and to destroy [all] the ungodly: and to convict all flesh of all the works [of their ungodliness]

which they have ungodly committed [and of all the hard things which] ungodly sinners [have spoken] against Him.[5]

Enoch 5

7c. And for you the godless there shall be a curse.

6i. And for all of you sinners there shall be no salvation,

7a. But for the elect there shall be light and grace and peace,

7b. And they shall inherit the earth.

8. And then there shall be bestowed upon the elect wisdom, and they shall all live and never again sin, either through ungodliness or through pride: but they who are wise shall be humble.

9. And they shall not again transgress, nor shall they sin all the days of their life, nor shall they die of (the divine) anger or wrath, but they shall complete the number of the days of their life. And their lives shall be increased in peace, and the years of their joy shall be multiplied, in eternal gladness and peace, all the days of their life.[6]

Enoch 25: *Michael, one of the holy and honoured angels*

1. And he said unto me: "Enoch, why dost thou ask me regarding the fragrance of the tree, and [why] dost thou wish to learn the truth?"

2. Then I answered him [saying]: "I wish to know about everything, but especially about this tree."

3. And he answered saying: "This high mountain [which thou hast seen], whose summit is like the throne of God, is His throne, where the Holy Great One, the Lord of Glory, the Eternal King, will sit, when He shall come down to visit the earth with goodness.

4. And as for this fragrant tree no mortal is permitted to touch it till the great judgement,

when He shall take vengeance on all and bring (everything) to its consummation for ever. It shall then be given to the righteous and holy.
5. Its fruit shall be for food to the elect: it shall be transplanted to the holy place, to the temple of the Lord, the Eternal King.
6. Then shall they rejoice with joy and be glad. And into the holy place shall they enter; and its fragrance shall be in their bones, and they shall live a long life on earth, such as thy fathers lived: and in their days shall no [sorrow or] plague or torment or calamity touch them."
7. Then blessed I the God of Glory, the Eternal King, who hath prepared such things for the righteous, and hath created them and promised to give to them.[7]

This false writer described the fate of two distinct groups of people—the righteous, meaning the Jews who kept the Law, and the sinners, meaning the rest of the world. God records Enoch's sermon[8] in Jude 1:14,15, which was used by the false Enoch in Enoch 1:9. The false writer and the Lord, however, have entirely different reasons for quoting Enoch. After severely condemning those godless people who had joined the Church and were dividing the believers, Jude implores, "Be merciful to those who doubt; snatch others from the fire and save them; to others show mercy, mixed with fear—hating even the clothing stained by corrupted flesh" (Jude 1:22,23). In contrast, the false writer does not plead with the wicked. There was no hope for them. He said, "And for you the godless there shall be a curse. And for all of you sinners there shall be no salvation" (Enoch 5:7c,6i).

The righteous, however, would inherit the earth; "nor shall they sin all the days of their life" (Enoch 5:9). They would feed on the fruit of a fragrant tree in the Lord's temple, and it would be a peaceful happy life. The eternal King would sit on his throne "when He shall come down to visit the earth with goodness" (Enoch 25:3). R. H. Charles points out, "The scene of the Messianic kingdom in 1-36 is Jerusalem and the earth purified from sin"[9] This false Enoch thinks that Messiah's kingdom will last forever although individual saints will eventually die. He is only concerned with the vindication of the righteous and with earthly dreams. He does not teach that death is the punishment for sin. Yet, by dying, the righteous prove that they are still under the condemnation of death. In contrast, this false author writes, "nor shall they die of (the divine) anger or wrath, but they shall complete the number of the days of their life" (Enoch 5:9). His writing does not portray his need for the Saviour to forgive his own sins. His concern is not spiritual salvation but a desire for an earthly Jewish kingdom.

> This false Enoch thinks that Messiah's kingdom will last forever although individual saints will eventually die.

3. The Desecration of the Temple, 168 B.C.[3]

"Moreover king Antiochus wrote to his whole kingdom, that all should be one people, And every one should leave his laws: so all the heathen agreed according to the commandment of the king. Yea, many also of the Israelites consented to his religion, and sacrificed unto idols, and profaned the sabbath" (1 Macc. 1:41-43, KJV). Whoever did not obey the king must die. Some Jews preferred to die rather than disobey the Law.[10] Many others renounced God's Law. They tore and burned any books of the Law that they could find. Then in 168 B.C., forces of Antiochus built an altar to Zeus on top of the altar of burnt offering. "Ten days later heathen sacrifice was offered on it."[11] What an abomination to God![12] Meanwhile those faithful to God and the Law fled for their lives. Mary and Joseph's ancestors were among the refugees who ended up in Galilee. Satan had no idea whether the line of the promised Seed was safe, but they were. Many years later

Jesus would grow up in obscurity, far from Jerusalem and safe from the danger of jealous rulers.

4. The Righteous Remnant

Turn from evil and do good; then you will dwell in the land forever. For the LORD loves the just and will not forsake his faithful ones. They will be protected forever, but the offspring of the wicked will be cut off; the righteous will inherit the land and dwell in it forever (Ps. 37:27-29).

A remnant will return, a remnant of Jacob will return to the Mighty God. Though your people, O Israel, be like the sand by the sea, only a remnant will return (Isa. 10:21,22).

One day a man ran up to Jesus.

"Good teacher," he asked, "what must I do to inherit eternal life?"

"Why do you call me good?" Jesus answered. "No one is good—except God alone. You know the commandments: 'Do not murder, do not commit adultery, do not steal, do not give false testimony, do not defraud, honor your father and mother.'"

"Teacher," he declared, "all these I have kept since I was a boy" (Mark 10:17-20).

This was the attitude of the righteous remnant. During the exile the Israelites loved the Law. As M. R. Wilson explains, "There was one thing Israel carried to Babylon and clung to dearly. It was the law, the Torah, for by it Israel was assured of its divine calling and mission."[13]

> By the time of Antiochus Epiphanes a group of Jews emerged who were very loyal to the Law.

By the time of Antiochus Epiphanes a group of Jews emerged who were very loyal to the Law. They believed that they were the righteous remnant who deserved to inherit the promised kingdom. These forerunners of the Pharisees called themselves Chasidim, meaning "godly men."[14] In their eyes they had fulfilled the conditions of the prophets. That is why Ladd writes:

> The prophets promised that a repentant, restored Israel would inherit the kingdom. Now Israel was restored to the land and was faithful to the law. According to the Jewish definition of righteousness, the conditions laid down by the prophets were satisfied; but the kingdom did not come. Instead came unprecedented suffering. Antiochus Epiphanes attempted to destroy the Jewish faith, inflicting tortures and martyrdoms upon the faithful.[15]

Were the Chasidim correct to expect a political Utopia on earth? Throughout the Old Testament God always had a remnant in Israel of those who truly loved and obeyed him. They acknowledged their sin and longed for the coming of the promised Seed to pay the penalty for sin. Unless a Chasid heeded the warnings of the prophets and repented of sin, that person was actually a non-believer. A loving and obedient heart attitude toward God is what counts. For most, following God's Law became an end in itself. As Wilson explains, "Gradually many Jews came to believe that here lay the only real proof of who was a true Jew: vigorous, unflinching obedience to the teachings of Torah."[16]

In an attempt to guard against breaking the Law, they added rules of their own making to the Torah. This became known as the oral law. Like the Israelites in Moses' day, they did not understand that they could never perfectly obey God in their own strength. In fact obedience to God's Law is not the prerequisite for inheriting the kingdom. Instead it is a loving heart attitude that has the desire to obey God. Such a person is heartbroken when he or she fails to live up to God's standards. That one earnestly waited for the arrival of the Saviour.

5. The Maccabean Revolt

5a. Mattathias Maccabeus, 167 B.C.[3]

Mattathias Maccabeus lamented:

> Woe is me! wherefore was I born to see this misery of my people, and of the holy city, and to dwell there, when it was delivered into the hand of the enemy, and the sanctuary into the hand of strangers? Her temple is become as a man without glory. Her glorious vessels are carried away into captivity, her infants are slain in the streets, her young men with the sword of the enemy…And, behold, our sanctuary, even our beauty and our glory, is laid waste, and the Gentiles have profaned it. To what end therefore shall we live any longer? (1 Macc. 2:7-13, KJV).

Mattathias and his five sons tore their clothes, put on sackcloth, and mourned. When the king's officers arrived in Modin and forced the people to sacrifice to idols, he was furious. Mattathias killed the Jew who was about to sacrifice on the heathen altar. After murdering the king's officer, he tore down the altar. Next Mattathias cried out, "Whosoever is zealous of the law, and maintaineth the covenant, let him follow me" (1 Macc. 2:27, KJV).

Immediately Mattathias and his five sons escaped to the mountains and left everything that they owned in the city. Many others also left to live in the wilderness. This was the beginning of a war for religious freedom that would last almost three years.

5b. Judas Maccabeus

Rule of Judas Maccabeus: 166-161 B.C.[3]

After the peaceful death of Mattathias, his son Judas became the new leader of the insurrection. Quickly he gained an honourable reputation in winning battles. "For he pursued the wicked, and sought them out, and burnt up those that vexed his people" (1 Macc. 3:5, KJV). Like Gideon of old, he fought the battle with few men. Some of his soldiers asked him:

> "How shall we be able, being so few, to fight against so great a multitude *and* so strong, seeing we are ready to faint with fasting all this day?"...
>
> [Judas replied,] "It is no hard matter for many to be shut up in the hands of a few; and with *the God of* heaven it is all one, to deliver with a great multitude, or a small company: For the victory of battle standeth not in the multitude of an host; but strength cometh from heaven" (1 Macc. 3:17-19, KJV).

When the neighbouring nations began to fear Judas, Antiochus Epiphanes was very angry. He ordered the extermination of the Jews and sent 40,000 footmen and 7,000 horsemen to Judea to destroy them. The Israelites fasted and rent their clothes. They cried out, "How shall we be able to stand against them, except thou, *O God,* be our help?" (1 Macc. 3:53, KJV).

> When the neighbouring nations began to fear Judas, Antiochus Epiphanes was very angry.

Judas answered, "Arm yourselves, and be valiant men, and see that ye be in readiness against the morning, that ye may fight with these nations, that are assembled together against us to destroy us and our sanctuary: For it is better for us to die in battle, than to behold the calamities of our people and our sanctuary. Nevertheless, as the will *of God* is in heaven, so let him do" (1 Macc. 3:58-60, KJV).

The Lord gave Judas success in the battle. On their way home, the army sang and praised God joyfully: "His mercy *endureth* for ever" (1 Macc. 4:24, KJV).

The next year, in 165 B.C., 60,000 footmen and 5,000 horsemen tried again, but Judas met them with 10,000 men.

He prayed, "Cast them down with the sword of them that love thee, and let all those that know thy name praise thee with thanksgiving" (1 Macc. 4:33, KJV).

Judas' army killed 5,000 of the enemy, and the rest ran away. As soon as Judas saw the Seleucid army fleeing, he entered Jerusalem and cleansed the temple of the heathen altar. The Jews immediately built a new altar for God and made new holy vessels. The people "offered sacrifice according to the law upon the new altar of burnt offerings, which they had made...Then all the people fell upon their faces, worshipping and praising the God of heaven, who had given them good success" (1 Macc. 4:53,55, KJV). Judas fought many other wars and was eventually killed in battle. The Jews, however, regained their religious freedom thanks to the bravery of the Maccabean family. No doubt Satan was vexed. God could still send the promised Seed.

6. Enoch: Chapters 83-90, 165 B.C.[3]

Enoch 90:
18. And I saw till the Lord of the sheep came unto them and took in His hand the staff of His wrath, and smote the earth, and the earth clave asunder, and all the beasts and all the birds of the heaven fell from among those sheep, and were swallowed up in the earth and it covered them.
37. And I saw that a white bull was born, with large horns, and all the beasts of the field and all the birds of the air feared him and made petition to him all the time.[17]

It is not surprising that the writing of this period would be nationalistic and vindictive after all of the persecution endured by the Jews faithful to God and the Law. According to Charles, the white bull represents the Messiah:

> He is a man only, but yet a glorified man; for he is described as a white bull to mark his superiority to

the rest of the community of the righteous who are symbolized by sheep...he has absolutely no function to perform, as he does not appear until the world's history is finally closed. Accordingly his presence here must be accounted for through literary reminiscence, and the Messiah-hope must be regarded as practically dead at this period. The nation, in fact, felt no need of such a personality so long as they had such a chief as Judas [Maccabeus].[18]

Is it not sad that most of the Jews appeared to place more importance on the leadership of Judas than on their need for a Saviour? How many in that generation cared that God promised to send the Shepherd King, the descendant of David? How many knew that God had announced the approximate time of the Messiah's birth to Daniel? Would we have waited patiently for the Saviour? Would we be more concerned with political than with spiritual salvation?

> Would we be more concerned with political than with spiritual salvation?

7. THE QUMRANIANS, 150 B.C.-A.D. 68[19]

Because God authorized the writing of Scripture, he expects people to study and meditate on the entire Bible in order to understand his message. Instead some have a tendency to concentrate only on his or her favourite part. For example, the Chasidim focused on the Law. In the process many of them became self-righteous and lost sight of their need for a Saviour. At this time other Jews, who belonged to a sect called Essenes, settled in Qumran on the northwest shore of the Dead Sea. Famous because of the Dead Sea Scrolls, they left the modern believer another legacy. The Qumranians became obsessed with prophecy. This is how William W. Klein describes them:

It regarded the Judaism centered in Jerusalem as apostate. So, led by its founder, a mysterious figure called the Teacher of Righteousness, its members withdrew to the wilderness of Judea to form a monastic community to prepare for the coming of the messianic age. Specifically, they awaited God's imminent judgment, which they expected to fall on their apostate religious competitors, and they anticipated his renewal of the covenant with only true, pure Israel—themselves. They saw themselves as the final generation about whom Biblical prophecy speaks.

> The Qumranians became obsessed with prophecy.

The interpretation of Hebrew Scriptures played a prominent role at Qumran. If the law of Moses entranced the rabbis, the OT prophets preoccupied the Qumranians. Alleging special divine inspiration, the Teacher of Righteousness claimed to show that events of that day, especially those involving the Qumran community, fulfilled OT prophecies. [19]

The Qumranians did not acknowledge their need for the Saviour or wait for the promised Seed to pay the penalty for their sin. Instead they encouraged three dangerous principles of interpretation: arbitrarily change God's original words to make them fit what they wanted to hear, contemporize prophecy by changing names or places from ancient ones to modern ones, and employ tunnel vision, which ignores not only the context of the passage, but also the teachings of the entire Bible.[20] Perhaps that is why the New Testament does not mention this sect of Judaism.

Does their method of interpretation sound familiar? How many have changed the text to suit their own ideas? How many have been positive that some particular prophecy applies to their generation? How many down through the ages have lost their credibility when time has proved them wrong?

Have any of those people ever admitted that they have made a mistake? How many employ tunnel vision and ignore clear teaching in other parts of the Bible? It is important to be honest and admit that it is easy to fall into any one of those traps.

8. The Second Jewish Commonwealth,[21] 142-63 B.C.

Rule of Simon Maccabeus: 143-135 B.C.[3]

In 143 B.C. Simon Maccabeus, Judas' older brother, gained independence from the Seleucids. The following year he was crowned king and high priest. [3] Durant comments:

> Judea became again a theocracy, under the Hasmonean dynasty of priest-kings. It has been a characteristic of Semitic societies that they closely associated the spiritual and temporal powers, in the family and in the state; they would have no sovereign but God.
> Recognizing the weakness of the little kingdom, the Hasmoneans spent two generations widening its borders by diplomacy and force. By 78 B.C. they had conquered and absorbed Samaria, Edom, Moab, Galilee, Idumea, Transjordania, Gadara, Pella, Gerasa, Raphia, and Gaza and had made Palestine as extensive as under Solomon. The descendants of those brave Maccabees who had fought for religious freedom enforced Judaism and circumcision upon their new subjects at the point of the sword.[21]

Let the saints rejoice in this honor and sing for joy on their beds. May the praise of God be in their mouths and a double-edged sword in their hands, to inflict vengeance on the nations and punishment on the peoples, to bind their kings with fetters, their nobles with shackles of iron, to carry out the sentence written against them. This is the glory of all his saints. Praise the Lord *(Ps. 149:5-9).*

Once again God granted Israel autonomy with borders as extensive as in Solomon's day. How sad that the Jews forced Judaism upon their new subjects! God did allow his people to praise him with their lips and to punish their enemies with the sword. The Lord did not give them the right, however, to forcibly convert people to the Jewish religion. What God desires is a loving heart attitude toward him. No one will truly love God with a sword poised at his or her throat. Before the Israelites entered the Promised Land, God commanded them, "Love the LORD your God with all your heart and with all your soul and with all your strength" (Deut. 6:5). God desires obedience arising from a loving heart. The Jews enforced an outward ritualistic religion on their captives. Because they did not try to win the hearts of their new subjects over to the Lord, God could not bless the nation any more than he did.

> No one will truly love God with a sword poised at his or her throat.

9. TESTAMENTS OF THE TWELVE PATRIARCHS, 125 B.C.[3]

Written in Palestine
Reign of John Hyrcanus: 135-105 B.C.[3]

Testament of Levi: Chapter 18

1. And after their punishment shall have come from the Lord, the priesthood shall fail.
2. Then shall the Lord raise up a new priest. And to him all the words of the Lord shall be revealed; and he shall execute a righteous judgement upon the earth for a multitude of days.
3. And his star shall arise in heaven as of a king, lighting up the light of knowledge as the sun the day, and he shall be magnified in the world.
4. He shall shine forth as the sun on the earth, and shall remove all darkness from under heaven,

and there shall be peace in all the earth.
5. The heavens shall exult in his days, and the earth shall be glad, and the clouds shall rejoice; [And the knowledge of the Lord shall be poured forth upon the earth, as the water of the seas;] and the angels of the glory of the presence of the Lord shall be glad in him.
6. The heavens shall be opened, and from the temple of glory shall come upon him sanctification, with the Father's voice as from Abraham to Isaac.
7. And the glory of the Most High shall be uttered over him, and the spirit of understanding and sanctification shall rest upon him…
8. For he shall give the majesty of the Lord to His sons in truth for evermore; and there shall none succeed him for all generations for ever.
9. And in his priesthood the Gentiles shall be multiplied in knowledge upon the earth, and enlightened through the grace of the Lord: In his priesthood shall sin come to an end, and the lawless shall cease to do evil. [And the just shall rest in him.]
10. And he shall open the gates of paradise, and shall remove the threatening sword against Adam.
11. And he shall give to the saints to eat from the tree of life, and the spirit of holiness shall be on them.
12. And Beliar shall be bound by him, and he shall give power to His children to tread upon evil spirits.
13. And the Lord shall rejoice in His children, and be well pleased in His beloved ones for ever.
14. Then shall Abraham and Isaac and Jacob exult, and I will be glad, and all the saints shall clothe themselves with joy.[22]

Testament of Judah: Chapter 24

1. And after these things shall arise the star of peace, and he shall walk with men in meekness

and righteousness.
2. And the heavens shall be opened unto him, and the blessings of the Holy Father will be poured down upon him.
3. And He will pour down upon us the spirit of grace, and ye shall be His true children by adoption, and ye shall walk in His commandments first and last.
4. [Then a branch shall go forth from me.]
5. And the sceptre of my kingdom shall shine forth; and from your root shall arise a stem;
6. And from it shall grow up the rod of righteousness unto the Gentiles, to judge and to save all that call upon the Lord.[23]

Testament of Judah: Chapter 25

1. And after these things shall Abraham and Isaac and Jacob arise unto life, and I and my brethren shall be chiefs of the tribes [of Israel]: Levi first, I the second, Joseph [the son of Jacob] third, Benjamin fourth, Simeon fifth, Issachar sixth, and so all in order.
2. And the Lord blessed Levi, and the Angel of the Presence, me; the powers of glory, Simeon; the heaven, Reuben; the earth, Issachar; the sea, Zebulon; the mountains, Joseph [the son of Jacob]; the tabernacle, Benjamin; the luminaries, Dan; Eden, Naphtali; the sun, Gad; the moon, Asher.
3. And ye shall be the people of the Lord, and have one tongue; and there shall be there no spirit of deceit of [Beliar], for he shall be cast into the fire for ever.
4. And they who have died in grief shall arise [in joy], [and they who were poor for the Lord's sake shall be made rich,] and they who are put to death for the Lord's sake shall awake [to life].

5. And the harts of Jacob shall run [in joyfulness], and the eagles of Israel shall fly [in gladness]; and all the peoples shall glorify the Lord for ever.[24]

Because the thoughts of this false writer were focused on the earth, any spiritual benefits related to the earth. "There shall be peace in all the earth...And in his priesthood the Gentiles shall be multiplied in knowledge upon the earth...And Beliar shall be bound by him" (Test. of Levi 18:4,9,12). Since fellowship shall be restored between God and his people, he "shall remove the threatening sword against Adam. And he shall give to the saints to eat from the tree of life" (Test. of Levi 18:10,11). One day Satan "shall be cast into the fire for ever," and the righteous will rise from the dead (Test. of Judah 25:3,4). Then this kingdom shall last forever. "And all the peoples shall glorify the Lord forever" (Test. of Judah 25:5).

Most Chasidim supported the Maccabees, the descendants of Levi, but not of Aaron. That is why Charles writes:

> Won over by the purity of life, nobility of character, and pre-eminent gifts of the Maccabees as high priests, civil rulers, and military commanders, the Chasids, or early Pharisees, had some decades earlier attached themselves to this new high-priesthood, though with many a misgiving on account of the break in the high-priestly succession. The approval thus won from the reluctant Chasids, the Maccabees had deepened and strengthened by their achievements every year in every province of their activity, till the thought was begotten in many a breast, that at last the hope of Israel had come, and, in defiance of all ancient prophecy, was sprung from the house and lineage of Levi.[25]

Although the Bible was clear that the Messiah would descend from Judah, the people began to doubt the truth of God's promise.

Although the Bible was clear that the Messiah would descend from Judah, the people began to doubt the truth of God's promise. How sad the Lord must have been that his chosen people were not patient enough to wait for the coming of the promised Seed! Would you have resisted popular opinion? Would you have remained true to God's Word?

10. THE BOOK OF JUBILEES, 110 B.C.[3]

Written in Palestine

Chapter 23: the Messianic Woes

18. Behold the earth will be destroyed on account of all their works, and there will be no seed of the vine, and no oil; for their works are altogether faithless, and they will all perish together, beasts and cattle and birds, and all the fish of the sea, on account of the children of men.
19. And they will strive one with another, the young with the old, and the old with the young, the poor with the rich, and the lowly with the great, and the beggar with the prince, on account of the law and the covenant; for they have forgotten commandment, and covenant, and feasts, and months, and Sabbaths, and jubilees, and all judgements.
20. And they will stand (with bows and) swords and war to turn them back into the way; but they will not return until much blood hath been shed on the earth, one by another.
21. And those who have escaped will not return from their wickedness to the way of righteousness, but they will all exalt themselves to deceit and wealth, that they may each take all that is his neighbour's, and they will name the great name, but not in truth and not in righteousness, and they will defile the holy of holies with their uncleanness and the corruption of their pollution.

22. And a great punishment will befall the deeds of this generation from the Lord, and He will give them over to the sword and to judgement and to captivity, and to be plundered and devoured.
23. And He will wake up against them the sinners of the Gentiles, who have neither mercy nor compassion, and who will respect the person of none, neither old nor young, nor any one, for they are more wicked and strong to do evil than all the children of men. And they will use violence against Israel and transgression against Jacob, and much blood will be shed upon the earth, and there will be none to gather and none to bury.
24. In those days they will cry aloud, and call and pray that they may be saved from the hand of the sinners, the Gentiles; but none will be saved.
25. And the heads of the children will be white with grey hair, and a child of three weeks will appear old like a man of one hundred years, and their stature will be destroyed by tribulation and oppression.

**Renewed Study of the Law Followed
by a Renewal of Mankind
The Messianic Kingdom and the
Blessedness of the Righteous**

26. And in those days the children will begin to study the laws, and to seek the commandments, and to return to the path of righteousness.
27. And the days will begin to grow many and increase amongst those children of men, till their days draw nigh to one thousand years, and to a greater number of years than (before) was the number of the days.
28. And there will be no old man nor one who is not satisfied with his days, for all will be (as) children and youths.

29. And all their days they will complete and live in peace and in joy, and there will be no Satan nor any evil destroyer; for all their days will be days of blessing and healing,
30. And at that time the Lord will heal His servants, and they will rise up and see great peace, and drive out their adversaries, and the righteous will see and be thankful, and rejoice with joy for ever and ever, and will see all their judgements and all their curses on their enemies.
31. And their bones will rest in the earth, and their spirits will have much joy, and they will know that it is the Lord who executeth judgement, and showeth mercy to hundreds and thousands and to all that love Him.
32. And do thou, Moses, write down these words; for thus are they written, and they record (them) on the heavenly tables for a testimony for the generations for ever.[26]

In the eyes of the ordinary Jew, God was blessing them. John Hyrcanus was popular because he had conquered more land for Israel. The people were truly autonomous again. At first this false writer painted a terrifying picture of the persecution of Antiochus Epiphanes. He explained that it had happened because they had "forgotten commandment, and covenant, and feasts, and months, and Sabbaths, and jubilees, and all judgements" (Book of Jub. 23:19). Then the people had prayed for salvation from "the hand of the sinners, the Gentiles" (Book of Jub. 23:24). They returned to a study of the Law (Book of Jub. 23:26). Sadly, they did not acknowledge that they were sinful like the wicked Gentiles.

This false writer believed that, by following the Law, the messianic age would gradually come. History seemed to support this theory, because the Maccabees had gradually enlarged the borders of Israel to those of Solomon's day. This author does not need a messiah to fulfill his hopes for a political Utopia. The

> This author does not need a messiah to fulfill his hopes for a political Utopia.

absence of any longing for the promised Seed's arrival is proof that God neither authorized nor approved of this writing. As far as this false writer is concerned, the saints will begin to live longer until "their days draw nigh to one thousand years...there will be no Satan nor any evil destroyer...they will rise up and see great peace...and rejoice with joy for ever and ever" (Book of Jub. 23:27,29,30). Individual saints, however, would eventually die (Book of Jub. 23:31). Curse the enemies of the righteous! Long live the saints!

11. Enoch: Chapters 37-71, 91-105, 108

Reign of Alexandra, wife of Alexander Jannaeus: 78-68 B.C.[27] 75f. B.C. [27] *The time is 67 years after Israel became an independent state under Simon and 91 years after Judas began to rule.*

Enoch 91: *The Last Three Weeks [in the apocalypse of weeks]*

12. And after that there shall be another, the eighth week, that of righteousness, and a sword shall be given to it that a righteous judgement may be executed on the oppressors, and sinners shall be delivered into the hands of the righteous.
13. And at its close they shall acquire houses through their righteousness, and a house shall be built for the Great King in glory for evermore,

14d. And all mankind shall look to the path of uprightness.

14a. And after that, in the ninth week, the righteous judgement shall be revealed to the whole world,
 b. And all the works of the godless shall vanish from all the earth,
 c. And the world shall be written down for destruction.

15. And after this, in the tenth week in the seventh part, there shall be the great eternal judgement, in which He will execute vengeance amongst the angels.
16. And the first heaven shall depart and pass away, and a new heaven shall appear, and all the powers of the heavens shall give sevenfold light.
17. And after that there will be many weeks without number for ever, and all shall be in goodness and righteousness, and sin shall no more be mentioned for ever.[28]

Almost 100 years had passed since the persecution of Antiochus Epiphanes. Since then the Jews had steadily engaged in battles to gain more land until Alexandra took the throne. Now there were no more military campaigns, but life inside Israel was not as peaceful and joyous as it ought to have been. There was dissension between the Pharisees, the teachers of the Law, and the Sadducees, the priests. Perhaps this world was too sinful to exist forever. Yet this false Enoch was not willing to give up the hope of an earthly kingdom. Therefore he decided that it would be temporary. Thus for one week, which was an undetermined amount of time, "all the works of the godless shall vanish from all the earth" (Enoch 91:14b). Afterwards "there shall be the great eternal judgement" (Enoch 91:15). Then the Lord would usher in a new heaven that would last forever. "Sin shall no more be mentioned for ever" (Enoch 91:17).

> Perhaps this world was too sinful to exist forever.

12. Conquered Again, 63 B.C.[27]

Before Alexandra's death her two sons Hyrcanus and Aristobulus began to fight over who should succeed her. Later, when a victorious Pompey was at Damascus, both of them appealed to him for the right to rule Judea. This is how Durant describes the situation:

> When Pompey decided for Hyrcanus, Aristobulus fortified himself with his army in Jerusalem. Pompey laid siege to the capital and gained its lower sections; but the followers of Aristobulus took refuge in the walled precincts of the Temple and held out for three months. Their piety, we are told, helped Pompey to overcome them; for perceiving that they would not fight on the Sabbath, he had his men prepare unhindered on each Sabbath the mounds and battering rams for the next day's assault. Meanwhile the priests offered the usual prayers and sacrifices in the Temple. When the ramparts fell 12,000 Jews were slaughtered; few resisted, none surrendered, many leaped to death from the walls. Pompey ordered his men to leave the treasures of the Temple untouched, but he exacted an indemnity of 10,000 talents ($3,600,000) from the nation. The cities that the Hasmoneans had conquered were transferred from the Judean to the Roman power; Hyrcanus II was made high priest and nominal ruler of Judea, but as the ward of Antipater the Idumean, who had helped Rome. The independent monarchy was ended, and Judea became part of the Roman province of Syria.[29]

13. Psalms of Solomon, 50 B.C[27]

Written in Palestine
The time is 13 years after Rome had conquered Judea

p. 40. Behold, O Lord, and raise up for them their king, the son of David, at the time which Thou, our God, knowest, that Thy servant...should reign over

Israel; and gird him with power to beat down unrighteous rulers...and he shall gather together the holy people which he shall guide in righteousness, and shall judge the tribes of the people hallowed by the Lord his God. And he shall not suffer unrighteousness to dwell in the midst of them, and no wicked man at all shall abide with them;

p. 41. For he will know them that they are all the children of God, and he will distribute them in their tribes upon the land. And the stranger and the foreigner shall no more sojourn among them; he shall judge the peoples and nations in the wisdom of his righteousness. He shall have the peoples of the Gentiles to serve him under his yoke, and he shall glorify the Lord by the submission of all the earth, and he shall cleanse Jerusalem with sanctification as from the beginning, that Gentiles may come from the ends of the earth to see his glory, bringing as offerings her way-worn children, yea, to see the glory of the Lord wherewith God hath glorified her. And he is the righteous king over them, taught of God. There is no injustice in his days in their midst, for they shall all be holy, and their king shall be christ the Lord. He shall not trust in horse or rider or bow, nor multiply to himself gold and silver for war, nor gather hope from arms in the day of battle; the Lord Himself is his king, the hope of the mighty one is in the hope of God, and he will set all the nations before him in fear; for he will smite the earth with the word of his mouth for ever, and bless the people of the Lord in wisdom with gladness. He himself is pure from sin that he may govern a great people, rebuke princes, and remove sinners by the power of his word. And, trusting upon his God, he shall not be weak in his days because God hath made him mighty by His holy spirit, and wise in the counsel of prudence, with power and righteousness. And the blessing of the Lord shall be with him in power, and his hope in the Lord shall not be weak;

p. 42. And who shall prevail against him? Mighty is he in his works, and strong in the fear of God. Tending the flock of the Lord in faith and righteousness, he will let none among them in their pasture to be weak.... Blessed are they who live in those days, to see the good things of the Lord which He will do in the generation to come, under the rod of the correction of christ the Lord in the fear of his God, in the wisdom of the spirit and of righteousness and power.[30]

According to Bruce, "The Hasmonaean rulers are denounced for having 'laid waste the throne of David', but they have received due judgement at the hands of the Romans, who in their turn will be overthrown by the true Messiah."[32] Sadly, this false writer only looked forward to a human messiah, the son of David, who would "not suffer unrighteousness to dwell in the midst of them" (p. 40). Each tribe would receive their portion of the land (p. 41), and the whole world would live in submission to the Jews. The Gentiles would "serve him under his yoke" (p. 41). The messiah would "smite the earth with the word of his mouth for ever" (p. 41). Being sinless he would have the power to "rebuke princes, and remove sinners" (p. 41). Trusting in his God, "he shall not be weak in his days" (p. 41). Regarding the length of messiah's kingdom, Leslie E. Fuller comments, "The final Judgment comes at the close of the temporary kingdom, and precedes the ushering in of the heavenly kingdom. No time limit is fixed for the duration of the earthly kingdom. Possibly it was to last only during the lifetime of the Messiah."[32]

I felt shocked as I studied the events and writings of the 400 years between the Old and New Testaments. Nobody had ever taught me that the Jewish hope for deliverance from the Romans originated from a false writer. Through Daniel, the Lord had told the Jews the due date for the birth of his Son.

Moreover Malachi had prophesied about a messenger who would prepare the way for the promised Seed. God expected his people to wait for the birth of their Saviour. For 400 years God was silent, but people were not. It was soon time for the advent of God's Son. Yet most of God's people were waiting for a political deliverer—not the promised Seed who would deliver them from the bondage of sin. Why? They believed the teachings of this false writer.

> God expected his people to wait for the birth of their Saviour. For 400 years God was silent, but people were not.

Points to Ponder

1. The printed word is not necessarily true. We can only count on the Scriptures to be true.
2. It is wrong to care more about God's Law or prophecy than about the Lord himself.
3. In the Old Testament, God intended a powerful Jewish kingdom to be a reward for their loving devotion to him, not the prime focus of their thoughts.
4. At first the false writers expected an eternal Jewish kingdom. As time passed, the later writers only anticipated a temporary one.
5. No false writer allowed Satan any more power in this world once Messiah's kingdom began.

Part 2:

Responding to the Promised Seed

Chapter One

The Birth of the Promised Seed

1. Mary and Joseph

6/5 B.C.[1] Mary was engaged to Joseph of Nazareth

ONE summer's evening Barry hurried down the stairs. He was on his way outside to cut the grass. In the front vestibule he unexpectedly met my cousin and me. I really did not want to be there, because Barry's sister and my cousin were planning a wedding. I would only be in the way. At this time Barry was a staunch atheist who was actively searching for objective truth. When he asked me out a couple of weeks later, he spent a lot of time asking me about my beliefs. Little did we realize how much our lives would change. We would eventually marry. In the same way, Mary was taken aback by the unexpected visit of the angel Gabriel, who said:

> *"Do not be afraid, Mary, you have found favor with God. You will be with child and give birth to a son, and you are to give him the name Jesus. He will be great and will be called the Son of the Most High. The Lord God will give him the throne of his father David, and he will reign over the house of Jacob forever; his kingdom will never end."*
>
> *"How will this be,"* Mary asked the angel, *"since I am a virgin?"*
>
> The angel answered, *"The Holy Spirit will come upon*

288 A Tale of Two Kingdoms

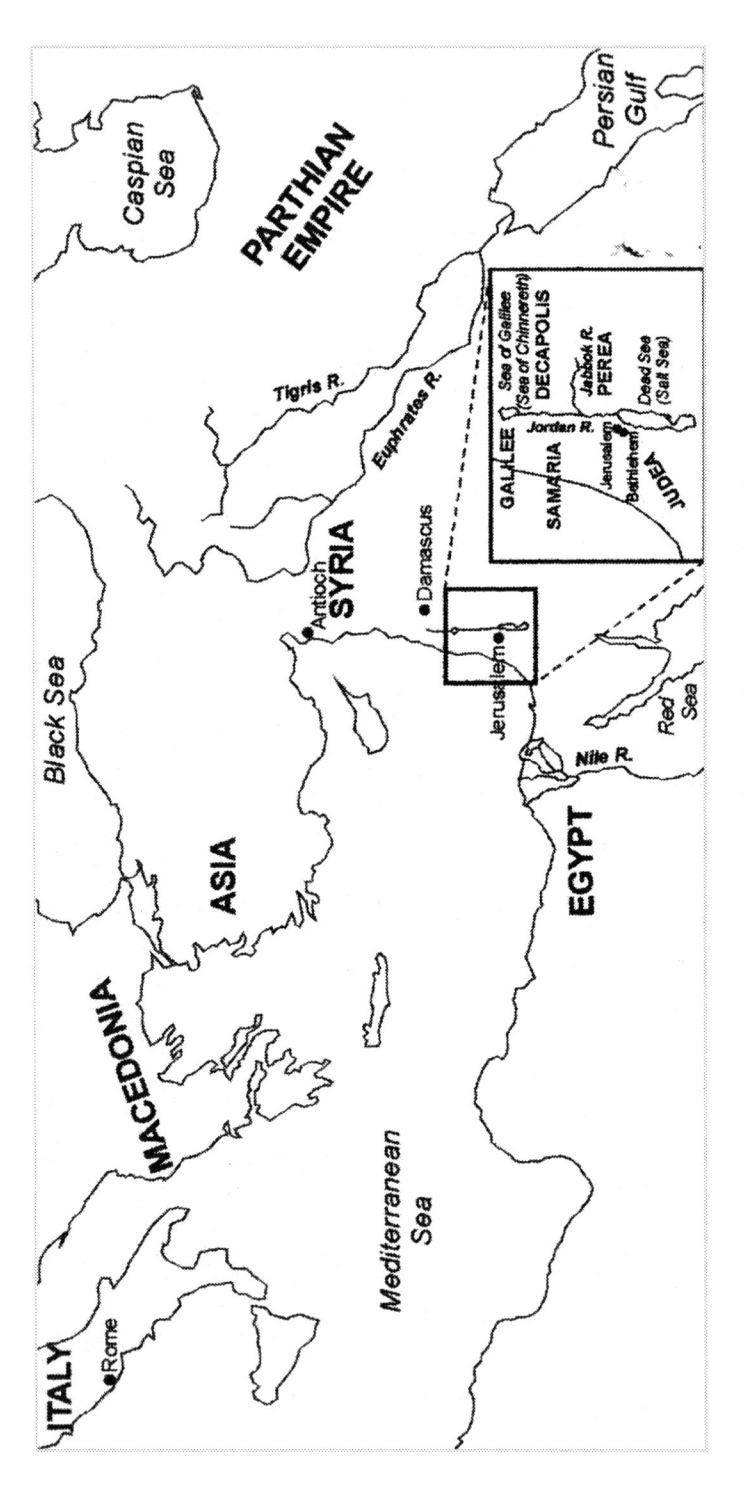

Figure 5: World of Jesus, the Promised Seed

you, and the power of the Most High will overshadow you. So the holy one to be born will be called the Son of God..."
"*I am the Lord's servant,*" Mary answered. "*May it be to me as you have said*" (Luke 1:30-38).

Mary and Joseph believed that God was telling them the truth.[2] Obeying God was no easy task for them. Did she tell her parents? Did they think that she was insane? Joseph tried to keep her pregnancy a secret. Yet, did some people gossip? Did they know that the promised Seed was to be born in Bethlehem? (Micah 5:2). Were they surprised when Caesar Augustus ordered a census of the entire Roman Empire? When he did this, God was working out his plan of salvation. Because Joseph was a descendant of David, they had to register in Bethlehem (Luke 2:1-4). Soon after they arrived there, Mary gave birth to her firstborn son, Jesus (Luke 2:6-7). Did Mary and Joseph praise God for keeping his promise in such an unusual way?

> Obeying God was no easy task for them.

God the Father did not invite aristocrats, priests, or Pharisees to celebrate the birth of his Son. Instead he invited some shepherds, because they gladly accepted spiritual realities. As they tended their flocks that night, an angel of the Lord appeared to them. The angel said, "Do not be afraid. I bring you good news of great joy that will be for all the people. Today in the town of David a Savior has been born to you; he is Christ the Lord. This will be a sign to you: You will find a baby wrapped in cloths and lying in a manger" (Luke 2:10-12).

Then a choir of angels praised God. "Glory to God in the highest, and on earth peace to men on whom his favor rests" (Luke 2:14).

Eagerly the shepherds hurried to Bethlehem to find the baby—the long-awaited promised Seed. After they had seen the child, the shepherds spread the word that the Saviour was born.

2. Herod: Trying to Destroy the Promised Seed

Reign of Herod the Great, king of Judea: 37-4 B.C.[1]
5/4 B.C.[1]

One night some wise men, who were likely from the Parthian Empire, were busy charting the stars when they noticed a bright new star hovering over the region of Judea. Unlike the Israelites, these men did not know the Scriptures. Instead they were probably the priests of Zoroaster, an ancient religion of Persia. In spite of many wrong ideas, these wise men believed in two important facts. Truth exists and can be discovered. Also, a special king would be born to the Jews, one whose coming would be heralded by a star in the sky. Assuming that the logical place to find the king would be in the capital, they made the long arduous journey to Jerusalem. As soon as they reached it, they began to ask, "Where is the one who has been born king of the Jews? We saw his star in the east and have come to worship him" (Matt. 2:2). They never doubted if he had been born. They only needed to know where he was.

> At once Herod realized that they were searching for the Messiah, not him.

Word soon reached King Herod that some wise men from the east were looking for the king of the Jews. At once Herod realized that they were searching for the Messiah, not him. He asked the chief priests and the teachers of the Law where the Messiah would be born. They read to him from a scroll, "But you, Bethlehem Ephrathah, though you are small among the clans of Judah, out of you will come for me one who will be ruler over Israel, whose origins are from of old, from ancient times" (Micah 5:2).

Herod secretly asked the wise men exactly when they first saw the star. Then he sent them to Bethlehem and said, "Go and make a careful search for the child. As soon as you find him, report to me, so that I too may go and worship him" (Matt. 2:8).

The Birth of the Promised Seed   291

Although Bethlehem was only a two-hour journey southwest from Jerusalem,[3] Herod and the rest of the people in Jerusalem were too lazy to search for the Messiah themselves. Instead they let the foreign wise men do it. How ecstatic those wise men were to see the star moving away from Jerusalem towards Bethlehem! They followed the star to the house where Jesus was living. When they saw him, they bowed down and worshipped Him. They gave Jesus the respect and devotion that only God deserved. Then they presented him with their treasures—gold, frankincense, and myrrh, the usual gifts that one would give to a more powerful king. After visiting with Jesus and his family, the wise men returned home a different way, because the Lord warned them in a dream not to go near Herod (Matt. 2:9-12).

As soon as they were gone, God directed Joseph in a dream, "Get up…take the child and his mother and escape to Egypt. Stay there until I tell you, for Herod is going to search for the child to kill him" (Matt. 2:13).

Immediately Mary and Joseph fled with Jesus into Egypt. After a while Herod realized that the wise men were not coming back to Jerusalem. Because he had asked the wise men when they had first seen the star, Herod furiously ordered his soldiers to kill all the boys, two years old and under, in Bethlehem and its vicinity (Matt. 2:16). Satan had tried throughout the centuries to prevent the birth of the promised Seed. Now he wanted to kill Jesus while he was a helpless young child, but God protected him. Mary and Joseph remained in Egypt until after Herod had died. Then they returned to their hometown of Nazareth. The promised Seed would indeed crush the head of the serpent! Satan could not thwart the plan of God.

3. A SIGN OF THE TIMES: ATTEMPTING TO ABOLISH THE KINGSHIP

Reign of Archelaus, son of Herod the Great: 4 B.C.-A.D. 6[4]

While a few believers were overjoyed at the birth of the promised Seed, most of the Jews did not realize that the Messiah had entered this world. The only king that they recognized was

Herod. In 40 B.C. the Roman Senate had declared Antipater's son, Herod the Great, to be the king of Judea. Meanwhile, the Parthians had placed Antigonus, the son of Aristobulus, on the throne. Herod, however, supported by Rome, prevailed against the Parthians. In 37 B.C. he officially became the uncontested king of Judea. Then the Pharisees accepted Herod's rule as God's judgment on his people.[5] As a descendant of Esau, Herod was a distant relative who publicly appeared to worship God. He did make the temple beautiful for the Jews. At his death, however, nationalists refused to acknowledge his son, Archelaus, as their king. Eventually, "A delegation of leading Jews went to Rome," writes Durant, "and begged Augustus to abolish the kingship in Judea. Augustus removed Archelaus, and made Judea a Roman province of the second class, under a procurator responsible to the governor of Syria (A.D. 6)."[6]

> It is not surprising that the Jews hated Rome so much for taking away their freedom or that some outwardly rebelled at Herod's death.

It is not surprising that the Jews hated Rome so much for taking away their freedom or that some outwardly rebelled at Herod's death. Yet it is significant that some Jews begged Augustus to get rid of their king. They likely wanted to restore peace in the land diplomatically. They were certainly unaware that the Messiah was alive or that their actions announced his birth. To God, the Jews already had a living king—Jesus. From that time on any human king sitting on the throne of Judea was an insult to his majesty.

Points to Ponder

1. God shows his sovereignty by working out his plan of salvation through a Roman emperor.
2. At Jesus' birth, the angels proclaimed a spiritual salvation available to all people.

3. The foreign wise men had a greater desire to meet the Saviour than anyone in Jerusalem had.

4. God protected his Son from Satan's fury for our sakes and his glory.

5. The massacre of innocent babies is a terrible picture of unbridled sin.

Chapter Two

The Ministry of Jesus

A.D. 26/27—30[1] God's plan of salvation is accomplished through the life, death, and resurrection of Jesus

1. John the Baptist: The Messenger of Malachi

A.D. 26[2]

IN January 1971 Barry was busy cataloguing books in the church library. The previous July we had moved to London so that he could go to library school at Western University. At the time I did not realize that he had made a bargain with the Lord. He had promised to believe in Jesus if God gave me a job. By the end of August I had found work, but Barry did not keep his promise. Then in October I was unexpectedly offered an even better position when I wasn't even looking for work. Barry still did not surrender to the Lord. Finally, alone in the church library, Barry confessed his sin, forsook atheism, and embraced Jesus as his Lord and Saviour. What a time of rejoicing when he told me that evening! The spiritual wall between us was gone. A few weeks later Rev. Douglas Dakin baptized him. At the service he pointed out God's sovereign grace in drawing a determined atheist to himself. Likewise, John the Baptist preached by the Jordan River and baptized anyone who confessed that he or she was a sinner. Filled with the Holy Spirit, he cried out, "Repent, for the kingdom of heaven is near" (Matt. 3:2).

Gradually word spread so that crowds flocked to hear John preach. The silent years were finally over! Once again God spoke just as he had through the prophets of old. Through John, God implored, "Produce fruit in keeping with repentance. And do not begin to say to yourselves, 'We have Abraham as our father.' For I tell you that out of these stones God can raise up children for Abraham" (Luke 3:8).

> The silent years were finally over!

John the Baptist was unlike previous prophets in two ways. The Old Testament prophets did not baptize anyone. In contrast, John baptized those who repented of their sins and wanted God to forgive them. He also refused to baptize those not willing to turn from their evil ways and to confess their sins. In addition, the Old Testament prophets looked forward to a future day when the promised Seed would procure their salvation. Instead, John the Baptist believed that the day of salvation was near.

2. Satan: Tempting Jesus

One day Jesus asked his cousin John to baptize him. At first John objected, but Jesus insisted and then explained, "Let it be so now; it is proper for us to do this to fulfill all righteousness" (Matt. 3:15).

As soon as John had baptized Jesus, he saw the Holy Spirit come down from heaven like a dove and rest on Jesus. In this way God anointed Jesus and consecrated him for his public ministry. Next God the Father said, "This is my Son, whom I love; with him I am well pleased" (Matt. 3:17). Immediately the Holy Spirit led Jesus into the desert where the devil could tempt him.

Jesus was hungry! (Matt. 4:1-2). After not eating for forty days and nights, he was also very vulnerable. How Satan desired to entice the promised Seed to sin! If Satan could succeed in tripping up Jesus, then God would no longer be pleased

The Ministry of Jesus

with his Son. In fact the Lord would not be able to keep his promise to Adam and Eve. The Saviour would never be able to crush the serpent's head. No one could ever be restored to fellowship with God, and this earth would belong to Satan forever. God's plan would be foiled. Therefore, while Jesus was in a weakened state physically and before he had a chance to begin his public ministry, Satan found him in the desert. He said, "If you are the Son of God, tell these stones to become bread" (Matt. 4:3).

> If Satan could succeed in tripping up Jesus, then God would no longer be pleased with his Son.

Jesus refused to satisfy his physical hunger by obeying the will of Satan. Instead he answered, "It is written: 'Man does not live on bread alone, but on every word that comes from the mouth of God'" (Matt. 4:4).

Next the Devil tempted Jesus emotionally. He said, "If you are the Son of God...throw yourself down. For it is written: 'He will command his angels concerning you, and they will lift you up in their hands, so that you will not strike your foot against a stone'" (Matt. 4:6).

Satan hoped that Jesus would be willing to prove his deity by relying on the providential care of God. Jesus, however, knew that it was wrong to deliberately test God by putting himself in a dangerous situation. He answered, "It is also written: 'Do not put the Lord your God to the test'" (Matt. 4:7).

Finally the Devil tempted Jesus spiritually. How Satan has desired to receive the worship due only to God! That is why he rebelled and coveted God's throne.[3] After he had shown Jesus all the kingdoms of the world, he said, "All this I will give you...if you will bow down and worship me" (Matt. 4:8).

Jesus replied, "Away from me, Satan! For it is written: 'Worship the Lord your God, and serve him only'" (Matt. 4:10).

A defeated Satan left Jesus alone. Then angels gathered around Jesus to look after him. The next day John saw him and cried, "Look, the Lamb of God, who takes away the sin of the world!" (John 1:29). Then he witnessed to others who were standing nearby that Jesus is the Son of God.

3. JESUS: EXPLAINING THE NECESSITY OF SPIRITUAL BIRTH

Soon after Jesus began his public ministry in Galilee, he travelled to Jerusalem for the Passover, where he preached in the temple and performed miracles. Word spread throughout Jerusalem, and many believed in him. Jesus, however, did not commit himself to those people, because he knew what was in their hearts. Many likely wavered in their faith, not sure what to believe. Others were hypocritical, while a few may have had dangerous political intentions. Certainly the general population was eagerly awaiting the arrival of the Messiah who would overthrow Rome and establish Israel as the dominant world power.

Nicodemus, a ruler of the Jews, wanted to meet Jesus privately. One night after finding him, Nicodemus said, "Rabbi, we know you are a teacher who has come from God. For no one could perform the miraculous signs you are doing if God were not with him" (John 3:2).

Jesus knew that Nicodemus was expecting a physical kingdom of God and that he was curious about the miracles. Instead of satisfying his curiosity, Jesus told Nicodemus what he needed to hear, not what he wanted to hear. He directed his attention toward the spiritual nature of the kingdom by telling Nicodemus that he must be born again. Therefore Jesus answered, "I tell you the truth, no one can see the kingdom of God unless he is born again" (John 3:3).

Thinking in only physical terms, Nicodemus asked, "How can a man be born when he is old?...Surely he cannot enter a second time into his mother's womb to be born!" (John 3:4).

Nicodemus needed to learn that, in order to belong to God's kingdom,

> Nicodemus needed to learn that, in order to belong to God's kingdom, his heart attitude must be changed.

his heart attitude must be changed. He must turn from hating to loving God. First he must be born into the physical world. Then he must be born into the spiritual kingdom of God. That is why Jesus tenderly answered:

> *"I tell you the truth, no one can enter the kingdom of God unless he is born of water and the Spirit. Flesh gives birth to flesh, but the Spirit gives birth to spirit. You should not be surprised at my saying, 'You must be born again.' The wind blows wherever it pleases. You hear its sound, but you cannot tell where it comes from or where it is going. So it is with everyone born of the Spirit"* (John 3:5-8).

Moving like the wind, the Holy Spirit enters the one who believes. That person becomes a child in the kingdom of God. Nicodemus questioned, "How can this be?" (John 3:9).

Jesus patiently explained that the Son of Man must be lifted up so that all believers may have eternal life (John 3:14,15). He said, "For God so loved the world that he gave his one and only Son, that whoever believes in him shall not perish but have eternal life" (John 3:16). Jesus wanted Nicodemus to take his eyes off the physical world and to concentrate on spiritual realities. In effect Jesus was saying, "God the Father loves you, Nicodemus. I love you. I am going to be lifted up so that you may have eternal life with God. Only trust me."

Like us, Nicodemus had a choice to make—whether to believe or not. Jesus lovingly warned him, "Whoever believes in him is not condemned, but whoever does not believe stands condemned already because he has not believed in the name of God's one and only Son" (John 3:18).

After Jesus died, Nicodemus accompanied Joseph of Arimathea, another secret believer, to the cross. As they took down his body and buried him in a tomb, Nicodemus likely remembered Jesus' teaching that he must be lifted up. Only then would Nicodemus realize that Jesus had been talking of his death on the cross.

4. Jesus: Declaring His Divinity

Walking past the pool of Bethesda, Jesus saw a man who had been an invalid for thirty-eight years. Filled with compassion, Jesus asked him if he would like to get well.

"Sir," the invalid replied, "I have no one to help me into the pool when the water is stirred. While I am trying to get in, someone else goes down ahead of me."

Then Jesus said to him, "Get up! Pick up your mat and walk" (John 5:2-8).

Immediately the invalid was healed and obeyed Jesus. As he walked down the street, some Jews warned him not to carry his mat on the Sabbath. But he replied, "The man who made me well said to me, 'Pick up your mat and walk'" (John 5:11).

When the Jews asked the invalid who had healed him, he did not know. Afterwards in the temple, Jesus found the man and said, "See, you are well again. Stop sinning or something worse may happen to you" (John 5:14).

> Those Jews were so angry that they wanted Jesus dead

At once the man told the Jews that Jesus had healed him. They were upset and persecuted Jesus, because he had healed the man on the Sabbath. Then Jesus informed them, "My Father is always at his work to this very day, and I, too, am working" (John 5:17).

Those Jews were so angry that they wanted Jesus dead (John 5:18). He had made himself equal to God the Father. This was blasphemy. How would you have responded to the promised Seed?

5. The Sermon on the Mount, Matthew 5-7

Walking throughout Galilee, Jesus taught in the synagogues. He proclaimed, "The time has come...The kingdom of God is near. Repent and believe the good news!" (Mark 1:15). Wherever he went, he healed the sick and those who were demon possessed. No wonder "large crowds from Galilee, the Decapolis, Jerusalem, Judea and the region across the Jordan followed him" (Matt. 4:25). Then one night Jesus spent all night alone in prayer before choosing the twelve men who would become his special disciples. After calling them, Jesus sat down on the mountainside to teach his disciples while the crowds listened nearby. What did he teach those who would help him announce the arrival of the kingdom? Did he explain their roles in a political kingdom? No! Instead Jesus directed their thoughts toward spiritual realities rather than an earthly kingdom. He began by explaining the characteristics of those blessed by God.

> *"Blessed are the poor in spirit, for theirs is the kingdom of heaven. Blessed are those who mourn, for they will be comforted. Blessed are the meek, for they will inherit the earth. Blessed are those who hunger and thirst for righteousness, for they will be filled. Blessed are the merciful, for they will be shown mercy. Blessed are the pure in heart, for they will see God. Blessed are the peacemakers, for they will be called sons of God. Blessed are those who are persecuted because of righteousness, for theirs is the kingdom of heaven"* (Matt. 5:3-10).

The poor in spirit understand "their need for God" (Matt. 5:3, Phillips). They mourn because they have been rebellious sinners. Knowing that they deserve to be punished by a holy righteous God, they "claim nothing" (Matt. 5:5, Phillips). Believers hunger and thirst for God and his truth. Because God has forgiven them, they willingly and gladly forgive others who have hurt them. Such people are pure in the eyes of God. As peacemakers they lead others to acknowledge their need for God's forgiveness—but not everyone will believe. They can expect persecution from non-believers.

Those who belong to the kingdom of heaven are lights in a world of darkness (Matt. 5:14-16). This means that a believer thinks and acts differently than others. For example, the scribes and Pharisees were concerned with the visible outward obedience of the Law. Instead Jesus taught that obedience to the Law begins with the right heart attitude. He said, "You have heard that it was said, 'Do not commit adultery.' But I tell you that anyone who looks at a woman lustfully has already committed adultery with her in his heart" (Matt. 5:27,28).

Believers trust in the providential care of God to supply the necessary food, clothes, and shelter. A loving heavenly Father gives "good gifts to those who ask him" (Matt. 7:11). Jesus promised, "But seek first his kingdom and his righteousness, and all these things will be given to you as well" (Matt. 6:33). Next Jesus taught his disciples how to treat others. "So in everything, do to others what you would have them do to you, for this sums up the Law and the Prophets" (Matt. 7:12).

Actions are a yardstick of a person's beliefs. Do you truly care about another's feelings? Can you forgive someone who has wronged you? Are you willing to point out wrong ideas or wicked behaviour in a loving manner? Can you accept criticism gracefully? Do you love God and others? There are two kinds of people, those who hear and obey Jesus and those who do not. The believer is "like a wise man who built his house on the rock" (Matt. 7:24). When the rain comes, the foundation of the house will be secure. In contrast, the non-believer is "like a foolish man who built his house on sand" (Matt. 7:26). When the rain comes, the house will crash to the ground. That is why Jesus warned his disciples, "Not everyone who says to me, 'Lord, Lord,' will enter the kingdom of heaven, but only he who does the will of my Father who is in heaven" (Matt. 7:21). This sermon is an invitation for people to trust God. Those who listen and believe are promised entrance into the kingdom of heaven. Are you foolish or wise? How are you responding to the promised Seed?

> This sermon is an invitation for people to trust God. Those who listen and believe are promised entrance into the kingdom of heaven.

6. Jesus: Driving Out Demons

Some friends led a demon-possessed man who was blind and mute to Jesus. After Jesus had healed him, everyone was astonished that the man could now talk and see. They wondered, "Could this be the Son of David?" (Matt. 12:23).

When the Pharisees heard this, they said, "It is only by Beelzebub, the prince of demons, that this fellow drives out demons" (Matt. 12:24).

Knowing their thoughts, Jesus rebuked them:

> *"Every kingdom divided against itself will be ruined, and every city or household divided against itself will not stand. If Satan drives out Satan, he is divided against himself. How then can his kingdom stand? And if I drive out demons by Beelzebub, by whom do your people drive them out? So then, they will be your judges. But if I drive out demons by the Spirit of God, then the kingdom of God has come upon you. Or again, how can anyone enter a strong man's house and carry off his possessions unless he first ties up the strong man? Then he can rob his house. He who is not with me is against me, and he who does not gather with me scatters"* (Matt. 12:25-30).

The Pharisees were so eager to discredit Jesus that they accused him of exorcising demons by the power of Satan. How ridiculous! Nobody tries to increase his kingdom by killing his own soldiers. Why would Satan weaken his conquests by eliminating his demons' influence in the lives of people? Instead of proving himself to be an emissary of Satan, Jesus pointed out that his onslaught against demons was actually a sign that the kingdom of God was present. There are two sides in the battle to control people—Satan's kingdom and God's. Just as a robber does not help a householder but renders him powerless, Satan's armies and God's are mutually exclusive.

7. Jesus: Explaining the Growth of the Kingdom

When Jesus was teaching in a synagogue, he asked the congregation, "What is the kingdom of God like? What shall I compare it to? It is like a mustard seed, which a man took and planted in his garden. It grew and became a tree, and the birds of the air perched in its branches" (Luke 13:18,19). Although a mustard seed is very tiny, it will grow into a huge tree. Similarly, the kingdom of God begins very small but over time grows larger and larger. To emphasize his point, Jesus also asked, "What shall I compare the kingdom of God to? It is like yeast that a woman took and mixed into a large amount of flour until it worked all through the dough" (Luke 13:20,21). When yeast is first mixed with flour, it is impossible to see it. Soon the yeast forces the flour to rise, until it becomes a large loaf of bread. Likewise, at first the kingdom of God was small and apparently insignificant. As time passes, however, the kingdom of God will grow much larger, because more people will accept God's gift of salvation.

8. A Clash of Opinion Concerning the Kingdom

Intrigued and excited by the healing miracles of Jesus, crowds followed him to a remote place by the Sea of Galilee. After spending most of the day preaching, Jesus knew that they were hungry. He asked his disciple Philip, "Where shall we buy bread for these people to eat?" (John 6:5).

Surprised, Philip exclaimed, "Eight months' wages would not buy enough bread for each one to have a bite!" (John 6:7).

Meanwhile Andrew found a boy with five small barley loaves and two small fish. Yet he wondered, "How far will they go among so many?" (John 6:9).

Jesus compassionately answered, "Have the people sit down" (John 6:10).

Then 5000 men, besides women and children, sat down in groups of fifty. After Jesus thanked his Father for the food, he distributed it to the crowd. When everyone had finished eating, his disciples gathered the excess—twelve baskets.

After the people witnessed this miracle they speculated, "Surely this is the Prophet who is to come into the world" (John 6:14).

The Jews saw in Jesus the political Messiah whom they were waiting for. Knowing that the crowd would try to forcefully crown him king, Jesus slipped away to be by himself. Instead of welcoming the opportunity, Jesus quietly rejected their intended offer. As the promised Seed, he could have become the visible king of earthly Israel if he had wanted. Instead he disappeared up the mountain to pray.

The next day the crowd found him in Capernaum. Jesus knew that he was only popular because he had provided them with free bread and fish. Imagine living in a country where the leader would heal all of your sicknesses and provide you with plenty to eat! No more toiling in the fields! Utopia! Instead of encouraging the Jews to focus on the physical world, Jesus pointed them to spiritual realities. Knowing that the crowds had been looking for him, Jesus said sadly:

> *"I tell you the truth, you are looking for me, not because you saw miraculous signs but because you ate the loaves and had your fill. Do not work for food that spoils, but for food that endures to eternal life, which the Son of Man will give you. On him God the Father has placed his seal of approval...I tell you the truth, it is not Moses who has given you the bread from heaven, but it is my Father who gives you the true bread from heaven. For the bread of God is he who comes down from heaven and gives life to the world"* (John 6:26-33).

The people responded, "Sir...from now on give us this bread" (John 6:34). They still wanted a limitless supply of ordinary bread.

Jesus replied lovingly, "I am the bread of life. He who comes to me will never go hungry, and he who believes in me will never be thirsty...For my Father's will is that everyone who looks to the Son and believes in him shall have eternal life, and I will raise him up at the last day" (John 6:35-40).

> The Jews began to grumble because Jesus was offering them eternal life and not physical bread.

The Jews began to grumble because Jesus was offering them eternal life and not physical bread. Some of his followers pondered, "This is a hard teaching. Who can accept it?" (John 6:60).

Jesus asked, "Does this offend you? What if you see the Son of Man ascend to where he was before! The Spirit gives life; the flesh counts for nothing. The words I have spoken to you are spirit and they are life. Yet there are some of you who do not believe" (John 6:61-64).

Sadly, many people were not interested in the spiritual bread that Jesus offered. They were only interested in the physical world. They rejected him and went away.

9. Peter's Confession

Throughout the Gospels Jesus continually called himself the Son of Man. This is a direct allusion to the son of man who approaches the Ancient of Days in Daniel 7. D. H. Wallace points out the reason:

> It has long been wondered why Jesus did not appropriate the title Messiah to himself instead of the less clear title Son of man. The former was probably avoided out of political considerations, for if Jesus had publicly used "Messiah" of himself it would have ignited political aspirations in his hearers to appoint him as king, principally a nationalistic figure, and to seek to drive out the Roman occupiers. This is precisely the import of the Jews' actions at

the triumphal entry. Jesus seized on the title Son of man to veil to his hearers his messianic mission but to reveal that mission to his disciples.[4]

While touring Caesarea Philippi, Jesus asked his disciples:

> *"Who do people say the Son of Man is?"*
> They replied, *"Some say John the Baptist; others say Elijah; and still others, Jeremiah or one of the prophets."*
> *"But what about you?"* he asked. *"Who do you say I am?"*
> Simon Peter answered, *"You are the Christ, the Son of the living God."*
> Jesus replied, *"Blessed are you, Simon son of Jonah, for this was not revealed to you by man, but by my Father in heaven. And I tell you that you are Peter, and on this rock I will build my church, and the gates of Hades will not overcome it. I will give you the keys of the kingdom of heaven; whatever you bind on earth will be bound in heaven, and whatever you loose on earth will be loosed in heaven"* (Matt. 16:13-19).

First Jesus praised Peter, because he understood that Jesus was the Messiah, the long-awaited Saviour, and also the Son of God. These are the two truths upon which the New Testament Church was established. The pastors or elders of every church are responsible for preaching the whole truth of God, for discerning and cultivating true faith, and for disciplining believers who tarnish the name of Jesus by their sinful behaviour. Jesus describes these responsibilities as binding and loosening. In Revelation 1-3, John sees the Lord judging how well the pastors of seven churches are fulfilling their calling.

> Knowing that they expected a political Messiah, Jesus gently began to correct their thinking.

Jesus was glad that his disciples believed that he was the Messiah, but, while he was alive, he did not want them to tell anyone else. Knowing that they expected a political Messiah, Jesus gently began to correct their thinking. "From that time on Jesus began to explain to his disciples that he must go to Jerusalem and suffer many things at the hands of the elders, chief priests and teachers of the law, and that he must be killed and on the third day be raised to life" (Matt. 16:21).

Such teaching offended Peter. He rebuked Jesus: "Never, Lord!...This shall never happen to you!" (Matt. 16:22). Would you have reacted the same way?

Jesus answered quickly and sadly, "Get behind me, Satan! You are a stumbling block to me; you do not have in mind the things of God, but the things of men" (Matt. 16:23).

As Jennings reminds his readers, "Are we not compelled to gather from this, and does it not confirm what we have seen, that whoever, or whatever, tends to put aside the atoning work of the Cross is utterly Satanic?"[5]

> *What good will it be for a man if he gains the whole world, yet forfeits his soul? Or what can a man give in exchange for his soul? For the Son of Man is going to come in his Father's glory with his angels, and then he will reward each person according to what he has done. I tell you the truth, some who are standing here will not taste death before they see the Son of Man coming in his kingdom* (Matt. 16:26-28).

In other words, Jesus implored, "Don't you realize that spiritual realities are more important than earthly concerns? Nothing is more important than regaining fellowship with God. I will be coming back to judge every person who has ever lived. Some of you will see my kingdom before you die."

Did Jesus tell the truth? Did his kingdom come in the lifetime of the disciples? If not, then he is a liar and a fraud. How confused the disciples were! First Jesus admitted that he was the Messiah. Then he talked about his death. Six days later Jesus led Peter, James, and John up a mountain. He graciously comforted his three closest disciples by allowing them to see him in his glory. "There he was transfigured before them. His face shone like the sun, and his clothes became as white as the light" (Matt. 17:2).

10. Abraham's Children

As Jesus taught in the temple, many Jews appeared to believe him, but he knew that they did not really understand his message or love him. To weed out the non-believers, he said, "If you hold to my teaching, you are really my disciples. Then you will know the truth, and the truth will set you free" (John 8:31,32).

His listeners were offended. They replied, "We are Abraham's descendants and have never been slaves of anyone. How can you say that we shall be set free?" (John 8:33).

How sad Jesus must have been! One purpose of the sacrificial system was to continually remind the Israelites of their sinfulness and of their need for a Saviour. Yet these people were oblivious to their sin. Jesus patiently explained to them:

> *"I tell you the truth, everyone who sins is a slave to sin. Now a slave has no permanent place in the family, but a son belongs to it forever. So if the Son sets you free, you will be free indeed. I know you are Abraham's descendants. Yet you are ready to kill me, because you have no room for my word. I am telling you what I have seen in the Father's presence, and you do what you have heard from your father"* (John 8:34-38).

Jesus graciously offered them assurance of salvation, but they rejected it. "Us a slave to sin! Preposterous! Surely because we are Abraham's descendants, he is our father," they thought. To Jesus they replied, "Abraham is our father" (John 8:39).

Jesus taught them, "If you were Abraham's children...then you would do the things Abraham did. As it is, you are determined to kill me, a man who has told you the truth that I heard from God. Abraham did not do such things. You are doing the things your own father does" (John 8:39-41).

They needed to understand that their heart attitude determines if they are truly Abraham's children. Physical lineage is not important. How Jesus yearned for them to have the same love for God as Abraham had! Incensed, they protested, "We are not illegitimate children...The only Father we have is God himself" (John 8:41).

> Physical lineage is not important.

If you were in the audience, how would you have reacted to the teachings of Jesus? As a child you were taught that you belonged to God's special people forever because you are a descendant of Abraham. Would you have admitted that you are a slave of sin? Would you have accepted the gift of salvation so freely and lovingly offered by the Saviour? How willing are you to give up the traditions of your spiritual fathers and accept correction?

Ever since the fall of Adam and Eve, there have been two rival kingdoms in this world. Everyone belongs to one or to the other. Those who belong to the kingdom of God are called the children of God; those who belong to the kingdom of Satan are called the children of Satan. Because his listeners rejected his teaching, Jesus declared that they were the children of Satan. If they had accepted his word, then they would have been transferred from the kingdom of darkness to the kingdom of light. Instead Jesus sadly rebuked them:

> *"If God were your Father, you would love me, for I came from God and now am here. I have not come on my own; but he sent me. Why is my language not clear to you? Because you are unable to hear what I say. You belong to your father, the devil, and you want to carry out your father's desire. He was a murderer from the beginning, not holding to the truth, for there is no truth in him. When he lies, he speaks his native language, for he is a liar and the father of lies"* (John 8:42-44).

11. LAZARUS

Lazarus had been dead for four days when Jesus showed up in Bethany, a town at the Mount of Olives and less than two miles east of Jerusalem (John 11:18). Many Jews had walked there to pay their respects. When Martha heard that Jesus was approaching the town, she went to meet him.

> "Lord," Martha said to Jesus, "if you had been here, my brother would not have died. But I know that even now God will give you whatever you ask."
> Jesus said to her, "Your brother will rise again."
> Martha answered, "I know he will rise again in the resurrection at the last day."
> Jesus said to her, "I am the resurrection and the life. He who believes in me will live, even though he dies; and whoever lives and believes in me will never die. Do you believe this?" (John 11:21-26).

Jesus is the source of all life, whether spiritual or physical. Anyone who believes in Jesus as his or her Saviour will continue to live in the spiritual realm after physical death. Jesus also has power over physical death. He promised Martha that the physical bodies of believers would come back to life. As Henry explains, "Man consists of body and soul, and provision is made for the happiness of both."[6]

Martha believed Jesus. She answered, "Yes, Lord...I believe that you are the Christ, the Son of God, who was to come into the world" (John 11:27).

Immediately Martha hurried home to tell her sister Mary that Jesus had come. When Mary rushed to see Jesus, all of the Jews followed her. When they saw how upset Jesus was, some said, "See how he loved him!" (John 11:36).

Others retorted, "Could not he who opened the eyes of the blind man have kept this man from dying?" (John 11:37).

Jesus approached the tomb and ordered some people to remove the stone. Martha objected, "But, Lord...by this time there is a bad odor, for he has been there four days" (John 11:39).

Gently Jesus asked her, "Did I not tell you that if you believed, you would see the glory of God?" (John 11:40). After they rolled the stone away, Jesus yelled, "Lazarus, come out!" (John 11:43).

At once Lazarus stood up and walked out of the cave. Many people believed in Jesus as a result of this miracle. Jesus knew that the scribes and Pharisees opposed him because he did not comply with their ideas concerning the Law. At this point Jesus also raised the ire of the Sadducees, who did not believe in a resurrection from the dead. Yet there was no way to refute the fact of Lazarus' death or resurrection. Many witnesses knew that after four days Lazarus' body had started to decay. How could the Sadducees deny that he who was dead now lived?

Soon afterward the chief priests and the Pharisees called a meeting of the Sanhedrin, the Jewish high council. They complained, "What are we accomplishing?...Here is this man performing many miraculous signs. If we let him go on like this, everyone will believe in him, and then the Romans will come and take away both our place and our nation" (John 11:47,48).

They chose preserving their jobs over believing in the Messiah. Caiphas, the high priest, spoke up. "You know nothing at all! You do not realize that it is better for you that one man die for the people than that the whole nation perish" (John 11:49,50).

Caiphas spoke about the physical world. If Jesus was killed, the Romans would not be tempted to squash a rebellion and thus destroy the entire Jewish nation. Caiphas did not realize that the Holy Spirit also used him to prophesy concerning the spiritual realm. Jesus took our place and died for us so that we could become the children of God. Through John, God promised, "Jesus would die for the Jewish nation, and not only for that nation but also for the scattered children of God, to bring them together and

> Lazarus was the catalyst that led to Jesus' death.

make them one" (John 11:51,52). When he died on the cross, Jesus took the punishment that each of us deserves in order to reconcile us to God. Lazarus was the catalyst that led to Jesus' death. "So from that day on they plotted to take his life" (John 11:53).

12. Jesus: Describing the Nature of the Kingdom

Once, having been asked by the Pharisees when the kingdom of God would come, Jesus replied, "The kingdom of God does not come with your careful observation, nor will people say, 'Here it is,' or 'There it is,' because the kingdom of God is within [among] you" (Luke 17:20,21).

As far as the Pharisees were concerned, kingdoms were political entities that occupied a certain geographical area. Therefore they expected that they would be able to observe the location and the physical reality of the kingdom of God. At some point in time they would be able to see how God's kingdom had overthrown all worldly kingdoms. Such an event would be visible and dateable by all. Much to their surprise Jesus explained that his kingdom would not be physically visible or limited to one geographical area. Just before his death Jesus also told Pilate:

> "My kingdom is not of this world. If it were, my servants would fight to prevent my arrest by the Jews. But now my kingdom is from another place."
> "You are a king, then!" said Pilate.
> Jesus answered, "You are right in saying I am a king. In fact, for this reason I was born, and for this I came into the world, to testify to the truth. Everyone on the side of truth listens to me" (John 18:36,37).

Jesus stated that his kingdom is not of this world.

Jesus stated that his kingdom is not of this world. If it is not a physical kingdom, then it must be a spiritual kingdom. Jesus was born to announce God's truth to a sinful, dying world. In speaking to Zacchaeus, Jesus declared, "For the Son of Man came to seek and to save what was lost" (Luke 19:10). How much he loves us! He wants you to accept his gift of salvation and restore you to fellowship with God. Will you believe God's truth and receive his gift of love? If you do, then you will become a member of Jesus' kingdom.

13. THE AMBITION OF JAMES AND JOHN

Once Peter reminded Jesus that he and the other disciples had given up everything to follow him. Curious about the future, Peter asked, "What then will there be for us?" (Matt. 19:27).

> *"I tell you the truth, at the renewal of all things, when the Son of Man sits on his glorious throne, you who have followed me will also sit on twelve thrones, judging the twelve tribes of Israel. And everyone who has left houses or brothers or sisters or father or mother or children or fields for my sake will receive a hundred times as much and will inherit eternal life. But many who are first will be last, and many who are last will be first"* (Matt. 19:28-30).

Jesus promised that those who remained committed to him would inherit eternal life at the renewal of all things. Yet there would be many surprises. Some thought that they were more important in the spiritual realm than others, but they were wrong. Others would actually receive greater honours. Some think that if they have accepted God's gift of salvation first, then they are more important than one who is a newer believer. Jesus, however, judges by their heart attitude. How much do they love and obey God? For example, Jesus will judge the willingness of believers to choose the Lord over material possessions and their family. Jesus also promised his disciples that they would sit on thrones and judge Israel at the end of time. Paul writes, "Do you not know that the saints will judge the world?" (1 Cor. 6:2). At the Final Judgment believers will hear and affirm Jesus' sentence of condemnation on non-believers.

Sadly, the disciples did not ponder what a world would be like without sin. No fleshly cravings within would tempt a person to sin. No one would try to influence another to sin. Not only would Satan be banished but also all of the other fallen angels. Nowhere in the entire world would there be any taint of sin, because everyone would willingly and joyfully love God. It would be a world where believers would live forever in fellowship with God. Instead, steeped in Jewish tradition, the disciples wanted political power. Their ears likely heard the words, "You will each have thrones." That is why James and John confronted Jesus:

> "Teacher," they said, "we want you to do for us whatever we ask."
> "What do you want me to do for you?" he asked.
> They replied, "Let one of us sit at your right hand and the other at your left in your glory" (Mark 10:35-37).

Those brothers wanted the most important positions in the coming political kingdom. They unwittingly tempted Jesus to choose an earthly kingdom over their spiritual salvation. Max Lucado recognizes the conflict that faced Jesus. "People wanted him to redeem Israel, but he knew better. He would rather his people be temporarily oppressed than eternally lost...He said no to what they wanted and yes to what they needed. He said no to a liberated Israel and yes to a liberated humanity."[7]

14. Jesus: Teaching the Separation of Church and State

Tuesday of his last week, Jesus speaks in the court of the temple[8]

By now both the Pharisees and the Sadducees wanted a reason to arrest Jesus. They decided that the best way to trap him was in his speech. That is why some Pharisees and Herodians asked, "Teacher, we know you are a man of integrity. You aren't swayed by men, because you pay no attention to who they are; but you teach the way of God in accordance with the truth. Is it right to pay taxes to Caesar or not? Should we pay or shouldn't we?" (Mark 12:14,15).

They thought that they had surely trapped him. What a dilemma! If he answered, "Yes, it is right to pay taxes to Caesar," they could accuse him of being pro-Roman. Then the Pharisees could easily arouse the anger of the mob against Jesus, because they wanted a Messiah who would destroy Rome. If he answered, "No, it is wrong to pay taxes to Caesar," they could accuse him of being anti-Roman. Because the Herodians were for Rome, they would soon complain to the governor that Jesus was an insurrectionist. Jesus, however, shocked everyone.

> "Why are you trying to trap me?" he asked. "Bring me a denarius and let me look at it." They brought the coin, and he asked them, "Whose portrait is this? And whose inscription?"
>
> "Caesar's," they replied.
>
> Then Jesus said to them, "Give to Caesar what is Caesar's and to God what is God's" (Mark 12:15-17).

In the mindset of those people, religion and the state were inseparable. To be forced to pay taxes to Rome irked the Jews. They had no desire to worship Roman gods. On the other hand, the Herodians were willing to overlook this issue because they were employed by Rome. As far as his listeners were concerned, Jesus had announced a revolutionary idea. Religion and the state are separate. No one sacrifices their religious beliefs by paying taxes. The government needs money to carry on its earthly business, and this has absolutely nothing to do with the worship of God. Also, the development of a believer's spiritual growth is dependent on the work of the Holy Spirit, not the government. Similarly, Satan and his demons encourage the rebellion of non-believers, not the government. Because the spiritual realm is more powerful than the physical world, both God and Satan influence governments, either for good or evil.

15. THE MOUNT OF OLIVES DISCOURSE, MATTHEW 24-25

Tuesday afternoon of his last week[9]

In his last public address earlier in the day, Jesus had upbraided the Pharisees for their hypocrisy. In their hearts they had said, "If we had lived in the days of our forefathers, we would not have taken part with them in shedding the blood of the prophets" (Matt. 23:30).

Jesus, however, knew that they were about to kill the Son of God. He had lamented, "O Jerusalem, Jerusalem, you who kill the prophets and stone those sent to you, how often I have longed to gather your children together, as a hen gathers her chicks under her wings, but you were not willing. Look, your house is left to you desolate" (Matt. 23:37,38).

As they had left the temple, his disciples had pointed to its buildings. Jesus had asked them, "Do you see all these things?...I tell you the truth, not one stone here will be left on another; every one will be thrown down" (Matt. 24:2).

Later on the Mount of Olives, his disciples privately asked him, "Tell us...when will this happen, and what will be the sign of your coming and of the end of the age?" (Matt. 24:3).

They wanted to know when the temple would be destroyed and when Jesus would come back to set up his kingdom. Jesus answered their first question in Matthew 24:4-35. He finished that section by promising that people living in A.D. 30 would certainly see the destruction of the temple. He said, "I tell you the truth, this generation will certainly not pass away until all these things have happened"(Matt. 24:34).

All these are the beginning of birth pains (Matt. 24:8).

Since time began, there had been wars, famines, and earthquakes. These events would intensify until the destruction of Jerusalem. They will continue to increase in strength and frequency until the end of the world. Similarly, the persecution of believers began when Cain murdered Abel and has continued to this day.

Soon the disciples would suffer persecution and would die for their faith. Moreover, many impostors would claim to be the Messiah, while throughout history false teachers would always teach lies as truth. Deception, persecution, wars, famines, and earthquakes are common occurrences that will happen more often until the end of time. In addition, their consequences will become increasingly more severe. This is just like the pain of childbirth. Every mother is very thankful when her baby is finally born. I know.

> "Because of the increase of wickedness, the love of most will grow cold, but he who stands firm to the end will be saved. And this gospel of the kingdom will be preached in the whole world as a testimony to all nations, and then the end will come" (Matt. 24:12-14).

Thankfully, we can count on God to tell the truth and to keep his promises. In spite of the continual development of Satan's kingdom, Jesus promised us two things. Our salvation is secure, and the kingdom of God will grow throughout the world until the end of time.

> "So when you see standing in the holy place 'the abomination that causes desolation,' spoken of through the prophet Daniel—let the reader understand—then let those who are in Judea flee to the mountains" (Matt. 24:15,16).

As soon as the Romans would destroy the temple, over 1500 years of Mosaic rule would also die. God would allow his beloved city to crumble because the people in it rejected his Son Jesus as their Messiah. He did not live up to their expectations. Concerning the Law and the prescribed festivals, Paul explains, "These are a shadow of the things that were to come; the reality, however, is found in Christ" (Col. 2:17). This was very difficult teaching for the devout Jew to grasp. Would you have accepted it?

> God would allow his beloved city to crumble because the people in it rejected his Son Jesus as their Messiah.

God would not allow the continuation of animal sacrifices after the promised Seed had completed his mission. Jesus is the sinless Lamb of God who paid the penalty for sin. To continue sacrificing animals is an insult to the finished work of Christ on Calvary.

Because of God's mercy, some Jews became the first believers to accept Jesus as their Saviour. Those precious Christians were the beginning of the New Testament Church. The Lord warned them to get out of Jerusalem before the Roman army would destroy it. He gave them a sign—the abomination that causes desolation standing in the holy place. In a parallel passage Luke writes, "When you see Jerusalem being surrounded by armies, you will know that its desolation is near" (Luke 21:20). According to E. F. Kevan:

> The word *bdelygma* refers to that which causes nausea and abhorrence... Anything which outraged the religious feelings of the Jewish people might be so described....Writing for Gentiles, it would seem that Luke has replaced the obscure and mysterious word *bdelygma* by a term more intelligible to his readers. This is not, as some have said, to alter the Lord's meaning, but to explain it. On the principle of interpreting Scripture by Scripture, therefore, the "abomination of

desolation" must mean the Roman troops…The word *bdelygma* was not too strong an expression to describe this invasion, for it was detestable indeed that heathen feet should defile the holy land and that the ungodly should come into the heritage of the Lord.[10]

How difficult it would be for pregnant women or for those with babies to flee! Realizing that the Lord was about to destroy Jerusalem, the believers would know that they must leave the city quickly. "For then there will be great distress, unequaled from the beginning of the world until now—and never to be equaled again" (Matt. 24:21). At no other time in history has a nation been judged for rejecting the physical presence of the Messiah, the promised Seed. It will never happen again.

It was possible that some believers would not leave Jerusalem. "If those days had not been cut short, no one would survive, but for the sake of the elect those days will be shortened" (Matt. 24:22). Desperately expecting God to rescue them from the tribulation, some would mistake false Christs for the Son of God. "At that time if anyone says to you, 'Look, here is the Christ!' or, 'There he is!' do not believe it. For false Christs and false prophets will appear and perform great signs and miracles to deceive even the elect—if that were possible" (Matt. 24:23,24). Christianity has been plagued with false prophets since its beginning. It will continue to struggle with false teachers until the end of the world.

> *"Immediately after the distress of those days 'the sun will be darkened, and the moon will not give its light; the stars will fall from the sky, and the heavenly bodies will be shaken.' At that time the sign of the Son of Man will appear in the sky, and all the nations of the earth will mourn. They will see the Son of Man coming on the clouds of the sky, with power and great glory. And he will send his angels with a loud trumpet call, and they will gather his elect from the four winds, from one end of the heavens to the other"* (Matt. 24:29-31).

God often used imagery about the sun and the moon to signify judgment on nations.[11] Although the primary fulfillment of this passage is Jerusalem's destruction, it is a mistake to relegate Jesus' Second Coming to a figurative event in the past. Significantly, John writes in a similar vein after the destruction of Jerusalem. "Look, he is coming with the clouds, and every eye will see him, even those who pierced him; and all the peoples of the earth will mourn because of him" (Rev. 1:7). The secondary but grander fulfillment is the Second Coming of Jesus. "Every eye will see him" when he returns for believers and to punish the wicked.

"No one knows about that day or hour, not even the angels in heaven, nor the Son, but only the Father" (Matt. 24:36).

Jesus answered the disciples second question directly in Matthew 24:36 to the end of chapter 25. Unlike the destruction of Jerusalem, no one can be certain exactly when Jesus will return, because God the Father is the only one who knows. Beware of anyone who is sure that they have figured out the time of his Second Coming. It is not scriptural. Nevertheless, people keep trying to figure it out. According to Jesus, life will be proceeding normally just as in the days of Noah. If you knew what time a thief would break into your house, you would prevent the theft by being prepared. Like a thief, "the Son of Man will come at an hour when you do not expect him" (Matt. 24:44).

Jesus taught his disciples how to wait for his return. "Therefore keep watch, because you do not know on what day your Lord will come" (Matt. 24:42). The faithful and wise servant will be prepared. He or she will be diligently carrying out the Master's work. "It will be good for that servant whose master finds him doing so when he returns" (Matt. 24:46). Then

Jesus told his disciples two parables to help them understand how to watch and be ready.

One day ten virgins were waiting for the bridegroom to come for his bride. Five were foolish and did not bring extra oil to keep their lamps lit, but the five wise virgins did. When the bridegroom was slow in coming, "they all became drowsy and fell asleep" (Matt. 25:5). At midnight someone yelled, "Here's the bridegroom! Come out to meet him!" (Matt. 25:6).

As soon as the five foolish virgins realized that they were low in oil, they begged the wise virgins, "Give us some of your oil; our lamps are going out" (Matt. 25:8).

The wise virgins answered, "No...there may not be enough for both us and you. Instead, go to those who sell oil and buy some for yourselves" (Matt. 25:9).

After the foolish virgins had gone to buy oil, "the bridegroom arrived. The virgins who were ready went in with him to the wedding banquet. And the door was shut" (Matt. 25:10). When the foolish virgins came back, they cried, "Sir! Sir!...Open the door for us!" (Matt. 25:11).

Instead of welcoming them, the bridegroom said, "I tell you the truth, I don't know you" (Matt. 25:12).

Then Jesus repeated the warning, "Therefore keep watch, because you do not know the day or the hour" (Matt. 25:13).

If Jesus came back today, would you be prepared? Have you accepted his gift of salvation? When he comes back, it will be too late. If you accept his gift, then you will be filled with the Holy Spirit just as the lamps were filled with oil. Becoming a believer is only the first step, however. Jesus told his disciples a second parable. Before leaving on a journey, a master gave some money to each of his servants for safekeeping. "To one he gave five talents of money, to another two talents, and to another one talent, each according to his ability" (Matt. 25:15). A long time later he returned to find out how the servants had taken care of his money.

The master found that the servant with five talents had earned five more. Therefore he said, "Well done, good and faithful servant! You have been faithful with a few things; I will put you in charge of many things. Come and share your master's happiness!" (Matt. 25:21).

Likewise the servant with two talents had earned two more. The master commended him in the same fashion as the first. Then the servant who had received only one talent said, "Master...I knew that you are a hard man, harvesting where you have not sown and gathering where you have not scattered seed. So I was afraid and went out and hid your talent in the ground. See, here is what belongs to you" (Matt. 25:24,25).

The master replied:

> *"You wicked, lazy servant!...Take the talent from him and give it to the one who has the ten talents. For everyone who has will be given more, and he will have an abundance. Whoever does not have, even what he has will be taken from him. And throw that worthless servant outside, into the darkness, where there will be weeping and gnashing of teeth"* (Matt. 25:26-30).

Watching for the Lord's return does not mean lazily staring up at the sky. God expects a believer to diligently use the talents that God has given him or her. One day Jesus will return to sit on his throne in heavenly glory, and everyone ever born will stand before him (Matt. 25:31,32). Then Jesus will separate the sheep from the goats. In other words, he will split believers from non-believers. To believers Jesus will say, "Come, you who are blessed by my Father; take your inheritance, the kingdom prepared for you since the creation of the world" (Matt. 25:34). To non-believers he will say, "Depart from me, you who are cursed, into the eternal fire prepared for the devil and his angels" (Matt. 25:41).

There are two kinds of people, believers and non-believers. There are two destinies, heaven or hell. At Jesus' Second

Coming, he will determine who goes where. Believers will go to eternal life while non-believers will go away to eternal punishment (Matt. 25:46). Are you prepared? Do you love other believers? King Jesus said, "I tell you the truth, whatever you did for one of the least of these brothers of mine, you did for me" (Matt. 25:40).

16. Judas Iscariot

Tuesday evening of his last week[12]

Whenever Jesus visited Jerusalem, he enjoyed spending time with his friends Mary, Martha, and Lazarus of nearby Bethany. One evening a neighbour had invited the three of them to dinner, along with Jesus and his disciples. While they were eating, Mary broke an alabaster jar containing precious perfume and poured it over Jesus' head and feet. Then she wiped his feet with her hair (John 12:1-3).

Judas Iscariot objected, "Why wasn't this perfume sold and the money given to the poor? It was worth a year's wages" (John 12:5). Judas did not really care about the poor. As the treasurer he often stole some of the money entrusted to him.

Jesus answered, "Leave her alone…It was intended that she should save this perfume for the day of my burial. You will always have the poor among you, but you will not always have me" (John 12:7,8).

Mary's loving devotion toward Jesus was the catalyst that Satan needed. Judas was utterly disgusted. "Then Satan entered Judas, called Iscariot, one of the Twelve. And Judas went to the chief priests and the officers of the temple guard and discussed with them how he might betray Jesus. They were delighted and agreed to give him money" (Luke 22:3-5).

17. The Upper Room

Thursday, the evening before his crucifixion[13]

While they ate the Passover meal, Jesus remarked to his disciples, "I tell you the truth, one of you will betray me—one who is eating with me" (Mark 14:18).

One by one they sadly asked, "Surely not I?" (Mark 14:19).

> *Leaning back against Jesus, he [John] asked him, "Lord, who is it?"*
>
> *Jesus answered, "It is the one to whom I will give this piece of bread when I have dipped it in the dish." Then, dipping the piece of bread, he gave it to Judas Iscariot, son of Simon. As soon as Judas took the bread, Satan entered into him.*
>
> *"What you are about to do, do quickly," Jesus told him, but no one at the meal understood why Jesus said this to him* (John 13:25-28).

Judas left immediately. Next, "Jesus took bread, gave thanks and broke it, and gave it to his disciples, saying, 'Take and eat; this is my body.' Then he took the cup, gave thanks and offered it to them, saying, 'Drink from it, all of you. This is my blood of the covenant, which is poured out for many for the forgiveness of sins'" (Matt. 26:26-28).

This was the beginning of a new era. The Saviour of the long-awaited everlasting covenant would soon complete his part in God's plan of salvation. The old covenant based on the blood of animals would soon be unnecessary. Instead, the shed blood of Jesus would be the sacrifice of the new covenant. His blood would be "poured out for many for the forgiveness of sins." At last the promised Seed would restore fellowship permanently between God and believers.

> During this meal Jesus made the transition from the old to the new.

During this meal Jesus made the transition from the old to the new. First he celebrated the Passover supper with his disciples. Then he instituted a new kind of remembrance service that focused on his blood, not the sacrificial blood of animals.

At this point Jesus was faced with a difficult task. The hopes and dreams of his disciples were about to be shattered. He wanted to comfort and encourage them to keep the faith. In order to strengthen them, Jesus taught them two wonderful truths. He is coming back, and the Holy Spirit would be their Comforter in his absence.

Almost 2000 years have passed. Yet believers today may still claim those two truths for themselves. Jesus is coming back. The Holy Spirit is our Comforter.

Jesus encouraged them, "Do not let your hearts be troubled. Trust in God; trust also in me...And if I go and prepare a place for you, I will come back and take you to be with me that you also may be where I am. You know the way to the place where I am going" (John 14:1-4).

Thomas was confused. He said, "Lord, we don't know where you are going, so how can we know the way?" (John 14:5).

Jesus replied, "I am the way and the truth and the life. No one comes to the Father except through me" (John 14:6).

There is only one way to have fellowship restored between a person and God. Jesus is "the way and the truth and the life." Jesus knew that he was about to go back home to God the Father, but he promised to come back someday to take his disciples to heaven. He knew that his absence would cause a terrible void in their lives. They would begin to wonder if they had wasted three and one-half years. That is why he told them, "I will ask the Father, and he will give you another Counselor to be with you forever—the Spirit of truth" (John 14:16,17). He lovingly comforted them, "But the Counselor, the Holy Spirit, whom the Father will send in my name, will teach you all things and will remind you of everything I have said to you. Peace I leave with you; my peace I give you. I do not give to you as the world gives. Do not let your hearts be troubled and do not be afraid" (John 14:26,27).

What a wonderful hope! Jesus would give them peace in the midst of despair. The Holy Spirit would remind them of everything that Jesus had taught them. Concerning the Holy Spirit, he explained, "But you know him, for he lives with you and will be in you" (John 14:17). Henry writes:

> The best knowledge of the Spirit of truth is that which is got by experience; *Ye know him, for he dwelleth with you.* Christ had dwelt with them, and by their acquaintance with him they could not but know *the Spirit of truth.* They had themselves been endued with the Spirit in some measure. What enabled them to leave all to follow Christ, and to continue with him in his temptations? What enabled them to preach the gospel, and work miracles, but the *Spirit dwelling in them*?[14]

Jesus concluded their time together by saying:

> *"You heard me say, 'I am going away and I am coming back to you.' If you loved me, you would be glad that I am going to the Father, for the Father is greater than I. I have told you now before it happens, so that when it does happen you will believe. I will not speak with you much longer, for the prince of this world is coming. He has no hold on me, but the world must learn that I love the Father and that I do exactly what my Father has commanded me. Come now; let us leave"* (John 14:28-31).

Like the Holy Spirit, Satan was already working in the world. Yet Jesus said that "the prince of this world is coming." In what sense would he come? Satan was about to launch his final and most powerful attack against the promised Seed. During those dark days Jesus wanted

> Satan was about to launch his final and most powerful attack against the promised Seed.

his disciples to remember that God is in control of every situation. The Lord is more powerful than Satan.

18. The Significance of the Cross[15]

One day Jesus told a parable:

> *"A man planted a vineyard, rented it to some farmers and went away for a long time. At harvest time he sent a servant to the tenants so they would give him some of the fruit of the vineyard. But the tenants beat him and sent him away empty-handed. He sent another servant, but that one also they beat and treated shamefully and sent away empty-handed. He sent still a third, and they wounded him and threw him out. Then the owner of the vineyard said, 'What shall I do? I will send my son, whom I love; perhaps they will respect him'"* (Luke 20:9-13).

After discussing the situation, the tenants agreed, "This is the heir...Let's kill him, and the inheritance will be ours" (Luke 20:14).

This was likely what Satan thought as Jesus was dying on the cross. Many times Satan had tried to exterminate the Jewish people before the birth of the promised Seed. Afterwards Herod had murdered all the boys aged two and under in Bethlehem. Finally, Satan was sure that, if he could kill Jesus, then he would triumph over God.

> *We have already made the charge that Jews and Gentiles alike are all under sin. As it is written: "There is no one righteous, not even one"* (Rom. 3:9,10).

Ever since Satan rebelled against God, he believed that justice and mercy were mutually exclusive. How could God love someone and then punish that person? After sinning, people could never be restored to fellowship with God. Satan knew that everyone had rebelled against God and deserved to be punished for his or her sin. This means that we must die physically and spiritually. How the promised Seed could ever restore fellowship between God and people was beyond Satan's comprehension, but he did not want to take any chances. He would thwart the plan of God by killing the promised Seed. This strategy backfired. Paul writes, "When we were God's enemies, we were reconciled to him through the death of his Son" (Rom. 5:10). Before the cross, Satan continually tried to prevent believers from entering heaven. For example, he argued with the archangel Michael over Moses' body (Jude 1:9). As far as Satan understood, everyone must pay the penalty for his or her sins. Not one believer had the right to be in heaven. Imagine how gleefully Satan approached God after Jesus' death! He thought that he had won the war. That is why Herman Hoeksema writes:

> Satan actually must have had the hope in his devilish heart that he could so thwart the purpose of the Almighty that the Christ would never be born, would never pay for the sins of the people of God, would never enter into everlasting glory with them. And therefore, according to Satan's view of the matter, all these saints of the Old Testament entered into glory as sinners upon whom he had a righteous claim, as sinners who deserved to go to hell because their sins had not yet been atoned for. God acted according to His counsel, however; and that counsel was certain as to its fulfillment. But Satan took the historical view of the matter, and maintained that all these souls who entered into glory belonged rightfully to him, that they had sinned against the Almighty, that they according to His own sentence were condemned to death, and that therefore they

might not be in heaven. And thus we imagine that the devil goes to heaven to accuse the brethren.[16]

> *This is love: not that we loved God, but that he loved us and sent his Son as an atoning sacrifice for our sins* (1 John 4:10).

> *God presented him as a sacrifice of atonement, through faith in his blood. He did this to demonstrate his justice, because in his forbearance he had left the sins committed beforehand unpunished—he did it to demonstrate his justice at the present time, so as to be just and the one who justifies those who have faith in Jesus* (Rom. 3:25,26).

On the cross Jesus substituted himself for us. He became the sacrifice required to pay the penalty for our sins and also for the sins of the Old Testament believers. Jesus took the place of sinners, because he loves us. "This is how we know what love is: Jesus Christ laid down his life for us" (1 John 3:16). According to E. J. Young, "That is at the very foundation, you might say, of the Gospel, that God must be propitiated. Our sins have alienated us from God, and if God is justly to forgive us our sins He must be propitiated. There must be a sacrifice that will satisfy God's justice and render Him propitious to us."[17] Justice and mercy wed at the cross. To deny either the holiness or the love of God is to deny who God is. He proved his love by satisfying his justice. How reassuring! The price for our salvation is paid in full.

> *Since the children have flesh and blood, he too shared in their humanity so that by his death he might destroy him who holds the power of death—that is, the devil—and free those who all their lives were held in slavery by their fear of death* (Heb. 2:14,15).

Whenever a person repents of sin and accepts God's gift of salvation, Satan loses one more subject from his kingdom.

"For he has rescued us from the dominion of darkness and brought us into the kingdom of the Son he loves" (Col. 1:13). The Lord kept his promise and worked out his plan of salvation. God always tells the truth.

Points to Ponder

1. Spiritual realities are more important to Jesus than this physical world is.
2. Jesus used miracles in the physical world to illustrate spiritual truths.
3. Jesus consistently refused to be the Jewish political Messiah who would liberate them from the Romans.
4. Jesus fulfilled his part in God's plan of salvation when he died a sinless sacrifice and then came back to life.
5. Satan indwelt Judas and used him like a pawn in the plot to kill the promised Seed. God's sovereign will allowed Satan to succeed so that believers could be saved.

Chapter Three

The Early Church

GOD has worked through time to accomplish his plan of salvation. From now on some people will accept that Jesus is the promised Seed and others will reject him.

1. Resurrection Sunday, A.D. 30[1]

In Sudbury we usually tied our dog up to a pin in the front yard. This was not an ordinary day, however, because we were moving to North Bay. The movers needed the front door open so that they could carry our belongings onto the truck. Since the sky was threatening rain, I felt mean tying her up in the backyard. Instead I decided to keep an eye on her. What a mistake! The last time that I saw her, she was quietly lying on the grass. Then she was gone. Our dog of thirteen years had run away. As you can imagine, the drive to North Bay was very sad because we had lost a family member.

One of our neighbours very kindly kept in touch with the dog pound, but there was only silence. We feared the worst. If she had wandered into the woods, she would not know how to survive. Then about five weeks later the pound phoned me to say that she had been found. Philip and I jumped into the car and drove the one and one-half hours back to Sudbury. Our sadness turned to joy and thankfulness!

Of course, our grief cannot truly compare to the shock and sorrow of the believers when Jesus was crucified. They mourned for three days. Terrified of the Jews, the disciples and

> Terrified of the Jews, the disciples and some others hid inside a locked room.

some others hid inside a locked room. Then early Sunday morning Jesus talked to Mary Magdalene, one of the believers, when she went to visit the tomb. Although she told the others that Jesus was alive, they did not believe her. That afternoon Jesus walked with two other believers to Emmaus. They had no idea that the man who was explaining the Scriptures to them was Jesus. Late in the day the three of them sat down to eat. As soon as Jesus gave thanks for the food, their eyes were opened. Immediately Jesus disappeared. Those two believers hurried back to the others who were hiding in the locked room. Suddenly Jesus stood before them and said, "Peace be with you!" (John 20:19). Sadness turned to joy! During the next forty days Jesus appeared to them and spoke about the kingdom of God.

2. The Significance of the Resurrection

And being found in appearance as a man, he humbled himself and became obedient to death—even death on a cross! Therefore God exalted him to the highest place and gave him the name that is above every name, that at the name of Jesus every knee should bow, in heaven and on earth and under the earth, and every tongue confess that Jesus Christ is Lord, to the glory of God the Father (Phil. 2:8-11).

Satan thought that he had won the war when Jesus died. Then a miracle happened. "God exalted him to the highest place." Jesus rose from the dead and began to reign as King over all creation. At Calvary Pilate had ordered that a sign be placed on the cross that read "JESUS OF NAZARETH, THE KING OF THE JEWS" (John 19:19). Pilate proclaimed the truth—unwittingly. As Bruce points out, "Pilate might not be interested, but to many who read these words when first they were published, and to many more who have read them since, they spoke and still speak of a King and a kingdom of enduring importance and authority...the theme of Christ reigning from the tree is central to Christian belief." [2] The resurrection is the proof that Jesus does indeed reign now. He is the long-awaited Messiah. The writer to the Hebrews says, "After he had provided purification for sins, he sat down at the right hand of the Majesty in heaven" (Heb. 1:3). As a result Jesus could tell his disciples, "All authority in heaven and on earth has been given to me" (Matt. 28:18). King Jesus truly reigns now over all creation.

> King Jesus truly reigns now over all creation.

Once Jesus instructed them, "Do not leave Jerusalem, but wait for the gift my Father promised, which you have heard me speak about. For John baptized with water, but in a few days you will be baptized with the Holy Spirit" (Acts 1:4,5).

Slowly the disciples began to dream that their hopes would come true. They thought, "Jesus is the Messiah! He is alive! Perhaps soon the Roman oppression will be over. God's people will be vindicated before an amazed world." Therefore they excitedly asked him, "Lord, are you at this time going to restore the kingdom to Israel?" (Acts 1:6).

He replied patiently, "It is not for you to know the times or dates the Father has set by his own authority. But you will receive power when the Holy Spirit comes on you; and you will be my witnesses in Jerusalem, and in all Judea and Samaria, and to the ends of the earth" (Acts 1:7,8). This was the same message that he had given to them on the day of his resurrection. "As the Father has sent me, I am sending you" (John 20:21). After breathing on them, Jesus had then said, "Receive the Holy Spirit" (John 20:22). In other words, "I am sending you to be my witnesses in the whole world. The Holy Spirit will give you the power to accomplish this task."

At this point the disciples did not understand that their mission was solely to preach the good news of salvation. They

> At this point the disciples did not understand that their mission was solely to preach the good news of salvation.

certainly did not realize how God's plan of salvation included saving Gentiles directly by the blood of Jesus. Paton G. Gloag ponders their dilemma:

> The apostles connected the outpouring of the Spirit with the establishment of the Messianic kingdom; and therefore, when our Lord promised that after a few days they would be baptized with the Holy Ghost, they regarded this as an indirect indication that He would then restore the kingdom of Israel. It is, however, not very clear what ideas the apostles attached to the restoration of the kingdom to Israel. No doubt they shared in the erroneous notions of the Jews in general concerning a temporal Messiah. They still clung to the idea that the Messiah would restore to Israel the palmy days of David and Solomon; that He would rescue Judea from the Roman yoke, and establish His throne in Jerusalem...They probably imagined that the world would be gradually converted to Judaism, and that Jerusalem, the holy city, would be the resort of all nations: most evidently they had not the slightest conception of any other way by which the Gentiles could be admitted into the kingdom of God, except by embracing the Jewish religion.[3]

Finally one day, while standing on the Mount of Olives, Jesus told his disciples to wait in Jerusalem for the outpouring of the Holy Spirit. Then he rose up into the sky and out of sight. Two angels asked those present, "Men of Galilee...why do you stand here looking into the sky? This same Jesus, who has been taken from you into heaven, will come back in the same way you have seen him go into heaven" (Acts 1:11).

The Old Testament prophets foretold the death, resurrection, and glorious reign of Christ. Until it happened, no one had the spiritual ability to understand. How could death be glorious? How could a king begin his reign in such shame? Besides, a dead person cannot be a king. Monarchs are flesh and blood. Nevertheless the promised Seed came at exactly the expected moment. He died, rose again, and set up his kingdom. Surely we can trust that Jesus will come back! God does not lie.

3. The Significance of Pentecost

There are 50 days inclusive from the resurrection to Pentecost[4]

For ten long days the believers waited for the gift of the Holy Spirit. Suddenly, looking like tongues of fire, the Holy Spirit settled on them. How could uneducated Galileans begin to preach to the multitudes in languages unknown to them beforehand? Yet that is exactly what happened. The Holy Spirit descended on them in power to evangelize their world. He used language to communicate the good news of Jesus' death and the resurrection. The result was the birth of the Church as we know it today. Up until Pentecost true believers worshipped the Lord in spirit and in truth. They waited for the promised Seed to restore them to fellowship with God. The Church was like a baby inside its mother's womb. Only after Pentecost could believers fully understand the significance of Jesus' death and resurrection. When Peter preached on that day, about 3000 people repented of their sins and were baptized in the name of the Father, Son, and Holy Spirit. The Church was born. At that point the disciples became known as apostles.

> The result was the birth of the Church as we know it today.

When he comes, he will convict the world of guilt in regard to sin and righteousness and judgment (John 16:8).

Because a holy God has judged everyone guilty of sin, the Holy Spirit longs to convince people that they are sinners. Paul preaches, "Godly sorrow brings repentance that leads to salvation and leaves no regret, but worldly sorrow brings death" (2 Cor. 7:10). Before Pentecost, few listened to the prophets and repented. After Pentecost, the Holy Spirit commended those ancients who had faith for being "a great cloud of witnesses" (Heb. 12:1). To all who have believed since that day to the present, the coming of the Holy Spirit so visibly is "the great and glorious day of the Lord" (Acts 2:20). To nonbelievers, however, the day of Pentecost is "the great and dreadful day of the Lord" (Joel 2:31).[5] Ever since that day, the Holy Spirit has been launching a continuously successful attack against the kingdom of Satan.

4. The Foiled Sadducees

As Peter and John entered the temple, they saw a crippled man begging at the gate. Peter said, "Look at us!" (Acts 3:4). After gaining the man's attention, he said, "Silver or gold I do not have, but what I have I give you. In the name of Jesus Christ of Nazareth, walk" (Acts 3:6).

Immediately the man jumped up and praised God. When the people saw the lame man "walking and jumping, and praising God" (Acts 3:8), they were astonished and flocked toward Peter. Giving all the glory for the miracle to God, Peter preached:

> *You disowned the Holy and Righteous One and asked that a murderer be released to you. You killed the author of life, but God raised him from the dead. We are witnesses of this. By faith in the name of Jesus, this man whom you see and know was made strong. It is Jesus' name and the faith that comes through him that has given this complete healing to him, as you can all see. Now, brothers, I know that you acted in ignorance, as did your leaders. But this is how God fulfilled what he had*

foretold through all the prophets, saying that his Christ would suffer (Acts 3:14-18).

After urging them to repent of their sins, Peter explained, "He [Jesus] must remain in heaven until the time comes for God to restore everything, as he promised long ago through his holy prophets" (Acts 3:21).

Ever since Jesus' ascension into heaven, there has been tension between the present reality of believers and our glorious future. Paul writes, "We know that the whole creation has been groaning as in the pains of childbirth right up to the present time. Not only so, but we ourselves, who have the firstfruits of the Spirit, groan inwardly as we wait eagerly for our adoption as sons, the redemption of our bodies" (Rom. 8:22,23). Anyone who has accepted God's gift of salvation belongs to his kingdom now. Since the Holy Spirit is living within every member of that kingdom, each believer will experience God's power to root out sin and live pleasing to him. Yet we long for the day when we will see Jesus face to face. Then we will live forever in a kingdom that will be free of sin.

Meanwhile the Sadducees were upset at Peter. No doubt they thought that they had rid themselves of a problem when they contrived to have Jesus killed. Not so. Since the apostles would not stop talking about Jesus' miraculous resurrection, thousands were joining this new sect. Instead of one problem, Jesus, they had many people testifying to the resurrection of this one man. Talk about a multiplication problem. They had it. Satan must not have been pleased. No created being is able to thwart the plan of God. As long as this present world exists, many will continue to accept the wonderful salvation offered by the Lord. How are you responding to the promised Seed?

> Talk about a multiplication problem. They had it.

5. Gamaliel

The Sadducees were so jealous of the apostles' popularity that they arrested them and put them in jail. Then during the night an angel opened the prison doors to free them (Acts 5:17-19). The next day the Sanhedrin, the Jewish council of religious leaders, assembled together to question them. When officers were sent to fetch the prisoners, they discovered that the apostles were no longer in jail. Instead they found them preaching in the temple courts. Fearing the people, the officers brought them from the temple to the council without using force. Then the high priest said, "We gave you strict orders not to teach in this name...Yet you have filled Jerusalem with your teaching and are determined to make us guilty of this man's blood" (Acts 5:28).

Peter and the other apostles replied, "We must obey God rather than men! The God of our fathers raised Jesus from the dead—whom you had killed by hanging him on a tree. God exalted him to his own right hand as Prince and Savior that he might give repentance and forgiveness of sins to Israel" (Acts 5:29-31).

The council furiously wanted to kill them all, but Gamaliel wisely advised them to let the apostles go:

> *"Men of Israel, consider carefully what you intend to do to these men. Some time ago Theudas appeared, claiming to be somebody, and about four hundred men rallied to him. He was killed, all his followers were dispersed, and it all came to nothing. After him, Judas the Galilean appeared in the days of the census and led a band of people in revolt. He too was killed, and all his followers were scattered. Therefore, in the present case I advise you: Leave these men alone! Let them go! For if their purpose or activity is of human origin, it will fail. But if it is from God, you*

Yet Gamaliel realized that if God were not in it, the sect would die.

will not be able to stop these men; you will only find yourselves fighting against God" (Acts 5:35-39).

To the Jews, this was an heretical sect of Judaism. Yet Gamaliel realized that if God were not in it, the sect would die. If God were in it, pity those who would fight against him.

6. The First Persecution, A.D. 35[6]

Around the time of the crucifixion, devout Jews from Cyrene, Alexandria, Cilicia, and Asia had travelled a long way to worship God at the temple in Jerusalem. They were thankful to be there, because back home they were far from the temple. Many of them had remained in Jerusalem after Pentecost. As time passed, a large number of those Grecian Jews became believers. Meanwhile many priests and Jews from Judea and Galilee had also accepted God's gift of salvation. Eventually tensions arose between the two factions over the distribution of food to the widows. The Grecians insisted that the Hebrew widows were receiving preferential treatment. The apostles knew that they were responsible to pray and preach the Word of God to this growing Church. Therefore the whole group chose seven men as deacons to make sure that all widows were treated equally. One of the seven was called Stephen (Acts 6:1-6).

Some non-believing Grecian Jews did not like Stephen for his words of wisdom. Because of their efforts Stephen was forced to appear before the Sanhedrin to answer false charges (Acts 6:9-12). He was accused of continually speaking out against the Law and against the holy place, meaning Jerusalem or, more likely, the temple. In his defense Stephen emphasized some important truths about Israel's history. God became a friend of Abraham while he was still a heathen living in Mesopotamia. Thus the first Jew was originally a Gentile. Abraham lived in the Promised Land as a stranger, and his descendants did not possess the land until 400 years later. At first the Israelites rejected Moses as their deliverer from slavery in Egypt. Afterwards, while Moses was receiving the Law from God, the people became impatient and worshipped a golden calf. Furthermore the temple did not exist until the time of Solomon. Obviously, the Israelites worshipped God for years without the Law or the temple, and outside the Promised Land. Stephen then explained to the council that God does not live in a physical house. Instead God declares, "Heaven is my throne, and the earth is my footstool" (Acts 7:49). In conclusion, Stephen sadly denounced the Israelites for continually resisting the Holy Spirit. Their ancestors persecuted the prophets, and the present generation murdered the Righteous One, meaning Jesus, the Messiah. As God's special people, the Israelites had received the Law, but they did not obey it (Acts 7:51-53).

At that point bedlam ensued. As far as those men were concerned, Stephen had just violated their sacred trust. It was the Sanhedrin's duty to uphold the Law. To be accused of not obeying it incensed them. Furiously refusing to listen to another word, they covered their ears and yelled loudly. If you were brought up a devout Jew, one of God's special people, how easily would you have embraced those truths? Without the Holy Spirit working in your heart, you would probably be as horrified and upset.

> *They all rushed at him, dragged him out of the city and began to stone him. Meanwhile, the witnesses laid their clothes at the feet of a young man named Saul. While they were stoning him, Stephen prayed, "Lord Jesus, receive my spirit." Then he fell on his knees and cried out, "Lord, do not hold this sin against them." When he had said this, he fell asleep* (Acts 7:57-60).

Saul, whose name was Paul in Greek, listened and approved of Stephen's murder. He rejected the truths in Stephen's sermon that race, temple, land, and Law are not necessary prerequisites for properly worshipping God. Therefore Saul zealously led the first persecution against believers. Luke records, "On that day a great persecution broke out against the church at Jerusalem, and all except the apostles were scattered throughout Judea and Samaria...But Saul began to destroy the church. Going from house to house, he dragged off men and women and put them in prison" (Acts 8:1-3).

7. THE CONVERSION OF SAUL, A.D. 35[6]

Saul continued to aggressively search for believers and throw them in jail. One day, in his zeal to destroy this new sect, he asked the high priest for permission to arrest believers in Damascus and bring them to Jerusalem.

> *As he neared Damascus on his journey, suddenly a light from heaven flashed around him. He fell to the ground and heard a voice say to him, "Saul, Saul, why do you persecute me?"*
> *"Who are you Lord?" Saul asked.*
> *"I am Jesus, whom you are persecuting," he replied. "Now get up and go into the city, and you will be told what you must do"* (Acts 9:3-6).

Those who travelled with Saul were in shock. They had heard Jesus' voice, but they did not see or understand him. Because the bright light had blinded him, Saul needed his friends to guide him into the city. "For three days he was blind, and did not eat or drink anything" (Acts 9:9).

Afterwards God called to Ananias in a vision, and he answered, "Yes, Lord" (Acts 9:10).

The Lord told Ananias where to find Saul and that Saul was expecting him. God said that Ananias must place his hands on Saul to restore his sight. Ananias was afraid of Saul, however.

> *"Lord," Ananias answered, "I have heard many reports about this man and all the harm he has done to your*

saints in Jerusalem. And he has come here with authority from the chief priests to arrest all who call on your name."
But the Lord said to Ananias, "Go! This man is my chosen instrument to carry my name before the Gentiles and their kings and before the people of Israel" (Acts 9:13-15).

As soon as Ananias found Saul, he placed his hands on him and said, "Brother Saul, the Lord—Jesus, who appeared to you on the road as you were coming here—has sent me so that you may see again and be filled with the Holy Spirit" (Acts 9:17).

Immediately Saul could see again. After he was baptized, Saul ate and regained his strength. "At once he began to preach in the synagogues that Jesus is the Son of God" (Acts 9:20). Everyone was amazed, because they knew that he had come to Damascus to arrest all the believers. Instead, he was preaching the same message they were preaching. Shortly afterwards Saul retired to Arabia for three years, where he was alone with God. On his return to Damascus, the non-believing Jews soon plotted to kill him because his preaching was so powerful. One night some believers ruined their plans by lowering Saul in a basket over the city wall (Acts 9:23-25). In Jerusalem Saul had similar problems as in Damascus. Believers were afraid to trust the man who had so zealously tried to destroy them, but Barnabas befriended Saul and took him to the apostles. For fifteen days Saul visited Peter. Meanwhile non-believers were angry at his message and tried to kill him. Encouraged by the believers to leave, Saul went home to Tarsus (Acts 9:26-30).

8. Peter and Cornelius

After Saul's conversion the Church "enjoyed a time of peace" (Acts 9:31). One day Peter visited the believers in Lydda and Joppa. While up on a roof praying and waiting for lunch, Peter fell into a trance. He saw a large sheet, full of four-footed animals, reptiles and birds, coming down towards him.

Three times he heard a voice saying, "Get up, Peter. Kill and eat."

"Surely not, Lord!" Peter replied. "I have never eaten anything impure or unclean."

The voice answered, "Do not call anything impure that God has made clean" (Acts 10:13-15).

As the sheet disappeared into the sky, Peter wondered why the Lord had given him such a vision. Meanwhile men from a God-fearing Roman centurion called Cornelius were knocking at the door. The Holy Spirit said to Peter, "Simon, three men are looking for you. So get up and go downstairs. Do not hesitate to go with them, for I have sent them" (Acts 10:19,20).

Cornelius was so glad when Peter arrived at his door in Caesarea that he bowed down in reverence. Peter exclaimed, "Stand up...I am only a man myself" (Acts 10:26). Soon Peter told the crowd who had gathered, "You are well aware that it is against our law for a Jew to associate with a Gentile or visit him. But God has shown me that I should not call any man impure or unclean. So when I was sent for, I came without raising any objection. May I ask why you sent for me?" (Acts 10:28,29).

Cornelius replied that an angel had instructed him to send for Peter and had even explained how to find him. Therefore Peter responded by saying:

> *"I now realize how true it is that God does not show favoritism but accepts men from every nation who fear him and do what is right. You know the message God sent to the people of Israel, telling the good news of peace through Jesus Christ, who is Lord of all. You know what has happened throughout Judea, beginning in Galilee after the baptism that John preached—how God anointed Jesus of Nazareth with the Holy Spirit and power, and how he went around doing good and healing all who were under the power of the devil, because God was with him"* (Acts 10:34-38).

While Peter was preaching, "the Holy Spirit came on all who heard the message" (Acts 10:44). Peter and the Jewish believers who had accompanied him "were astonished that the gift of the Holy Spirit had been poured out even on the Gentiles" (Acts 10:45). They assumed that Cornelius and his relatives only had access to God through the Jewish religion, but Paul contradicts this notion. "This mystery is that through the gospel the Gentiles are heirs together with Israel, members together of one body, and sharers together in the promise in Christ Jesus" (Eph. 3:6). The truth of an open door to heaven for all is at the heart of the gospel invitation. Everyone has direct access to God through Jesus. "For there is one God and one mediator between God and men, the man Christ Jesus" (1 Tim. 2:5). The Holy Spirit welcomed those Gentiles into the kingdom of heaven. As proof of their salvation, they spoke in tongues (or other languages) and praised God (Acts 10:46).

> The truth of an open door to heaven for all is at the heart of the gospel invitation.

Meanwhile Peter and his friends learned a valuable lesson, something that they had not known or understood before. God loves and saves Gentiles in the same way that he loves and saves Jews—through the blood of Jesus. Recognizing the reality of their faith, Peter ordered that the new believers be baptized. During the next few days they likely united together to worship God. This is the first time in Scripture that "the dividing wall of hostility" (Eph. 2:14), the barrier that had so long divided Jew and Gentile, was visibly destroyed by the Lord Jesus. In the Church, faith in Christ is what counts—not race, religion, or government. Paul writes, "For through him we both have access to the Father by one Spirit" (Eph. 2:18).

By A.D. 43[7] some of the believers had "traveled as far as Phoenicia, Cyprus and Antioch, telling the message only to Jews" (Acts 11:19). Eventually some from Cyprus and Cyrene went to Antioch and also witnessed to the Greeks. A great number accepted God's gift of salvation. When the church at

Jerusalem heard about the Greeks believing in Jesus, they sent Barnabas, Saul's friend, to find out what was happening. "He was glad and encouraged them all to remain true to the Lord with all their hearts" (Acts 11:23). Afterwards Barnabas went to look for Saul in Tarsus so that he could help with the work at Antioch. "The disciples were called Christians first at Antioch" (Acts 11:26).

9. Paul's First Missionary Journey, A.D. 46-48[6]

One day while the church at Antioch was worshipping God and fasting, the Holy Spirit said, "Set apart for me Barnabas and Saul for the work to which I have called them" (Acts 13:2).

God had accomplished his plan of salvation through the death and resurrection of Jesus. Now he was about to expand his kingdom by reaching the Gentiles who lived throughout the Roman Empire. That is why Barnabas and Saul became the first missionaries sent by God to establish local churches in other places. After being officially set apart for this work by the Church, they set sail for Cyprus with John Mark as their helper. After travelling and preaching throughout the island, they sailed to Perga in Pamphylia, where, sadly, John left them and returned to Jerusalem. In every place they first preached at the local synagogue. In Pisidian Antioch some Jews, and also some Gentile converts to Judaism, were very interested in their message and asked them to speak again. The non-believing Jews were jealous when almost the entire city gathered the next Sabbath to listen to the good news of salvation.

Paul and Barnabas responded boldly, "We had to speak the word of God to you first. Since you reject it and do not consider yourselves worthy of eternal life, we now turn to the Gentiles" (Acts 13:46).

"When the Gentiles heard this, they were glad and honored the word of the Lord; and all who were appointed for eternal life believed" (Acts 13:48). God blessed their preaching by establishing churches in several towns in modern-day Turkey.

> Although many Jews and Gentiles accepted God's gift of salvation, others were violently opposed.

Although many Jews and Gentiles accepted God's gift of salvation, others were violently opposed. In Lystra a crowd stoned Paul, dragged him out of the city, and left him for dead. He got up and walked back into the city (Acts 14:19,20). During this first trip Paul and Barnabas were away two years and travelled about 1,500 miles.[8] After their journey was over, they reported to the church at Antioch "all that God had done through them and how he had opened the door of faith to the Gentiles" (Acts 14:27).

10. The First Christian Council at Jerusalem, A.D. 50[6]

Not surprisingly, there were Jews who insisted that the only way for Gentiles to receive Christ was through Judaism. Such people became known as Judaizers. One day some Judaizers from Jerusalem visited Antioch to teach their doctrine to the Gentile believers. They self-righteously demanded, "Unless you are circumcised, according to the custom taught by Moses, you cannot be saved" (Acts 15:1).

Paul and Barnabas were so upset that they travelled to Jerusalem to discuss the issue with the apostles and elders. At the meeting some believers who were Pharisees persisted, "The Gentiles must be circumcised and required to obey the law of Moses" (Acts 15:5).

Peter addressed the council first:

> *"Brothers, you know that some time ago God made a choice among you that the Gentiles might hear from my lips the message of the gospel and believe. God, who knows the heart, showed that he accepted them by giving the Holy Spirit to them, just as he did to us. He made no distinction between us and them, for he purified their hearts by faith. Now then, why do you try to test God by putting on the necks of the disciples a yoke that neither*

we nor our fathers have been able to bear? No! We believe that it is through the grace of our Lord Jesus that we are saved, just as they are" (Acts 15:7-11).

Afterwards everyone quietly listened to the testimonies of Paul and Barnabas concerning the "miraculous signs and wonders God had done among the Gentiles through them" (Acts 15:12). Then based on Amos 9:11,12, James explained:

"Brothers, listen to me. Simon has described to us how God at first showed his concern by taking from the Gentiles a people for himself...It is my judgment, therefore, that we should not make it difficult for the Gentiles who are turning to God. Instead we should write to them, telling them to abstain from food polluted by idols, from sexual immorality, from the meat of strangled animals and from blood" (Acts 15:13-20).

Then the apostles and elders wrote a letter to the Gentile believers in Antioch to say:

We have heard that some went out from us without our authorization and disturbed you, troubling your minds by what they said...It seemed good to the Holy Spirit and to us not to burden you with anything beyond the following requirements: You are to abstain from food sacrificed to idols, from blood, from the meat of strangled animals and from sexual immorality. You will do well to avoid these things (Acts 15:24-29).

These suggestions wisely encouraged the Gentile believers to avoid any hint of paganism. It was not an attempt to insist that certain laws be obeyed in order to guarantee salvation. It was very important for Paul

> It was very important for Paul to convince the council that the Gentiles had received salvation apart from the Law.

to convince the council that the Gentiles had received salvation apart from the Law. Not to do so would jeopardize the effectiveness of the finished work of Christ on Calvary. Thankfully, the council decided that circumcision was not necessary for salvation, and the Judaizers were unable to sway the council in their direction.

11. Paul's Second Missionary Journey, A.D. 50-52[6]

Paul was eager to return to the towns where he and Barnabas had founded local churches. When Barnabas wanted to take John Mark again, Paul refused. He did not trust John, because he had deserted them in Pamphylia previously. Since they could not resolve their disagreement, Barnabas sailed to Cyprus with John Mark. Meanwhile Paul chose Silas to accompany him to Syria and Cilicia. "As they travelled from town to town, they delivered the decisions reached by the apostles and elders in Jerusalem for the people to obey. So the churches were strengthened in the faith and grew daily in numbers" (Acts 16:4,5). After he had travelled through Phrygia and Galatia, Paul wanted to spend time in Asia, but the Holy Spirit would not let him. "During the night Paul had a vision of a man of Macedonia standing and begging him, 'Come over to Macedonia and help us'" (Acts 16:9). By obeying the Lord, Paul was instrumental in reaching the Gentiles in Macedonia, Greece, and ultimately throughout the Roman Empire. On this particular trip local churches grew in many towns and cities in Macedonia and Greece. Those believers accepted God's gift of salvation and became members of God's kingdom. In three years Paul travelled about 3500 miles.[8] Half of this time he spent in Corinth.

12. Paul's Third Missionary Journey, A.D. 53-57[9]

After a short visit to Jerusalem and Antioch, Paul set out once again. This time he spent two years at Ephesus in Asia. During those trips Paul suffered much persecution, but he never stopped preaching the good news that Jesus died and rose again to pay the penalty for sin. Then, on his last visit to Jerusalem, Paul was falsely accused and arrested. The non-believing Jews hated his message of forgiveness through Jesus' blood. They refused to believe that Jesus was God's Son and their Messiah. For two years Paul remained in jail in Caesarea. God, however, continued to work out his plan to reach Gentiles through Paul. Eventually Paul would preach in Rome.

13. Paul Explaining the Hope of Israel, A.D. 57-59

Paul imprisoned in Caesarea[9]

As procurator of Judea, Festus had a problem. The Jews had laid charges against Paul, who had testified, "I have done nothing wrong against the law of the Jews or against the temple or against Caesar" (Acts 25:8).

Paul had also refused to go to trial at Jerusalem; instead he had appealed to Caesar. Festus, therefore, decided to ask King Agrippa for help. He said:

> *"King Agrippa, and all who are present with us, you see this man! The whole Jewish community has petitioned me about him in Jerusalem and here in Caesarea, shouting that he ought not to live any longer. I found he had done nothing deserving of death, but because he made his appeal to the Emperor I decided to send him to Rome. But I have nothing definite to write to His Majesty about him. Therefore I have brought him before all of you, and especially before you, King Agrippa, so that as a result of this investigation I may have something to write. For I*

think it is unreasonable to send on a prisoner without specifying the charges against him" (Acts 25:24-27).

When King Agrippa invited Paul to speak, he defended himself in this way:

"The Jews all know the way I have lived ever since I was a child, from the beginning of my life in my own country, and also in Jerusalem. They have known me for a long time and can testify, if they are willing, that according to the strictest sect of our religion, I lived as a Pharisee. And now it is because of my hope in what God has promised our fathers that I am on trial today. This is the promise our twelve tribes are hoping to see fulfilled as they earnestly serve God day and night. O king, it is because of this hope that the Jews are accusing me. Why should any of you consider it incredible that God raises the dead?" (Acts 26:4-8).

After listening to Paul's defense, Festus and Agrippa left the room to talk privately. They both agreed that Paul had not done anything to deserve death or imprisonment. Agrippa said to Festus, "This man could have been set free if he had not appealed to Caesar" (Acts 26:32).

Paul finally reached Rome, where he preached to a group of Jews. He told them, "It is because of the hope of Israel that I am bound with this chain" (Acts 28:20). Some believed, and some did not. To those who refused to believe Paul said, "Therefore I want you to know that God's salvation has been sent to the Gentiles, and they will listen!" (Acts 28:28).

> The Jews imprisoned their fellow countryman Paul because he taught salvation from sin through the shed blood of Jesus.

There are two hopes of Israel—one from God and one from those who think that he promised Israel world dominance under any circumstance. Such people refuse to believe that God would ever apply the law for nations to Israel (Jer. 18:7-10).[10] The Jews imprisoned their fellow countryman Paul because he taught salvation from sin through the shed blood of Jesus. This was the hope of the prophets, for they longed for the arrival of the promised Seed, the Saviour who would restore fellowship between God and believers. In contrast, the non-believing Jews taught strict adherence to the Law and a political dominance of the world. Mauro ponders the resulting conflict:

> What then *is* the true and biblical "Hope of Israel"? To obtain a full answer to this question it is necessary that we search the Scriptures from beginning to end...
>
> Inasmuch as what Paul had been preaching, both to the Jews and also to the Gentiles, was the gospel of Jesus Christ, and nothing else, it follows that the true "hope of Israel" is an essential part of that gospel; and therefore it is a matter regarding which we cannot afford to be mistaken.
>
> The above quoted statement of Paul to the Jewish leaders at the imperial city is very illuminating. It shows, to begin with, that, whatever it was he had been preaching as "the hope of Israel," it was something *so contrary to the current Jewish notion thereof* that it caused the people to clamor for his death (Acts 22:22), and led to his being formally accused before the Roman Governor as "a pestilent fellow, and a mover of sedition among all the Jews throughout the world" (Acts 24:5 [KJV]). Had he been preaching what the Jews themselves believed to be, and what their rabbis had given them as, the true interpretation of the prophesies (namely, that God's promise to Israel was a kingdom of earthly character that should have dominion over all the world), they would have heard him with intense satisfaction. But what Paul and all the apostles preached was that what God had promised afore by His prophets in the Holy Scriptures was a kingdom over which Jesus Christ of

the seed of David should reign in *resurrection*, a kingdom that flesh and blood *cannot inherit*, a kingdom which does *not* clash with the duly constituted governments of this world, and one into which Gentiles are *called upon terms of perfect equality* with Jews...

Thus the teaching of Christ and His apostles in respect to the vitally important subject of the Kingdom of God, the hope of Israel, came into violent collision with that of the leaders of Israel; and because of this *He* was crucified and *they* were persecuted.[11]

14. The Separation of Christianity from Judaism, A.D. 66[12]

For almost 130 years the Roman Empire had ruled Judea. If God keeps his promises, the Messiah should have been born by now (Dan. 9:25,26). Why had he not set up his kingdom? Although the false writer of the Psalms of Solomon promised that the Gentiles would live in submission under the yoke of the Messiah,[13] it had not happened yet. Filled with a smouldering hatred of Rome, many Zealots openly revolted. It was no surprise when Rome retaliated. This is how Keller recounts the disintegration of peace between Judea and Rome:

> This mounting anger broke into open revolt in May 66, when the procurator, Florus, demanded 17 talents from the Temple treasury. The Roman garrison was overrun. Jerusalem fell into the hands of the rebels. The prohibition of the daily sacrifices to the emperor meant an open declaration of war against the Roman world empire. Tiny Jerusalem threw down the gauntlet at Rome's feet and challenged the great Imperium Romanum.
>
> This was the signal for the whole country. Rebellion flared up everywhere. Florus was no longer in command of the situation. The governor of the province of Syria, C. Cestius Gallus, marched to the rescue with one legion and a large number of auxiliary troops, but

was forced to retire with heavy losses. The rebels controlled the country.

Being certain that Rome would strike back with all its might, they hastened to fortify the cities.[14]

The believers in Jerusalem expected that Roman legions would soon come and squash the rebellion. They remembered Jesus' instructions to flee as soon as armies surrounded the city (Luke 21:20). Therefore they left Jerusalem and moved to Pella, a town east of the Jordan River in Decapolis. In this way God protected the church in Jerusalem from destruction. Such behaviour angered the non-believing Jews. As Durant points out, "From that hour Judaism and Christianity parted. The Jews accused the Christians of treason and cowardice, and the Christians hailed the destruction of the Temple by Titus as a fulfillment of Christ's prophecy."[15]

Due to persecution after Stephen's martyrdom, many Jewish believers had gradually travelled as far north as Antioch and as far west as Cyprus. In addition, most of the Grecian Jews present during the crucifixion had likely gone back home. Many of them had heard Peter's sermon at Pentecost and had accepted Jesus as their Saviour. Because of this exodus from Judea, other Jews and Gentiles believed in God's wonderful plan of salvation and established local churches. One example is the church at Rome. Then, sent by the Holy Spirit, Paul and Barnabas became the first missionaries to spread the news of salvation and establish local churches of believers wherever they went. In accordance with God's plan, Paul ended up in Rome, the capital of the Roman Empire. From there more believers spread the gospel over the rest of the Empire.

The promised Seed has paid the penalty for sin. Now God's plan is to continue the expansion of his kingdom through local churches. He will do this until the end of time. No one can thwart the plan of God.

Aren't you glad that God's plan of salvation includes people from every race? Aren't you glad that Paul was willing to be an obedient servant of the Lord?

Points to Ponder

1. Before his death Jesus warned the disciples that he would die and then come back to life. Their spiritual eyes were blind and unable to understand until they saw the risen Christ for themselves.

2. At first it was difficult for the disciples to fathom how the Gentiles would or could be saved.

3. At Pentecost the Holy Spirit began convincing many people that they are sinners in need of a Saviour. The result was an explosion in Church growth.

4. Gamaliel had enough spiritual discernment to know that men's plans will fail while God's will always succeed.

5. Paul stood firm that only believing in the finished work of Jesus on Calvary can save.

Chapter Four

Letters to the Churches

THE early Church needed to be grounded in God's truth in order to grow spiritually. We need the same teaching today. That is why the Holy Spirit spoke through letters to the churches. Each one has a particular message for that generation and for us also. What did the authors write about God's plan of salvation? What did they say about Jesus' kingdom or about his return?

1. James

Date written: probably A.D. 49, before the first Christian council.[1]
Written by James, half brother of Jesus and the first bishop of the church in Jerusalem.

Debra was a teaching assistant in the geology department when she first went to the University of Calgary. Although she was a graduate student, Debra was still determined to put the Lord first in her finances. Therefore she began sponsoring a needy child overseas. After a couple of years she continued to support the child in spite of a decreasing bank balance. She did it, because she loved the Lord, not to earn her salvation. This is the point of James' book. He is emphasizing the practical result of faith in God's gift of salvation.

> *Do not merely listen to the word, and so deceive yourselves. Do what it says* (Jas. 1:22).

Listening to God's Word without acting on his promises is meaningless. If a person truly believes what God says, then that person will obey God's instructions. His or her actions will be the result of a loving heart attitude to the Lord. In thinking about this verse, it is wise, however, to consider the progressive nature of God's revelation to us. He revealed more of himself to Moses than to Adam, more to David than to Moses, and more to the apostles than to anyone in the Old Testament. To insist on obeying all of the laws of the sacrificial system after Jesus' resurrection is wrong. The Judaizers had tunnel vision when they did not understand that Jesus' sacrifice paid the penalty for sins once for all. The sacrifices that God demanded in the Old Testament were a reminder of the sinfulness of people and a picture of what his Son would accomplish on the cross.

> *For whoever keeps the whole law and yet stumbles at just one point is guilty of breaking all of it* (Jas. 2:10).

Around this time Judaizers claimed that obeying the Law was as necessary for salvation as believing in the work of Jesus on the cross. That is why they insisted that Gentiles must be circumcised. James wrote this letter to Jewish believers so that they would understand the proper relationship between Law and salvation. Since nobody can keep the whole Law, everyone is guilty of breaking it. This means that no one can be saved through the Law. Circumcision will not save a person; only by God's grace is anyone saved. For someone brought up in the Law and also the myriad of man-made commandments surrounding it, this was difficult teaching.

> *As the body without the spirit is dead, so faith without deeds is dead* (Jas. 2:26).

Godly works are the result of faith. They are the proof that faith is based on the promises of God, not the vain dreams of people. Just as a body is not alive when the spirit has departed from it at death, likewise the evidence that God has saved a person will be shown through his or her works. For example, God considered Abraham righteous when he offered Isaac on the altar. "You see that his faith and his actions were working together, and his faith was made complete by what he did" (Jas. 2:22).

2. Paul

2a. Letter to the Galatians

Date written: A.D. 49, from Antioch[2]

> *But even if we or an angel from heaven should preach a gospel other than the one we preached to you, let him be eternally condemned!* (Gal. 1:8).

There is only one way to have fellowship restored between God and humanity—through the gospel of the Lord Jesus Christ. There is no other way. If anyone adds anything to it, "let him be eternally condemned!" There are not multiple ways to heaven. In essence the Judaizers said, "The gospel of Jesus plus our customs is the way to heaven. Yes, Lord, we accept your free gift of salvation, but we also want to obey the old covenant. It does not hurt to carry a little extra insurance." Faith plus works. Is faith enough for you?

> There are not multiple ways to heaven.

> *May I never boast except in the cross of our Lord Jesus Christ, through which the world has been crucified to me, and I to the world* (Gal. 6:14).

Is this your prayer? Do you believe that Jesus' cross is the only way to be reconciled to God? Is it sufficient to pay for your sins? Is the cross of Christ of prime importance in your life? Is everything else secondary? It was for Paul. He was killed because he upheld the truth.

> *"Get rid of the slave woman and her son, for the slave woman's son will never share in the inheritance with the free woman's son"* (Gal. 4:30).

Paul recalled the story of Abraham and his two sons, Ishmael and Isaac. Ishmael was born "in the ordinary way" by Hagar, but Isaac was born "as the result of a promise" by Sarah (Gal. 4:23). Then Paul explains:

> *These things may be taken figuratively, for the women represent two covenants. One covenant is from Mount Sinai and bears children who are to be slaves: This is Hagar. Now Hagar stands for Mount Sinai in Arabia and corresponds to the present city of Jerusalem, because she is in slavery with her children. But the Jerusalem that is above is free, and she is our mother* (Gal. 4:24-26).

Note that this is God's allegory, not Paul's. The Lord is teaching that the old covenant has been replaced by the new covenant. Those who remain faithful to the old covenant "will never share in the inheritance." Under the old covenant, most Israelites expected a physical kingdom for their inheritance, but the chance for such an earthly Utopia is over. In contrast, the new covenant is a spiritual agreement between God and people from many different nationalities. That is why the New Testament is silent about the subject of an earthly kingdom.

2b. Two Letters to the Thessalonians

1 Thessalonians

Date written: about A.D. 51, from Corinth[3]

Some of the Thessalonian believers misunderstood Paul's teaching on the Second Coming of Jesus. They neglected to work for a living, because they thought that Jesus would return right away. In this letter Paul corrected them, "Make it your ambition to lead a quiet life, to mind your own business and to work with your hands, just as we told you, so that your daily life may win the respect of outsiders and so that you will not be dependent on anybody" (1 Thess. 4:11,12). Other believers mourned because their loved ones had died before Jesus' return. God promised them that someday they would be reunited with those who had died. They must not grieve like non-believers without hope. Then Paul explained:

> They must not grieve like non-believers without hope.

For the Lord himself will come down from heaven, with a loud command, with the voice of the archangel and with the trumpet call of God, and the dead in Christ will rise first. After that, we who are still alive and are left will be caught up together with them in the clouds to meet the Lord in the air. And so we will be with the Lord forever (1 Thess. 4:16,17).

For you know very well that the day of the Lord will come like a thief in the night (1 Thess. 5:2).

God used the Old Testament phrase *the day of the Lord* to describe Jesus' Second Coming. In his Mount of Olives discourse, Jesus had warned his disciples that he would come like a thief in the night—unexpectedly. Paul told the believers how to prepare for that day. "Let us be self-controlled, putting on faith and love as a breastplate, and the hope of salvation as a helmet. For God did not appoint us to suffer wrath but to receive salvation through our Lord Jesus Christ. He died for us so that, whether we are awake or asleep, we may live together with him" (1 Thess.5:8-10). Believers have the assurance that, whether they are alive or dead physically, they are always alive spiritually. When the day of the Lord comes, non-believers will face God's wrath, whereas believers will be united with Jesus and their loved ones in the Lord.

2 Thessalonians

Date written: about A.D. 51 or 52, from Corinth[4]

Some people were upset, because they thought that they had missed the day of the Lord (2 Thess. 2:1,2). Paul chided them:

> *Don't let anyone deceive you in any way, for (that day will not come) until the rebellion occurs and the man of lawlessness is revealed, the man doomed to destruction. He will oppose and will exalt himself over everything that is called God or is worshiped, so that he sets himself up in God's temple, proclaiming himself to be God. Don't you remember that when I was with you I used to tell you these things?* (2 Thess. 2:3-5).

At this time the temple was still standing in Jerusalem, but Jesus had promised that one day it would be completely destroyed. Obviously, he could not return until after that had happened. Soon Zealots would openly rebel against Rome. Then Titus and his army would surround Jerusalem. As emperor, Titus would demand the worship due only to God. Thus he is the abomination of desolation promised by Jesus.

Paul reminded them, "And now you know what is holding him back, so that he may be revealed at the proper time" (2 Thess. 2:6). History has revealed that the Jewish state is what prevented Rome from persecuting God's infant Church. At this point Jews and Romans alike regarded Christianity as a sect of Judaism. As such it was protected under Roman law, because subject states were allowed to retain their own religions.[5] After Jerusalem's destruction, many Roman emperors unleashed their fury against the Church. Yet the Jewish state was only the vehicle that restrained evil. The power that held Rome in check was actually the Holy Spirit. He alone has the ability to prevent evil from spreading or to allow it full reign. Without God's gracious control over this world, every human being would belong to Satan's kingdom.

> *And then the lawless one will be revealed, whom the Lord Jesus will overthrow with the breath of his mouth and destroy by the splendor of his coming* (2 Thess. 2:8).

Paul expected that Jesus would return and overthrow the man of sin. Like the prophets of old, Paul only understood the primary fulfillment of his prophecy, whereas God also looked ahead to the future. Many years before, Antiochus Epiphanes had persecuted those Jews who remained faithful to the Law. In Paul's day believers were about to suffer at the hands of Rome. Likewise the political beast of Revelation will persecute believers at the end of time. Satan will continue to fight God every chance that he gets, but he will not win. Because of Jesus' death and resurrection, God will be the victor.

> Satan will continue to fight God every chance that he gets, but he will not win.

2c. Two Letters to the Corinthians

1 Corinthians

Date written: about A.D. 55, from Ephesus[6]

> *For as in Adam all die, so in Christ all will be made alive. But each in his own turn: Christ, the firstfruits; then, when he comes, those who belong to him. Then the end will come, when he hands over the kingdom to God the Father after he has destroyed all dominion, authority and power. For he must reign until he has put all his enemies under his feet. The last enemy to be destroyed is death* (1 Cor. 15:22-26).

Through Paul, God promises believers that they will rise from the dead at Jesus' Second Coming. "Then the end will come." At that point Jesus will hand over his kingdom to God the Father. While Jesus is reigning, he will be busy putting "all his enemies under his feet. The last enemy to be destroyed is death." In other words, life will go on until the end of time. As soon as there is no more death, there will be no more earth, as we know it. As long as time continues, King Jesus will keep on subduing his enemies. After death is conquered, no other enemy will ever arise to challenge God or believers. Satan will never be able to hurt us again.

> *I declare to you, brothers, that flesh and blood cannot inherit the kingdom of God, nor does the perishable inherit the imperishable. Listen, I tell you a mystery: We will not all sleep, but we will all be changed—in a flash, in the twinkling of an eye, at the last trumpet. For the trumpet will sound, the dead will be raised imperishable, and we will be changed. For the perishable must clothe itself with the imperishable, and the mortal with immortality. When the perishable has been clothed with the imperishable, and the mortal with immortality, then the saying that is written will come true: "Death has been swallowed up in victory"* (1 Cor. 15:50-54).

> When Jesus comes back to visibly establish the kingdom of God, there will be no mortals there.

When Jesus comes back to visibly establish the kingdom of God, there will be no mortals there. At the last trumpet the dead will rise with new immortal bodies while those alive will have their bodies changed also. Death will be gone forever, and believers will live forevermore with God. What a precious promise! How much he loves us!

2 Corinthians

Date written: about A.D. 55-57, from Macedonia[7]

For we must all appear before the judgment seat of Christ, that each one may receive what is due him for the things done while in the body, whether good or bad (2 Cor. 5:10).

Paul is writing to the Corinthian believers to warn them that they must answer to Jesus one day for their actions. Their works will not determine their salvation, but their rewards.

I tell you, now is the time of God's favor, now is the day of salvation (2 Cor. 6:2).

Now is the time to accept God's gift of salvation. When Jesus returns, it will be forever too late. No one can be saved after Jesus returns. Have you received his gift?

2d. Romans

Date written: about A.D. 57, from Corinth[8]
Paul had never been to Rome and longed to preach the gospel to them in person.

For all have sinned and fall short of the glory of God (Rom. 3:23).

A sinner is a person who prefers his or her own way instead of God's. The result is a hatred of God and his Law. As far as sin is concerned, there is no difference between the races. Everyone has been born with the sin nature. Because of this we readily sin. Each person must take responsibility for the fact that he or she has disobeyed God. As sinners we can never attain the purity or holiness of God.

> *For the wages of sin is death, but the gift of God is eternal life in Christ Jesus our Lord* (Rom. 6:23).

Because we are sinners, we deserve to die physically and spiritually. Before the world began, God devised a marvellous plan of salvation. He would offer sinners a precious gift—eternal life through the work of his Son Jesus. Just as a person earns wages for working, likewise we deserve punishment for our sinful thoughts and actions. In contrast, God's gift of salvation, eternal life, can never be earned by anything that we do.

> *This righteousness from God comes through faith in Jesus Christ to all who believe* (Rom. 3:22).

God promises to clothe believers with Christ's righteousness. When he looks at us, he will see the purity and holiness of Jesus, not our sinfulness. We can receive this righteousness by having faith that Jesus took the punishment for our sins when he died on Calvary.

> *Therefore, since we have been justified through faith, we have peace with God through our Lord Jesus Christ* (Rom. 5:1).

Since we have been declared righteous and our sins have been forgiven, believers have peace with God. We are no longer enemies, but his children. How much this must upset Satan!

> *You see, at just the right time, when we were still powerless, Christ died for the ungodly. Very rarely will anyone die for a righteous man, though for a good man someone might possibly dare to die. But God demonstrates his own love for us in this: While we were still sinners, Christ died for us* (Rom. 5:6-8).

This is God's wonderful plan of salvation. He loved us while we were still rebellious God-haters. Because he loved us,

Jesus took the punishment that we deserve. Justice and mercy wed at the cross.

> *Therefore, there is now no condemnation for those who are in Christ Jesus, because through Christ Jesus the law of the Spirit of life set me free from the law of sin and death* (Rom. 8:1,2).

Believers are no longer condemned sinners, because Jesus paid the punishment that we deserve. Since the Holy Spirit dwells within each believer, we are no longer controlled by sin. This does not mean that we will never sin. Paul himself struggled with the sin nature. It is only in the new heaven and new earth where there will be no sin ever.

> *It [salvation] does not, therefore, depend on man's desire or effort, but on God's mercy* (Rom. 9:16).

The Lord is the potter while people are the clay (Isa. 64:8). Because of our sinful nature, it irks us that we are only weak vessels. As rebellious sinners no one has the will or ability to turn to God with a repentant heart, and everyone deserves to be separated eternally from our Creator. Our salvation is entirely up to the sovereign God. By his grace and mercy he lovingly saves whom he will. Each of us willingly chooses to go his or her own way. Once we follow down that path, only the love of God will draw us into his kingdom.

> Each of us willingly chooses to go his or her own way. Once we follow down that path, only the love of God will draw us into his kingdom.

> *Therefore, I urge you, brothers, in view of God's mercy, to offer your bodies as living sacrifices, holy and pleasing to God—this is your spiritual act of worship* (Rom. 12:1).

Can we do anything less than give ourselves completely to God for his service? He loved us before we were born. He died for us while we were rebellious God-haters. His Holy Spirit lives within us. What better way to show our love and gratitude to God Almighty than to yield completely to his Spirit?

2e. Ephesians

Date written: about A.D. 60, from Rome[9]

In him [Jesus] we have redemption through his blood, the forgiveness of sins, in accordance with the riches of God's grace that he lavished on us with all wisdom and understanding (Eph. 1:7).

Because of God's love and mercy, he lavished so many blessings on believers. He bought us as his own by Jesus' blood and forgave our sins. Now we no longer belong to Satan's kingdom, but we have become God's children.

As for you, you were dead in your transgressions and sins, in which you used to live when you followed the ways of this world and of the ruler of the kingdom of the air, the spirit who is now at work in those who are disobedient (Eph. 2:1).

Paul reminds believers that they once belonged to Satan's kingdom. As such they were the walking dead—alive physically, but dead spiritually. A dead person cannot talk or respond to outside stimuli. In the same way, spiritually dead people have no ability to make themselves come to life. Some people have a more dramatic testimony. For example, Barry turned from atheism to God. My heart needed changing as much as his did, even though I was only a child when I accepted Jesus as my Saviour. We were both dead and unable to respond spiritually to God.

For it is by grace you have been saved, through faith—and this not from yourselves, it is the gift of God—not by works, so that no one can boast. For we are God's workmanship, created in Christ Jesus to do good works, which God prepared in advance for us to do (Eph. 2:8-10).

Salvation is "the gift of God." Before the world existed, God planned for believers "to do good works" in Jesus' name. It is only by the grace of God that we are saved through Jesus' blood and are able to accomplish what God has ordained. There is nothing that we can do to save ourselves. Even faith is God's gift. Only the Holy Spirit is able to open our spiritual eyes and enable us to accept the marvellous salvation offered by God.

> There is nothing that we can do to save ourselves. Even faith is God's gift.

2f. Philippians

Date written: about A.D. 61, from Rome[10]

Your attitude should be the same as that of Christ Jesus: Who, being in very nature God, did not consider equality with God something to be grasped, but made himself nothing, taking the very nature of a servant, being made in human likeness. And being found in appearance as a man, he humbled himself and became obedient to death—even death on a cross! (Phil. 2:5-8).

Jesus did not need to prove that he was God to himself or others, because he knew that he was. Therefore he willingly became a human and gave up all of his rights as the Creator. Not only did he humble himself by becoming a man, but he also died a cursed death on a cross. If Jesus could give up his rights for us, can we not give up our supposed rights for him?

> *Continue to work out your salvation with fear and trembling, for it is God who works in you to will and to act according to his good purpose* (Phil. 2:12,13).

Paul encourages the Philippians to continue working out their salvation. Yet they may only do this as God works in their hearts to accomplish his purposes. Just as Paul presses on "toward the goal to win the prize" (Phil. 3:14), likewise every believer runs the race toward heaven. Yearning to please the Lord, believers fear to fall short of God's standard but gladly give him the glory for any spiritual success.

3. Two Letters by Peter

1 Peter

Date written: about A.D. 62—64, possibly from Rome[11]

> *In his great mercy he has given us new birth into a living hope through the resurrection of Jesus Christ from the dead, and into an inheritance that can never perish, spoil or fade—kept in heaven for you, who through faith are shielded by God's power until the coming of the salvation that is ready to be revealed in the last time* (1 Pet. 1:3-5).

Knowing that his readers were suffering persecution, Peter comforted them by reminding them of God's salvation. He expressed a tension in these verses, however. Because believers are born into a new relationship with the Lord, we have a present living hope. We are children of the King now. Nevertheless, we are also waiting for our inheritance. The kingdom that we belong to is both present and future.

> *The kingdom that we belong to is both present and future.*

> *But you are a chosen people, a royal priesthood, a holy*

nation, a people belonging to God, that you may declare the praises of him who called you out of darkness into his wonderful light (1 Pet. 2:9).

Many years before at Mount Sinai, God had promised the Israelites they would be his treasured possession, a kingdom of priests, and a holy nation (Exod. 19:5,6). This was the founding of the physical nation of Israel. The Lord had nurtured and protected them so that the promised Seed could be born into a nation who knew God and his Law. As soon as Jesus accomplished his work on earth and ascended to heaven, God quickly began to build his Church, the New Israel. Since then believers are God's "chosen people, a royal priesthood," and "a holy nation." One's physical race is not important. Repentance and belief in the finished work of Jesus on Calvary is what counts.

He himself bore our sins in his body on the tree, so that we might die to sins and live for righteousness (1 Pet. 2:24).

For Christ died for sins once for all, the righteous for the unrighteous, to bring you to God (1 Pet. 3:18).

Peter, the apostle to the Jews, preached the same gospel as Paul, the apostle to the Gentiles. Jesus shed his blood in order to restore our fellowship with God. He paid the penalty for our sins. Like Paul, Peter taught believers to be self-controlled. Like Jesus, Peter instructed them to be alert and watchful, since "your enemy the devil prowls around like a roaring lion looking for someone to devour" (1 Pet. 5:8).

You also, like living stones, are being built into a spiritual house to be a holy priesthood, offering spiritual sacrifices acceptable to God through Jesus Christ (1 Pet. 2:5).

Believers are living stones of a spiritual house that God is building. In the earthly Jerusalem, priests offered animal sacrifices that looked forward to the perfect sacrifice of Jesus on the cross. In the heavenly Jerusalem, every believer is a priest who presents "spiritual sacrifices acceptable to God through Jesus Christ."

2 Peter

Date written: about A.D. 67, three years after 1 Peter was written, possibly from Rome[12]

God promises believers two things. "His divine power has given us everything we need for life and godliness" (2 Pet. 1:3). In this present world the Holy Spirit provides everything that believers require to persevere and grow in the Christian life. Also, "and you will receive a rich welcome into the eternal kingdom of our Lord and Savior Jesus Christ" (2 Pet. 1:11). Believers look forward to an eternal kingdom, not a temporary one when Jesus returns. This was a momentous statement for Peter to make, because most Jews were longing for an earthly Jewish kingdom. After Jesus' resurrection the disciples had wanted to know when God would restore the kingdom to Israel. Over thirty years later, Peter did not mention such a kingdom.

For prophecy never had its origin in the will of man, but men spoke from God as they were carried along by the Holy Spirit. But there were also false prophets among the people, just as there will be false teachers among you (2 Pet. 1:21; 2:1).

> Sadly, there have always been, and always will be, false teachers.

The Holy Spirit gave us the Scriptures through human authors. Sadly, there have always been, and always will be, false teachers. These people claim to speak with the authority of God, but "they will secretly introduce destructive heresies" (2 Pet. 2:1). Beware of those who are afraid to have their beliefs challenged by the Scriptures.

With the Lord a day is like a thousand years, and a thousand years are like a day. The Lord is not slow in keeping his promise, as some understand slowness. He is patient with you, not wanting anyone to perish, but everyone to come to repentance. But the day of the Lord will come like a thief. The heavens will disappear with a roar; the elements will be destroyed by fire, and the earth and everything in it will be laid bare (2 Pet. 3:8-10).

Just before Jesus returns, scoffers will jeer, "Where is this 'coming' he promised? Ever since our fathers died, everything goes on as it has since the beginning of creation" (2 Pet. 3:4). Peter, however, explained that God is above time. He created the world and then later destroyed it by water. If God says that he will destroy the earth by fire, then he will, but why is he waiting so long? Be thankful. Otherwise you would not have been born or have accepted his gift of salvation. Be thankful, because your loved ones have a chance to believe. When Jesus does come back, it will be like a thief—unexpectedly.

Peter looked forward to "a new heaven and a new earth, the home of righteousness" (2 Pet. 3:13). This is significant. Because of his upbringing, he was conditioned to expect that the Messiah would overthrow the Romans and usher in peace and prosperity to this wartorn world. In contrast, Peter longed for a new world truly without sin—the new heaven and new earth.

4. Hebrews

Date written: probably before the destruction of the temple in Jerusalem in A.D. 70[13]
Writer unknown

The point of what we are saying is this: We do have such a high priest, who sat down at the right hand of the throne of the Majesty in heaven, and who serves in the sanctuary, the true tabernacle set up by the Lord, not by man (Heb. 8:1,2).

On the cross Jesus was the sacrificial Lamb of God, but at his ascension he changed roles. As High Priest he entered the Most Holy Place, namely heaven, and presented his blood, which was the blood of the new covenant, to God. Moses' tabernacle is only "a copy and shadow of what is in heaven" (Heb. 8:5). In it, "only the high priest entered the inner room, and that only once a year, and never without blood, which he offered for himself and for the sins the people had committed in ignorance" (Heb. 9:7). In contrast:

> *When Christ came as high priest...he went through the greater and more perfect tabernacle that is not man-made, that is to say, not a part of this creation. He did not enter by means of the blood of goats and calves; but he entered the Most Holy Place once for all by his own blood, having obtained eternal redemption...For Christ did not enter a man-made sanctuary that was only a copy of the true one; he entered heaven itself, now to appear for us in God's presence* (Heb. 9:11-24).

> When Jesus offered his blood to God, the new covenant was officially ratified.

When Jesus offered his blood to God, the new covenant was officially ratified. He died as a willing sacrifice to obtain our salvation. His ministry was completed as soon as the Father accepted his sacrifice. What a celebration!

> *Day after day every priest stands and performs his religious duties; again and again he offers the same sacrifices, which can never take away sins. But when this priest had offered for all time one sacrifice for sins, he sat down at the right hand of God* (Heb. 10:11,12).

Unlike earthly priests who continually had to offer sacrifices, the offering that Jesus presented to God the Father was accepted once for all. Thus by his death and resurrection Jesus procured salvation for all who would believe. Then Jesus sat on his throne at the right hand of God the Father. Because King Jesus earned the right to rule with all authority, he was allowed to open the seven seals in Revelation 5. He also deserves the loving adoration of all people, living and dead (Rev. 5:13). The plan of God was completed, and Satan was furious (Rev. 12:12). His hope for an eternal kingdom is dashed, and he can never oust any believers from heaven. Satan can only try to prevent others from becoming believers.

5. Revelation

Probably about A.D. 95, by John from Patmos[14]
Persecution under Domitian, emperor of the Roman Empire:
A.D. 90-95[14]

While in exile on the island of Patmos, the apostle John received a revelation from God—a glimpse into the spiritual realm. In the midst of persecution, the early Christians needed reassurance that God had indeed won the war against Satan when Jesus died on the cross. Today we also need comfort, because we have been waiting so long for Jesus' return. John, therefore, described Jesus in his glory, the ongoing battle between God and Satan, and God's final victory. Although the Lord wants each generation of believers to trust in his providential care, he especially wants to comfort those who are suffering persecution for the sake of Christ. Because Satan wants to weaken every Christian's faith in God, he periodically forces some to endure severe tribulation. Those persecuted Christians need to know that God has not forsaken them and that his promises are trustworthy.

5a. King Jesus and His Kingdom

Revelation 1-3

Grace and peace to you...from Jesus Christ, who is the faithful witness, the firstborn from the dead, and the ruler of the kings of the earth. To him who loves us and has freed us from our sins by his blood, and has made us to be a kingdom and priests to serve his God and Father—to him be glory and power for ever and ever! Amen (Rev. 1: 4-6).

Whether his authority is acknowledged or not, King Jesus is now ruling over all the kings of the earth. Moreover, believers are priests and servants of God in Jesus' kingdom. This was true in John's day and is also true in ours.

I turned round to see the voice that was speaking to me. And when I turned I saw seven golden lampstands, and among the lampstands was someone "like a son of man," dressed in a robe reaching down to his feet and with a golden sash around his chest. His head and hair were white like wool, as white as snow, and his eyes were like blazing fire. His feet were like bronze glowing in a furnace, and his voice was like the sound of rushing waters. In his right hand he held seven stars, and out of his mouth came a sharp double-edged sword. His face was like the sun shining in all its brilliance (Rev. 1:12-16).

At the sight of the Son of Man, John collapsed at his feet as if he were dead. Then Jesus lovingly encouraged him, "Do not be afraid. I am the First and the Last. I am the Living One; I was dead, and behold I am alive for ever and ever!" (Rev. 1:17,18). Next Jesus explained, "The seven stars are the angels of the seven churches, and the seven lampstands are the seven churches" (Rev. 1:20).

With authority Jesus holds pastors in his loving, protective hand. John writes to the church of Philadelphia, "These are the words of him who is holy and true, who holds the key of David. What he opens no one can shut, and what he shuts no one can

> Jesus has believers as his loyal subjects.

open" (Rev. 3:7). Long ago Eliakim held the key to the house of David during the reign of Hezekiah. As second in command he had authority to rule Jerusalem. David's key on his shoulder represented his control over government (Isa. 22:22). Eliakim only reigned in the physical world, whereas King Jesus rules over everything physical and spiritual. Thus Eliakim is a picture of the present reign of Christ. Jesus has believers as his loyal subjects. These members of his kingdom are in local churches. This kingdom defies physical boundaries. It is worldwide.

5b. The Coronation of God's Lamb

Revelation 4, 5

"Worthy is the Lamb, who was slain, to receive power and wealth and wisdom and strength and honor and glory and praise!" (Rev. 5:12).

Here we find the basis for his authority. Jesus is pictured as a Lamb, "looking as if it had been slain" (Rev. 5:6). John saw a mighty angel cry out, "Who is worthy to break the seals and open the scroll?" (Rev. 5:2).

Then John wept, because no one was found who was "worthy to open the scroll or look inside" (Rev. 5:4). One of the elders implored, "Do not weep! See, the Lion of the tribe of Judah, the Root of David, has triumphed. He is able to open the scroll and its seven seals" (Rev. 5:5).

Because of his death and resurrection, Jesus is the only one worthy to take the scroll from God the Father. When Jesus received the scroll, he was given authority over the entire world. How comforting this must have been to John's readers! How encouraging to us!

> When Jesus received the scroll, he was given authority over the entire world.

Once Jesus told the story of a woman who had lost one of her ten silver coins. She searched the house until she found it. (I can easily empathize with that woman. Once I searched for my contact lens in the backyard and some other times on the kitchen floor. I never gave up until I found it.) Immediately she called her friends to a party. She said, "Rejoice with me; I have found my lost coin" (Luke 15:9).

Likewise, what a celebration there must have been when the Lord Jesus approached the throne of God as the sacrificial lamb! What joy when the sacrifice was accepted! What happiness when all authority was given to King Jesus! This story never grows old. For all eternity the redeemed will cry out, "Worthy is the Lamb, who was slain."

5c. The First Six Seals: The Consequences of Sin

Revelation 6
A brief synopsis of sin's effect on this world and also
of the continual war between God and Satan from
the beginning of time to the end.

After he was given the scroll, Jesus opened up the seals. Opening the first seal revealed a white horse on which a conqueror rode out to battle (Rev. 6:1,2). The same white horse and rider appear in Revelation 19. "His name is the Word of God" (Rev. 19:13). As Henry notes, "The Lord Jesus appears riding on *a white horse*; *white horses* are generally refused in war, because they make the rider a mark for the enemy; but our Lord Redeemer was sure of the victory and a glorious triumph, and he rides on the *white horse* of a pure but despised gospel, with great swiftness through the world." [15] Opening the second seal revealed a rider on a red horse who was given "power to take peace from the earth and to make men slay each other. To him was given a large sword" (Rev. 6:4). War has been around since sin first entered the world and Cain killed Abel. Opening the third seal revealed a rider on a black horse who held "a pair of scales in his hand" (Rev. 6:5). A voice cried out, "A quart of wheat for a day's wages, and three quarts of barley for a day's wages, and do not damage the oil and the wine!" (Rev. 6:6). People have struggled with famine since the beginning of time. The first recorded famine was in Abraham's day. Opening the fourth seal revealed a rider on a pale horse who was named "Death" (Rev. 6:8). Death and Hades were given "power over a fourth of the earth to kill by sword, famine and plague, and by the wild beasts of the earth" (Rev. 6:8). Since sin entered the world, death has held sway over all people. None can escape. The fifth seal revealed the souls of those slain because of their testimony. They cried out, "How long, Sovereign Lord, holy and true, until you judge the inhabitants of the earth and avenge our blood?" (Rev. 6:10). As time passes, more and more believers enter heaven violently and wait for their blood to be avenged by the Righteous Judge of all.

> Wherever the first horseman goes, the next three are bound to pursue. Thus while the gospel goes forth, war, famine, and death follow.

Wherever the first horseman goes, the next three are bound to pursue. Thus while the gospel goes forth, war, famine, and death follow. Meanwhile, in making war against the kingdom of God, Satan often murders believers. As soon as Adam and Eve sinned, they looked forward to the coming of the promised Seed, who would crush the head of the serpent. War, famine, disease, death, and the martyrdom of saints are the present realities of life. Satan hopes that those things will prevent the spread of the gospel. Notice that death has the power to kill one-quarter of the earth, which represents "the ordinary death-rate of the world." [16]

When the sixth seal was opened:

> *There was a great earthquake. The sun turned black like sackcloth made of goat hair, the whole moon turned blood red, and the stars in the sky fell to earth, as late figs drop from a fig tree when shaken by a strong wind. The sky receded like a scroll, rolling up, and every mountain and island was removed from its place* (Rev. 6:12-14).

Natural calamities such as earthquakes are also a part of life, but one day Jesus will come back. When he does, those who are non-believers, both living and dead, will partake of the great wrath of God. "For the great day of their wrath has come, and who can stand?" (Rev. 6:17). Thus the earthquake described in the sixth seal is also a picture of the Final Judgment of God. In that day people will hide in caves and under rocks in an attempt to hide from God (Rev. 6:15). Do you fear that day? There is no need to fear if you are trusting in God to protect and save you.

5d. Missionaries for Jesus

Revelation 7

And you also were included in Christ when you heard the word of truth, the gospel of your salvation. Having believed, you were marked in him with a seal, the promised Holy Spirit, who is a deposit guaranteeing our inheritance (Eph. 1:13,14).

And do not grieve the Holy Spirit of God, with whom you were sealed for the day of redemption (Eph. 4:30).

The Jews were the first to receive the gospel—the good news that Jesus had died in their place to pay the punishment for their sins. When those first believers accepted God's gift of salvation, they received the seal of the Holy Spirit (Rev. 7:3,4). Thousands of them spread throughout the world and told others the good news. The result of their missionary efforts was "a great multitude that no one could count, from every nation, tribe, people and language, standing before the throne and in front of the Lamb" (Rev. 7:9). Every day heaven welcomes a believer into

> We need to thank those first Jewish missionaries for their zealousness and bravery in the face of persecution.

its midst. "Precious in the sight of the LORD is the death of his saints" (Ps. 116:15). We need to thank those first Jewish missionaries for their zealousness and bravery in the face of persecution. Without them, none of us would know how much God loves us!

Because John's readers were going through great tribulation (Rev. 7:14), God lovingly comforted them. They could know for sure that those believers, who had been killed for their faith, were alive in heaven and were worshipping the Lord. "God will wipe away every tear from their eyes" (Rev. 7:17).

5e. The First Four Trumpets: Disasters of Increasing Intensity

Revelation 8. The seventh seal describes more details about the end of time. It is divided into seven trumpets.

At the first trumpet, "a third of the earth was burned up" (Rev. 8:7) by a hail-and-fire storm. At the second trumpet, "a third of the sea turned into blood, a third of the living creatures in the sea died, and a third of the ships were destroyed" (Rev. 8:8,9) by a fiery mountain falling into the sea. At the third trumpet, "a third of the waters turned bitter, and many people died from the waters that had become bitter" (Rev. 8:11). At the fourth trumpet, "a third of the day was without light, and also a third of the night" (Rev. 8:12). Until this point in time, Death and Hades have had power over one-fourth of the earth; now one-third of the earth will die from natural calamities. Because these disasters have increased in intensity, the natural death rate will become "just a little more" than previously.[17] Hail and lightning storms, earthquakes, poisoned water, and lack of sunlight will devastate the earth. Long ago in Egypt the Israelites

Similarly, both believers and non-believers will experience the effects of the first four trumpets.

suffered, as well as the Egyptians, during the first three plagues. Similarly, both believers and non-believers will experience the effects of the first four trumpets. Jesus controls the destiny of worldly kingdoms by weather and other natural disasters.[17]

5f. The Three Woes

Revelation 9-11. Trumpets five through seven are also called the three woes, because non-believers will suffer severely under God's judgment.

At the first woe the key to the Abyss is given to a star that had fallen from the sky to the earth (Rev. 9:1). This fallen angel is Satan (Isa. 14:12), who immediately unlocks the Abyss. Like smoke from a gigantic furnace, the king of the Abyss descends upon the earth with his locusts (Rev. 9:2). His name is Abaddon in Hebrew and Apollyon in Greek, meaning "Destroyer" (Rev. 9:11). This is how Fausset explains the two names. "The giving of *both* the Hebrew and the Greek name implies that he is the destroyer of both Hebrew and Gentile alike...Jesus unites Hebrew and Gentile in a common salvation; Satan combines both in a common 'destruction.'"[18]

At Pentecost the Holy Spirit descended on believers in the likeness of fire. Near the end of the world, Satan and his demons will come down on non-believers like smoke. These locusts will be powerless against believers, because the seal of God will protect them (Rev. 9:4). In contrast, the demons will be allowed to torture, but not to kill, any non-believer for five months. "And the agony they suffered was like that of the sting of a scorpion when it strikes a man. During those days men will seek death, but will not find it; they will long to die, but death will elude them" (Rev. 9:5,6). While the Israelites were protected from the plagues in Egypt, they had a wonderful opportunity to witness to their Egyptian neighbours about the awesome power and loving-kindness of the Lord. Similarly, believers can do the same thing once again.

The second woe describes another aspect of the climax at

the very end of time. God has bound four angels at the Euphrates River until a certain hour, day, month, and year (Rev. 9:15). Historically the Euphrates River has been the boundary between the East and the West (Rev. 16:12). At a particular moment decreed by the Lord, 200 million riders will incite a war that will kill one-third of the earth's population. God knows the exact hour when the war will begin. He will allow this war between the East and the West in order to judge some and to encourage others to repent of their sins. How much God yearns for non-believers to accept his gift of salvation! Just as the death rate for natural disasters will increase from one-quarter to one-third, likewise war will claim "just a little more" victims than previously.[19] God controls the destiny of the world by war as well as by natural disasters.

"A third of mankind was killed by the three plagues of fire, smoke and sulfur that came out of their mouths" (Rev. 9:18). Fire is red, which is reminiscent of the red horse and rider (seal two) that brings war. Smoke is black, which reminds us of the black horse and rider (seal three) that brings famine. Sulphur is pale yellow, which suggests a picture of the pale horse and rider (seal 4) that brings death by the sword, famine, plague, and by wild beasts.[19]

> Sadly, an increase in plagues will not soften the hearts of non-believers. Like Pharaoh of old, their hearts will only be hardened further.

The rest of mankind that were not killed by these plagues still did not repent of the work of their hands; they did not stop worshiping demons, and idols of gold, silver, bronze, stone and wood—idols that cannot see or hear or walk. Nor did they repent of their murders, their magic arts, their sexual immorality or their thefts (Rev. 9:20,21).

Sadly, an increase in plagues will not soften the hearts of non-believers. Like Pharaoh of old, their hearts will only be hardened further. Satan will be jubilant!

It is very easy for believers to be distracted and upset over life's difficulties. How delighted Satan is when this happens! God, on the other hand, wants us to be "more than conquerors through him who loved us" (Rom. 8:37). He does not want us to be discouraged or to think that he has forgotten us and no longer loves us. Therefore Revelation 10 and 11 reveal how God continually takes care of his people—even in times of trouble. In fact, during the second woe, Jesus is still building his Church just as he promised (Matt. 16:18). Notice the similarity between the description of Jesus in Revelation 1 and the mighty angel in Revelation 10. This mighty angel reminds believers of two important truths: God is in control, and he keeps his promises. How comforting to those in the midst of natural calamities or religious persecution! Do you trust the Lord to keep his promises? Standing on the land and the sea, and swearing by God the Creator, the mighty angel promised, "There will be no more delay! But in the days when the seventh angel is about to sound his trumpet, the mystery of God will be accomplished, just as he announced to his servants the prophets" (Rev. 10:6,7).

In his Mount of Olives discourse Jesus warned his disciples that after the destruction of Jerusalem in A.D. 70, the city would "be trampled on by the Gentiles until the times of the Gentiles are fulfilled" (Luke 21:24). During the time of the second woe, the Gentiles are still trampling on Jerusalem (Rev. 11:2,14). Because the third woe is the end of this present world, this indicates that the Jews have permanently lost complete control of Jerusalem. When John wrote Revelation, both the temple and Jerusalem lay in ruins. Nevertheless, in this chapter the temple of God and two witnesses are physically present in the actual city of Jerusalem where Jesus was crucified (Rev. 11:8). How amazing! Unlike other cities, which will have passed into oblivion, Jerusalem will once again become a thriving metropolis.

Before anyone has built God a house of worship, the Lord has always given instructions regarding its construction. Consider Moses, David, and Ezekiel. In New Testament times God has replaced the temple with the Church. Paul teaches,

"We are the temple of the living God" (2 Cor. 6:16). God would not utterly forsake his beloved city. He would establish a church there. That is why John was instructed to measure the temple of God and those who worshipped there. God reserves both for his honour and glory. The two witnesses are likely the pastors of this church. They have the inner grace from the Lord to witness to an apostate audience just as Enoch and Elijah did. Having the power to stop the rain brings back memories of Elijah, while having the ability to instigate plagues reminds us of Moses.

For 1260 days the two witnesses will preach to the people in Jerusalem, which is the same amount of time allowed by God for Satan to set up his kingdom of Antichrist (Rev. 13:5). In other words, both God and Satan will actively continue to recruit members for their respective kingdoms until the end of time. No one will be able to harm the witnesses. In contrast, they will have great power "to strike the earth with every kind of plague as often as they want" (Rev. 11:6). How reassuring to know that God will always have witnesses and a Church, no matter what Satan accomplishes in his kingdom!

> In other words, both God and Satan will actively continue to recruit members for their respective kingdoms until the end of time.

> *Now when they have finished their testimony, the beast that comes up from the Abyss will attack them, and overpower and kill them. Their bodies will lie in the street of the great city, which is figuratively called Sodom and Egypt, where also their Lord was crucified. For three and a half days men from every people, tribe, language and nation will gaze on their bodies and refuse them burial* (Rev. 11:7-9).

This is quite possible today because of satellite television. Then three and one-half days later, after rising from the dead, the two witnesses will strike terror in those who see them. "And they went up to heaven in a cloud, while their enemies looked on. At that very hour there was a severe earthquake and a tenth of the city collapsed. Seven thousand people were killed in the earthquake, and the survivors were terrified and gave glory to the God of heaven" (Rev. 11:12,13). This is the end of the second woe. In giving glory to God, many will accept the gift of salvation and trust Jesus as their Lord and Saviour.

Next, the third woe will occur. The angel will sound the seventh and last trumpet. At that point three important things will happen. The eternal kingdom will be inaugurated; the dead will be judged; and believers will be rewarded (Rev. 11:15-18).

5g. The Woman and the Dragon

Revelation 12

Ever since Satan coveted the throne of God, he has been waging a war against God Almighty. First he persuaded one-third of the angels to follow him (Rev. 12:4). Next, as soon as God created people, Satan attacked them in an attempt to prove that God is not worthy to rule.[20] When Adam and Eve sinned, the Lord promised to send them a Saviour, the promised Seed. Therefore in the Old Testament Satan continually tried to destroy the ancestors of the promised Seed, but he never succeeded. Then at the time appointed God sent his Son Jesus into the world.

In Revelation 12 the Lord explains the spiritual battle that ensued at Jesus' birth. John saw two contrasting signs in heaven, a pregnant woman, crying out in pain, "as she was about to give birth," and "an enormous red dragon with seven heads and ten horns and seven crowns on his heads" (Rev. 12:2,3). "The dragon stood in front of the woman who was about to give birth, so that he might devour her child the moment it was born" (Rev. 12:4). The woman gave birth to a son, a ruler, who "was snatched up to God and to his throne. The woman fled into the desert to a place prepared for her by God, where she might be taken care of for 1,260 days" (Rev. 12:5,6).

The woman symbolizes the believers in Israel. Those people belonged to the Church in the protective womb of Israel before its birth at Pentecost. One of those believers was Mary of Nazareth, who literally cried out in pain at the birth of Jesus. The Dragon, who is Satan, wanted to kill Jesus the moment that he was born. That is why Herod killed all of the boy babies in Bethlehem two years old and under, but he did not succeed in murdering Jesus. Later on, at his ascension, Jesus sat down at the right hand of God. Then before the destruction of Jerusalem, the church fled to Pella, where it was safe from Satan.[21] Meanwhile Michael and his angels had kicked Satan and his demons out of heaven. They overcame Satan by the blood of the Lamb. After Calvary every believer has overcome the attacks of Satan by the blood of the Lamb.

Satan is furious because he knows that his time is short (Rev. 12:12). You may be thinking that 2000 years is not a short time. Satan, however, knows that each person's life is short. He only has opportunity to thwart God's plan for your life as long as you are alive. Satan found the woman in the desert and "spewed water like a river, to overtake the woman and sweep her away with the torrent" (Rev. 12:15). Mercifully, the Lord protected the church of Jerusalem from all of Satan's efforts to destroy it. Enraged, Satan focused his hatred on other believers. He made war with "those who obey God's commandments and hold to the testimony of Jesus" (Rev. 12:17). Although a war is raging now between God and Satan, the final outcome has been determined at the cross. The blood of the Lamb will always prevent Satan from succeeding in his desire to destroy the kingdom of light. Moreover, every Christian today is a spiritual child of the woman, who is the early Church. Consequently, no matter

> The blood of the Lamb will always prevent Satan from succeeding in his desire to destroy the kingdom of light.

what tactics Satan uses against believers, God promises to protect them from spiritual harm. Finally, unlike God, Satan cannot be everywhere at the same time. He focused his energy first on one group of people and then on another. These facts are comforting to the persecuted Church.

5h. The Unholy Trinity

Revelation 13

While standing by the seashore, Satan came up with a plan of attack. Being a copycat, he formed his own trinity. God consists of the Father, Son, and Holy Spirit, all of whom are working to promote his kingdom of light. Likewise Satan uses himself, the beast over government, and the false lamb over religion to establish his kingdom of darkness. Since the origin of city states, Satan has encouraged the union of religion and government. Anyone born in a certain region automatically worshipped the god of that particular area. Not to do so would have caused economic hardship. John's readers saw in the Roman emperors the beast of government and the religion that they espoused. Even in our own day some governments foster a religion forced on its citizens. In such countries the union of religion and the state has always made it difficult to be a believer.

> Since the origin of city states, Satan has encouraged the union of religion and government.

Nevertheless, there is a future element in this vision. Near the end of time, the political beast will lead the worst rebellion against God ever. Satan will give this person "his power and his throne and great authority" (Rev.13:2). Antichrist will be like Antiochus Epiphanes, because he will "utter proud words and blasphemies" (Rev.13:5). For forty-two months Antichrist will persecute the saints so that some will become slaves and others will be killed. "This calls for patient endurance and faithfulness on the part of the saints" (Rev.13:10). Will that generation of believers be found faithful, just as the Maccabees were during the persecution of Antiochus Epiphanes or just as the early Church was in the time of the Roman Empire? "All inhabitants of the earth will worship the beast—all whose names have not been written in the book of life belonging to the Lamb that was slain before the creation of the world" (Rev. 13:8). Moreover, the false lamb will force "everyone, small and great, rich and poor, free and slave, to receive a mark on his right hand or on his forehead" (Rev. 13:16). Satan puts a mark on the members of his kingdom, just as the Holy Spirit seals those who belong to God's kingdom.

5i. The Great Winepress of God's Wrath

Revelation 14-16

> *Then I saw another angel flying in midair, and he had the eternal gospel to proclaim to those who live on the earth—to every nation, tribe, language and people...A second angel followed and said, "Fallen! Fallen is Babylon the Great, which made all the nations drink the maddening wine of her adulteries." A third angel followed them and said in a loud voice: "If anyone worships the beast and his image and receives his mark on the forehead or on the hand, he, too, will drink of the wine of God's fury, which has been poured full strength into the cup of his wrath. He will be tormented with burning sulfur in the presence of the holy angels and of the Lamb. And the smoke of their torment rises for ever and ever"* (Rev. 14:6-11).

The Lord encourages the persecuted Church not to forget three important truths. God's gospel is eternal. It will never end. In contrast, Babylon, the capital of Satan's kingdom, will be destroyed. Then all of Satan's followers will suffer God's wrath forever.

> *For God did not appoint us to suffer wrath but to receive salvation through our Lord Jesus Christ* (1 Thess. 5:9).

"One 'like a son of man' with a crown of gold on his head and a sharp sickle in his hand" was seated on a cloud (Rev. 14:14). An angel called out to the Son of Man, "Take your sickle and reap, because the time to reap has come, for the harvest of the earth is ripe" (Rev. 14:15).

At the seventh trumpet or the third woe Jesus will sit on the clouds ready to pour out the wrath of God on the nonbelievers living on the earth, but where will the believers be? "And I saw what looked like a sea of glass mixed with fire and, standing beside the sea, those who had been victorious over the beast and his image and over the number of his name. They held harps given them by God and sang the song of Moses the servant of God and the song of the Lamb" (Rev. 15:2,3). Believers need not fear the seven golden bowls filled with the wrath of God, because Jesus promised to come back for us. Then we will live with him forever.

> Believers need not fear the seven golden bowls filled with the wrath of God, because Jesus promised to come back for us.

John saw seven angels pouring out "the seven bowls of God's wrath on the earth" (Rev. 16:1). The first bowl produced "ugly and painful sores" (Rev. 16:2). The second bowl turned the sea to blood and "every living thing in the sea died" (Rev. 16:3). The third bowl turned the rivers and springs to blood (Rev. 16:4). The fourth bowl caused the sun "to scorch people with fire" (Rev. 16:8). Yet those who were suffering "refused to repent and glorify him" (Rev. 16:9). The fifth bowl plunged the kingdom of the beast into darkness (Rev. 16:10), but they still "refused to repent of what they had done" (Rev. 16:11). Instead, they cursed God. The sixth bowl dried up the water in the Euphrates River "to prepare the way for the kings from the East" (Rev. 16:12). Afterwards the unholy trinity, consisting of Satan, Antichrist, and the false prophet, sent three evil spirits to convince the kings of the whole world that they could fight against God Almighty at Armageddon (Rev. 16:14,16). These kings contrast with the wise men from the East who came to worship the Messiah at the first advent. When the seventh angel poured the seventh bowl, a loud voice from the throne cried, "It is done!" (Rev. 16:17). Babylon the Great drank the cup of God's wrath (Rev. 16:19). The war between Satan and God was finally over. Mountains were levelled. The earth was ravaged with earthquakes. Hailstones, 100 pounds each, fell on the people. Yet they continued to curse God (Rev. 16:18-21).

5j. Babylon the Great

Revelation 17, 18

In this passage John goes into more detail about the fall of that great city, Mystery Babylon the Great, which was first mentioned in Revelation 14:8. Lest anyone thinks that God intends to revive the ancient city of Babylon, which had been doomed to eternal extinction, the Lord calls this city "Mystery Babylon." It is a mystery for two reasons. The Lord is speaking to John's readers and to the final generation on earth. Therefore he is talking about two different cities. In his vision John saw a woman dressed in purple and scarlet riding on a beast with seven heads and ten horns. An angel explained, "The woman you saw is the great city that rules over the kings of the earth" (Rev. 17:18). "The seven heads are seven hills on which the woman sits" (Rev. 17:9). Without him actually naming the city, John's readers would realize that he was talking about Rome. Nevertheless, to the final generation on earth, God warns that another city will be utterly destroyed. John wrote, "In her was found the blood of prophets and of the saints, and of all who have been killed on the earth" (Rev. 18:24). There is only one city guilty of killing the prophets of God—Jerusalem. Although the Lord has always had a special place in his heart for Jerusalem, he punished the city in A.D. 70 for rejecting his Son, the Messiah. Yet, because of God's grace and mercy, it exists today.

> The woman is not only a city; she is also a prostitute.

The woman is not only a city; she is also a prostitute. "With her the kings of the earth committed adultery" (Rev. 17:2). In other words, this woman represents false religion that is opposed to the true worship of God. Just as God described his Church as a woman in Revelation 12, Satan's false religion is represented by another woman. This prostitute sits on a scarlet beast that has seven heads and ten horns (Rev. 17:3). Both Satan and the Antichrist look exactly like that beast (Rev. 12:3; 13:1). Thus the Lord paints a hideous picture of the union of false religion and the state. Yet even in false religions, God claims a remnant of people whom he loves. Therefore he pleads, "Come out of her, my people, so that you will not share in her sins, so that you will not receive any of her plagues" (Rev. 18:4).

5k. The Wedding Supper of the Lamb

Revelation 19

"Blessed are those who are invited to the wedding supper of the Lamb!" (Rev. 19:9).

What a wonderful celebration that will be! Every believer from the beginning of time to the end will be gathered together in heaven to be with Jesus forever! Jew and Gentile will unite together to praise the Lord. A great multitude will shout joyfully, "Hallelujah! Salvation and glory and power belong to our God, for true and just are his judgments...Hallelujah! For our Lord God Almighty reigns. Let us rejoice and be glad and give him glory!" (Rev. 19:1-7). Are you looking forward to that day?

> *He is dressed in a robe dipped in blood, and his name is the Word of God. The armies of heaven were following him, riding on white horses and dressed in fine linen, white and clean. Out of his mouth comes a sharp sword with which to strike down the nations* (Rev. 19:13-15).

Ever since Satan first coveted the throne of God, he has been trying to discredit the Lord. As soon as God created people, Satan tried to win them over to his kingdom of darkness. When Eve succumbed and ate the forbidden fruit, Adam followed suit. The Lord responded by promising to send the Saviour, the promised Seed. After that Satan spent centuries trying to prevent God from carrying out his plan of salvation. In killing Jesus, Satan merely fulfilled God's plan. Since Jesus' death and resurrection, Satan has been constantly fighting to stop the spread of the kingdom of light—to no avail. In God's time this present world will end, and he will create a new heaven and a new earth that will last for eternity. Revelation 19 is a description of the final battle between Satan and God. It is a picture of the physical end of the world as we know it. The kingdom of darkness will be forever gone.

> Jew and Gentile will unite together to praise the Lord.

51. Life after Death

I saw thrones on which were seated those who had been given authority to judge. And I saw the souls of those who had been beheaded because of their testimony for Jesus and because of the word of God. They had not worshiped the beast or his image and had not received his mark on their foreheads or their hands. They came to life and reigned with Christ for a thousand years. (The rest of the dead did not come to life until the thousand years were ended.) This is the first resurrection (Rev. 20:4,5).

Many of John's readers were sorrowing over the loss of their loved ones who had been killed because they were Christians. For this reason God compassionately revealed the spiritual realities of life after death in order to comfort those left behind. While people on earth are busy with the joys and concerns of physical life, the dead are in the intermediate state between physical death and eternity. They are disembodied spirits waiting for the moment when they will receive their spiritual bodies. Although many believers in John's day were beheaded for their faith, "they came to life and reigned with Christ for a thousand years." In other words, those martyrs in John's day are alive and reigning now during this gospel age.

Christians who are physically dead are literally alive in the spiritual realm. Yet, what does it mean to be alive without a body? Jesus once told a story about a wicked rich man and a beggar called Lazarus. After a while Lazarus died and went to heaven. Later on the rich man died and went to hell (Luke 16:19-31). Because both of them were able to talk, communication alone is not a sign of life in the spiritual realm.[22]

Non-believers that died physically *"did not come to life."* In contrast, believers "came to life and reigned with Christ." In heaven they have an active part in overseeing the destruction of Satan's kingdom and the success of God's. This is the difference between believers and non-believers in the life after death. The former have the ability to influence others. They have authority, whereas the latter are powerless. How reassuring to know that every believer who has died physically is alive and reigning in heaven today! On the other hand, when non-believers die, they are helpless. When I think about my parents, these facts give me so much comfort and happiness.

> How reassuring to know that every believer who has died physically is alive and reigning in heaven today! On the other hand, when non-believers die, they are helpless.

The result is that, during this gospel age, God's army becomes increasingly more powerful and Satan's more ineffective. Doesn't God have a sense of humour?

The war between Satan and God is not over after the completion of the thousand years, which is this present gospel age. On the contrary, the Lord will free Satan from his spiritual prison and will allow him to attack with all of his available forces of evil—human and demonic. By implication, the non-believers who have been helpless prisoners in their disembodied state will now have the ability to make war along with Satan. Every living being in the spirit world and on earth will be involved in the war. For a time Satan will even realize his dreams of grandeur. Whose side are you on?

God promises that believers will never suffer from the second death. It "has no power over them" (Rev. 20:6). Because of the curse of sin, everyone must die physically. This is the first death. Only those who reject God's wonderful gift of salvation will be condemned to eternal separation from God in the Lake of Fire. This is the second death (Rev. 20:14). Do you believe that God has already won the war because of Jesus' death and resurrection? God is the Victor! Do not fear the future!

5m. The Final Judgment

> *Then I saw a great white throne and him who was seated on it. Earth and sky fled from his presence, and there was no place for them. And I saw the dead, great and small, standing before the throne, and books were opened. Another book was opened, which is the book of life. The dead were judged according to what they had done as recorded in the books. The sea gave up the dead that were in it, and death and Hades gave up the dead that were in them, and each person was judged according to what he had done...If anyone's name was not found written in the book of life, he was thrown into the lake of fire* (Rev. 20:11-15).

One day all the dead, great and small, will physically stand before the great white throne. Each person will be judged according to what he or she has done. Believers need not fear the Final Judgment, because the blood of the Lamb covers them. When God looks at believers, he sees the righteousness of Christ. Although our works will not save us, this does not mean that God does not care how we behave. He will judge our actions to determine our rewards (see Rom. 14:10-12). In contrast, anyone who has not trusted Jesus to take away his or her sins has much to fear. If anyone's name is not found written in the Book of Life, he will be thrown into the Lake of Fire. Will you repent of your sin and accept the gift of salvation lovingly offered by God?

5n. The New Heaven and New Earth

Blessed are those who wash their robes, that they may have the right to the tree of life and may go through the gates into the city. Outside are the dogs, those who practice magic arts, the sexually immoral, the murderers, the idolaters and everyone who loves and practices falsehood (Rev. 22:14,15).

Since the time of Cain and Abel there have been two types of people. Those who trust the Lord to forgive their sins can look forward to restored fellowship with their Creator. Those who refuse his gift will be forever shunned in the Lake of Fire, the second death. John saw the new heaven and new earth. "The first heaven and the first earth had passed away" (Rev. 21:1). God said, "I am making everything new!" (Rev. 21:5).

It is marvellous that the new earth and heaven will be paradise restored, even better than the old. Satan entered the original paradise and wreaked havoc. In contrast, sin will never destroy the new heaven or new earth. There is no need for a temple there, because the Triune God will be the temple. Most Old Testament prophets looked forward to the day when Israel would become a dominant political force. The Lord graciously allowed his people to expand their borders more than once. The New Testament is silent about this subject. Instead we

> Instead we are encouraged to look for the new heaven and new earth where the Lord will be in close fellowship with his people, believers from many nations.

are encouraged to look for the new heaven and new earth where the Lord will be in close fellowship with his people, believers from many nations.

Jesus said, "Behold, I am coming soon!" (Rev. 22:7).

Skeptics may rightly reply, "Soon! It has been 2000 years!"

Jesus, however, expressed what our attitude should properly be. "He is coming soon!"

Only God the Father knows exactly when the Second Coming of Christ will be. Until he does come, the invitation to accept God's gift of salvation is still available. "Whoever is thirsty, let him come; and whoever wishes, let him take the free gift of the water of life" (Rev. 22:17). The foolish virgins of Matthew 25 left to buy oil for their lamps. They lived as if there was plenty of time before the wedding banquet. The wise virgins did not know the exact time of the groom's arrival, but, knowing that it would be soon, they waited expectantly. In the same way non-believers, living only for the present, do not think about or expect Jesus to return. In contrast, believers fervently long for the soon arrival of their Lord. Indeed, he will come!

Points to Ponder

1. God's revelation is progressive in nature. Therefore we should interpret the Old Testament in light of the New—not vice versa.

2. The everlasting covenant to Abraham was fulfilled in Jesus, the sinless sacrifice of the new covenant. The old covenant was never meant to be permanent, only a temporary step of preparation for the new.

3. As God haters, nobody wants or deserves to go to heaven to live with the Triune God.

4. Like the prophets, the writers in the New Testament did not always understand the long-range intent of the Holy Spirit—neither do we.

5. Most of us are linear thinkers. When reading, we start at the beginning and progress through time to the end of the plot. The book of Revelation is not like that. It is like a painting in which God draws a broad outline of history and gradually fills in more and more of the details. His purpose is not to satisfy our minds about future events but to encourage us that he is the sovereign God who knows the end from the beginning.

CHAPTER FIVE

THE APOSTOLIC FATHERS

PHILIP is my prodigal son, not once but twice. He came home from university with credit card debt as well as student loans. Barry and I thought that he had learnt his lesson until recently. Then Philip admitted that he was badly in debt again, because of a desperate attempt to become a successful real estate agent. I am so happy that Debra and Stephen are not like the older brother in the story of the prodigal son. They are supporting and encouraging Philip. In contrast, the older brother in the Bible story was angry and jealous when his father threw a party to welcome the prodigal home.

Those first Jewish believers struggled with thoughts similar to the older brother. They thought that they deserved special favours from God because they had been faithful longer than the Gentile believers had. One day Jesus told his disciples a parable to explain what the kingdom of heaven is like. This story also explains how those first believers felt.

Early in the morning a landowner hired some men to work in his vineyard. They agreed to be paid one denarius (or one penny). At nine in the morning the landowner hired some more men. He said, "You also go and work in my vineyard, and I will pay you whatever is right" (Matt. 20:4).

At noon and three hours later the landowner again recruited more men to work in his vineyard. Finally at five o'clock he found some men who had not worked all day, and he enlisted them. One hour later the landowner paid everyone. First he gave a penny to those who had only worked one hour. Next he gave a penny to those who had worked three hours. As soon as everyone who had worked that day received a penny, those who were hired first complained:

> *"These men who were hired last worked only one hour," they said, "and you have made them equal to us who have borne the burden of the work and the heat of the day."*
>
> *But he answered one of them, "Friend, I am not being unfair to you. Didn't you agree to work for a denarius? Take your pay and go. I want to give the man who was hired last the same as I gave you. Don't I have the right to do what I want with my own money? Or are you envious because I am generous?"* (Matt. 20:12-15).

Beginning with Moses, God had set the Israelites apart from all other nations. He had been their God for centuries while the Gentiles had worshipped false gods. Surely they deserved to be treated differently than the Gentiles. Those Jewish believers were glad that God the Father had sent the promised Seed, the Saviour. They were also thankful that Jesus had accomplished his part in the plan of salvation. They knew that Jesus had lived a sinless life and was the perfect sacrifice for their sins. They joyfully accepted God's gift of salvation and fervently expected to see their Saviour soon. What did they expect to happen at Jesus' return, however?

> Those first Christians were no different than us. When they received Jesus as their Lord and Saviour, they were spiritual babies whose minds were filled with wrong ideas.

During the first century A.D., the Holy Spirit wrote through the apostles to reveal God's will for the Church. How did the apostolic Church respond? Those first Christians were no different than us. When they received Jesus as their Lord and Saviour, they were spiritual babies whose minds were filled with wrong ideas. For example, the Jews assumed that Gentiles must first be converted to Judaism and then to Christ. The Holy Spirit dwelt within each of them, but they did not have the completed Scriptures until approximately A.D. 100. Even then, it was years before the Holy Spirit convinced the Church what writings to authorize and what to reject.

During Jesus' time on earth, he often clashed with the Jewish notion of an earthly political kingdom. Because the first Christians were Jews, most of them continued to wait for that political Utopia. For the 400 years of God's silence between the Old and New Testaments, false writers, unauthorized by the Holy Spirit, had imagined what this kingdom would be like. Originally this kingdom was to last forever, but gradually it was shortened to an undetermined set length of time. False Jewish writers continued writing apocalyptic literature in the first century A.D., because they were still waiting for their Messiah. Slavonic Enoch, or 2 Enoch, written in A.D. 50,[1] is especially noteworthy. According to Fuller, "This is the only reference in Jewish literature to a temporary kingdom of one thousand years, that is, a millennium."[2] Le Roy Edwin Froom comments on Slavonic Enoch's 7,000-year theory:

> The most remarkable feature of this book, in respect to our quest, is that we find here, for the first time in Jewish literature, the equation that one day of creation corresponds to one thousand years of the world's history—a theory which has played an important role in both ancient and modern chiliasm, and which, consciously or subconsciously, has been accepted by many exegetes who attempted to compute the time to the end of the world.[3]

It is significant that Paul orders Titus not to pay attention to Jewish myths (Titus 1:14). Peter pointedly writes that God is not chained to time. "But do not forget this one thing, dear friends: With the Lord a day is like a thousand years, and a thousand years are like a day" (2 Pet. 3:8). When Jesus was alive, John eagerly desired an important position in a political kingdom. Then shortly before A.D. 100 John wrote his gospel. Instead of expecting a political Utopia he emphasized the spiritual nature of Jesus' kingdom.[4] Soon after Christianity spread to the Gentiles, the hope for a Jewish Utopia on earth was often replaced by the desire for a perfect Christian society. While some believers in the apostolic Church continued to envisage Jewish world dominance, others imagined a completely Christian Utopia.

Strictly speaking, the apostolic fathers lived during the time of the apostles or within a generation of them. Two examples of such authors are Barnabas of Alexandria and Clement of Rome. Clement, the third bishop of Rome, who wrote in approximately A.D. 96,[5] appears to be in the minority at this time. He does not mention a political kingdom on earth at Christ's return.

The First Epistle of Clement to the Corinthians

Chapter 24: "Let us consider, beloved, how the Lord continually proves to us that there shall be a future resurrection, of which He has rendered the Lord Jesus Christ the first fruits by raising Him from the dead."[6]

The Second Epistle of Clement to the Corinthians

Written by an unknown author about A.D. 130-140.[7]

Chapter 9: "And let no one of you say that this very flesh shall not be judged, nor rise again. Consider ye in what (state) ye were saved, in what ye received sight, if not while ye were in this flesh. We must therefore preserve the flesh as the temple of God. For as ye were called in the flesh, ye shall also come (to be judged) in the flesh."[8]

Chapter 19: "Blessed are they who obey these commandments, even if for a brief space they suffer in this world, and they will gather the imperishable fruit of the resurrection. Let not the godly man, therefore, grieve; if for the present he suffer affliction, blessed is the time that awaits him there; rising up to life again with the fathers he will rejoice for ever without a grief."[9]

Barnabas of Alexandria wrote between A.D. 70-100.[7] According to Hilgenfeld, he was a Gentile Christian determined to guard against a Judaic form of Christianity.[10] Unlike the Jewish author of Slavonic Enoch, Barnabas expected a purely Christian Utopia. Yet both of them used the story of creation as an allegory. Each day represented 1,000 years. On the seventh day God would remove the wicked from this world and usher in 1,000 years of peace. Time has proved both men wrong. Jesus should have returned and set up the millennial kingdom. In fact, we should be living in it now. Notice that Barnabas expected only one resurrection. Also, God would judge the wicked before the 1,000 years, not after.

The Epistle of Barnabas

Chapter 15: *the False and the True Sabbath*
The Sabbath is mentioned at the beginning of the creation [thus]: "And God made in six days the works of His hands, and made an end on the seventh day, and rested on it, and sanctified it" (Gen. 2:2). Attend, my children, to the meaning of this expression, "He finished in six days." This implieth that the Lord will finish all things in six thousand years, for a day is with Him a thousand years. And He Himself testifieth, saying, "Behold, to-day will be as a thousand years" (Ps. 90:4; 2 Pet. 3:8). Therefore, my children, in six days, that is, in six thousand years, all things will be finished. "And He rested on the seventh day."

This meaneth: when His Son, coming [again], shall destroy the time of the wicked man, and judge the ungodly, and change the sun, and the moon, and the stars, then shall He truly rest on the seventh day...Further, He says to them, "Your new moons and your Sabbaths I cannot endure" (Isa. 1:13). Ye perceive how He speaks: Your present Sabbaths are not acceptable to me, but that is which I have made, [namely this,] when, giving rest to all things, I shall make a beginning of the eighth day, that is, a beginning of another world. Wherefore, also, we keep the eighth day with joyfulness, the day also on which Jesus rose again from the dead. And when he had manifested Himself, He ascended into the heavens.[11]

Chapter 21: *Conclusion*

It is well, therefore, that he who has learned the judgments of the Lord, as many as have been written, should walk in them. For he who keepeth these shall be glorified in the kingdom of God, but he who chooseth other things shall be destroyed with his works. On this account there will be a resurrection, on this account a retribution. I beseech you who are superiors, if you will receive any council of my goodwill, have among yourselves those to whom you may show kindness: do not forsake them. For the day is at hand on which all things shall perish with the evil [one]. The Lord is near, and His reward.[12]

In the first three centuries A.D., believers struggled to defend and define their faith. For this reason it is worthwhile to consider those who wrote before the council of Nicaea in A.D. 325. This council was the first formal meeting of believers to settle a doctrinal issue since A.D. 50.[13] Technically those authors are not apostolic fathers. Yet they were instrumental in formulating Christian doctrine. For sixty-three years (A.D. 117-180)[14] all of the Christian writers were concerned with defending their faith, not explaining it.

Irenaeus, Bishop of Lyons, was born in Asia Minor (c. A.D. 120-202?).[15] In A.D. 180-190, Irenaeus wrote "Against Heresies." As the first Biblical theologian of the Church,[16] Irenaeus states:

Against Heresies: book 5, chapter 33

> 3. The blessing of Isaac with which he blessed his younger son Jacob has the same meaning, when he says, "Behold, the smell of my son is as the smell of a full field which the Lord has blessed" (Gen. 27:27, etc). But "the field is the world" (Matt. 13:38). And therefore he added, "God give to thee of the dew of heaven, and of the fatness of the earth, plenty of corn and wine. And let the nations serve thee, and kings bow down to thee; and be thou lord over thy brother, and thy father's sons shall bow down to thee: cursed shall be he who shall curse thee and blessed shall be he who shall bless thee" (Gen. 27:28,29). If any one, then, does not accept these things as referring to the appointed kingdom, he must fall into much contradiction and contrariety, as is the case with the Jews, who are involved in absolute perplexity.[17]

In this passage Irenaeus has invented his own allegory. In his mind he has substituted the word *field* in Genesis 27:27 with the word *world* used in Matthew 13:38. In reality Isaac thought that Jacob smelled like a field only because he was wearing Esau's clothes that smelled of the outdoors. Irenaeus, however, assumes that because Jacob smelled like a field, his descendants, the future nation of Israel, deserve to rule the world during the time of the appointed kingdom. In Genesis 27, God does promise Jacob that his descendants would rule other nations at some point in time, but he does not specifically promise that they would have authority over the entire world at the end of time. Moreover, God does not use this verse in the New Testament to point toward a future Jewish kingdom.

In contrast, Tertullian writes the following sometime after A.D. 202,[18] when he had joined the heretical sect of Montanus:

Against Marcion: chapter 25

> Besides, your Christ promises to the Jews their primitive condition, with the recovery of their country; and after this life's course is over, repose in Hades in Abraham's bosom. Oh, most excellent God, when He restores in amnesty what He took away in wrath! Oh, what a God is yours, who both wounds and heals, creates evil and makes peace! Oh, what a God, that is merciful even down to Hades! I shall have something to say about Abraham's bosom in the proper place. As for the restoration of Judaea, however, which even the Jews themselves, induced by the names of places and countries, hope for just as it is described, it would be tedious to state at length how the figurative interpretation is spiritually applicable to Christ and His Church, and to the character and fruits thereof.[19]

Although Irenaeus and Tertullian disagreed on the place of the Jews in the future kingdom, they both agreed that believers deserve happiness in this world to make up for their suffering. Irenaeus writes:

Against Heresies: book 5, chapter 32

> Inasmuch, therefore, as the opinions of certain [orthodox persons] are derived from heretical discourses, they are both ignorant of God's dispensations, and of

the mystery of the resurrection of the just, and of the [earthly] kingdom which is the commencement of incorruption, by means of which kingdom those who shall be worthy are accustomed gradually to partake of the divine nature...and it is necessary to tell them respecting those things, that it behoves the righteous first to receive the promise of the inheritance which God promised to the fathers, and to reign in it, when they rise again to behold God in this creation which is renovated, and that the judgment should take place afterwards. For it is just that in that very creation in which they toiled or were afflicted, being proved in every way by suffering, they should receive the reward of their suffering; and that in the creation in which they were slain because of their love to God, in that they should be revived again; and that in the creation in which they endured servitude, in that they should reign. For God is rich in all things, and all things are His. It is fitting, therefore, that the creation itself, being restored to its primeval condition, should without restraint be under the dominion of the righteous; and the apostle has made this plain in the Epistle to the Romans, when he thus speaks: "For the expectation of the creature waiteth for the manifestation of the sons of God. For the creature has been subjected to vanity, not willingly, but by reason of him who hath subjected the same in hope; since the creature itself shall also be delivered from the bondage of corruption into the glorious liberty of the sons of God" (Rom. 8:19).[20]

Likewise Tertullian expresses similar hopes:

Against Marcion: chapter 25

But we do confess that a kingdom is promised to us upon the earth, although before heaven, only

> in another state of existence; inasmuch as it will be after the resurrection for a thousand years in the divinely-built city of Jerusalem, "let down from heaven," (Rev. 21:2) which the apostle also calls "our mother from above;" (Gal. 4:26)...We say that this city has been provided by God for receiving the saints on their resurrection, and refreshing them with the abundance of all really spiritual blessings, as a recompence for those which in the world, we have either despised or lost; since it is both just and Godworthy that His servants should have their joy in the place where they have also suffered affliction for His name's sake. Of the heavenly kingdom this is the process. After its thousand years are over, within which period is completed the resurrection of the saints, who rise sooner or later according to their deserts, there will ensue the destruction of the world and the conflagration of all things at the judgment: we shall then be changed in a moment into the substance of angels, even by the investiture of an incorruptible nature, and so be removed to that kingdom in heaven.[21]

Irenaeus, like many believers, was fixated on physical prosperity during the millennium:

Against Heresies: book 5, chapter 33

> The predicted blessing, therefore, belongs unquestionably to the times of the kingdom, when the righteous shall bear rule upon their rising from the dead; when also the creation, having been renovated and set free, shall fructify with an abundance of all kinds of food, from the dew of heaven, and from the fertility of the earth: as the elders who saw John, the disciple of the Lord, related that they had

heard from him how the Lord used to teach in regard to these times, and say: The days will come, in which vines shall grow, each having ten thousand branches, and in each branch ten thousand twigs, and in each true twig ten thousand shoots, and in each one of the shoots ten thousand clusters, and on every one of the clusters ten thousand grapes, and every grape when pressed will give five and twenty metretes [measures] of wine. And when any one of the saints shall lay hold of a cluster, another shall cry out, "I am a better cluster, take me; bless the Lord through me." In like manner [the Lord declared] that a grain of wheat would produce ten thousand ears, and that every ear should have ten thousand grains, and every grain would yield ten pounds...of clear, pure, fine flour; and that all other fruit-bearing trees, and seeds and grass, would produce in similar proportions...and that all animals feeding [only] on the productions of the earth, should [in those days] become peaceful and harmonious among each other, and be in perfect subjection to man.

4. And these things are borne witness to in writing by Papias, the hearer of John, and a companion of Polycarp, in his fourth book; for there were five books compiled...by him.[22]

> As a prolific writer and a systematic theologian, Origen wrote books that challenged and changed the millennial beliefs of many.

Born in Alexandria in A.D. 185, Origen is the greatest teacher in the early Church.[23] As a prolific writer and a systematic theologian, Origen wrote books that challenged and changed the millennial beliefs of many. In his writing Origen considered both the present and the future reality of the kingdom. Concerning the present reality, Origen preaches:

Thy Kingdom Come

"Thy Kingdom come" (Matt. 6:10; Luke 11:2). If "the kingdom of God," according to the word of our Lord and Saviour, "cometh not with observation: neither shall they say, Lo, hear! or, Lo, there!" but "the kingdom of God is within us" (Luke 17:20,21)…it is evident that he who prays that "the kingdom" of God should come prays with good reason that the kingdom of God should spring up and bear fruit and be perfected in him. For every saint who takes God as his king and obeys the spiritual laws of God dwells in himself as in a well-ordered city, so to speak. Present with him are the Father and Christ who reigns with the Father in the soul that has been perfected, in accordance with the saying which I mentioned a short time ago: "we will come unto him, and make our abode with him" (John 14:23).[24]

Concerning the future kingdom, Origen expounds:

Commentary on St. Matthew

Those who have followed the Saviour will sit on twelve thrones and be judges over the twelve tribes of Israel (Matt. 19:28). They will receive this power when the dead rise again. It will be a rebirth, a new birth. They will be made new creatures. A new earth and a new heaven (Isa. 65:17) will be created for them; there will be a new covenant given and a new cup. The prelude to this rebirth is what Paul calls (Titus 3:5) the regenerating bath which, with the newness resulting from it, renews the spirit.[25]

Finally, the apostolic Church struggled to understand the proper relationship between the Old and New Testaments. This is how Origen understood their connection:

Commentary on Matthew 12:10

Thus, the killing of Christ in the earthly Jerusalem by the leading men of the earthly city is represented as the essential condition for the building of the Heavenly Jerusalem and the glorification of Christ by its leaders and scribes. The transition...from Israel to the Church, from the letter to the spirit, is seen to hinge on the drama of the Passion...The attitude of the Jews who opposed Christ is not just something that appeared at a given point in the past. Refusal to accept the abolition of the Law has been the Jewish attitude ever since and it always will be, just as it is and always will be the attitude of those who cling to the literal sense of the Old Testament. They too hold on to a figure which can no longer serve its original purpose. Thus refusal to accept the spiritual sense is equivalent to a refusal of history, is an anachronism. For Christ is at once the "new man" who succeeds the "old man" and the "spiritual Adam" who succeeds the "natural Adam" (cf. I Cor 15:44 et seq.).[26]

All the apostolic fathers I have quoted trusted in the finished work of Jesus on Calvary to take away their sins. All of them looked forward to the Second Coming of Christ. Yet they disagreed on the nature of the kingdom or what would happen at Jesus' return. They also had different opinions about God's promises in the Old Testament. Both Irenaeus and Tertullian assumed that the justice of God required a political kingdom on earth before the inauguration of eternity. Do believers have a right to expect that they should be happy someday on the very earth where they have suffered? Irenaeus also assumed that God meant to fulfill his promise to Abraham to bless Israel politically, not only in the time of the Old Testament, but also during the future millennial kingdom. Can these promises be wrested out of their time context? Is it correct to assume that God's promise to Abraham of blessing for Israel must override his promise to Moses of curses if the nation is disobedient?

After taking a journey through time, believers know for sure that God always tells the truth and always keeps his promises. God completed his plan to restore fellowship between himself and people. He sent the promised Seed, Jesus, to pay the penalty for sin. Because of his death and resurrection, King Jesus presently rules over everything, both physical and spiritual. He especially watches over those who belong to his kingdom. They may suffer and die in this world, but they are promised a wonderful future in the new heaven and new earth. We also know that God is sovereign and that his kingdom will continue to grow. Since Satan is defeated, his kingdom is doomed to destruction. Because God has kept his promises so far, believers are confident that Jesus will return again physically. At that point he will judge sinners and gather the redeemed into his kingdom. Let us join with the angels in singing, "Glory to God in the highest, and on earth peace to men on whom his favor rests" (Luke 2:14).

As time passes, more people will accept God's gift of salvation, the pearl of great price (Matt. 13:46, KJV). Perhaps you are wondering who will listen to you about Jesus. All of us have different spheres of influence. For me, a good place to start was with my family, because we spent a lot of time together. When Stephen was in high school science fairs, the two of us spent hours playing with wooden cars and wind tunnels. Debra catapulted marbles onto a tablecloth covered in flour. Of course, I was directly in the line of fire. Meanwhile Philip and I composted garbage under various conditions. As a young child Debra liked to watch me prepare my Sunday school lesson, especially since she was in my class. It was very easy to talk about God with my family, and I am very thankful that the three children have accepted Jesus as their Lord and Saviour. I pray that they will continue to grow in his grace. May all believers reach out to those around, point them to the Saviour, and teach them to pray, "Come, Lord Jesus. Come soon!"

Points to Ponder

1. Some Christians think that they deserve greater recognition from God than newer believers do.
2. Only by God's grace is anyone able to reject religious teachings instilled from childhood.
3. Slavonic Enoch contains the earliest reference we have to a 1000-year reign of Christ on earth.
4. Why do people constantly think that they have figured out when Jesus will return? If one date is wrong, then they blithely choose another. Jesus said that only God the Father knows.
5. If believers look forward to a new heaven and earth, why are we so preoccupied with the old ones?

APPENDIX

1. Dating the Founding Fathers

MANY scholars agree that David became king of Israel in 1010 B.C. There are serious differences of opinion concerning the date of the Exodus, however. According to Walton there are four chronological systems—Early Exodus Long Sojourn, Early Exodus Short Sojourn, Late Exodus, and Reconstructionist.[1] After studying the following Bible verses, I find myself in the "Early Exodus Short Sojourn" classification.

> *In the four hundred and eightieth year after the Israelites had come out of Egypt, in the fourth year of Solomon's reign over Israel, in the month of Ziv, the second month, he began to build the temple of the* Lord (1 Kings 6:1).

> 1446 B.C. Exodus from Egypt
> 1010 B.C. David king
> 970 B.C. Solomon king
> 967 B.C. Fourth year of Solomon's reign

> *Then the* Lord *said to him [Abram], "Know for certain that your descendants will be strangers in a country not their own, and they will be enslaved and mistreated four hundred years"* (Gen. 15:13).

The writer to the Hebrews says, "By faith he [Abraham] made his home in the promised land like a stranger in a foreign country; he lived in tents, as did Isaac and Jacob, who were heirs with him of the same promise" (Heb. 11:9). Abraham and his descendants did not have a home that they could call their own for 400 years. At first they lived in Canaan and then in Egypt. The Israelites did not become slaves of the Egyptians until they had been there for a while and Joseph's mighty deeds to save the people from starvation were forgotten (Exod. 1:8-14).

> *"In the fourth generation your descendants will come back here, for the sin of the Amorites has not yet reached its full measure" (Gen. 15:16).*

God promised that the Israelites would return to Canaan in the fourth generation. Thus only four generations of Hebrews would be born outside of Canaan. The genealogies in Matthew 1 and Luke 3 show that only four men were born in Egypt or the wilderness: Ram, Amminadab, Nahshon, and Salmon. Hezron, Ram's father, accompanied his great-grandfather Jacob to Egypt (Gen. 46:8-12). After entering the Promised Land, Salmon married Rahab, the prostitute from Jericho (Matt. 1:5).

> *Now the length of time the Israelite people lived in Egypt was 430 years* (Exod. 12:40).

This is very plain language. Both the Samaritan Pentateuch and the Septuagint, however, include the time spent in Canaan in the 430 years.[2] "And the sojourning of the children of Israel, while they sojourned in the land of Egypt and the land of Canaan, *was* four hundred and thirty years."[3]

    1951 B.C. Abraham's birth
    1876 B.C. Abraham moves to Canaan, Gen. 12:4 (age 75)
    1791 B.C. Jacob's birth, Gen. 21:5; 25:26
    1661 B.C. Jacob moves to Egypt, Gen. 47:28 (age 130)
    1446 B.C. Exodus from Egypt

What I mean is this: The law, introduced 430 years later, does not set aside the covenant previously established by God and thus do away with the promise. For if the inheritance depends on the law, then it no longer depends on a promise; but God in his grace gave it to Abraham through a promise (Gal. 3:17,18).

1876 B.C. God's covenant with Abraham
1446 B.C. Exodus from Egypt; Giving of the Law

The genealogy in Matthew 1 confirms Genesis 15 that only four generations would be born outside of Canaan. Furthermore the Septuagint verifies Galatians 3. Thus the length of the sojourn in Egypt must be 215 years.

2. The Pre-tribulation Rapture

None of the apostolic fathers conceived as complicated a system of end-time events as many do today. Certainly, none of them taught that Jesus would come back in two stages. It is not the purpose of this book to trace the development of such beliefs. The problem is that, according to some scholars, the apostolic fathers taught the pre-tribulation rapture. For example, Thomas Ice bases this belief on a sermon of Pseudo-Ephraem (A.D. 374-627). "For all the saints and elect of God are gathered, prior to the tribulation that is to come, and are taken to the Lord lest they see the confusion that is to overwhelm the world because of our sins."[4]

These writings are far too late to be considered apostolic. In addition, it is very dangerous to attribute such a complicated view of end times by reading one sentence. Thankfully, because of God's mercy, believers will not be present when the seven bowls of wrath are poured out on the last generation. Those judgments will be swift, severe, and certainly unprecedented in the world's history.[5]

Timeline of Key People and Events

From Creation to the Division of Israel

Adam and Eve
Cain and Abel
Enoch
Noah and the flood
Tower of Babel
1951–1776 B.C. Abraham
1851–1671 B.C. Isaac
1791–1644 B.C Jacob
1526–1406 B.C. Moses
1446 B.C. Exodus from Egypt
1010–970 B.C. David's reign
970–930 B.C. Solomon's reign
930 B.C. Kingdom divided

The Northern Kingdom of Israel

874–853 B.C. Ahab
865 B.C.? Elijah: Confronting Baal's prophets
841 B.C Elisha: Commissioning of Jehu
793–753 B.C. Jeroboam II
785–760 B.C. Jonah (from Israel): Preaching to Nineveh
760–750 B.C. Amos (from Judah): Preaching to Israel
753–715 B.C. Hosea (from Israel): Preaching to Israel
742–687 B.C. Micah (from Judah): Preaching to both
722 B.C. Fall of Samaria

663–612 B.C. Nahum (from Judah): Preaching to Assyria
612 B.C. Fall of Nineveh
Tiglath-Pileser III, king of Assyria: 745–727 B.C.
Sargon II, king of Assyria: 722–705 B.C.

The Southern Kingdom of Judah

872–848 B.C. Jehoshaphat
841–835 B.C. Athaliah
835–796 B.C. Joel (prophet)
792–740 B.C. Uzziah
740–724 B.C. Ahaz
740–681 B.C. Isaiah (prophet)
725–697 B.C. Hezekiah
640–621 B.C. Zephaniah (prophet)
640–609 B.C. Josiah
627–586 B.C. Jeremiah (prophet)
612–589 B.C. Habakkuk (prophet)
586 B.C. Fall of Jerusalem
Sennacherib, king of Assyria: 705–681 B.C.
Nebuchadnezzar, king of Babylon: 604–561 B.C.

From the Captivity to the Silent Years

605–536 B.C. Daniel (prophet)
593–571 B.C. Ezekiel (prophet)
586 B.C. Obadiah (prophet)
538 B.C. Edict of Cyrus
520 B.C. Haggai (prophet)
520–480 B.C. Zechariah (prophet)
516 B.C. Temple rebuilt
479–474 B.C. Esther
445 B.C. Walls of Jerusalem rebuilt
430 B.C. Malachi (prophet)
Kings of Persia: Cyrus (558–529 B.C.),
Darius (521–485 B.C.),
and Ahasuerus (485–465 B.C.).

The Silent Years

170 B.C. Enoch 1–36, 106, 107
168 B.C. Desecration of temple
167 B.C. Maccabean revolt
167, 166 B.C. Mattathias Maccabeus
166–161 B.C. Judas Maccabeus
165 B.C. Enoch 83–90, Altar rebuilt
143–135 B.C. Simon Maccabeus
143 B.C. Independence regained
135–105 B.C. John Hyrcanus
125 B.C. Testaments of the Twelve Patriarchs
110 B.C. The Book of Jubilees
78–68 B.C. Alexandra
75 B.C. f. Enoch 37–71, 91–105, 108
63 B.C. Conquered by Romans
50 B.C. Psalms of Solomon
Antiochus Epiphanes, king of the Seleucid Empire: 175–164 B.C.

From Jesus' Birth to the Book of Revelation

6/5 B.C. Jesus' birth
A.D. 26 Ministry of John the Baptist
A.D. 26/27–30 Ministry of Jesus
A.D. 35 Martyrdom of Stephen, First persecution
A.D. 35 Conversion of Saul (Paul)
A.D. 46–48 Paul: First missionary journey
A.D. 49 James, Galatians
A.D. 50 First Christian council at Jerusalem
A.D. 50–52 Paul: Second missionary journey
A.D. 51 1 Thessalonians
A.D. 51 or 52 2 Thessalonians
A.D. 53–57 Paul: Third missionary journey
A.D. 55 1 Corinthians
A.D. 55–57 2 Corinthians
A.D. 57 Romans
A.D. 60 Ephesians

A.D. 61 Philippians
A.D. 62–64 1 Peter
A.D. 67 2 Peter
Before A.D. 70 Hebrews
A.D. 70 Destruction of Jerusalem
A.D. 95 Revelation
Herod the Great, king of Judea: 37 B.C.–4 B.C.
Domitian, Roman emperor: A.D. 81–96.

Christian Writers up to the Council of Nicaea

A.D. 70–100 Barnabas of Alexandria: Epistle of Barnabas
A.D. 96 The First Epistle of Clement to the Corinthians
A.D. 125–126 Aristides: The Apology of Aristides
A.D. 130-140 The Second Epistle of Clement to the Corinthians
A.D. 180–190 Irenaus: Against Heresies
A.D. 202 Tertullian: Against Marcion
b. A.D. 185 Origen: Thy Kingdom Come, Commentary on St. Matthew
b. A.D. 260 Eusebius: Ecclesiastical History
A.D. 325 Council of Nicaea

Endnotes

PART 1: WAITING FOR THE PROMISED SEED

Chapter 1: The Beginning of the War

[1] F. C. Jennings, *Satan: His Person, Work, Place and Destiny* (Toronto: Haynes, n.d.) 129.

[2] Ibid., 92,104.

[3] R. Milligan, rev. ed., *An Exposition and Defense of the Scheme of Redemption* (St. Louis: Christian Publishing: 1885) 228,229.

Chapter 2: The Development of Satan's Kingdom

[1] Matthew Henry, *Matthew Henry's Commentary on the whole Bible,* vol. 1 (Marshallton: Sovereign Grace, p.d.) 31.

[2] Milligan, 207.

[3] A. R. Fausset, *Fausset's Bible Dictionary* (Grand Rapids: Zondervan, 1949) 647.

[4] Ira M. Price, Leslie E. Fuller, and Chester J. Attig, "Synchronous History of the Nations," *The New Standard Alphabetical Indexed Bible* (Chicago: John A. Hertel, 1963) 250.

[5] Robert W. Rogers, "Isaiah," eds. Frederick Carl Eiselen, Edwin Lewis, and David G. Downey, *The Abingdon Bible Commentary* (New York: Abingdon-Cokesbury, 1929) 631. Also see map p. 41.

[6] E. J. Young, *Old Testament Prophecy* (Toronto: Gospel Witness, n.d.) 77.

[7] See pp. 25, 26.

[8] Aristides, "The Apology of Aristides," Syriac trans., ed. Allan Menzies, *The Ante-Nicene Fathers. Translations of the Writings of the*

Fathers down to A.D. 325, vol. 9 (New York: Scribner's, 1926) 274.

[9] Origen, "Exhortation to Martyrdom," trans. and annotated by John J. O'Meara, *Ancient Christian Writers: The Works of the Fathers in Translation,* vol. 19 (Westminster: Newman, 1954) 188.

Chapter 3: The Founding Fathers of the Faith

[1] Theodore H. Robinson, "History of the Hebrew and Jewish People," *Abingdon Bible Commentary,* 61.

[2] Eusebius, "The Church History of Eusebius," eds. Philip Schaff and Henry Wace, 2nd series, trans. with prolegomena and notes by Arthur Cushman McGiffert, *A Select Library of Nicene and Post-Nicene Fathers of the Christian Church,* vol. 1 (New York: Christian Literature Co., 1892) 87.

[3] Ibid., 87,88.

[4] The word *offspring* in Gen. 12:7, 13:15, and 24:7 is singular.

[5] Philip Mauro, *The Hope of Israel: What is it?* (Swengel: Reiner, n.d.) 35.

[6] Price, 270.

[7] George H. Box, "The Historical and Religious Backgrounds of the Early Christian Movement," *Abingdon Bible Commentary,* 840.

[8] Fausset, 321.

[9] See pp. 271-275.

Chapter 4: The Establishment of Israel as a Nation

[1] See pp. 46, 47.

Chapter 5: King David

[1] David Maas, "A Chronology of Bible Events and World Events," *Life Application Study Bible* (Wheaton: Tyndale House, 1991) 431.

[2] See pp. 57, 58.

[3] Fausset, 738.

[4] George Smith, qtd. in Mauro, 224.

[5] D. H. Wallace, "Messiah," ed. Walter A. Elwell, *Evangelical Dictionary of Theology* (Grand Rapids: Baker Book House, 1984) 710.

[6] F. F. Bruce, *The New Testament Development of Old Testament Themes* (Grand Rapids: Eerdmans, 1969) 79.

[7] Henry, vol. 2,390.

[8] Robert Young, rev. Wm. B. Stevenson, 22nd Amer. ed., *Analytical Concordance to the Bible* (New York: Funk & Wagnall, 1936) 165,657. In Jesus' day, Greek was the universal language. The words *Christ* in Greek and *Messiah* in Aramaic are interchangeable and mean "the anointed king."

[9] Ibid., 619.

Chapter 6: The Northern Kingdom of Israel

[1] Maas, 431.
[2] See pp. 57, 58, 94-96.
[3] Maas, 598.
[4] Ibid., 599.
[5] See p. 144.
[6] Price, 254.
[7] Maas, 1559.
[8] Price, 256. This king was either Adad-nirari III or Shalmaneser IV.
[9] Maas, 1536.
[10] See pp. 113, 114.
[11] See pp. 147-151.
[12] See pp. 48-50.
[13] See pp. 93,94.
[14] Maas, 1502.
[15] Ibid., 1566.
[16] Henry, vol. 2, 1423.
[17] T. T. Shields, "Jesus of Bethlehem—and of the Days of Eternity," *The Gospel Witness*, 73,12, (Dec. 1, 1994) 13.
[18] See pp. 228, 229.
[19] Dr. Kac, qtd. in Hal Lindsey and C. C. Carlson, *The Late Great Planet Earth* (Grand Rapids: Zondervan, 1970) 51.
[20] *The Bethel Series New Testament,* (Madison: Adult Christian Foundation, 1981) 5.
[21] J. Ironside Still, *St. Paul On Trial* (New York: Doran, 1923) 37.
[22] Price, 256.
[23] Will Durant, *The Story of Civilization*: Part I, *Our Oriental Heritage* (1935; New York: Simon and Schuster, 1954) 267.

[24] Ibid., 270.

[25] Price, 256. Also see pp. 156, 157. Ahaz, the king of Judah, asked Tiglath-Pileser III to be his ally against Israel.

[26] Maas, 1580.

[27] Price, 258.

[28] Durant, *Our Oriental Heritage*, 283,284.

Chapter 7: The Southern Kingdom of Judah

[1] Maas, 598.

[2] See pp. 112, 113.

[3] Maas, 599.

[4] See p. 117.

[5] Maas, 1526.

[6] See pp. 33, 34.

[7] See p. 143.

[8] Henry, vol. 2, 1354.

[9] Maas, 600.

[10] Fausset, 312.

[11] Henry, vol. 2, 659.

[12] Price, 256.

[13] Fausset, 24.

[14] Young, *Old Testament Prophecy*, 101.

[15] Ibid., 102.

[16] John Urquhart, *The Wonders of Prophecy* (Harrisburg: Christian Publications, n.d.) 198.

[17] *The Bethel Series*, 5.

[18] See p. 394.

[19] Price, 258.

[20] Fausset, 290.

[21] For example, Isa. 41:14;48:17.

[22] For example, Isa. 44:21;48:20.

[23] See p. 24.

[24] Henry, vol. 2, 864.

Chapter 8: The Fall of Judah

[1] Maas, 1594.

[2] Henry, vol. 2, 1445.

[3] Maas, 1283.

[4] Ibid., 601.

[5] See pp. 270, 271.

[6] George B. Fletcher, *The Millennium What it is Not and What it is* (Sterling: Gam, n.d.) 25.

[7] Price, 258.

[8] Urquhart, 146.

[9] Werner Keller, Trans. William Neil. *The Bible as History* (1956; New York: Morrow, 1981) 290.

[10] Maas, 1587.

[11] Ibid., 601. Jehoiachin's short reign must have been near the end of 598 B.C.

Chapter 9: The Captivity

[1] Price, 258.

[2] See pp. 54, 55.

[3] See pp. 270, 271.

[4] See pp. 93, 94.

[5] Maas, 1399.

[6] Keller, 287.

[7] Ibid., 288, 289.

[8] D. A. Rausch, "Synagogue," *Evangelical Dictionary of Theology*, 1061.

[9] Loraine Boettner, rev. ed., *The Millennium* (Phillipsburg: Presbyterian and Reformed, 1984) 243.

[10] Maas, 1399.

[11] [Louis A. DeCaro], "Israel and Biblical Prophecy," final ed., *The Researcher* (Spring 1994) 26.

[12] Henry, vol. 2, 1117.

[13] Fletcher, 27.

[14] See pp. 394, 395.

[15] See pp. 207, 208.
[16] Mauro, 134.
[17] Ibid., 125.
[18] Ibid., 127, 128.
[19] Maas, 1473.
[20] See p. 195.
[21] See p. 307.
[22] Price, 262,263.
[23] "Palestine," *Encyclopedia Britannica: A New Survey of Universal Knowledge,* vol. 17 (Toronto: Benton, 1956) 127.
[24] Price, 264.
[25] Charles D. Alexander, "The Woman in the Wilderness," *The Researcher* 23, 4 (Winter 1994) 31. An exposition of Rev. 12:14.
[26] Price, 266.
[27] See pp. 354, 355.
[28] Maas, 771.
[29] Henry, vol. 2, 1281.
[30] Young, *Analytical Concordance,* 349.
[31] Ibid., 997.
[32] Ibid., 39.
[33] Fausset, 153.

Chapter 10: A Second Chance for Israel

[1] Price, 258.
[2] Ibid., 260.
[3] Maas, 1603.
[4] Ibid., 1608.
[5] Ibid., 771.
[6] Henry, vol. 2, 1488.
[7] See pp. 325, 326.
[8] Price, 266.
[9] See pp. 265-267, 270, 271.
[10] Fletcher, 33.
[11] See p. 34.

[12] See pp. 151, 161, 179, 180, 194.

[13] Maas, 821.

[14] Ibid., 1627.

Chapter 11: The Silent Years

[1] G. E. Ladd, "Apocalyptic," *Evangelical Dictionary of Theology*, 64.

[2] William J. Deane, *Pseudepigrapha: An Account of Certain Apocryphal Sacred Writings of the Jews and Early Christians* (Edinburgh: T. & T. Clark, 1891) 1.

[3] Price, 266.

[4] See p. 222.

[5] R. H. Charles, ed., trans. ed.'s Ethiopic text, *The Book of Enoch or 1 Enoch* (Oxford: Clarendon, 1912) 4,5,7,8.

[6] Ibid., 11-13.

[7] Ibid., 52-54.

[8] See pp. 29, 30.

[9] Charles, *The Book of Enoch*, sect. 2, intro. 66.

[10] Ladd, "Apocalyptic," *Evangelical Dictionary of Theology*, 63.

[11] E. F. Kevan, "Abomination of Desolation," *Evangelical Dictionary of Theology*, 3.

[12] This heathen altar is the abomination that causes desolation (Dan. 9:27; 1 Macc. 1:54).

[13] M. R. Wilson, "Judaism," *Evangelical Dictionary of Theology*, 589.

[14] Fausset, 566.

[15] Ladd, "Apocalyptic," *Evangelical Dictionary of Theology*, 63.

[16] Wilson, "Judaism," *Evangelical Dictionary of Theology*, 589.

[17] Charles, *The Book of Enoch*, 212,215.

[18] Ibid., 215n, 216n.

[19] William W. Klein, Craig L. Bloomberg, and Robert L. Hubbard Jr., consulting ed. Kermit A. Ecklebarger, *Introduction to Biblical Interpretation* (Dallas: Word, 1993) 27.

[20] Ibid., 27,28.

[21] Durant, *The Story of Civilization:* Part III, *Caesar and Christ* (New York: Simon and Schuster, 1944) 530.

[22] Charles, ed., trans. ed.'s Gr. text, *Testaments of the Twelve Patriarchs* (London: Adam and Charles Black, 1908) 62-67.

23 Ibid., 95-97.

24 Ibid., 97,98.

25 Ibid., intro. 15.

26 Charles, trans. Ethiopic text, intro. G. H. Box, *The Book of Jubilees or The Little Genesis* (New York: Macmillan, 1917) 130-132.

27 Price, 268.

28 Charles, *The Book of Enoch*, 232-234.

29 Durant, *Caesar and Christ*, 530,531.

30 Deane, 40-42.

31 Bruce, 76,77.

32 Leslie E. Fuller, "Religious Development of the Intertestamental Period," *Abingdon Bible Commentary*, 207.

PART 2: RESPONDING TO THE PROMISED SEED

Chapter 1: The Birth of the Promised Seed

1 Maas, 1636.

2 See pp. 156, 157.

3 Fausset, 90.

4 Price, 270.

5 "Herod," *Encyclopedia Britannica*, vol. 11, 511.

6 Durant, *Caesar and Christ*, 543.

Chapter 2: The Ministry of Jesus

1 Maas, 1637.

2 Ibid., 1723.

3 See pp. 19-21.

4 Wallace, "Messiah," *Evangelical Dictionary of Theology*, 711.

5 Jennings, 111,112.

6 Henry, vol. 3, 608. Also see pp. 392-395.

7 Max Lucado, *He Still Moves Stones* (Dallas: Word, 1993) 89.

8 A. T. Robertson, *A Harmony of the Gospels for Students of the Life of Christ* (New York: Harper and Row, 1950) 165.

9 Ibid., 173.

[10] Kevan, "Abomination of Desolation," *Evangelical Dictionary of Theology*, 4.

[11] See pp. 145, 148.

[12] Robertson, 187. Three passages record this incident about Mary of Bethany (Mark 14:3-9; Matt. 26:6-13; John 12:2-8).

[13] Ibid., 190.

[14] Henry, vol. 3, 645.

[15] For details on the story of the crucifixion, see pp. 107-109, 244, 245.

[16] Herman Hoeksema, ed. and partially rev. Homer C. Hoeksema, *Behold, He Cometh! An Exposition of the Book of Revelation* (Grand Rapids: Reformed Free, 1969) 432,433.

[17] Young, *Old Testament Prophecy*, 166.

Chapter 3: The Early Church

[1] Maas, 1867.

[2] Bruce, 31.

[3] Paton G. Gloag, qtd. in Fletcher, 43.

[4] Fausset, 557.

[5] See pp. 147, 148.

[6] Maas, 1940.

[7] Frank Charles Thompson, "An outline history of the evangelistic and missionary work in the early church," *The New Chain-Reference Bible* (Indianapolis: Kirkbride Bible Co., 1964) 294.

[8] Ibid., 295.

[9] Maas, 1941.

[10] See pp. 120, 121.

[11] Mauro, 10-12.

[12] Peritz, "The Chronology of the New Testament," *Abingdon Bible Commentary*, 879. See pp. 226, 227.

[13] Deane, 41.

[14] Keller, 365.

[15] Durant, *Caesar and Christ*, 577.

Chapter 4: Letters to the Churches

[1] Maas, 2243.
[2] Ibid., 2112.
[3] Ibid., 2169.
[4] Ibid., 2178.
[5] See pp. 135. 136.
[6] Maas, 2059.
[7] Ibid., 2091.
[8] Ibid., 2023.
[9] Ibid., 2128.
[10] Ibid., 2143.
[11] Ibid., 2254.
[12] Ibid., 2266.
[13] Ibid., 2217.
[14] Ibid., 2295.
[15] Henry, vol. 3, 1391.
[16] Hoeksema, 307.
[17] Ibid, 308.
[18] Fausset, 3.
[19] Hoeksema, 308,326-330.
[20] See pp. 19-24.
[21] See pp. 354, 355.
[22] See pp. 164, 165.

Chapter 5: The Apostolic Fathers

[1] Price, 270.

[2] Fuller, "The Literature of the Intertestamental Period," *Abingdon Bible Commentary*, 199.

[3] Le Roy Edwin Froom, *The Prophetic Faith of Our Fathers: The Historical Development of Prophetic Interpretation*, vol. 1 (Washington: Review and Herald, 1950) 195.

[4] See pp. 304-306, 313, 314.

[5] James Orr, *The History and Literature of the Early Church* (London: Hodder & Stoughton, 1913) 55.

Endnotes

[6] Clement, 3rd bishop of Rome, ed. Allan Menzies, *The Ante-Nicene Fathers,* vol. 9,236.

[7] Orr., 56.

[8] Clement, ed. Allan Menzies, *The Ante-Nicene Fathers,* Vol. 9, 253.

[9] Ibid, 256.

[10] Hilgenfeld, eds. Alexander Roberts and James Donaldson, *Ante-Nicene Christian Library: Translations of the Writings of the Fathers Down to A.D. 325,* vol. 1. *The Apostolic Fathers* (Edinburgh: T. & T. Clark, 1883) intro. 100.

[11] Barnabas of Alexandria, *Ante-Nicene Christian Library,* 127,128.

[12] Ibid., 134.

[13] See pp. 348-350.

[14] Orr, 66.

[15] Ibid., 110,111.

[16] Henry Bettenson, *The Early Church Fathers* (Toronto: Oxford University, 1956) 17.

[17] Irenaeus, eds. Alexander Roberts and James Donaldson, *The Ante-Nicene Fathers. Translations of the Writings of the Fathers down to A.D. 325,* vol. 1 (New York: Scribner's, 1908) 562.

[18] Orr, 113.

[19] Tertullian, eds. Alexander Roberts and James Donaldson, *The Ante-Nicene Fathers,* vol. 3, 342.

[20] Irenaeus, eds. Alexander Roberts and James Donaldson, *The Ante-Nicene Fathers,* vol. 1, 561.

[21] Tertullian, eds. Alexander Roberts and James Donaldson, *The Ante-Nicene Fathers,* vol. 3, 342,343.

[22] Irenaeus, eds. Alexander Roberts and James Donaldson, *The Ante-Nicene Fathers,* vol. 1, 562,563.

[23] Orr, 119.

[24] Origen, eds. John Ernest Leonard Oulton and Henry Chadwick, selected trans. of Clement and Origen, *Library of Christian Classics,* vol. 2, *Alexandrian Christianity* (Philadelphia: Westminster, 1954) 289.

[25] Origen, qtd. in Jean Daniélou, trans. Walter Mitchell, *Origen* (New York: Sheed and Ward, 1955) 60.

[26] Ibid., Origen, qtd. in Jean Daniélou, 152.

Appendix

[1] John H. Walton, *Chronological and Background Charts of the Old Testament* (Grand Rapids: Zondervan, 1978) 25.

[2] "Samaritan Pentateuch," May 6, 2000, Online posting, Eastons Bible Dictionary, Jan. 21, 2006, <http://www.htmlbible.com/kjv30/easton/east3203.htm>

[3] *Septuagint Version of the Old Testament*, Eng. trans. (New York: James Pott, n.d.) 86.

[4] Francis X. Gumerlock, *The Day and the Hour* (Atlanta: American Vision, 2000) 92.

[5] See pp. 389-391.

BIBLIOGRAPHY

Alexander, Charles D. "The Woman in the Wilderness." *The Researcher*, 23,4, Winter 1994, 22-34.

The Bethel Series New Testament. Madison: Adult Christian Education Foundation, 1981.

Bettenson, Henry. *The Early Church Fathers.* Toronto: Oxford University, 1956.

Boettner, Loraine. *The Millennium.* Rev. ed. Phillipsburg: Presbyterian and Reformed, 1984.

Bruce, F. F. *The New Testament Development of Old Testament Themes.* Grand Rapids: Eerdmans, 1969.

Charles, R. H., ed. *The Book of Enoch or 1 Enoch.* Trans. ed.'s Ethiopic text. Oxford: Clarendon, 1912.

—, ed. *The Book of Jubilees or The Little Genesis.* Trans. Ethiopic text. Intro. G. H. Box. New York: Macmillan, 1917.

—, ed. *The Testaments of the Twelve Patriarchs.* Trans. ed.'s Gr. text. London: Adam and Charles Black, 1908.

Daniélou, Jean. *Origen.* Trans. Walter Mitchell. New York: Sheed and Ward, 1955.

Deane, William J. *Pseudepigrapha: An Account of Certain Apocryphal Sacred Writings of the Jews and Early Christians.* Edinburgh: T. & T. Clark, 1891.

[DeCaro, Louis A.] "Israel and Biblical Prophecy." *The Researcher*. Final ed. (Spring 1994): 25-44.

Durant, Will. *The Story of Civilization*: Part I. *Our Oriental Heritage*. 1935. New York: Simon and Schuster, 1954.

—. *The Story of Civilization*: Part III: *Caesar and Christ*. New York: Simon and Schuster, 1944.

Eastons Bible Dictionary. May 6, 2000. Online posting. Jan. 21, 2006. <http://www.htmlbible.com/kjv30/easton/east3203.htm>

Eiselen, Frederick Carl, Edwin Lewis, and David G. Downey, eds. *The Abingdon Bible Commentary.* New York: Abingdon-Cokesbury, 1929.

Elwell, Walter A., ed. *Evangelical Dictionary of Theology.* Grand Rapids: Baker Book House, 1984.

Encyclopedia Britannica: A New Survey of Universal Knowledge. 24 vols. Toronto: Benton, 1956.

Fausset, A. R. *Fausset's Bible Dictionary.* Grand Rapids: Zondervan, 1949.

Fletcher, George B. *The Millennium What it is Not and What it is.* Sterling: Gam, n.d.

Froom, Le Roy Edwin. *The Prophetic Faith of Our Fathers: The Historical Development of Prophetic Interpretation.* 4 vols. Washington: Review and Herald, 1950.

Gumerlock, Francis X. *The Day and the Hour.* Atlanta: American Vision, 2000.

Henry, Matthew. *Matthew Henry's Commentary on the whole Bible.* 3 vols. Marshallton: Sovereign Grace, p.d.

Hoeksema, Herman. *Behold, He Cometh! An Exposition of the Book of Revelation.* Ed. and partially rev. Homer C. Hoeksema. Grand Rapids: Reformed Free, 1969.

The Holy Bible containing the Old and New Testaments and the Apocrypha. London: Cambridge University, n.d.

Jennings, F. C. *Satan: His Person, Work, Place and Destiny.* Toronto: Haynes, n.d.

Keller, Werner. *The Bible as History.* Trans. William Neil. 1956. New York: Morrow, 1981.

Klein, William W., Craig L. Bloomberg, and Robert L. Hubbard Jr. *Introduction to Biblical Interpretation.* Consulting ed. Kermit A. Ecklebarger. Dallas: Word, 1993.

Lindsey, Hal, and C. C. Carlson. *The Late Great Planet Earth.* Grand Rapids: Zondervan, 1970.

Lucado, Max. *He Still Moves Stones.* Dallas: Word, 1993.

Maas, David. "A Chronology of Bible Events and World Events." *Life Application Study Bible.* Wheaton: Tyndale House, 1991.

Mauro, Philip. *The Hope of Israel: What is it?* Swengel: Reiner, n.d.

Menzies, Allan, ed. *The Ante-Nicene Fathers. Translations of the Writings of the Fathers down to A. D. 325.* Vol. 9. New York: Scribner's, 1926.

Milligan, R. *An Exposition and Defense of the Scheme of Redemption.* Rev. ed. St. Louis: Christian Publishing, 1885.

O'Meara, John J., trans. and annotator. *Ancient Christian Writers: The Works of the Fathers in Translation.* Vol. 19. Westminster: Newman, 1954.

Orr, James. *The History and Literature of the Early Church.* London: Hodder & Stoughton, 1913.

Oulton, John Ernest Leonard, and Henry Chadwick, eds. *The Library of Christian Classics.* Vol. 2. *Alexandrian Christianity.* Selected trans. of Clement and Origen. Philadelphia: Westminster, 1954.

Price, Ira M., Leslie E. Fuller, and Chester J. Attig. "Synchronous History of the Nations." *The New Standard Alphabetical Indexed Bible.* Chicago: John A. Hertel, 1963.

Roberts, Alexander, and James Donaldson, eds. *Ante-Nicene Christian Library: Translations of the Writings of the Fathers Down to A.D. 325.* Vol. 1. *The Apostolic Fathers.* Edinburgh: T. & T. Clark, 1883.

—, eds. *The Ante-Nicene Fathers. Translations of the Writings of the Fathers down to A. D. 325.* Vols. 1, 3. New York: Scribner's, 1908.

Robertson, A. T. *A Harmony of the Gospels for Students of the Life of Christ.* New York: Harper & Row, 1950.

Schaff, Philip, and Henry Wace, eds. 2nd series. Trans. with prolegomena and notes by Arthur Cushman McGiffert. *A Select Library of Nicene and Post-Nicene Fathers of the Christian Church.* Vol. 1. New York: Christian Literature Co., 1892.

Septuagint Version of the Old Testament. Eng. trans. New York: James Pott, n.d.

Shields, T. T. "Jesus of Bethlehem—and of the Days of Eternity." *The Gospel Witness,* 73,12, (Dec. 1, 1994): 13.

Still, J. Ironside. *St. Paul On Trial.* New York: Doran, 1923.

Thompson, Frank Charles. "An outline history of the evangelistic and missionary work in the early church." *The New Chain-Reference Bible.* Indianapolis: Kirkbride Bible Co., 1964.

Urquhart, John. *The Wonders of Prophecy.* Harrisburg: Christian Publications, n.d.

Walton, John. H. *Chronological and Background Charts of the Old Testament.* Grand Rapids: Zondervan, 1978.

Young, E. J. *Old Testament Prophecy.* Toronto: Gospel Witness, n.d.

Young, Robert. *Analytical Concordance to the Bible.* 22nd Amer. ed. Rev.Wm. B. Stevenson. New York: Funk & Wagnall, 1936.

INDEX

Aaron, 62-65, 71-77, 114
Abednego, 204, 219
Abel, 26-28, 37, 318, 378, 396
Abomination of desolation, 226, 227, 262, 319, 320, 362
Abraham, 41-53, 58, 59, 63, 68, 83, 98, 99, 123, 131, 206, 207, 341, 359, 360, 379, 397, 415-417
Abraham's children, 188, 296, 309, 310
Adam and Eve, 21-26, 32, 33, 37, 72, 146, 160, 229, 230, 297, 310, 379, 386, 393
Agrippa, 351, 352
Ahab, 114-117, 141
Ahasuerus *See* Xerxes.
Ahaz, 156, 157
Ahaziah, 117, 144
Ahijah, 112
Alexander the Great, 222, 223
Alexandra, 278, 279
Amaziah, 123, 126
Ammon, 123, 142, 143, 152, 182
Amos, 121-126, 139
Amram, 62
Ananias, 343, 344

Andrew, 304
Angels, 20, 23, 24, 55, 149, 151, 248, 289, 292, 297, 308, 320, 321, 336, 383, 386-391
Antichrist (political beast), 223, 224, 363, 385, 388-392
Antigonus:
    of Phrygia, 222
    son of Aristobulus, 292
Antioch, 347-351, 355
Antiochus Epiphanes, 212, 213, 223-227, 246, 247, 259, 262, 264, 277
Antipater, 280
Aram, 117, 118, 156, 157, 195
Araunah, 89, 90
Archelaus, 291, 292
Aristides, 37, 38
Aristobulus, 279, 280
Armageddon, 391
Assyria, 36
Assyrian Empire, 116-121, 124, 127, 129, 131, 137-139, 157, 164, 167-169, 182, 209
Athaliah, 144
Augustus, 162, 163, 289, 292
Babel, tower of, 36, 37, 190

Babylon (the city), 145, 189-191, 241

Babylon, Mystery, 389-392

Babylonia, 36, 138

Babylonian Empire, 58, 164, 184, 191, 192, 195-197, 200, 220, 221, 235

Balaam, 78-81, 83

Balak, 78-81

Barnabas:
    friend of Paul, 344-350, 355
    of Alexandria, 402-404

Bathsheba, 87

Bethel, 56, 113, 121

Bethlehem, 132, 133, 237, 289-291, 328, 387

Bronze snake, 77, 78

Cain, 25-27, 37, 165, 318, 378, 396

Caiaphas, 312

Calvary (Golgotha), 52, 108, 109, 163, 177, 178, 232, 319, 334, 350, 356, 366, 371, 387, 411

Canaan, 33, 34, 42, 43, 46, 48, 68, 100, 194, 249, 416

Chasidim, 264, 268, 274

Christian council, first, 348-350

Church:
    beginning of, 218, 319, 337, 357, 362
    God's temple, 95, 214, 215, 384, 385
    Jew and Gentile in, 218, 344-348
    mission of, 231, 307, 335, 355
    New Israel, 371
    persecution of, 192, 193, 213, 341-343, 387, 389
    worship in, 93, 94, 203, 204, 316, 317

Circumcision:
    of body, 45-47, 83, 270, 348, 358
    of heart, 83, 188, 189, 215

Clement of Rome, 402

Cornelius, 344-346

Covenant:
    at Sinai, 68-71, 125
    everlasting, 46-50, 97-99, 163, 175, 210, 211, 397
    new, 185-189, 244, 325, 326, 374
    old, 75-77, 81-83, 183-185, 359, 360
    with Abraham, 44-46, 123, 131, 138, 207
    with David, 94-96, 100, 104, 124, 129, 131, 144

Crucifixion, 108, 231, 431

Cyrus, 128, 170, 210, 221, 222, 235-237

Dan, 113

Daniel, 219-233

David, 48, 49, 59, 85-112, 214

David's tent, 92-94, 123-125

David's throne, 58, 94-97, 104, 105, 112, 124, 130, 144, 158, 287, 292

Day:
    of Atonement, 73-75, 94
    of salvation, 296, 365
    of the Lord, 122, 147, 151, 164, 181-183, 254, 338, 361, 362, 373

Death:
    physical, 37, 164-166, 262, 395

Index

spiritual, 72, 329, 366, 368, 395
Eden. *See* Garden of Eden.
Edom, 124, 142, 143, 177, 200, 201, 234, 270
Egypt, 35, 62-68, 84, 168, 195-198, 202, 209, 222, 226, 242, 258, 259, 291, 382, 385
Eli, 91
Eliakim (Hezekiah's chief minister), 377
Elijah, 114-116, 188, 253, 254, 385
Elisha, 116
End of world (time), 149-151, 178, 182, 183, 213, 223, 224, 245, 247, 248, 254, 315, 318, 363, 364, 382, 385, 388, 393, 401
Enoch, 29, 30, 261, 385
Esau, 53-56, 177, 200, 201
Essenes, 268
Esther, 249-251
Eternal life, 18, 27, 78, 148, 165, 230, 299, 306, 314, 324, 347, 366
Eternal punishment, 148, 165, 166, 324, 359, 366, 395
Euphrates River, 36, 48, 49, 79, 111, 383, 390
Eusebius, 45
Eve. *See* Adam and Eve.
Exile in Babylon, 101, 134, 159, 169, 170, 175, 198, 201-206, 219, 263
Ezekiel, 204-218
Ezra, 228, 242
Faith, 34, 65, 103, 118, 193, 225, 230, 307, 321, 330, 358, 359, 366, 369, 370

False prophet (false lamb), 224, 388-390
Festus, 351, 352
Final judgment, 20, 27, 165, 166, 178, 179, 315, 380, 395, 396
Florus, 354
Gabriel, 228, 287
Galilee, 102, 137, 220, 232, 262, 298-301, 304, 336, 341, 345
Gallus, 354
Gamaliel, 340, 341
Garden:
    of Eden, 19, 22-26, 98, 145, 229
    of Gethsemane, 244, 245
Gedaliah, 197
Gentiles, 124, 125, 128, 129, 161, 162, 173, 253, 319, 328, 336, 346-350, 352, 358, 384, 400
Gentiles, in false writings, 49, 260, 261, 265, 272-277, 281
Gibeon, 93
God:
    attributes of, 18, 29, 30, 65, 67, 68, 128, 131, 152, 155, 204, 205, 228, 252, 321, 365, 367, 384, 395
    his throne, 20-24, 31, 51, 91, 108, 152, 168, 224, 297, 342, 373, 378, 380, 386, 391, 393, 395
    names of, 43, 67, 68, 95, 105, 123, 152, 194, 224
    work of, 17, 52, 99, 100, 102, 104, 143, 148, 151, 164, 166, 169-171, 182, 188, 225, 239, 247, 334, 369, 370, 395
Gog and Magog, 211-213
Goliath, 88, 89

Gomer, 127, 129
Greek Empire, 220-223
Habakkuk, 191-194
Hagar, 46, 360
Haggai, 237-238, 254
Ham, 33, 34, 146
Haman, 250, 251
Heart attitude, 26, 34, 37, 47, 77, 83, 125, 139, 148, 154, 201, 215, 264, 271, 299, 302, 310, 314, 358
Herod:
    the Great, 290-292, 328, 387
    the Tetrarch, 101
Herodians, 316
Hezekiah, 167-169, 377
Holy Spirit:
    at Pentecost 147-149, 217, 218, 337, 338
    attributes of, 214-218
    indwelling of, 171, 208, 212, 216, 231, 234, 295, 299, 322, 339, 344, 367, 368
    seal of, 206, 231, 305, 380, 382, 389
    work of, 157, 166, 176, 189, 215, 287, 289, 296, 312, 317, 326, 327, 335-338, 342, 345, 346, 362, 363, 369, 372, 397
Hosea, 126-130
Hyrcanus, son of Alexandra, 279, 280
Idolatry:
    Baal, 81, 114-117, 144
    Dagon, 91
    early development of, 35, 36
    God's condemnation on, 38, 39
    Zoroaster, 290

Intermediate state, 165, 393-395
Ipsus, battle of, 222
Irenaus, 405-409
Isaac, 48, 50-55, 58, 360
Isaiah, 152-180
Ishmael:
    David's descendant, 197
    Abraham's son, 46, 50, 360
Israel:
    God's plan for, 63, 66, 70, 90, 96, 97, 100, 128, 135, 164, 170, 171, 186, 198, 201, 204, 206, 236
    God's servant, 170, 173, 380, 381
    hope of, 48, 134, 162, 257, 262, 268, 274, 277, 279, 282, 283, 298, 305, 316, 351-354
    origin of, 57
Jacob, 48, 53-59
Jahaziel, 142
James:
    half brother of Jesus, 124, 349, 357-359
    the apostle, 308, 314, 315
Japheth, 33
Jebus, 89, 90, 200
Jehoahaz, 195
Jehoiachin, 196
Jehoiada, 144
Jehoiakim (Eliakim), 195
Jehoshaphat, 141-144, 149, 151
Jehosheba, 144
Jehu, 116-119
Jeremiah, 183-191
Jeroboam, 112-114, 122
Jeroboam II, 121, 129, 152

Index

Jerusalem, 43, 90, 95, 113, 133, 134, 145, 147, 149, 151, 162, 164, 170, 171, 183, 184, 195-197, 200, 205-207, 217, 227, 235-243, 247-249, 253, 301, 308, 317, 319, 321, 341, 348, 351, 371, 411

Jerusalem, New (heavenly), 151, 360, 371, 372, 411

Jesus:
    attributes of, 97, 98, 106, 135, 153, 177, 240, 365, 369, 373-378, 384
    birth of, 132, 133, 156, 157, 228, 229, 236, 237, 287-291, 386, 387
    his baptism, 296
    his death and resurrection, 45, 52, 58, 75, 77, 99-105, 108, 109, 134, 135, 148, 160-163, 172, 173, 177, 178, 194, 216, 225, 226, 229-233, 243-246, 295, 319, 328-341, 347, 350, 353, 354, 356, 358, 363, 366, 370, 371, 387
    his last week, 243-246, 316-327, 330
    his miracles, 136, 137, 300, 303-305, 311, 312
    his parables, 150, 151, 302, 304, 322, 323, 328, 377, 378, 397, 399, 400
    his throne, 58, 94-96, 101, 104, 105, 130, 158, 240, 287, 292, 314, 323, 336, 375
    names of, 18, 44, 58, 66, 101, 148, 158-160, 172, 342, 377, 392
    work of, 70, 75, 78, 105, 107-109, 128, 136, 159, 161, 173, 175-178, 210, 211, 229-232, 363, 366, 371, 373-376

Jew, spiritual definition of, 189

Jezebel, 114, 117

Joab, 87, 90

Joash, 144

Jochebed, 62

Joel, 145-151

John:
    Hyrcanus, 271, 277
    Mark, 347, 350
    the apostle, 101, 102, 308, 314, 315, 325, 338, 375-398
    the Baptist, 166, 171, 253, 254, 295-298, 335

Jonah, 118-121, 139

Joram, 117, 144

Joseph:
    of Arimathea, 299
    of Nazareth, 58, 156, 157, 262, 289, 291
    son of Jacob, 57, 62

Joshua:
    high priest, 236-240
    Moses' assistant, 48, 143

Josiah, 183, 195

Judah, 57-59, 86

Judaizers, 348-350, 358, 359

Judas:
    Iscariot, 244, 245, 324, 325, 331
    Maccabeus, 212, 213, 265-268
    the Galilean, 340

Judea, 58, 102, 213, 223, 227, 232, 237, 258, 266, 269, 270, 280, 290, 292, 301, 318, 335, 336, 341, 343, 345, 351, 354, 355

Judgment seat, 151, 365, 395, 396

Kingdom:
- earthly, 283, 301, 305, 306, 315, 335, 336, 360, 372, 373, 401-409
- of Christ, 94-96, 101, 105, 106, 133-137, 158, 185, 201, 220, 225, 226, 232-234, 243, 287, 308, 313, 314, 317, 335, 337, 353, 354, 357, 363, 364, 370, 372, 375-377
- of God, 24, 27, 34, 44, 83, 129, 220, 221, 223, 230, 298-300, 303, 304, 310, 318, 334, 339, 347, 350, 354, 355, 364, 367, 368, 379, 385, 386
- of heaven, 150, 151, 221, 295, 301, 302, 307, 346, 399, 400
- of Israel, 69, 70, 95, 96, 111-139, 210, 371
- of Judah, 113, 141-198
- of Messiah, in false writings, 257, 258, 262, 264, 273-283
- of Satan, 24, 27, 30, 33, 39, 72, 83, 103, 150, 229, 230, 241, 303, 304, 310, 318, 330, 331, 338, 363, 368, 375, 385-393
- united, 210, 270, 271

Last days, 129, 133, 134

Law:
- for nations, 120, 121, 125, 353
- purpose of, 71-73

Lazarus, 311-313, 324

Living water, 189, 216-218

Lot, 42, 43

Maccabean revolt, 265

Malachi, 252-255

Man of sin (lawlessness), 223, 362, 363

Martha, 311, 312, 324

Mary:
- Magdalene, 334
- of Bethany, 244, 311, 324
- of Nazareth, 106, 156, 157, 176, 262, 287, 289, 291

Mattathias Maccabeus, 265

Median Empire, 138

Medo-Persian Empire, 58, 128, 164, 170, 189, 190, 220, 221, 226, 236, 255

Melchizedek, 43, 44

Meshach, 204, 219

Micah, 130-137

Michael, 329, 387

Midian, 78

Millennium, 276-279, 373, 393, 394, 401-409

Miriam, 62, 67

Moab, 78-81, 123, 142, 143, 182

Mordecai, 250, 251

Moses, 61-84, 91-93, 116, 125, 132, 146, 214, 231, 329, 341, 374, 385, 390, 400

Mount:
- Carmel, 114-116
- Moriah, 51, 52
- of Olives, 247, 311, 317, 336
- Sinai, 69-71, 186, 360
- Zion (God's holy mountain), 68, 90-94, 133-137, 147, 160, 161, 201, 220

Nahum, 138, 139

Nathan, 87, 95

Nazareth, 156, 175, 176, 287, 291, 334

Nebuchadnezzar, 134, 189, 190, 195-197, 202, 204, 219-221, 223

Nebuzaradan, 197, 206
Nehemiah, 228, 242
New birth, 298-299, 370
New heaven and new earth (paradise restored), 161, 179, 180, 214, 218, 249, 315, 339, 367, 373, 396, 397, 412
Nicodemus, 298, 299
Nimrod, 36
Nineveh, 36, 118-121, 123, 125, 138, 169, 233
Noah, 30-34
Obadiah, 199-201
Obed-Edom, 92
Origen, 38, 409-411
Palestine, 49, 203, 212, 222, 259, 270
Parthian Empire, 290, 292
Passover, 63-66
Paul (Saul), 206, 342-344, 347-354, 359-370
Pax Romana, 135
Pella, 355, 387
Pentecost, 104, 107, 147, 148, 188, 207, 216-218, 245, 337, 338, 341, 355, 356, 382, 387
Persian Empire, *See* Medo-Persian Empire.
Peter, 101, 102, 104, 107, 147, 148, 207, 218, 221, 244, 245, 306-309, 314, 337-340, 344-346, 348, 355, 370-373
Pharisees, 106, 108, 136, 211, 264, 274, 279, 289, 292, 302, 303, 312, 313, 316, 317, 348
Philip, 304
Philistia, 88, 89, 91, 118, 123, 152, 246
Pompey, 280

Pontius Pilate, 101, 245, 313, 334
Pseudepigrapha, 49, 257, 401
Pseudo-Ephraem, 417
Ptolemaeus, 222
Ptolemaic Empire, 223
Qumranians, 268-270
Rahab, 193, 416
Rebekah, 53, 54
Redemption:
    physical, 65, 68, 100, 166, 170, 171, 173, 175, 248, 339, 380, 412
    spiritual, 65, 66, 99, 169-180, 315, 368, 374, 378
Rehoboam, 112, 113, 141
Religion and the state, 37, 66, 110, 113, 121, 130, 159, 316, 317, 392
Remnant, believing, 153, 182, 188, 206, 207, 264, 392
Resurrection:
    physical, 311, 312, 352, 363, 364, 385, 386, 395
    spiritual, 298, 299, 311-313, 366-369, 370, 371, 393, 394
Reuel, 63
Roman Empire, 135, 136, 217, 220, 221, 280, 282, 289, 292, 298, 316, 319, 350, 354, 355, 362, 363, 389
Rome, 292, 351, 355, 365, 391
Sadducees, 101, 279, 312, 316, 338-340
Salem, 43
Salvation:
    assurance of, 34, 45, 97-99, 110, 131, 132, 163, 309, 318, 330, 346

God's gift of, 12, 47, 154-156, 158, 173-175, 178, 180, 183, 188, 201, 304, 306, 310, 314, 322, 330, 339, 341, 346, 348, 350, 359, 365, 369, 373, 380

God's plan of, 12, 13, 17, 18, 21, 23, 25, 27, 29, 33, 56, 58, 63, 70, 75, 77, 78, 86, 100, 118, 121, 124, 129, 138, 139, 172, 173, 216, 220-222, 228-232, 235, 236, 249, 289, 292, 295, 297, 325, 331, 333, 336, 339, 347, 355, 357, 366, 367, 386, 387, 393

Samaria:
city of, 114, 126, 127, 130, 137, 167
Roman district of, 189, 233, 335, 343

Samuel, 85, 86, 91

Sanhedrin, 102, 312, 340, 341, 342

Sarah, 42, 44, 46, 50, 51, 360

Sargon II, 137, 138

Satan:
attributes of, 19, 20, 22, 114, 121, 150, 195, 213, 223, 224, 239, 241, 255, 262, 293, 296-298, 308, 310, 317, 328-330, 363, 387, 392
indwelling of, 324, 325, 331
mark of, 389
names of, 19, 22, 32, 296, 303, 330, 382
work of, 12, 20-24, 36, 42, 103, 144, 169, 178, 222-224, 229, 250, 291, 303, 304, 327-329, 386-389, 394, 395

Saul, king, 86, 88

Scythians, 138, 213

Seleucid Empire, 212, 213, 222, 223, 258, 259, 265-267, 270

Seleucus Nicator, 222

Sennacherib, 167-169

Seraiah, 197

Shadrach, 204, 219

Shalmaneser III, 118

Shalmaneser V, 137

Shem, 33

Shinar, plain of, 36, 190

Silas, 350

Simon Maccabeus, 270

Slavery in Egypt, 62, 84, 202

Solomon, 95, 97, 111-113, 121, 270, 271, 277, 336

Solomon's temple, 124, 195-197, 214, 216, 237, 238, 342, 415

Stephen, 341-343

Syria (Roman province), 280, 292

Syria *see* Aram.

Tertullian, 406-408

Theudas, 340

Tiglath-Pileser III, 137, 157, 164

Titus, 227, 355, 362

Unholy trinity, 388, 389

Uriah, 87

Uzzah, 92

Uzziah (Azariah), 152

Xerxes, 249-251

Zealots, 354, 362

Zechariah, 239-249, 254

Zedekiah (Mattaniah), 196, 197

Zephaniah, 181-183

Zerubbabel, 58, 128, 185, 236-240

Zionism, 49, 207